Next page: Jacob van
Ruisdael, *The Mill at Wijk*
(detail). c.1670.
Canvas, 83 x 101 cm.
Rijksmuseum, Amsterdam.

THE

COUN

OW
TRIES

ARTS AND SOCIETY IN FLANDERS
AND THE NETHERLANDS
A YEARBOOK

1994-95

Published by the

Flemish-Netherlands Foundation 'Stichting Ons Erfdeel'

NX
553
.L69
v.2
1994 –
95

Contents

7

russels,

City of the Coming Century

Hidden bilingualism

Foreigners who come to live in Belgium soon realise that they have arrived in a bilingual country. Many of them, those who work for the European institutions and the private companies which cluster around them, live either in the centre of the capital city, Brussels, or else very nearby. I am constantly amazed by the fact that these people see Brussels as an exclusively French-speaking city. Even Dutch people, who speak the same language as Flemings, are able to miss the bilingualism of this city, which is so obvious to me. Worse still, a great many Flemings, themselves Belgians, assume without any further consideration that Brussels is French-speaking, even though Brussels is the capital of their own Flemish Community. Can these people not see? Can they not hear? All the street name plates and road signs are bilingual, with combinations which are sometimes very original, such as 'Schae/arbeek' or 'centre/um', and sometimes almost surrealistic, such as 'Treurenberg/Treurenberg'. Every notice in every town hall and post office is bilingual, and the counter staff have to be able to speak both languages. The metro and tram systems are completely bilingual, although some employees still obstinately refuse to understand simple phrases like 'one tram card please' or 'how much does this cost?' if they are said in Dutch. In the bars and on the streets I hear not only French, Turkish, Arabic, Portuguese, English and a dozen other languages every day, but also Dutch, and what is more – thank goodness – the Brabant dialect of Brussels, which is Dutch to the core. The confusion of tongues in Brussels is like the Tower of Babel, and yet foreigners still say again and again: Yes, of course Brussels is French-speaking. What else would it be?

Eight centuries of Dutch, two centuries of Frenchification

This city is just over a thousand years old. It is said that Bruocsella, a combination of old Dutch words which means 'settlement in the marsh', was founded in 979. The Brussels Region, in existence since 1988, includes the

Bilingual poster for the historical procession on the occasion of the 1930 centenary.

city itself and eighteen other municipalities. Until the beginning of the twentieth century, all but one of these (Elsene/Ixelles) were mainly Dutch-speaking, though, as far as road signs and public notices were concerned, just as French as the Walloon cities of Liège or Charleroi. At the moment the vast majority of the population of the Brussels Region is French-speaking, and the street scene is more bilingual than ever. In everyday life it is sometimes difficult to draw the dividing line between Dutch-speakers and French-speakers; there is still a very large number of *bilingual people,* even though the population of what is now the Brussels Region has certainly been Frenchified on a massive scale during the nineteenth and twentieth centuries.

This does *not* mean that Brussels is now mainly a Walloon (and hence French-speaking) city. The *geographical* language border between Flanders and Wallonia runs to the south of the Brussels Region, where it has been for centuries. Much more important was the *social* language border, which divided the higher classes in Flanders and Brussels, who spoke French, from the lower classes who spoke Dutch dialects.

After the Netherlands was split into a northern and southern part, as a disastrous consequence of the religious wars of the sixteenth and seventeenth centuries, the Dutch language blossomed in the North, while in the Southern part, which was occupied by the armies of Spain, the same language disintegrated into a number of ineffectual dialects, which soon came to be deeply despised by the elite. During the eighteenth century, the French language enjoyed a high degree of respect throughout Europe, and even more so in Flanders and Brussels, because there was nothing which looked like a cultural language to set against it. Nevertheless, the courts and local authorities continued to work almost exclusively in Dutch, as they had been doing for centuries. This was to change drastically at the end of the eighteenth century, as the southern Netherlands became part of revolutionary France.

The fatherland of 'liberté, égalité, fraternité' deprived all languages except French of their freedom, by treating them with appalling inequality. All official documents, for example birth certificates or deeds drawn up by a notary, *had to* be drawn up in French. Citizens were no longer tried in their own language, as they had been for centuries – another clear step backwards compared with the Ancien Régime. The sole language of the justice system was now French, whether the accused understood a word of it or not.

At this time, remember, virtually no one in Flanders, and at the most fifteen percent of the population in Brussels, spoke French. Not long before, Voltaire had written: 'Il n'y a à Bruxelles que les Flamands.'

A quarter of a century of French occupation (1790-1815) had very serious consequences for the Dutch language in Brussels: ordinary people became firmly convinced that their everyday language, the Brabant dialect, was common and low, and that it was undesirable or even dangerous to use that language in public life.

The period of reunification with the Northern Netherlands from 1815 to 1830, and the well-meaning but clumsy and ineffective attempts by the Dutch King William I to restore the national language to its rightful position, could not erase the Flemish people's deep-rooted contempt for their own language. In 1830, after a series of proletarian food riots got out of hand, the independent Kingdom of Belgium came into being. Like many other European countries, Belgium was governed by a small elite of no more than two percent of its citizens. This elite spoke French, and French was the only official language of this young, self-confident and in fact very liberal country, although the majority of the population could not speak it. Not even in the capital, Brussels; in 1830 only about one-quarter of the population of the city were more or less able to speak French.

In Brussels, the Frenchification of the civil service and the educational system was carried out in an extremely brutal fashion. Frenchification was not a spontaneous process: pressure was relentlessly and consistently applied over a long period, from the early nineteenth century until well into the 1970s. The consequences of this for the ordinary people of Brussels were disastrous. In the nineteenth century, Charles Buls, an alderman in charge of education who later became Mayor, observed during a schools inspection how a certain teacher, who of course spoke French, gave a half-hour lesson about a locomotive. The pupils spoke so little French that they thought the teacher was talking about a tree. From 1879 onwards Buls, who was French-speaking but had a keen awareness of the sufferings of the common people, diffidently attempted to introduce a little Dutch into primary schools in Brussels. He was shamelessly boycotted, and his well-meaning efforts came to nothing. It was not until the second half of the twentieth century that the Dutch language really began to make headway in Brussels.

For more than a century, French-speakers in Brussels worked to Frenchify the city by means of social control, depriving Dutch speakers of their livelihood, by slander and outright breach of the law and, if all else failed, by neatly circumventing the laws of Belgium. Officials behind Town

The Palace of Justice, designed by Joseph Poelaert and built between 1866-1883.

Hall counters shamelessly insulted or even threatened citizens. Identity cards are unknown in Anglo-Saxon countries, but in Belgium everybody has to carry one. Twenty years ago, anyone in Brussels who wanted to obtain a card in Dutch needed to have an argumentative disposition and nerves of steel. You had almost to assault some officials to claim your rights; for as a Fleming you did have a perfect right to a card in your own language. Most people, however, are relatively peaceable, so the majority of Flemings carried French-language identity cards. They were consequently considered to be French-speaking, and received all their official papers in French.

Moreover, a great many Flemings who settled in Brussels were quick to send their children to French-speaking schools. Until recently, French was the elite language in Belgium and Brussels. The French-speaking school was the preferred way to social advancement.

Despite all this, Brussels remained a bilingual city. That bilingualism is established by law, and this law is being implemented more and more effectively. For some years now the prestige of the Dutch language in Belgium, and hence also in Brussels, has been rising. This is related to the economic decline of Wallonia and the growth in the economy of the Flemish part of the country. The old climate of contempt for anyone who speaks Dutch has given way to a great deal of goodwill and good sense. Even the process of Frenchification through the educational system has been reversed. During the last few years, more and more pupils from French-speaking or mixed-language families have been firmly opting for Dutch-speaking schools.

However, in business circles a new bilingualism is emerging: French and English. Some hotels are not ashamed to make public announcements only in those two languages. There are shops where the sales staff speak good French and bad English, but shrug their shoulders at Dutch. Dutch is an official medium-sized EU language which enjoys parity with the other languages both in Belgium and in the European Union, but these people see it as an irritating remnant of the past. I do not know how they would react if you told them that contempt for another person's language is the same thing as contempt for a different skin colour.

The administrative organisation of the Brussels Region provides a good example of the legislative balance between the language groups. The Region's Council is directly elected. The Dutch-speaking delegates therefore constitute a small minority. However, in the regional Government a system of so-called quasi-parity exists. This means that there are two Dutch- and two French-speaking ministers: the law does not state what language the regional Prime Minister should speak, but at the time of writing the post is held by the socialist Charles Picqué, who is French-speaking but speaks good Dutch also. There are two French-speaking junior ministers, and one Dutch-speaking junior minister. Incidentally, the Belgian Government is also constituted according to the principle of parity, apart from the junior ministers and the national Prime Minister.

One typically Belgian aspect of this whole situation is that all these historical tensions have never resulted in serious violence. A series of language laws have been introduced, gradually and democratically, and their implementation has been patiently enforced, both in Belgium and in Brussels.

Hôtel Solvay, designed by Victor Horta and built between 1894-1898.

There have been a great many demonstrations, and quite a lot of abusive language, but the language struggle has claimed only two lives in the whole of Belgium, one Fleming and one French-speaking inhabitant of Brussels. Two is too many, but compared with other similar conflicts it is an honourable record.

Brusselisation

Brussels is the capital of Belgium, and the city has been made very aware of that fact. King Leopold II (1835-1909), in particular, wanted Brussels to look truly royal. Leopold II was more than just the bloody exploiter of the Congo – he had a real talent for urban planning. A series of splendid tree-lined avenues was built in Brussels at his instigation. Leopold II built the Palace of Justice and the Museums of Fine Arts, Natural Science and Central Africa (the latter in the peripheral municipality of Tervuren). He also created the Jubelpark (Cinquantenaire) and Woluwe Park. During the last quarter of the nineteenth century and the early years of the twentieth century, the population of Brussels tripled. I do not know of any city where there are so many large, beautifully ornamented, self-assured town houses, occupying neighbourhood after neighbourhood and street after street. There are thousands of them. The famous architect Victor Horta built the first Art Nouveau house in Brussels in 1893, and this style was to make its mark on the Brussels urban landscape more than any other. Around the turn of the century, Brussels was without any doubt the leading city in European architecture. Things have gone downhill since then.

The North and South Stations needed to be connected, right through the centre of the city. To this end, the first houses were demolished around the beginning of the century, but the North-South link (Jonction Nord-Midi) was not to be opened until after the Second World War. In the meantime, a swathe of demolition and destruction was cut through Brussels, and the wound has still not been healed. Foreigners sometimes ask themselves what terrible bombardment Brussels must have suffered around the Keizerslaan and the National Bank. The Belgian capital was fortunate enough to be spared the fate of Rotterdam or Dresden; but it was destroyed by non-military means.

Next, the beautiful avenues from the time of Leopold II met their doom. These were replaced by urban motorways, with large numbers of tunnels, to improve the traffic flow for the World Exhibition in 1958. Then the poor, friendly red-light district near the North Station was razed to the ground. Monumental planners, money-spinning property men and their political friends visualised a kind of Manhattan arising from the rubble there. The district around the North Station became known as a dirty, dismal grassy waste, and the development ground to a halt halfway through because the money ran out.

Since then, people in international urban planning circles speak of 'brusselisation', meaning the brutal demolition of large areas without building anything sensible to replace them. All these colossal projects were necessary to make Brussels a worthy capital of Belgium. Now Brussels wants to be the capital of the much larger European Community, or even the capital of Europe, although the latter suggestion is totally pretentious and unrealistic.

Belgian Governments have not lifted a finger to oppose this European megalomania – quite the opposite. Quiet, comfortable, pretty residential areas have disappeared to make room for craters hundreds of metres across,

The Jubelpark palace.

where arrogant heaps of stone slowly rise into the air. What is the most beautiful square in Europe? My own Grand' Place in Brussels? The Old Town Square in Prague? The Place des Vosges in Paris? I leave it to the reader to choose, as he probably knows other worthy city squares in our old continent which have their own poignant beauty. But I am quite sure which is the ugliest square in Europe. It lies at the heart of the European area of Brussels, and bears the name of one of the great designers of the European structure, Robert Schuman. It contains the empty Berlaymont building and the offices of the European Commission, which looks like the tomb of an oriental despot. If the way people build their cities indicates the level of their civilisation, then today's EU citizens, under the arrogant leadership of their Eurocrats, have fallen into a state of abject barbarism.

The Berlaymont building (Photo Sint-Lukasarchief, Brussels).

City of the coming century

The Brussels region has just under one million inhabitants. Almost three hundred thousand of these are foreigners, the majority of them from EU countries. That is not to say that all these people are employed by the European institutions; Italian, Greek, Spanish and Portuguese workers arrived in waves from 1945 onwards to work in Belgian factories. The first Moroccans arrived during the 1960s. Now they make up the largest group of foreigners in Brussels. The Turks arrived later still. The number of Zaireans is remarkably small. Unlike the Netherlands, France or England, the Belgian motherland has not attracted many immigrants from its (ex-) colony.

So far, the integration of all these ethnic groups has been both successful and unsuccesful. For example, there have been very few riots in Brussels, certainly nothing that even approaches the violence in Brixton or Liverpool. What is more, no real ghettos have developed yet, although the guest workers are of course very concentrated in the cheapest parts of the city, which means those most dilapidated and most neglected.

The trade unions have made praiseworthy efforts over the decades to maintain solidarity between Belgian and foreign workers. Few foreigners know that the trade unions in Belgium are among the strongest and most influential in Europe. Only the Scandinavian unions come close to the power of their Belgian counterparts.

Most immigrant children in Brussels end up in the French-language educational system. That system is failing dismally in its duty, flatly refusing to take account of people who speak other languages, just as it did decades ago with the Flemish children. The consequences cannot be ignored: disadvantaged schools, widespread truancy leading to petty street crime, poor job prospects, unemployment etc. It is noticeable that the Dutch-speaking educational system in Brussels is making efforts to organise bi-cultural education, although very few foreign parents in Brussels choose Flemish schools.

The single most important task of the coming century will be the integration of the immigrant groups; after all, it is they who guarantee the future of Brussels. For years they were responsible for more than forty percent of births in the nineteen municipalities; but that percentage is now falling, an

unmistakable sign that these people are becoming integrated into the basic cultural patterns of their Belgian surroundings. Brussels has been open to people of foreign origin for centuries. For more than a hundred and fifty years this city has wrestled with its own bilingualism and, slowly but surely, developed systems to cope with it. Brussels is a textbook example of a twenty-first century city: its inhabitants have blown in from all the four winds, and it has experience in accomodating minorities and having many different cultures living together. If the technocratic violence of Europe does not flatten this city, it has an unpredictable but very promising future: on the border between Latin and Germanic Europe, open to the Mediterranean basin and tomorrow, who knows, perhaps open to Central Europe as well, introverted but multi-faceted, peace-loving and down-to-earth. Brussels is certainly not the most beautiful city in Europe, Brussels is chaotic, because Brussels has been cruelly disfigured and violated, even by its own citizens. Nevertheless, many people still feel at home in what the Flemish Brussels singer Johan Verminnen calls the 'binnenzak', the snug inside pocket, of Brussels.

GEERT VAN ISTENDAEL
Translated by Steve Judd.

Islamic Centre (Photo Sint-Lukasarchief, Brussels).

LIKE Being Naughty!'

The Work of Annie M.G. Schmidt

Annie M.G. Schmidt in Oslo in 1988, with the Hans Christian Andersen Award 'for her contribution to children's literature' (Photo Letterkundig Museum, The Hague).

The writer Annie M.G. Schmidt (1911-) is often affectionately called the Grandmother of the Netherlands; or, if it doesn't sound too solemn, the Mother of the Fatherland. She owes this title to a combination of talents which it would be hard to find anywhere else. Children's literature has Astrid Lindgren and Roald Dahl, comedy has Alan Ayckbourn and Neil Simon. We have Kurt Tucholsky's satirical poems and Lewis Carroll's light verse, and all the witty lyrics of Noel Coward and Cole Porter. But Annie Schmidt excels in all these fields and she has been writing so much for so long that three generations of Dutch men and women have grown up with her work. You won't find anyone in the Netherlands who doesn't know at least a few lines of hers by heart.

Over the last few years, since the eve of her eightieth birthday, Annie Schmidt has been honoured by Queen Beatrix and praise and awards have been heaped upon her. She has received one prize after another – and has accepted them all with the slightly mocking amusement which has become her trademark. She is as Dutch as anyone can be, no great lover of fuss and hullabaloo, always quick to put things in perspective with a remark like 'Oh well, if you keep going long enough, and you get old enough, there comes a time when they simply can't ignore you any longer.' All those juries and committees have in fact been paying a debt of honour. While almost all the Netherlands adored her work, the literary world largely ignored it because it was merely entertainment – and for a long time now the literary world has attached little importance to entertainment. However, once Annie Schmidt was unmistakably a part of Dutch cultural history her work could no longer be ignored. She had become a grandmother; but not the sweet, unthreatening little granny familiar to us from so many films and children's books. Long before it became fashionable, Annie Schmidt was making a stand in her children's stories against bossy mothers and authority-figures who thought only of their own positions of power. In her books it's the children who usually run things, with at most the occasional assistance of a sensible adult. A kind father, perhaps; because the fathers in Annie Schmidt's books are usually much nicer than the mothers.

All her childrens' books are in fact a plea for imagination and freedom of thought and action, though she is never the least bit solemn about it. And she still runs her life on these principles, as she has made clear in the interviews to which she has submitted on various festive occasions. One chat show host wanted to know how anyone can live to such an age and still remain so young in spirit. 'Plenty of drinking and plenty of smoking,' she answered mischievously, lighting another cigarette to make her point. One of her books of children's verse has the title *I LIKE Being Naughty!* (Ik ben lekker stout, 1955), and that has become her motto, too.

Anna Maria Geertruida Schmidt was born in Zeeland, in the south-western part of the Netherlands, the daughter of a parson. This seems to be the ideal background for a satirist, for she is by no means the only parson's child to have found a place in the flourishing world of Dutch satire. Even as a child, she had a keen eye for the hypocrisy which tends to be the essential prerequisite for respectability in bourgeois circles. Her father kept hinting that he had stopped believing in God long ago, but had to keep up appearances because of his work. Her mother saw through this pretence and made derisive jokes about it. And the daughter watched, and did not understand why grown-ups always had to deceive themselves and everyone around them. The idea of a grown-up world where such rules apply has always filled her with horror. She once wrote, in the child's lullaby 'This is the World of the Grown-ups' ('Dit is de wereld van de grote mensen'): 'Don't be afraid, you don't have to go there yet.'

As a girl, what Annie Schmidt liked best was to bury herself in books. She dreamed herself into a make-believe world which was much more beautiful then the real one; just as later, when she had her own family, her husband and child would often find it impossible to talk to her because she would be walking round with yet another story in her head. 'Mother's got her head in the clouds again,' they said then.

At first it was not clear what her future would be. She began by studying to be a solicitor, because that's what her brother had done, but dropped it halfway through to take courses in shorthand and typing. For two years she worked as an au pair for three aristocratic sisters in Germany, where she

Bob and Jilly (Drawing by Fiep Westendorp).

became acquainted with the work of satirists such as Kurt Tucholsky and Erich Kästner, writers whom she has continued to admire all her life. 'That's where it all came from, from them,' she said recently, discussing her own sources of inspiration. 'People simply don't realise that this culture is one more thing that Adolf Hitler destroyed.'

Back in the Netherlands again in 1932, Annie Schmidt became a librarian – an enthusiastic young woman, who enjoyed reading good books out loud to rooms full of children. During the Second World War she came into contact with journalists from the underground newspaper *Het Parool,* and after the Liberation she became head of its documentation department. One of her colleagues discovered by chance that Miss Schmidt wrote the odd poem in her spare time. Perhaps she could write a few things for a staff party as well?

Her work caused little short of a sensation with its airy, laconic tone. Professional comedians promptly started fighting for material by her, and *Het Parool* published her children's stories, poems and columns in rapid succession. Annie Schmidt was already thirty-six when all this began. 'Writing was a release,' she said. 'It was as if I had always had to hold it in and then suddenly I could let it all out.' All at once the floodgates opened. The stories and poems and columns were collected into innumerable books and her song lyrics were heard in theatres and on the radio. In 1952 she was approached by a radio producer who wanted to make an American-style soap opera about a family, using a whole team of scriptwriters. Her reaction was: 'Can't I do it on my own?' And for seven years Annie Schmidt wrote the script for *Mr and Mrs Average* (De familie Doorsnee), Dutch radio's most popular series ever. For it she created a distinctive style, with the dialogue regularly interrupted by songs; a sort of ongoing radio musical. In 1958 she also began writing a TV series on the same pattern about the constantly rowing inhabitants of a boarding house called *Pension Hommeles.*

Annie Schmidt created a whole new brand of radio and television entertainment – totally Dutch in its warmth and homeliness, but with enough of an edge to stop it becoming saccharine. Progressive, but not blinkered by revolutionary dogma. Playful and teasing, but not fanatical. She took Dutch domesticity and flung its windows wide to let the fresh air in; but the pot plants on the windowsills remained neat and undisturbed. In 1963 a producer asked her if she would translate a musical for the theatre. She had only a vague idea of what a musical actually was, but said: 'While I've got so many ideas of my own, I'll write my own musical.' And so she did. And in her musicals, too, she created her own form: comedies with songs – and a bit sharper than had been possible on radio and television, because there was no censorship in the theatre. Typical of the exchanges in that first musical is this:

First woman: 'My thirteen-year-old daughter carries condoms in her handbag.'
Second woman: 'Gosh. So young and already she's got a handbag!'

Since then Annie Schmidt has written many more TV series, children's books and stage plays. Critics have sometimes remarked that her work could use rather more bite and less restraint. This was their verdict on her play *Shifting Sand* (Los zand, 1992) in which emotions are understated in the extreme. But in all likelihood this, like all her work, is simply a flawless reflection of the typical Dutchman, who doesn't go in for impassioned speeches and when he quarrels with someone just stalks round in a huff without realising how funny he looks to those watching his sulks. It is no coincidence that the play's funniest scene is one between two women, one of whom has a nasty feeling that her husband is sleeping with the other, while the other is on the point of confessing just that. But their conversation, what they actually say, is about small waffles and large waffles and what you have to look out for when you buy waffles at the baker's.

As yet Annie Schmidt has received little attention from the wider world. Some of her children's books have been translated – into Czech, Greek, Swedish, Norwegian, German, French and some other languages – but only a handful of isolated titles. To date there has been no attempt to promote her by publishing a representative selection of her work. The English-speaking world, in particular, has been badly served, apart from a nice selection of children's verses in the collection *Pink Lemonade* (1992). Yet any idea that her humour might be untranslatable was proved nonsense at the 1991 Story International festival in Rotterdam, where translators from a number of countries pounced on Annie Schmidt's work. The children's author Anthony Horowitz, in particular, produced adroit, humorous translations which delighted the writer herself.

Despite the limited number of translations, in 1988 she was awarded the Hans Christian Andersen Award by the International Board on Books for Young People (IBBY). In a witty acceptance speech, addressed to Andersen himself, Annie Schmidt did not hide her frustration at the lack of adequate translations of her work. 'It is a bit curious and frustrating to make a speech in English, when my best books are not available in that language,' she said. 'The international jury had to read my work in German or Japanese or Danish, perhaps to their irritation. The Dutch BBY kept saying: Oh, she's very popular in Holland. So is football, the jury replied, but because she is on the nomination list since 1960, we'll take the risk. And so they did.' And then she ended her speech with a striking self-portrait: 'Dear Hans, I have been an ugly duckling for a long time, now I am an old and ugly swan. But still a swan.'

HENK VAN GELDER
Translated by Julian Ross.

The Fairy-Tale Man

I know a fairy-tale writer, a man
who starts work each morning as soon as he can.

From a quarter past six until two o'clock he's
writing tales about witches, hobgoblins and fairies.

From a quarter past two till about six he writes
about dashing princes, princesses and knights.

Then he sleeps and begins again early next day.
One inkwell won't do him, not by a long way.

So he keeps all his ink in a garden pond
with a ring of dark bushes planted all round,

and whenever he needs to have a good think
he dips his nib into that pond full of ink.

Ten thousand stories already he's done,
and he's just started work on another one.

And if he spends all his life sitting there – why,
maybe he'll have written the whole pond dry.

The Porcupine's Lullaby

Hush-a-bye my Prickly-one, outside the moon is high,
you are a little porcupine, but there's no need to cry;
you are a little porcupine, and you know you are.
The lions have their manes, the tigers have their stripy fur
and our auntie squirrel has a fine red woolly tail,
but you've got lots and lots of spines, and they'll do you very well.
Go to sleep, my Prickly-one, then you'll grow big and sturdy,
you'll be a proper porcupine just like me and your Daddy.
The elephant he has a trunk, the bears they have their claws,
the fish have fins for swimming, the cattle have their horns,
and the giraffe our uncle has a neck that's really long,
but you've got lots and lots of spines, and so you can't go wrong.
Hush-a-bye my Prickles, the night is getting on,
you're the loveliest little porcupine that ever there was born.
The pussy-cats have whiskers that they use for purring through,
the parrot has his feathers, some green ones and some blue,
and our cousin otter has a sleek brown coat of velvet,
but you have lots and lots of spines, and they'll come in handy yet.

Never Build a Nest out of Chewing-Gum

Once there were two little birds, and they were getting married;
One day they were considering what kind of nest they wanted.
One made of twigs, the cock-bird said, small twigs would be the best,
Twigs and down are what every bird uses to build its nest.
Oh no, not twigs, the hen complained, they're really out of date;
I'd so like something different – modern, but nice and neat.
What about plastic, said the cock, or would concrete suit you better,
Or maybe wire, or rubber, or corrugated paper?
Just tell me what you'd like to have, I'll give it you, you'll see;
If you want a nest of chewing-gum it's all the same to me!

Chewing-gum … said the hen-bird, now that would be quite neat;
It's clean, it's soft and springy, it's got some give to it.
So they started in to build it, deep in the woods somewhere –
The very first nest of chewing-gum ever built anywhere!
And when they had it finished it was quite a pretty sight;
Just look at it, the hen-bird said, it's lovely! It's just right!
She laid five little eggs in it, and said: Oh well, that's that.
You go and get some worms now, but watch out for the cat!

But when she'd sat there for a while, it was the oddest thing …
That nest became extremely long, it stretched and kept on stretching!
Out of the eggs the babies came, and Cheep! they sweetly cried;
But you could hardly see them, they were so deep inside.
That nest was like a stocking, it had got so very long;
The poor birds couldn't work it out. Something was very wrong!
And all the birds for miles around just laughed till they were sick
And cried: Oh, will you look at that! A nest made of elastic!

The little cock-bird said: You see? Now are you satisfied?
Oh, what a shame! It was so nice at first! the hen replied,
Now it's like a collecting bag. It won't do. It's no good.
So then they built another nest as quickly as they could,
Of twiglets and of feathers and of fur shed by the cat,
Of bits of straw and bits of down and bits of this and that.
And as soon as it was ready they moved all five young ones there,
Well, said the hen, what a mistake that was, I do declare!
All her life she told her children: Now you hear what I say –
Never build a nest out of chewing-gum, it's simply not the way.

All poems from *There You are, the 347 Poems for Children (Ziezo, de 347 kinderverzen, 1987).* Translated by Tanis Guest.

Bob and Jilly (Tr. Lance Salway / Ill. Carolyn Dinan). London, 1976.

Bob and Jilly Are Friends (Tr. Lance Salway / Ill. Carolyn Dinan). London, 1977.

The Empty House (Tr. Margo Logan). Milton, 1977.

Grandpa's Glasses (Tr. Margo Logan). Milton, 1977.

Highland Low (Tr. Margo Logan). Milton, 1977.

The Tunned (Tr. Margo Logan). Milton, 1977.

Dusty and Smudge and the Bride (Tr. Lance Salway / Ill. Fiep Westendorp). London, 1977.

Dusty and Smudge and the Soap Studs (Tr. Lance Salway / Ill. Fiep Westendorp). London, 1977.

Dusty and Smudge Spill the Paint (Tr. Lance Salway / Ill. Fiep Westendorp). London, 1977.

Dusty and Smudge Keep Cool (Tr. Lance Salway / Ill. Fiep Westendorp). London, 1977.

Dusty and Smudge and the Cake (Tr. Lance Salway / Ill. Fiep Westendorp). London, 1979.

Bob and Jilly Splash the Soup (Tr. Lance Salway / Ill. Fiep Westendorp). London, 1979.

Bob and Jilly in Trouble (Tr. Lance Salway / Ill. Carolyn Dinan). London, 1980.

Minnie (Tr. Lance Salway / Ill. P. Vos). Woodchester, 1992.

Pink Lemonade: Poems (Tr. Henrietta ten Harmsel / Ill. Timothy Foley). Grand Rapids, 1992.

ive

Times Two Picture-Poems

It's inevitable – a language-area famous above all for its painters is bound also to produce a good many poets who allow themselves to be inspired by paintings. And it does. The *Almanac of Contemporary Dutch and Flemish Literature* (Almanach zur niederländischen und flämischen Literatur der Gegenwart), published in August 1993 in connection with the Frankfurt Book Fair in October of the same year, which had the Dutch-speaking area as its focal point, includes some sixty poets; and more than half of them write, or wrote, picture-poems. That is a very high proportion. Their favourite painters are Hieronymus Bosch, Pieter Brueghel, Hercules Seghers, Rembrandt, Johannes Vermeer and Vincent van Gogh; noticeably rare, by contrast, are celebrations of works by Jan Steen, Frans Hals and Piet Mondrian. Poets with a particular feeling for the visual arts are, from the past, Albert Verwey and especially S. Vestdijk; and from the present generation Willem van Toorn, Hans Faverey, C.O. Jellema and J. Bernlef. The picture-poem is a popular genre, and some masterpieces are particularly favoured by poets. Brueghel's *Landscape with the Fall of Icarus,* for instance, inspired not only W.H. Auden in his famous 'Musée des Beaux-Arts', but also at least ten of his Dutch-speaking colleagues; while Rembrandt's *The Jewish Bride* has provided us with eight poems. Yet the best-known Dutch picture-poem by a long way derives not from the obvious source, our own Dutch Golden Age, but from a watercolour in Vienna's Albertina by the German Albrecht Dürer. This is 'The Columbine' by Ida Gerhardt, the grand old lady of Dutch poetry:

When that little plant he found,
he thoughtfully stooped to the ground
and then, around the roots and moss there,
he dug out the fine earth, with care,
to do no damage with his hand …

A good second in the popularity stakes comes Lucebert's 'Fisherman of Ma Yuan' – again, a far from indigenous subject:

under clouds the birds sail by
under waves the fishes fly
but between the fisher rests

waves to lofty clouds do turn
clouds turn into lofty waves
but meanwhile the fisher rests.

No poem about Rembrandt's *Nightwatch,* Paulus Potter's *Bull,* Vermeer's *Little Street* or van Gogh's *Sunflowers* approaches the popularity of these two poems inspired by works of art from elsewhere.

It is also striking how very rarely poets provide illustrations of the works of art to which their poems owe their existence. The most notable exception is S. Vestdijk; in 1956, Rembrandt Year, he published a volume of poems (his last) on works by the Master, with his source pictures reproduced at the end of the book. Poets evidently consider that the reader should be satisfied with the poems themselves.

However that may be, it is worth the reader's while to compare the source (the painting) with the result (the poem) and so try to work out to what extent, and in what way, the poet has bent the picture to his own theme. For that is what, if he is successful, the poet does with the painting. He does not describe it, he looks at it with a poet's eye and re-creates it in words; if not in his own likeness, at least tailored to fit his own view of the world. In the last resort, after all, what he sees in the painting is what he himself is and what he stands for. And that is what he extracts from it.

Pieter Pourbus, *Portrait of Jacquemyne Buuck.* 1551. Panel, 97.5 x 71.2 cm. Groeningemuseum, Bruges.

ANTON KORTEWEG
Translated by Tanis Guest.

E. Du Perron (1899-1940)
Adriana de Buuck

A sixteenth-century lady, not yet twenty;
the brow is narrow but young and smooth, and round
it the hair is piously combed back and brown,
with a fine gauze cap set on it lightly.

The figure stands unmoving, all in black, and where,
slipping out from the fur, the sleeves impress
some life with their warm crimson on that funereal dress,
the hands lie stiff together; little colour there.

And calm, too calm is this young woman's face. We may
guess at a fire those soft red lips betray,
deep down within those staring eyes suppressed.

A starved emotion, by a brutish lord,
church-going, languid gesture, modest words,
unworthy of the Virgin, as if by steel oppressed.

From *Collected Works, vol. I* (Verzameld werk 1, 1955)
Translated by Tanis Guest.

E. Du Perron (1899-1940)
Da Capo (6 years later)

That's what I wrote. What meant your sins to me –
me, on tiptoe under your portrait there?
No child could grasp your noble soul. As lovely
you seemed to me then as a tranquil prayer.

The mouths your mouth had salved I did not see,
nor how you'd constantly saved those who'd been
wounded beyond salvation by your beauty,
giving yourself, searing, pure and serene.

In this poor life the single gift, no more,
of god or devil who to us life gave,
poison-and-antidote, before the unfailing grave!

And what was written in your eyes, for sure:
contempt for punishment and a cool hate
and bitter grief that you could not give more.

From *Collected Works, vol. I* (Verzameld werk 1, 1955)
Translated by Tanis Guest.

Rembrandt H. Van Rijn,
The Jewish Bride. c.1665.
Canvas, 121.5 x 166.5 cm.
Rijksmuseum, Amsterdam.

Lenze L. Bouwers (1940-)

you are my bridegroom and I am your bride,
your man's arm stronger than my meek esteem,
your right hand touches words of heart and dream,
my left the answer that on your skin abides,
you are my bridegroom and I am your bride;
like a golden sparkle quiet along seam
and neck, richer than any merchant's minted pride;
you are my bridegroom and I am your bride

From *The Route of the Sightseeing-Boat* (De route van de rondvaartboot, 1987)
Translated by André Lefevere.

Pierre Kemp (1886-1967)
The Red of the Jewish Bride

I have loved the Red of the Jewish Bride
from the first time I saw it,
not realising yet
what kind of courtship I began that day.
I went there also when the sky was grey,
or the sun's light showed for a moment only
and flowed away in an unsteady line,
and then I sought the nuance that so tenderly,
yet never with passion enough,
asked me to stay a long time.
I saw the Bride with her left hand
play the piano on the right hand of
her husband made diffident by time
and I was not jealous. That was *their* bond.
I did not come to intrude upon their loving,
I am concerned with the Red of her dress
and with nothing else,
not even their entourage in golden-green.
Just to see *that* colour as a colour of today,
as though Rembrandt were beside me playing with it
amidst the bronzes of the background scene
and, whatever other colours he painted in,
still found that one colour for all time.
Whether or not the maulstick was used in her making,
it's his Red in which he sang the young Bride's dress;
it is my Red, surrounding her right hand,
not jewels, no, not fringes or lace,
it is only red, the Red, that I adore,
above all when I sit by Rembrandt in the sun.

From *Collected Works, vol. II* (Verzameld werk II, 1976)
Translated by Tanis Guest.

Rutger Kopland (1934-)
Brueghel's Winter

Roland Jooris (1936-)
Brueghel

Winter by Brueghel, the hill with hunters
and dogs, at their feet the valley with the village.
Almost home, but their dead-tired attitudes, their steps
in the snow – a return, but almost as

slow as arrest. At their feet the depths
grow and grow, become wider and further,
until the landscape vanishes into a landscape
that must be there, is there, but only

as a longing is there.

Ahead of them a jet-black bird dives down. Is it mockery
of this laboured attempt to return to the life
down there: the children skating on the pond,
the farms with women waiting and cattle?

An arrow underway, and it laughs at its target.

From *All Those Fine Promises* (Al die mooie beloften, 1978)
Translated by James Brockway (in 'A World Beyond Myself', London, 1991)

a bird,
sitting on a branch
of a tree in a
winter landscape like
in a painting
by Brueghel, has a
meaning one need
seek no further
than in its sharp
black presence
against the white
occurrence of a
space;

as though a bird defines
what visibly surrounds us
and illuminates it;

but does a bird
do that? does it not
sit still on its branch
with hunger and look
as sharp as its beak,
when the air, when the
cold cuts in the
winter light.

From *Poems 1958-1978*
(Gedichten 1958-1978, 1978)
Translated by Paul Vincent.

Pieter Brueghel, *Hunters in the Snow.* 1565. Canvas, 117 x 162 cm. Kunsthistorisches Museum, Vienna.

Johannes Vermeer,
View of Delft. c.1661.
Canvas, 98.5 x 117.5 cm.
Mauritshuis, The Hague.

Albert Verwey (1865-1937)
Vermeer seeing Delft as he will paint it

'A town on yonder side,
With towers and roofs and gateways,
Embankment and long barges,
Cloud-shadow, sunny light.

From here we can descry
The joint-marks in her buildings,
The cool glaze of her colours,
Things distant and near by.

How far she does outshine
Her image in the water! –
Will so God's City later
Outshine this town of mine?'

From *Collected Poems, vol. II* (Verzameld dichtwerk II, 1938)
Translated by Theodoor Weevers (in 'Vision and Form',
London, 1986).

Willem van Toorn (1935-)
Vermeer: View of Delft

I make you appear in this.
Your shadow announces you
round a corner. Had run some errands
in invisible alleys. Quivering

painted sunlight touches you
when you turn up on the quay.
Hatted governors are waiting
for dead vessels.

Their eyes follow you. Young miss. For certain
I'll let one of them sleep with you
tonight, if I keep you alive,
three hundred years from here.

From *A Crow near Siena* (Een kraai bij Siena, 1979)
Translated by Ria Leigh-Loohuizen.

Adriaen Coorte, *Still-Life with Asparagus, Goose-berries and Strawberries.* 1690. Canvas, 36.5 x 44 cm. Dordrechts Museum, Dordrecht.

Ed Leeflang (1929-)

Adriaen Coorte

Painter of asparagus and raspberries,
he's added lemons too and gooseberries
in tangible magnificence.
He sets them down, depicts their shape.
A rigid order they communicate,
stubbornness that helps the viewer share
durable pretence.
Things edible and perishable as
men are, have for a brief space been
wilfully set apart and raised
above nature's breathlessness. They must
and would transcend it, before becoming
indistinct remnants on a dinner-plate
or scrap heap.

From *Inhabited as I Am* (Bewoond als ik ben, 1981)
Translated by Paul Vincent.

Hans Faverey (1933-1990)

Blinds

before the white.
Snowscreens

against themselves. Pelican,
pecking its own breast,
stone plinth, without whom
nothing takes place.

As if ice-bound: error-flow,
permanently trickled.
Still air, the absence
of something, steadily beating

in gooseberry, raspberry,
the creamiest of asparagus.

From *Collected Poems* (Verzamelde gedichten, 1993)
Translated by Francis R. Jones.

Between

Theatre and Cinema

The Films of Alex van Warmerdam

Alex van Warmerdam in
Abel (1986).

Coming from the world of the theatre, the young Alex van Warmerdam (1952-) occupies a special place in the still not fully developed field of the Dutch feature film. To date he has made only two features, *Abel* (1986) and *The Northerners* (De Noorderlingen, 1992). A small output, as yet; and it is for its quality rather than its quantity that we shall be considering it here. This question of its quality led to fierce debate in the Dutch film world: was it filmed theatre or pure cinema?

The slightly absurdist characters, the lengthy dialogues, the disconcerting camera work and lighting and the more than artificial design occasioned considerable confusion in a film culture in which realism, both in documentaries and features, had always played a major role. But both sides in the debate were agreed on one point: *Abel* and *The Northerners* offered a unique view of what may be called the Dutch character.

Alex van Warmerdam was a complete novice when he became part of the film scene with his debut *Abel*. After studying graphics and going to art school in Amsterdam he seemed destined to become a painter. Perhaps inspired by his father, who was a stage manager, he made theatre his hobby. When he moved to Amsterdam he came into contact with a music group who were developing a kind of total theatre. He joined the group, along with his brothers Mark and Vincent (now an award-winning composer of film music). Under the name Hauser Orkater it was to play an important part in creating an unconventional kind of theatre.

Van Warmerdam's interest in cinema arose from his work on two television films made by Hauser Orkater, which included drawing the storyboards. With the type of logic characteristic of his work, he says: 'On the one hand it became clear how difficult film is, but on the other a kind of simplicity emerged. You shoot something, for example someone going out of a door. Then you pick that up on the other side, splice it together and it looks as if he's going through the door.'

Starting from this optimistic simplicity, Van Warmerdam set to work on the scenario for *Abel*. Out of long dialogues between three people developed the story of Abel, the withdrawn son who is too afraid of the outside world to leave home but is finally driven out by his father.

Without going in for detailed psychological explanations ('I don't like psychology. It completely throws me.'), Van Warmerdam gives his characters individual peculiarities. Throughout the film, for example, Abel is preoccupied with cutting buzzing flies in half, while his father wolfs down one copious meal after another on the grounds that: 'We must eat well because we're not working class'. In her own idiosyncratic fashion the seemingly docile mother, Duif, opposes the father's decision to turn Abel on to the streets.

'The smell of sprouts' is an expression in Dutch denoting everything that is petit bourgeois and small-minded, and in *Abel* Van Warmerdam uses an abundance of fish and fishy smells to underline these traits in his characters, in whom they are exaggerated and absurd but still recognisable. He abhors and mocks this small-mindedness while at the same time cherishing it as his inevitable heritage. Both in *Abel* and *The Northerners* there is a fascinating contrast between the almost affectionate depiction of pettiness and the design, in which this man of the theatre turns his slight fear of theatricality into a style.

Abel was shot almost entirely in the studio, using completely artificial sets, colours and lighting. Fake snow swirls round an old villa whose windows look out on to ultramodern skyscrapers. The characters always wear the same clothes, like figures in cartoons. Distances are all wrong, and the few locations are turned into sets. The streets are deserted; trees, lampposts and cars are carefully kept out of the picture, except for an occasional red Lada. Everything is redolent of cardboard and fakery.

Through their quasi-naturalistic acting Henri Garcin as the father, Olga Zuiderhoek as the mother and Alex van Warmerdam himself as Abel succeed in giving a tragicomic and at times moving logic to this illogical universe.

Van Warmerdam's debut caused a sensation in a national cinema balancing unsteadily between art and commerce, between small-scale, state-funded art films and big, relatively expensive commercial films, also subsidised, aimed at the international market. Other Dutch films released with varying degrees of success in the same year as *Abel* included the Oscar-winning *The Assault* (De Aanslag) by Fons Rademakers, the box-office hit

The housing estate in
The Northerners (1992).

The butcher and his wife in *The Northerners* (1992).

Flodder by Dick Maas (co-producer with Laurens Geels of *Abel*), the thoughtful *I Love Dollars* by Johan van der Keuken, the absurdist *The Pointsman* (De Wisselwachter) by Jos Stelling and the populist *The Good Hope* (Op Hoop van Zegen) by Guido Pieters.

With fifteen features and any number of documentaries being produced each year, it was widely felt that the Dutch film industry had come of age. The output was quite large and varied, ranging from commercial hits to artistic gems of high quality. Films such as *The Pointsman* and *Abel* even led to talk of a Dutch New Wave, the Holland School, excelling in caricaturing national traits and in its pronounced Dutch identity. The strong element of caricature gave rise to some concern about what other nations might think of the odd people in the smooth-shaven swampy delta called the Netherlands. But there was general agreement that the Holland School produced original and highly individual films. There was still hope for a small country forced to compete with giant European coproductions.

Eight years on the hopes of a Dutch New Wave have been dashed and the film industry is in deeper trouble than ever. Nonetheless, Alex van Warmerdam scored a success in 1992 with his second feature, *The Northerners,* which won the European Film Prize, the Felix, for best film by a young filmmaker.

Here again a story as improbable as it is recognisable is played out in an artificial setting. This time it is a new, unfinished and typically Dutch housing estate among the polders, fringed by carefully laid out woods. The inhabitants can be called the Postman, the Hunter, the Butcher and the Boy. They are emblems rather than people; their outlines largely determine their characters, as in comic strips and cartoons.

The story develops through their interaction. Outside events seldom affect its progress. In *The Northerners* the world stops at the edge of the woods surrounding the estate. A bus comes and goes but it brings only anonymous extras, the sole sign of life beyond the film location.

The postman (played by Alex van Warmerdam) functions as a *deus ex machina*. He knows what everyone is up to because he reads the post in the woods before delivering it. The hunter rules the woods and sees himself as the conscience of the community. He tries to hide his impotence and sterility behind inappropriately authoritarian behaviour. His wife meanwhile finds consolation in the arms of the far from impotent butcher, who has taken advantage of various of his employees because his wife is frigid and suffers from religious mania. When she goes on hunger strike, the estate soon becomes a place of pilgrimage which is even honoured with a visit from the bishop.

Once the characters have been described, so has the film. *The Northerners* is not much more than a collection of anecdotes and jokes which serve to reveal Dutch sensitivities and to expose characteristic mores and customs. Sharper, harder, more dryly comic and less theatrical than *Abel,* this film uses measured scenes to make clear what it is like to live in a country that is at once Catholic and Calvinist, petty and narrow-minded, progressive and spiritual. Instead of the smell of sprouts or fish, here we have a palette of familiar odours, such as those of roast meat, unwashed socks, new-mown grass, pine trees and exhaust gases.

For all these reasons, *The Northerners* deserves praise. But when it comes to cinematic qualities – the technique of propelling the story forward through an organic sequence of image and sound in which each scene develops from a previous one and points forward to a later one and in which the action is influenced or strengthened by the camera work – in short, when conventional film criteria are applied, all is confusion.

The camera work in *The Northerners* is more static than ever and has no driving force. The cutting is dull and often slow, the soundtrack plain and barely supportive. Other problems arise from the disappearance of the protagonist (the postman) half way through, the failure of the other characters really to come to life, the lack of a strong plot leading towards the end and the fact that nothing is fully resolved. All these are reasons why we should, in the end, give a negative answer to the question whether Van Warmerdam's work is truly cinematic. But how much does that really matter? He steers his own idiosyncratic and highly inventive course between theatre and cinema, with the dialogue, the anecdote, the always slightly theatrical design and the often archetypal characters combining to create a completely unique picture of a world which appears very Dutch. When that world contains so much that is recognisable and enjoyable, the whole debate as to whether or not it is film pales into insignificance.

GERDIN LINTHORST
Translated by John Rudge.

'Read me in full or not at all'

The Poetry of Leonard Nolens

It is not particularly difficult to write a purely informative introduction on a generally acclaimed poet from a smallish language area – in this case Dutch – for an international audience. However, it is a more interesting but also much trickier task to try to give some indication of the writer's international relevance. In the specific case of the Fleming Leonard Nolens (1947-), the problematic relationship between his own, exporting, source culture on the one hand and the foreign, recipient, target culture on the other is if anything even more complex. While it is true that in the Netherlands and Flanders his work is generally highly regarded by virtue of its non-conformist but very authentic tone – a recognition reflected in the award of the Dutch Jan Campert Prize and the Flemish Three-Yearly Poetry Prize – attention is invariably drawn to the unusual, unconventional character of his poetry. This ambivalent attitude is linked to Nolens' highly individual style, which certainly has its share of rhetoric and pathos. And it is precisely that combination of autobiographical authenticity and rhetorical embellishment which presents an additional problem for the export of his work, certainly to the Anglo-Saxon world, where a very different concept of poetry prevails. In this short essay, I hope nevertheless to be able to make out a case for this very unusual and absorbing poetry.

The reader of Nolens' poems is soon struck by the monomaniacal, quasi-obsessional nature of the work. The omnibus volume *Heart to Heart. Poems 1975-1990* (Hart tegen hart. Gedichten 1975-1990, 1991) is based almost entirely on only a few underlying themes and dominant motifs. The very titles of his successive volumes can in fact be interpreted as a condensed poetic programme: *Two Forms of Silence* (1975), *Incantation* (1977), *All the Time in the World* (1979), *Homage* (1981), *Vertigo* (1983), *The Dreamed Figure* (1986), *Certificate of Birth* (1988), *Love Declarations* (1990) and *Discord* (1992).[1] It is striking that with Nolens language does not function as a non-problematical means of communication, but on the contrary incorporates a complex range of speech acts, from invocation and incantation, to homage and declarations of love – both about and addressed to love, as well as spoken by love itself – through to an equally significant silence. However, this poetic discourse is not a self-contained, purely introspective activity, but is inherently relational, addressed to a definite other person. Finally there is the speaking I, which is given definition only in the highly problematical relationship with the other person and with language. Language, the Other and the I are the crucial coordinates of Nolens' poetic œuvre.

In general terms Nolens' poetry can be characterised as 'second-person lyricism'. As a poet Nolens clearly needs a sounding board to find his voice; he makes continual, insistent appeals to the presence of the other, and through him/her tries indirectly to situate himself as a subject. Pronouns like 'jij' (you) and 'Gij' (Thou) are used with striking frequency, since the concrete other affords an unmistakable glimpse of the unattainable absolute Other. Through constant reference to the second person, the reader is also, more directly than usual, involved in the poetic process as an active participant instead of an outside observer. The volume *Love Declarations,* for example, opens with a programmatic poem, 'To whom it may concern' ('Lectori salutem'), in which the reader becomes an accomplice by virtue of being addressed: 'So read me. Read me in full or not at all. (…) I wanted to speak, here, on everyone's behalf. / Am I a bottle at sea, a sermon in the dark?' However, at the same time the second person refers just as strongly to the poet, communicating and debating with himself … This creates a significant tension between dialogue and monologue, provocation and confession; the fact that Leonard Nolens attaches such importance to writing and publishing a *literary* diary – in which the close interconnection between Nolens the writer and Nolens the man is forcefully demonstrated – is eloquent proof of this.

This complex relationship between the I and the various manifestations of the Other forms the central axis of Nolens' work. In fact, the Other may assume a wide variety of forms. On the one hand there are various characters from the poet's immediate environment: father and mother, close friends and of course the beloved woman. On the other hand authors with whom he feels an affinity are regularly introduced into the poems, helping to give fuller form to the problematic poetics. However, on closer inspection one notices that all these figures – despite their disparity – are in fact extensions of each other. Again and again we encounter 'reflections', representations with which the poet Nolens may enter into an intense confrontation, but from which at the same time he attempts to derive his own identity.

In the earlier work particularly there are a large number of poems which are addressed to other writers: the Flemish experimentalists Hugues C. Pernath and Marcel van Maele, but also writers like Cesare Pavese, Edmond Jabès and Paul Celan are never far away in these poems, giving Nolens' writing an eminently international flavour. The first thing which attracts Nolens in such symbolic fathers is their exemplary tragedy, their tormented and non-conformist humanity, precisely because in their work there is maximum convergence of life and artistic commitment. In this respect they constitute an ideal starting point for an impassioned paean of praise to the poetic word and the radical individual existence without compromise or limitations. At the same time that passionate relationship with the other as model, master *and* rival is evoked in highly imaginative, sometimes even homo-erotic images. This is the true world of Leonard Nolens: not that of mutedly emotional Romanticism, but of confrontation which penetrates to the marrow.

Leonard Nolens (1947-)
(Photo by Herman
Selleslags).

The same ambivalence defines his relationship with both parents, which runs like a thread through the work. Nolens certainly shows a strong genealogical awareness, in which the poetic I constantly tries to define itself in relation to its 'origin' and its own autobiographical past. For example, in the 'In memoriam matris' section of *Two Forms of Silence,* the mother's portrait is placed between the two paradoxical extremes 'I shall die you. (…) I shall live you.' On the one hand she is 'A garment I'm outgrowing', but on the other hand the memory of her persists in monumental form, as both origin and future. In that imaginary relationship pattern the two antagonists are interchangeable; the emphatic presence of the mother is compared to an unborn child, and the son in his turn with a mother failing in her duty. It is no coincidence that the mother should be herself finally transformed into a poetic creation. And conversely, in the recent collection *Discord,* the usual cliché of the poet as 'pregnant' with thoughts is radicalised into its most oppressive physical consequences. The poet carries and gives birth to the verse like a child, and thus as it were achieves his own birth. The subject is created only through the poetic word, not as a definite given, but as a permanently provisional 'becoming'; indeed, that truth is not a voluntary choice, but rather an obligation or even a doom.

The role of the father is just as ambivalent. First and foremost the father is the symbol par excellence of everything from which the I is struggling to free itself: the paralysing law, the oppressive weight of the past, the family prehistory and the claustrophobic surroundings. On the other hand the son becomes a father in his turn, and eventually finds himself partially identifying with the despised father.

Finally the beloved woman appears as an incarnation of the uncanny other, who remains both terribly familiar and essentially unknown. Though by her presence she allows the I figure to achieve optimal self-realisation, at the same time she too is recalcitrant, a stranger who constantly stands in the way of a boundless narcissistic expansion of the I. Leonard Nolens has been able to transform the resulting dichotomy between wanting to be alone to (be able to) find oneself and the simultaneous tragic awareness that any identity can only be provided by the other, into a number of impressive passionate love poems: 'Come and touch me. I want to be alone again.'

Partly because of this necessary detour via the Other, the poetic I never appears in these texts as something axiomatic and given, but is on the contrary marked by a fundamental sense of fragmentation; the I is essentially alien to itself and tries laboriously, via the confrontation with the other and with the word to (re)construct itself as a subject. In this respect there are two typical strategies. First there is negativity, because of which the I figure (whether out of impotence or disinclination) refuses to characterise itself as a positive entity, but generally resorts to negative assertions: 'I'm no longer a son, no longer a seer. (...) I'm no longer a man, no longer a lover. (...) I'm no longer a poet, no longer a poem.' In addition it is striking how often Nolens in his poetry evokes the spectre of the 'fragmented body'; in Lacanian psychoanalysis that term is used to denote a stage in which the infant does not yet see itself as an entity or continuous identity, but on the contrary experiences itself as fragmented, chaotic, centrifugal. Characteristic of this are the large number of words referring to primitive bodily functions (faeces, urine, sperm and sweat) and the way in which the body, via the objectifying gaze, is represented as an anonymous matter or a huge hole. Within this precarious play of tensions between identity and otherness the linguistic order plays a crucial role. In numerous poetical texts the poet reflects on his craft and his medium. The (poetic) word is alternately equated with an eroticised or on the contrary decaying body, with a journey of adventure or banishment, with wordless music, with a process of mystical introspection or on the contrary inadequate exteriorisation, all metaphors with which both the complexity and the ambivalences of poetry are very suggestively analysed. In the cycle 'Homage to the Word' ('Hommage aan het woord') in *Homage* the ultimate poetic Word is addressed as 'the restless place where I don't yet exist', 'the hour which must fill all my cracks' or even 'the hunger / Which eats me and may well satisfy me'.

The solemn, evocative tone, the expansive rhetoric and the strikingly apodictic use of language are, to put it mildly, highly unusual in Dutch literature and may well initially disturb readers from the English language-area. Yet that unfashionable pathos accords perfectly with Nolens' striving to evoke in plain terms precisely those fundamental existential experiences which most people prefer to pass over in silence or with euphemism. And instead of believing in the naive illusion of transparent communication – which is supposed to enable the reader to make direct contact with the poet's personality and world through the words of the text – Nolens resolutely opts for the opposite: the impenetrability and materiality (literalness) of language. In consequence repetition and variation are far from being neutral stylistic devices in this œuvre, but are completely bound up with the ambiguity and paradoxical nature of the intangible human experiences which Nolens attempts to make tangible. Thus the numerous imperative forms are by no means a monotonous feature. They reveal something of that complex vision, by being used alternately (and just as frequently simultaneously) to express an authoritarian command, an invocation, an exhortation, a wish or an entreaty ... And the insistent repetitions suggest an impetus allied not only to impatience but also to unease and rejection; at the same time they provide subtle shifts of meanings and connections, by integrating the same words and phrases in constantly changing contexts.

Precisely because of this, Nolens' work is perhaps best read as the monumental symbolisation of an autobiography. A life which obsessively writes and rewrites itself as an auto-graphy. Which paradoxically resorts to the living letter, against the threatening background of dead script. Or which, conversely, from fear of the transience of language, inscribes itself in graphic characters.

DIRK DE GEEST
Translated by Paul Vincent.

NOTE   1. Original titles: *Twee vormen van zwijgen* (1975), *Incantatie* (1977), *Alle tijd van de wereld* (1979), *Hommage* (1981), *Vertigo* (1983), *De gedroomde figuur* (1986), *Geboortebewijs* (1988), *Liefdes verklaringen* (1990), *Tweedracht* (1992).

Four Poems by Leonard Nolens

Kiss

With you away my time has overflowed.
Gone are the banks which were my vantage point,
Gone are the firm contours of our presence.
You directed all waters, brought the Greek river
Of passing time to our house and put it to sleep
In our bed, we could see it through ourselves.

Tomorrow when you return the hours can converge again here

At our door and flow straight and true on their course.
We shall be clearly reflected up here,
High up on the banks, now submerged, we shall sit
To join hands and relinquish the chaos.
We'll embrace to delimit dry land,
To define emptiness with a kiss.

From *Heart to Heart. Poems 1975-1990* (Hart tegen hart. Gedichten 1975-1990, 1991)
Translated by Paul Vincent.

Tributary

She sleeps and all is still. Snow falls in the rooms
Of the house I live in with my lover.
She lies there naked, white, a breathing stone,
A large and tiresome statue I can't help bumping into,
A harsh weight that I must carry every day,
Every night that her sleep keeps me awake.

I am alone with her. Only with her do I
Make it down the years, since her name shows me the way
And in her eyes I see my blind time reflected.
She lies there naked, white, a breathing stone
On which I have whetted my whole blunt existence
And do still, even when I sleep and call to her in dreams.

From *Heart to Heart. Poems 1975-1990* (Hart tegen hart. Gedichten 1975-1990,1991)
Translated by Paul Vincent.

To whom it may concern

I've brought you with me to this halfway-house.
The loft's abuzz with voices like a hive.
Hatred and love help swell the honeycombs
With the poems to be consumed elsewhere.

Thus I portray, poison and antidote, transformed,
What I've purloined from you, a little world
Paid for with my capture of your mystery.
Only you gain freedom here in black and white.

So read me. Read me in full or not at all.
This was my wish, I'd not do this alone,
I wanted to speak, here, on everyone's behalf.
Am I a bottle at sea, a sermon in the dark?

I was still young, I dreamt that I appeared here
Like one walking singing over yonder hills.
I dreamt I wrote like a dead man speaks
With all the gift of tongues his absence brings.

From *Heart to Heart. Poems 1975-1990*
(Hart tegen hart. Gedichten 1975-1990,1991)
Translated by Paul Vincent.

Last Wishes

At that moment it will all be easy,
Mother there'll be pregnant
With the same son,
On father's stone

Reconciliation, large as life,
Its case will be consigned
To the sea, at that moment
Going will be easy.

So take my coat off then,
I wore it for form's sake.
And take my trousers off,
As I did every day.

And lay me slowly, slowly
In a box, for I was slow.
And keep me in a grave,
I don't want an oven.

Don't burn my bones.
I've been on fire enough.
I've long since baked right through.
Don't turn my crumbs to ash.

Lower me, haltingly,
As I have always lived.
And bless that bread with a cross
Just as my mother did.

Carve my name, my dates,
So even the blind can see me.
For me alone my life's in vain,
And was in vain. But not for us.

From *Discord* (Tweedracht, 1992)
Translated by Paul Vincent.

Spinoza and the Golden Age of the Dutch Republic

When philosophers write about other philosophers who are long dead and so cannot reply, they usually do so in order to highlight the relevance of those earlier thinkers to current issues. Instead of studying old philosophical texts whith an eye to the texts themselves, they claim rather that what they are doing is above all of great significance for the current debate. Significant, of course, for the philosophical debate. Anglo-Saxon philosophers are particularly reluctant to admit that they are interested in their subject's past for the sake of the past itself. This essentially unhistorical concern for philosophy's past has produced some fine books – on Plato and Aristotle, Descartes and Leibniz, Kant, Hegel and Wittgenstein. But for the layman those books are often extremely boring, if not totally unintelligible. Anyone who does not spend sleepless nights worrying about the problem of free will or the definition of substantiality is far better off with an answer to the question of how earlier thinkers related to their own times.

Take, for instance, the seventeenth-century philosopher Spinoza (1632-1677), undoubtedly the most famous philosopher in the history of the Netherlands, particularly for his *Ethics,* the book published soon after his death. At first sight the book's form adheres strictly to the timeless aspirations of philosophy as such. Modelled on Euclid's *Elements,* it consists of five parts in which propositions are derived from definitions and axioms – *more geometrico,* as the mathematicians call it, though Spinoza's propositions are not concerned with points, straight lines or triangles, but with God, the human spirit, passions and freedom. This geometrical expression of his ideas certainly makes him the ideal 'philosophers' philosopher', if only because of the unique opportunity it gives the reader to check the – quite astonishing – consistency of his concepts.

But every historian knows that this fascination with mathematics is a hallmark of the seventeenth century. Moreover, only a historical approach can at least try to explain how Spinoza was *possible,* in other words how he could be a product of the Dutch Republic of that time. For Spinoza is actually in many respects an exceptional philosopher. For a start he was a Dutchman, and our view of the Dutch Golden Age is still determined by painters. Everyone knows of Rembrandt, Vermeer, Frans Hals, Jan Steen,

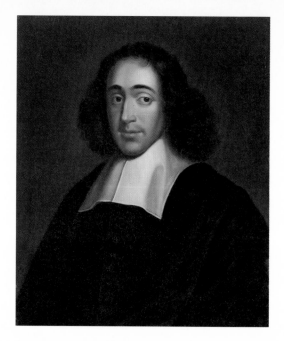

Portrait of Spinoza.
Dutch School, after 1650.
Canvas. Historisch Museum,
The Hague.

Saenredam, Gerard Dou and many others, and Dutch masters from the Golden Age of the United Provinces are treasured in every international art gallery. That the seventeenth-century Republic also spawned great scientists, outstanding statesmen, remarkably successful merchants and fine seamen is also well known; but when we think of the Netherlands, even of the Netherlands of the Golden Age, we do not immediately think of philosophical achievements. Yet the Golden Age apparently offered fertile ground for the emergence of this remarkable Spinozan philosophy, as well as of a Rembrandt, a Johan de Witt, a Michiel Adriaansz de Ruyter, a Leeuwenhoek and a Boerhaave. And it is clear from recent research that the history of philosophy in the Dutch Republic is in fact of considerable importance.

We might start by looking at the organisation of philosophical activities in the seventeenth century. Professional philosophers today generally regard their field as an essentially academic discipline. One studies philosophy at university, and philosophers *work* almost exclusively in universities. Things were rather different in the seventeenth century. Of the great philosophers of the early modern period, only one or two were attached to academies. Descartes, Hobbes, Locke, Leibniz and Hume were never professors. Only since Kant have the great philosophers been professional academics. Spinoza, too, never worked in a university. When, in 1673, he was offered a chair in Heidelberg, he declined politely and emphatically. He preferred to write his books as a free-lance outsider rather than a civil servant. He was self-employed and, so it seems, thought too highly of philosophy to become a professor of it; for the standing of philosophy at the university was somewhat uncertain. Traditionally, philosophy was a preliminary course for students going on to read a 'real' subject in one of the three major faculties of theology, medicine or law. It was only in the course of the seventeenth century that philosophy became a subject in its own right and no longer merely a foundation course for those intending to become clergymen, doctors or lawyers.

Indeed, at first there was no indication that Spinoza would become a scholar. Less than twenty years before his invitation to Heidelberg he was dealing in Mediterranean fruits. After attending the yeshiva run by the religious society Ets Haim in Amsterdam, he ran the firm Bento y Gabriël de Spinoza with his brother. But in 1656, when he was twenty-three, he was banned, and all his links with the Sephardic community in his home-town were thereby cut. Unlike many other outcasts – it was by no means exceptional to be (temporarily) banned from the synagogue – Spinoza accepted the break as irreversible, and started looking for a new way of life. He dropped the name Baruch in favour of Benedict, probably attended lectures for a time at Leiden University, and found a new source of income. He became a lens grinder.

Why the rabbis of Amsterdam no longer wanted the young Baruch in their congregation is unknown. Probably they could no longer put up with his impertinent questions about *Tenach* (what Christians call the Old Testament). Probably in the mid-1650s Spinoza had already written the nucleus of what was to appear anonymously in 1670 as his *Tractatus theologico-politicus*. However that may be, in 1656 Spinoza is literally and metaphorically out on the street. But he finds a new home with Franciscus van den Enden, a one-time Jesuit from Antwerp who had established a Latin school in the heart of the city, right behind the Dam, among dozens of bookshops. There the sons of the city's patriciate were initiated into the classics, and there Descartes was read. This interest in Descartes in Amsterdam in the middle of the seventeenth century is not in itself remarkable. Descartes had lived for twenty years in the Netherlands, he had published his most important works in Amsterdam and Leiden and acquired his first serious following in Dutch universities; and that *was* remarkable.

As we have said, the universities of Europe in the early modern period were not exactly hotbeds of philosophical innovation. In Oxford and Cambridge as well as Paris, not to mention the southern universities, Aristotle was read right up to the eighteenth century as if time had stood still. Though academic Aristotelianism was not – as was believed for a long time – a medieval anachronism, but rather the result of a sixteenth-century Aristotle 'revival', it hardly encouraged intellectual acceptance of the one intellectual challenge that fascinated the progressive minds of the seventeenth century: the so-called 'mechanisation of the world picture'. Descartes' ideas were, however, largely based on this very mechanisation, so that in the middle of the seventeenth century Cartesianism, which had provided the sciences with an entirely new foundation, was considered to be the 'modern' philosophy. There were, however, deep divisions about the desirability of this new philosophy. Many theologians in particular were far from enthusiastic.

Yet around 1650, the year in which Descartes succumbed in Stockholm to the exhausting regime of Queen Christina's court and died, there was in the Dutch Republic an extensive academic network of theologians, physicists and philosophers who were very attracted to Cartesianism. The regents who served on the boards of the universities listened courteously to the orthodox Calvinists' opposition to Cartesian metaphysics and numerous

other aspects of Descartes' legacy, but no action was taken. If a ban was imposed, or if the Cartesian professors were maybe advised to keep a low profile, such measures were usually ignored. It was through the Cartesian influence on higher education in the Republic that philosophy developed as it did, into an autonomous discipline. It also laid the foundation in the second half of the seventeenth century for the crucial part to be played by Leiden University in disseminating Newtonianism in the first half of the eighteenth century. But that is another story.

In fact, the Dutch regent patriciate turned non-intervention in politics into a fine art. Even books that were proscribed, such as those by Hobbes and the Socinians, and finally Spinoza's, remained available on the open market, to the chagrin of the orthodox calvinists, not surprisingly, and to the amaze-ment of several foreign visitors to the Netherlands, who could not believe their eyes, unaccustomed as they were to this kind of government indiffer-ence. It was also quite clear to foreigners that the Republic was in no way ill-served by this deliberate indifference to the religious or philosophical views of its subjects. The Republican faction in the Netherlands of the time, to which Spinoza also belonged, defiantly formulated the advantages of this indifference: the success of the Republic depended on trade, and the trader selling or purchasing should not have to wonder whether his supplier or

Letter from Spinoza to Gottfried Wilhelm Leibniz, written in The Hague on 9 November 1671 (facsimile: original in the Niedersächsische Landesbibliothek, Hannover).

customer was a Calvinist, Lutheran, Catholic or Turk. Just so long as he supplied or paid. This, combined with the essentially theological Erasmian tradition of tolerance, provided such a cast-iron battery of arguments in favour of mutual tolerance that it survives honourably to this day in the Netherlands.

What is more, if the government really was minded to take firm action, the extensive decentralisation of public authorities severely limited the possibilities of implementing any more restrictive policy. There has never been a Versailles in the Netherlands. The provinces and the large cities in those provinces simply refused to give up their autonomy. Just as they had refused to yield to the Spanish Habsburgs and the Roman popes, so now they positively declined to bend the knee to the States-General in The Hague or the doctrinal authority of the synods of the Reformed Church. It cannot be overemphasised that in the Netherlands it was not just the university government but all public administration that was in the hands of the regents; and they were descended from families that had made their fortunes in commerce.

It was relatively easy for a young Jewish exile, such as Spinoza in the 1650s, in every way a marginal figure, to flourish on the fringes offered by the Republic to outsiders. He could easily acquire books by Descartes, and numerous commentaries on them by the latest Cartesian professors at

Leiden and Utrecht. There was nothing to stop him discussing recent developments in philosophy and science with his new friends. In this climate, where the diehard right wing of the Dutch Reformed Church was steadily losing its hold on public opinion, where the field seemed to be open to a staggering diversity of religious and philosophical societies, where the most exotic books were published and read, in this climate Spinoza must have been in his element. He made friends with liberal Mennonites who had broken away from all church doctrine, entering in complete freedom into debates on the Bible, on God and man, on good and evil, without the services of any minister. Descartes' call to use your own judgement rather than relying on tradition found a ready hearing in these circles. Away with preconceived ideas! For if by using reason you can arrive at the course of the planets, why should you not then be able rationally to debate the necessity of baptism or the authenticity of the books of the Bible? Our reason is after all God-given? When all is said and done, is reason not actually the divine *in* us?

Franciscus van den Enden and his friends went even further. Was Descartes' rationalism itself actually all that rationalistic? Why was Descartes so cautious where theology was involved? And why had Descartes never formulated a political philosophy? Precisely what Van den Enden taught his pupils we do not know. But in the early 1660s dangerous rumours were already circulating in Amsterdam. Van den Enden was said to lead a circle of disaffected Cartesians, of 'naturalists', of *atheists*. Van den Enden himself came to a sorry end. In 1670 he closed his school, reappearing soon after in Paris where he became closely involved with a notorious plot against Louis XIV. But he was betrayed, and in 1674 he was hanged in the Place de la Bastille.

Spinoza was more circumspect. There may have been considerable freedom in the Netherlands, but Spinoza realised that even in the Netherlands there were limits to tolerance. He withdrew to smaller towns like Rijnsburg and Voorburg. In 1663 he published a brilliant – geometrically arranged – *Principia Cartesianae Philosophiae,* in which he also warily indicated that he himself was not a fully committed Cartesian. But how he proposed to 'improve' on Descartes remained a mystery. When in 1669 his friend Adriaan Koerbagh perished in the Amsterdam gaol after the first impression of his highly Spinozistic *A Light Shining in Dark Places* (Een ligt schijnende in de duystere plaatsen, 1668) had been impounded, Spinoza became even more cautious. His *Tractatus theologico-politicus* appeared anonymously the following year. Not that that made much difference, since everyone knew immediately who the author was. And the book was butchered. Although the critics all agreed that they were up against an exceptionally gifted opponent, all the theological factions – the Calvinists, Arminians, the Cartesians and even the universally despised Socinians – took fright at Spinoza's thinly disguised atheism. For that, in their view, was what Spinozism was all about. Spinoza, after all, had maintained that the powers of nature were the same as God's, and that real miracles did not exist, that the prophets in the Bible were simply endowed with lively imaginations, that Moses could not possibly have written the first five books of the Old Testament, that theology and philosophy were two entirely different disciplines and that only philosophy was capable of formulating truths, so that philosophers must be allowed freedom of thought, that democracy was the most natural form of government, and a whole lot more. It was all equally appalling, but what else could you expect from an atheist?

Spinoza was deeply hurt. He decided to keep his masterpiece, the *Ethics,* under wraps. He was about to publish it in 1675, having moved in the meantime to The Hague, but had second thoughts at the last moment. Not until two years later, just after his death, was it published by his friends as part of the so-called *Opera Posthuma.* It does then indeed become apparent that he identifies God with nature, that he attempts to interpret man as a perfectly natural being, that he believes that nature is governed by an absolute determinism, but that this need not lead to fatalism, because knowledge of the causal mechanism by which everything is made what it is, turns passive feelings into active and ultimately leads to what he calls 'amor intellectualis Dei'. This provoked further torrents of refutation. Until well into the eighteenth century he was attacked as the most dangerous atheist of his day, but he was also read – in France, for instance, by the radical wing of the Enlightenment and by the authors and copyists of the clandestine manuscript circuit. Later he was reinstated by the trend-setters of German Idealism, after which he gained his established place in the pantheon of western philosophy.

At this point emerges the myth of the isolated genius, the man rising above his time and place. Nor is that myth entirely absurd. Myths seldom are. Spinoza was certainly isolated, inasmuch as he proclaimed utterly revolutionary ideas. Moreover, anyone who writes such an *Ethics* as Spinoza wrote, cannot avoid shutting himself up for years in his study. The writing of such a book demands peace and quiet. But this should not eclipse the fact that Spinoza did indeed find that peace and quiet in the Netherlands. We have already seen that Spinoza as a Dutch philosopher was a remarkable phenomenon of international stature, even allowing for the fact that Dutch universities in the seventeenth and eighteenth centuries made an outstanding contribution to the history of early modern philosophy.

Yet from a historical perspective, Spinoza's uniqueness must be accounted for in other ways: in his relationship to other – mainly older – philosophers who were also of the opinion that freedom in a prescribed universe

Reconstruction of Spinoza's library in Rijnsburg (Photo by Theo van der Werf).

consists in an understanding of the principles of that universal determinism. Isaiah Berlin once remarked (in *Four Essays on Liberty,* 1969) that such a concept of freedom *'seems to arise when the external world has proved exceptionally arid, cruel, or unjust (…). In a world where man seeking happiness or justice or freedom (in whatever sense) can do little, because he finds too many avenues of action blocked to him, the temptation to withdraw into himself may become irresistible. It may have been so in Greece, where the Stoic ideal cannot be wholly unconnected with the fall of the independent democracies before centralised Macedonian autocracy. It was so in Rome, for analogous reasons, after the end of the Republic.'*

The unique quality of Spinoza's ideas seems to be just this, that he was a 'Stoic' who did not reject the world around him, but embraced it as the inescapable product of the necessity that is the universe.

In the *Tractatus theologico-politicus* he said in so many words that he reckoned himself fortunate in living at a time and in a country where freedom was also nurtured by the authorities:

'Take the city of Amsterdam, which enjoys the fruits of this freedom, to its own considerable prosperity and the admiration of the world. In this flourishing state, a city of the highest renown, men of every race and sect live in complete harmony; and before entrusting their property to some person they will want to know no more than this, whether he is rich or poor and whether he has been honest or dishonest in his dealings. As for religion or sect, that is of no account, because such considerations are regarded as irrelevant in a court of law; and no sect whatsoever is so hated that its adherents – provided that they injure no one, render to each what is his own, and live upright lives – are denied the protection of the civil authorities.'

One of the most important propositions in the *Ethics* – it is the 29th in the first book – is this: 'In nature there is nothing contingent, but all things have been determined from the necessity of the divine nature to exist and produce an effect in a certain way.'

You do not need to be a Spinozist to see how the Golden Age of the Dutch Republic at the very least made Spinoza possible. The Republic did that by giving space to outsiders, to fringe figures, to minorities. And you need not go looking for the relevance of the past in order to find it.

WIEP VAN BUNGE
Translated by Peter King.

BENNETT, JONATHAN, *A Study of Spinoza's Ethics.* Cambridge, 1984.

BOUCHER, WAYNE I., *Spinoza in English. A Bibliography from the Seventeenth Century to the Present.* Leiden, 1991.

CURLEY, EDWIN, *Behind the Geometrical Method. A Reading of Spinoza's Ethics.* Princeton, 1989.

CURLEY, EDWIN and PIERRE-FRANCOIS MOREAU, *Spinoza. Issues and Directions. The Proceedings of the Chicago Spinoza Conference.* Leiden, 1990.

DONAGAN, ALAN, *Spinoza.* New York, 1988.

HAMPSHIRE, STUART, *Spinoza. An Introduction to his Philosophical Thought.* Harmondsworth, 1987 (1951).

POPKIN, RICHARD, *The History of Scepticism from Erasmus to Spinoza.* Berkeley, 1979.

VERBEEK, THEO, *Descartes and the Dutch. Early Reactions to Cartesian Philosophy 1637-1650.* Edwardsville / Carbondale, 1992.

YOVEL, YIRMIYAHU, *Spinoza and Other Heretics.* Princeton, 1989, 2 vols.

LIST OF TRANSLATIONS

Tractatus theologico-politicus (Tr. Samuel Shirley with an introduction by Brad S. Gregory). Leiden, 1989.

The Collected Works of Spinoza. Volume 1 (ed. and tr. Edwin Curley). Princeton, 1985.

THE INTERNATIONAL SPINOZA SOCIETY IN THE NETHERLANDS

When the house in Rijnsburg in which Spinoza had lived for a number of years was for sale in 1896, the *Vereniging Het Spinozahuis* was founded for the purpose of buying and establishing it as a Spinoza Museum. At present it houses, among many other things, the collection of books Spinoza possessed at the time of his death. One of the main objectives of the Society – in addition to managing the museum and keeping the building in good repair – is the advancement of the study of Spinoza's works. This is primarily done by means of organising meetings, publishing scholarly papers in the series *Mededelingen* and the distribution of a Newsletter, containing information about congresses, symposia, Spinoza-research and recent publications. The Society also has a Library and Reading room in *Domus Spinozana* in The Hague, the house in which Spinoza died in 1677.

For further information, please write to:
Secretary *Vereniging Het Spinozahuis*
Paganinidreef 66 / 2253 SK Voorschoten / The Netherlands

Euthanasia

in the Netherlands

Facts and Moral Arguments

The year is 1990, and the place a University Hospital in France. The medical staff is confronted with a problem: a considerable number of cancer patients have tried to commit suicide by jumping from the roof of the hospital. When asked why, the patients answer that 'they cannot stand the treatment anymore'.

The first moral principle: respect for patients

A situation like this is unthinkable in the Netherlands. In that country most (cancer) patients are well-informed, they know their diagnoses and prognoses, and if they cannot bear the treatment any longer, they have the absolute right to refuse. Even if such a refusal will lead to a quick death, this right can be sustained. In the Dutch view, respect for patients means that they have such a right at any moment during the course of treatment.

It is this same respect which may also lead to a positive reaction to a request for euthanasia – the active procurement of a gentle death – by terminal patients confronted with a difficult and painful process of dying, and especially with loss of human dignity in the last weeks of their lives.

The debate about the moral acceptability of euthanasia is in the Netherlands indeed closely associated with the moral principle of respect for the patient, with his right not to be treated against his wishes, and with his right to die in full control of the situation. To provide a gentle death within the context of the entire medical treatment is generally felt to be a moral duty of physicians.

Necessary conditions for the euthanasia debate

Of course, most health care professionals in western countries will hold the view that patients are entitled to respect. But the association between respect for patients and euthanasia is seldom made. It seems that only in the Netherlands has a real moral debate taken place on euthanasia, or gentle death. Indeed, more than simply respect for patients is required for an open debate on this issue.

First of all, society at large has to acknowledge death as an inescapable human reality which cannot always be postponed by medical treatment. It may be that the core of the resistance to euthanasia is a denial of mortality – and also of the limits of medicine.

For that is the second condition for a debate about, and the practice of, euthanasia: physicians as well as patients must be aware of the limits of medicine. Medicine, although at times very successful, cannot cure all diseases, and certainly cancer patients may experience the tragic limits of medical intervention.

A third condition has to do with a specific view of the dying person. Discussions about euthanasia are based on the supposition that the dying patient is still a moral actor, and not only a passive victim of his disease. It is one of the results of modern medicine that dying, this so far unmanageable part of human existence, has become manageable, at least to a certain extent.

Factual changes leading to the necessity of discussing euthanasia

Apart from these more or less moral considerations, some factual developments in medicine may also explain the need felt in the Netherlands to discuss and sometimes to perform euthanasia.

First, there has been a major change in the patterns of dying and causes of mortality in the last fifty years. As late as 1918-1920, 20 million people all over the world died of influenza, as many as were killed in the entire First World War. But generally speaking, they died 'gently'; no medical interference was needed to kill their pain or agony. Infectious diseases with their usually gentle dying process were the major cause of death until antibiotics were discovered. Then a sudden change in mortality took place: cardiac failure and cancer became the predominant causes of death, the latter especially often culminating in a difficult process of dying. Moreover, the dying process is often prolonged as a result of medical technology. Both facts contribute to the need to discuss the gentle death; death has become less and less gentle.

A further consideration is that, at least in the Netherlands, a very obvious change has occurred in the patient-doctor relationship: patients and doctors tend more and more to decide together on the treatment and its conclusion; we may speak of a certain democratisation of their relationship.

Situations and definitions

We have defined euthanasia as 'the active procurement of a gentle death'. But there are other possible courses of action at the end of life. We can define at least the following situations:

a. *Refusal of treatment.* Sometimes patients refuse (further) medical treatment, for two reasons: because they dislike the sort of treatment that has been offered, or because they feel that their life has come to its end and that death is no longer an enemy. Such a refusal may cause a moral dilemma for the doctors or the patient's family, but is morally justifiable and legally permitted: although medicine is of great benefit for patients, there can be no obligation to be treated.

b. Non-treatment decisions. Not only patients, but also doctors may decide to forgo futile medical treatment. Morally this is especially problematic with respect to incompetent persons, like comatose patients, psychogeriatric patients, and newborns, because of the plural meaning of the word 'futile'. In the Netherlands, non-treatment decisions are not only widely accepted, but are considered a necessary part of humane medicine. This surely is the case all over the world. In the Remmelink Investigation[1], which yielded a great deal of data on the actions of doctors and patients regarding the end of life in the Netherlands, it is estimated that in one out of three cases (50,000 a year) some kind of decision is made by a doctor or a patient to withhold treatment, also from incompetent patients. Moreover, in 1,000 cases physicians decided, after such a decision, to ease the incompetent patient's dying by pain killing medication, so that death was somewhat hastened, but never by more than a few days. In fact this last practice is an instance of:

c. Indirect euthanasia. This means that relief from pain is the objective, while death is accepted as a concurrent result. This is an example of the well-known principle of the double effect, long ago conditionally accepted by the Roman Catholic doctrine. Indirect euthanasia is practised both on request and without the request of a patient, but always concerns only dying patients. The new Dutch law requires a thorough investigation of each case of pain relief which results in death where a non-competent patient is involved.

d. Active euthanasia. Death is actively caused by intravenous drugs, by injection (rarely) or by pills, provided by a physician, and always at the request of the patient.

e. Assisted suicide. In the Netherlands the term 'assisted suicide' is generally reserved for something different from active euthanasia. Assisted suicide refers to persons who are not suffering from a terminal disease, but who still have reasons for wishing to die. This is a serious problem and should be treated differently from euthanasia. That means that we reserve the word *euthanasia* for reference to patients *dying of a terminal disease.* Because refusal of treatment by patients, non-treatment decisions by doctors, and pain relief resulting in death are legally permitted, the Dutch political debate has been concentrated on active (requested) euthanasia alone.

The present situation in the Netherlands

Each year there are about 2,300 cases of active euthanasia in the Netherlands. Physicians will not be prosecuted if these criteria are met:
– the patient has persistently requested euthanasia
– the patient is in a hopeless and intolerable situation
– the physician has consulted another physician about the diagnosis and prognosis
– the physician can provide a written report with all the relevant medical data about the disease and the death of the patient.

All these conditions have to be met at the same time. These criteria are based on jurisdiction and on agreements between prosecutors and organisations of physicians, and are confirmed in the recent new law, which in fact supplements existing legislation concerning the disposal of the dead.

At the same time, however, euthanasia and assisted suicide continue to be punishable under Articles 293 and 294 of the Penal Code. The new law of 1993 provides for a report procedure for each separate case; the physician can reasonably *expect* not to be prosecuted if he adheres to the criteria, but has no certainty of this.

This means that in fact the law does not go far enough for the advocates of freely available euthanasia, while for their opponents it goes too far.

Thus, the then Catholic Minister of Justice (who belongs to the CDA, the Christian Democratic Appeal) appeared to regard the new law as a means of further restricting the practice of euthanasia. The PvdA (Labour Party), on the other hand, collaborated on the law in order to increase the availability of euthanasia. The result is that it is considered by non-politicians as an awkward compromise; what its precise effects will be, only time will tell.

Apart from that, when the law was passed the Vatican immediately let it be known that in their view this law was not far removed from the notorious practices of Nazi Germany. This accusation was received with indignation in the Netherlands and prompted the then Prime Minister (also a Catholic) to protest strongly against the Vatican's attitude.

Most people in the Netherlands hope that the present carefully controlled practice of euthanasia will continue. After all, three quarters of the Dutch population considers euthanasia morally acceptable and would like more liberal euthanasia legislation.

Some moral aspects of euthanasia: The arguments against

First, we shall discuss some moral arguments against euthanasia: the Christian commandment 'Do not kill', the respect for life or the sanctity of life, the principle of non-maleficence 'Do no harm', the oath of Hippocrates, and some so-called 'slippery slope' arguments.

One of the most obvious moral restraints on euthanasia seems to be the commandment 'Thou shalt not kill'. Of course this commandment, whether of Judeo-Christian or other origin, is the basis of every decent society. Transgression of this principle requires a very strong justification indeed. The Dutch view is that a persistent request by a patient can constitute such a justification. Another justification is to be found in the intention of shortening a patient's suffering. Most people, even those with a pro-life view, acknowledge the necessity of pain-killing drugs in some situations, even to an extent at which death follows more quickly. Although they purport to be against euthanasia, they view death as an acceptable outcome of pain-killing medication. The question then arises, how they can at the same time consistently reject euthanasia on grounds of the prohibition of killing. It seems to have to do with power or authority: in cases in which pain relief culminates in death it is often the physician who takes the initiative, while in cases of so-called 'active euthanasia', it is the patient who is the centre of the decision-making process.

The respect for life or the sanctity of life: should not this most basic moral principle oblige us to refrain from euthanasia? It is often argued that euthanasia implies a lack of respect for life, or – stronger – flatly conflicts with this principle. It is true that we all agree that respect for life, that is, respect for each other and for other living beings including animals and even plants, is a very proper starting-point for moral reflection and moral behaviour. But respect for life does not necessarily imply that for fear of killing living beings in general, we should harm individual patients by causing them to suffer and by refusing to carry out their wishes. Neither the principle of respect for life nor the principle of the sanctity of life[2] compel us to cruelty and negligence towards human beings in distress who ask for a shortening of their dying process. On the contrary, those two basic principles seem to be perfectly compatible with euthanasia in certain situations.

Another important moral principle that should also be borne in mind is that of non-maleficence (do no harm). According to many ethicists all over the world, the duty to do no harm is an even stronger moral duty than the duty of 'beneficence'.[3] However, the duty to do no harm is not inconsistent with active euthanasia. Although it is certainly true that death is generally considered harmful, this is clearly not the case for the patient who requests euthanasia, and it is his death which is in question. The implication is not that death is never deplorable, only that in some cases it can be desirable.

An argument often cited against euthanasia is based on the oath of Hippocrates, which is alleged to condemn all actions against life. Apart from what this ancient oath may or may not mean, there is one obvious reaction to this argument: why should we allow our present decisions to be influenced by someone, however venerable, who lived 2,500 years ago, in a entirely different culture? Do we still look to the codex Hammurabi for a penal code?

One last argument also often used against euthanasia is the so-called 'slippery slope' argument. This is phrased in several ways. Sometimes it is used to point out that society will coarsen, if practices such as euthanasia become accepted, and worse, that we are moving down a slippery slope that will bring us in the end to condoning even greater sins.[4] This famous 'slippery slope' argument is based on several assumptions, all of them highly questionable. First of all there is the assumption that in former times people were more human and more inclined to adhere to moral values than we are today. This claim cannot be justified. People have behaved badly and cruelly in all periods of history, but probably more so in earlier times, and there is no proof at all that nowadays people who discuss the gentle death are moving down a slippery slope toward murdering or killing one another. In cases of active euthanasia it is the patient who judges his own life; no value judgments are made about the lives of others.

Another assumption of the 'slippery slope' argument is that people in present times may have become too 'soft' and are not inclined to accept suffering anymore. This is also untrue: as soon as opiates were discovered the use of these drugs became common. And the need to relieve the pain and the distress that may accompany the dying process has always existed.[5] In earlier centuries dying people were sometimes suffocated with pillows by their families to avert further suffering.

In some instances there was indeed a great need for pain killing drugs, but as has been argued, many people died quickly, mostly as a result of infection.

The 'slippery slope' argument alleges also that a moral justification for active requested euthanasia will lead to acceptance of the killing of patients who have not asked for a gentle death. History shows, however, that societies have always been able to distinguish among the various ways of killing. In many countries the law makes a distinction, for instance, between murder, manslaughter, killing in self defence, accidental killing, etc. Obviously people are able to draw the line, and they do. Why should they suddenly lose that ability?

One last comment on the 'slippery slope' argument: it may be that people who use it are often not completely sure as to their own opinion. Would they perhaps like to accept requested euthanasia, but dread the negative consequences, and therefore reject it? Or are they truly opposed to euthanasia, even if persistently requested by terminal patients and carefully carried out? In such a case they should not be referring to the slippery slope but to euthanasia as such.

This survey of the five arguments against euthanasia and their refutation makes it clear that most such arguments cannot be convincingly sustained. Maybe the conclusion is that, in the absence of convincing moral arguments against euthanasia, the rejection of it probably has more to do with a person's logical make-up than with moral argumentation.

Arguments in favour of euthanasia

On the other hand, there are some strong arguments in favour of this practice: the respect for self-determination, the principle of beneficence, the absence of a moral duty to live under all circumstances, and the acceptance of tolerance as a major moral virtue especially in relation to actions with no, or only very limited, consequences for others. All the arguments in favour of euthanasia are based on principles that are central to today's bioethics.[3]

First, there is the principle of respect for self-determination. Precisely the circumstance that the dying or terminal patient expresses his desire to die leads us to the issue of self-determination: we may very well ask how we can justify refusing patients relief from their agony, something they strongly wish, when – and this is very important – no other human being will be harmed by compliance with their wishes. Some people wish to remain in control of the last stage of their life, and why should we deny them this control? It is often said that dying patients are not rational any more, and that their wishes are irrelevant. This may be true in some cases, but it can never be a general rule that all dying patients should be considered incompetent.

Secondly, there is the principle of beneficence. It seems that this principle and respect for self-determination coincide and enhance one another, if we consider requested euthanasia. It is clear that there is a request, which means that there is a person with certain wishes. The dying person claims respect for this decision, and appeals at the same time to our duty to do well (to be beneficent). Complying with his wishes can be considered as acting in accordance with the principle of beneficence.

The refusal to consider seriously a request for euthanasia means in fact that a person is compelled to live. People in favour of the principle of self-determination are, however, inclined to think that the decision to go on living or to die should be left to the person involved. It is his life, his suffering, and his death. Some may argue that self-determination is acceptable but should not extend to decisions about life and death. Of course, everyone is entitled to hold this opinion, certainly with respect to themselves. But there is no moral justification for forcing this view on people who think differently. No one is obliged to request euthanasia; on the other hand, no one should be denied the freedom to do so. Here we have come to the last argument in favour of euthanasia: the principle of tolerance. In the Dutch view this is in fact the strongest and most irrefutable argument. We can not imagine how anyone can deny the strength of this argument. Why should we burden each other with our personal views of life, illness and dying? Why is it not possible to accept that people have different opinions about the really personal issues of life and death? Why not accept a moral plurality concerning the end of life? This is the issue that every society with highly advanced medical care has to address. Tolerance is of course not the ultimate value, but it could become so in situations where the actions of individuals have no consequences for others.

Almost no one wants to die sooner than is necessary. Life is surely our most precious possession, and people often cling even to a life with only a minimum of quality. The implication is that people who request euthanasia may have good reasons to do so. In a humane society their wishes should be granted.

H.M. DUPUIS

REFERENCES

1. *Medical Decisions about the End of Life. Report of the Committee Investigations of the Medical Practice Related to Euthanasia.* The Hague, 1991.

2. KUHSE, H. and P. SINGER, *Should the baby live?*. New York, 1985; pp. 118-139.

3. BEAUCHAMP, T. and JF. CHILDRESS, *Principles of Biomedical Ethics.* New York, 1988.

4. RACHELS, J., *The End of Life.* New York, 1986; pp. 170-179.

5. EIJK, W.J., *De zelfgekozen dood naar aanleiding van een dodelijke en ongeneeslijke ziekte.* Bruges, 1987.

Adaption of this article by permission of Kluwer Academic Publishers. The original version was published as 'Euthanasia in the Netherlands', *Annals of Oncology* 4 (1993), pp. 447-450.

A

dventuress

in the Thickets of Postmodernism

A Reflection on the Work of Anne Teresa de Keersmaeker

The two graduate students from my class at New York University's Tisch School of the Arts almost knocked the styrofoam coffee cup out of my hand as they rushed up, saying, 'You *have* to see Teresa's dance; the second show is just starting!' This was in April 1981, and we were at the State University of New York at Purchase – just north of New York City – attending a series of panels and performances that focused on the early years of American modern dance. I took one look at the students' faces and went across the campus to the studio where dance trainees from various New York colleges and universities were showing off their work.

Anne Teresa de Keers-
maeker in *Asch* (1980)
(Photo Rosas, Brussels).

To see the untitled solo by NYU student Anne Teresa de Keersmaeker (1960-), one had first to sit through a composition-class dance by five lumpy young women, and an earnest, not very accomplished reconstruction of Charles Weidman's *Lynchtown* (1936). When De Keersmaeker began to dance, to a tape of Steve Reich's *Violin Phase*, the very air in the room

became fresher, sharper, more invigorating. Wearing white shoes and socks and a loose pink dress printed with white flowers that looked as if it might have been worn in the 1930s by a much heavier woman, De Keersmaeker began to journey along a circular path; on each step-dig, step-dig of her feet, her arms lashed out and wrapped around her body – now to the right, now to the left. As she travelled, she very gradually added beautifully chosen gestures – a stretch of one arm, a kick forward, a lunge, a turn, a hop, a leg swing. Without losing its purity of purpose or its hypnotic repeating base, the movement increased in impetus and complexity until it acquired the verve of a postmodern folk dance. When De Keersmaeker suddenly threw her arms up and stopped, the spectators – who knew a good thing when they saw it – yelled and screamed their approval.

De Keersmaeker returned to the city in my car, along with two visiting teachers from England's Laban Centre. How had she structured the dance?, they wanted to know. De Keersmaeker, still wearing the pink dress she had performed in, said that she hadn't known exactly what Reich's structure was, but had worked out a system for herself that seemed appropriate. As I remember, it was ingeniously simple, entailing a ratio between new movements added and old ones eliminated.

I never did figure out why this gifted twenty-one-year-old had enrolled as an undergraduate in Tisch's conservatory program. She only stayed there for a year. During that time, she also created a duet for two women that brilliantly caught the suppressed and cyclical violence of Reich's *Come Out to Show;* along with *Violin Phase,* it was to become part of her first big European success, *Fase* (1982).

Fase (1982) (Photo Kaaitheater, Brussels).

Looking now at a video of De Keersmaeker dancing *Violin Phase* thirteen years ago, I am moved all over again by her pristine structure, her musicality, her appetite for movement (the camera, moving in close to scrutinise the performance, often captured a half smile of pure pleasure hovering around her lips). Interviewed about her methods, years later in 1991, she said that she worked to find little molecules that expressed 'the energy as well as the architecture of the musical cells'. It was this approach that I sensed then, and it is this, I think, that has given her pieces their peculiar intensity.

When De Keersmaeker and her company Rosas returned to New York in 1985 with *Rosas danst Rosas* (1983), she was, deservedly, a heroine in Belgium and a name to be reckoned with all over Europe. What immediately struck most American critics about this long and arduous work for four women was the tension between the austerity of De Keersmaeker's forms and the natural human heat of her movement. (It is perhaps significant that the flyer for her very first work, *Asch* (1980), had announced that 'stumbles are made with the greatest possible care …').

When it came to minimalism or repetition, we were used to the ritualistic circlings of Laura Dean's dancers and to Lucinda Childs' frosty, neutrally executed patterns of what *The New Yorker* critic Arlene Croce once likened to prehistoric ballet. De Keersmaeker's brand of repetition was nothing like this. It was also nothing like Pina Bausch's blankly mechanical reiterations of dramatic and painful moves, or those Bauschian sequences in which an action escalates in violence until you can hardly bear to watch it. In the first place, the litanies of steps and gestures performed by De Keersmaeker and her colleagues often looked like the involuntary movements that one might

Rosas danst Rosas (1983)
(Photo by Jean Luc Tanghe /
Kaaitheater, Brussels).

make alone in one's room or while waiting for a train. The women raked their fingers through their hair, slumped in their chairs, dropped their heads into their hands. And not only did the movements carry a subtle, unaffected human weight in themselves, but, together with the travelling steps and the simple changes of position (fall, roll, stand), they almost never looked the same twice. By varying the dynamics, inserting pauses, breaking up a phrase, De Keersmaeker made everyday movement into dancing and gave dancing the changeable rhythms of life.

Also, De Keersmaeker, unlike Bausch, made it clear that she had not lost faith in the expressive powers of choreography. In this she has not changed, although, on occasion, she appears to have been attracted to the accoutrements of *Tanztheater.* At the beginning of the unaccountably sad *Elena's Aria* (1984), I wondered what slips and high-heeled shoes had to do with de Keersmaeker; certainly *she* never wore them. But here, too, despite the distraction of film and barely heard texts, the movement was what counted: an initial phrase (rising from a chair to grip its back, whirling to sit again, twisting to press against it) grew in complexity and spawned variations, as the recorded arias increased in volume, and the lights became brighter. This time, De Keersmaeker offered her dancers in solos, but even when the five women of Rosas were performing the same gestures, De Keersmaeker willed you to see them as individuals.

De Keersmaeker has said that she is not interested in emotions per se, but in how an image might change if another image or emotional layer were put over it. Perhaps this excitement about how context alters perception accounts for her recycling movements from *Ottone Ottone* into *Stella* (1990), and phrases from *Stella,* plus music by Gyorgi Ligeti, into *Achterland.* She also makes us see virtuosity in actions that have little in common with the heroic and polished feats we normally term virtuosic (in this she resembles vanguard American choreographers who began in the late 1960s to substitute risk for conventional virtuosity). In *Stella,* a somewhat disappointing collage of isolated theatrical acts set in what looked like a chaotic backstage of the mind (or one of those clothes-strewn, ego-strewn rooms that mothers are always yelling at their teen-aged daughters to clean up), the most memorable moment for me was not the extravagant delivery of speeches from *A Streetcar Named Desire* and *Rashomon,* but when a woman tried by degrees to get as much of herself as possible off the stool she was sitting on. Her balances became more and more precarious until, just as she was about to fall, another woman placed a second stool as a goal for her to attain. As concentrated as an animal, the woman didn't agonise over her predicament, and the tension between the matter-of-fact performance and the strangely perilous task was thrilling.

Achterland, made the same year, seemed to be all about this kind of rigour. Nothing could have been farther from the volatile and messy atmosphere of *Stella* than the stylish white platforms of this dance. In the gleaming arena, the interplay between *Achterland*'s male and female dancers and the musicians (playing virtuosic and complicated music by Ligeti and Ysaye) stripped theatre to the bone. The images suggested both preparation and performance. The rhythms were shaped not only by the music but by the actions: the performers might try something, pause, try again, change clothes, then tear into a passage of dancing as if plunging headlong into a river of music; no amount of practice could fully prepare any dancer for that moment of total commitment. Whether the men were hurling themselves to the ground, or the women sitting on little individual platforms to play what looked like demanding hand games with air, they all appeared something more than performers involved in the private agonies of professionalism; they were a society of losers and achievers striving for unity as well as for mastery.

Both in Europe and America, choreographers these days seem to trust dancing less and less. Some of them, whose complex political or dramatic narratives demand the spoken word, have demoted choreography to an often inchoate emotional subtext. Only four of De Keersmaeker's big pieces have been performed in the Unites States, alas. However, from what I hear of her recent work – despite her interest in non-linear narrative and despite the theatrical luxuries that she has access to – she's still engaged by the emotional power generated by formal manipulations of movement in relation to music. For instance, *Stella* includes a performance of Ligeti's *Symphonic Poem for 100 Metronomes.* Watching and listening to a row of metronomes – set at different speeds, wound to different degrees of tension, sliding in and out of phase with one another and gradually dropping their voices from the chorus – can be a profound experience. De Keersmaeker's ability to see the world in such designs may well be her greatest strength as an artist.

DEBORAH JOWITT

Elena's Aria (1984) (Photo by Herman Sorgeloos / Kaaitheater, Brussels).

'Nothing helps'

The Poems of Hans Faverey

The spring of 1993, almost three years after his death, saw the publication of the *Collected Poems* of Hans Faverey (1933-1990): just over five hundred poems in one sober volume on india paper, in an almost classical format. Although the book contained no surprises, no posthumous work or enlightening variants, Dutch literary critics immediately responded with page-length reviews, as they had done on the appearance, two days before his death, of his eighth and last volume, *The Lacking* (Het ontbroken, 1990). As then, too, the critics wholeheartedly agreed that Faverey's poetry is among the most important in all twentieth-century Dutch literature.

Such copious and unanimous praise for a poet may be remarkable enough in itself, but it becomes even more so when we consider that for a long time – and with almost equal unanimity – Faverey's poetry had been regarded as totally inaccessible, bizarre and unpoetic. Until the publication in 1977 of his third collection, *Chrysanthemums, Rowers* (Chrysanten, roeiers), hardly any periodical would publish his work; the one exception was *Raster,* the 'Structuralist' literary review edited singlehandedly by the poet, prose writer and translator H.C. ten Berge. And up until then there had been only one critic with any real understanding of his work, as his lengthy and favourable reviews showed: the film-maker and fellow-poet Rein Bloem. What had happened in the fifteen years between his debut in a periodical (in 1962; his first collection appeared in 1968) and *Chrysanthemums, Rowers?* Had Faverey's poetry become so much more accessible? Had the poet learnt to read his critics? Had the earlier harsh criticism been due mainly to the laziness, inertia and literary conservatism with which experimental writers so often have to contend?

Probably all of this is to some extent the case. But it is also possible that some critics, for whatever reason, now go too far in their understanding of Faverey's work. In my experience, many of the poems, and certainly many individual lines, remain obscure even after repeated reading, even after reading other people's commentaries on them; and this is almost inevitable, since a measure of obscurity is the essence of this poetry. I should not be surprised, then, if opinions of Faverey suddenly swung back again, or even if there were to be a collective change of attitude; all poetry is vulnerable, and this poetry probably more than any other. It offers the reader, and certainly the unsympathetic reader, every opportunity to tear it to pieces.

It is hardly surprising that many readers had problems with Faverey's first collection, *Poems* (Gedichten, 1968). His verses are spare, abstract, recalcitrant, and have no connection with anything outside themselves; not with the work of other poets active at the time (though there are some slight traces of the Fifties experimentalist Gerrit Kouwenaar), let alone with any established trend or group in poetry, and certainly not with any more-or-less recognisable real world. There are (almost) no proper names, no quotations, no allusions (though this was to change in later volumes); there is nothing to give these poems a context, in a critical or any other sense. Rather, they seem to repel any context, of any kind. Also, the poet seems not to care whether anyone reads him or not; he has dispensed with everything that could point to a communicative environment where normal linguistic, social or psychological rules apply. There are no anecdotal layers, often there are not even sentences. What remains has at best the status of 'semantic snippets'. And if a sentence does suddenly turn up among all those disparate (but not always desperate) words, it will not give the reader any sense of being drawn into a sort of poetic community by the poet: 'yes, there is communication, / but of the kind that bites / its tail and with that tail's / sting strikes its head.'

There is thus one general respect in which Faverey's poems do indeed conform with 'modern' poetry: they want to stand on their own. This also means that they want to be taken absolutely literally. The reader should not look for underlying meanings; he must follow the linguistic process which *is* the poem. Of course, this is true of all poetry, and of modern poetry in particular; but it applies especially to Faverey's work, which denies any context, begins in nothingness, and ends there too.

The words are introduced with a minimum of referential force, and handled in such a way as to yield nothing: no worldly wisdom, no word of comfort, no view of anything outside the poem; only nothing, literally Nothing. It is as if every word, every image that emerges is at once busy disappearing, being erased. 'I … enter / the inn, athrob with leavetaking', he writes somewhere, and this seems to go for practically *every* word in his work; they all seem to throb with the urge to take their leave, often long before the end of the poem – and taking their contexts with them. And the end is usually not a definitive ending, as a few of his early closing lines immediately make clear: 'no understanding'; 'the true isolation'; 'then stayed lying almost still'; 'better to say nothing'; 'having hardly ever been there' – the mere possibility of remembering the poem is sabotaged even as we read it.

To a greater extent than that of other poets, Faverey's work plays itself out between the first word and the last of each poem; as he puts it metapoetically and in (for his early work) rare complete sentences:

No metaphor's

appropriate here.
The match,

in accordance with its task,
communicated in burning.

Of course one can read a pessimistic view of life into this. Communication has nothing to do with freedom, it does not refer to a faculty which has enabled man to emancipate himself to some extent from his natural limitations. Far from it; in so far as 'communication' exists, it is one-sided and determined by the nature of whoever or whatever is 'communicating', it is a by-product of his own inescapable transitoriness. In this way 'communication' seems to have been reduced to a direct physical, almost Pavlovian 'expression' of an unstoppable demolition process. 'Cessation / while building, demolition / while building'. These are the first lines of the first *Poems,* and they say it all; there seems as little place for an open beginning as for an open ending.

But still …

But still, the question is how long such a 'pessimistic' reading will last. Is this poetry really all about anything as tedious as 'the impossibility of human communication'? There is in any case also, from the very beginning, a counterpoint – dry, laconic, amongst all the cessation and demolition in a strange way receptive to life, even on occasion subtly humorous.

In considering the reception of Faverey's work it is not without significance that the publication of his last, overwhelming work should have almost exactly coincided with the death of the poet (who had been aware for some six months that he was terminally ill). In such circumstances it goes without saying that a connection will be made between the processes of disappearance in these final poems, however autonomous they may – still – be, and that biological fact. It is equally obvious that this will produce a tendency to see the workings of death in everything, including the earlier work. And while I would hesitate to claim that there is *no* shadow of death hanging, from the very beginning, over all those processes of demolition and disappearance, it is still better to leave the words vague where possible and not disturb their ambiguity. And then on closer study we are faced with the question of just how definitive Faverey's reductions are; and above all, just how negatively we should view those reductions, and the situations resulting from them. Let me quote another brief poem from the first volume:

With a heavily blindfolded mole

into a fog –.
What to do?

(I don't feel like this).

Things could not be worse: the mole has by nature very limited eyesight; a 'blindfolded' – no, a 'heavily blindfolded' mole would seem to be the very quintessence of blindness. Yet, not content with this, in the second line the poet sends him in addition 'into a fog –'. Which means, figuratively as well as literally, that he doesn't know where he is going. It is quite logical that the poet should not feel like accompanying the mole. The problem is that he evidently had no choice. So, having reached that point of desperation where he finds himself in a dead end, he wonders: 'What to do?' There is not much left: to feel. But that too is unproductive; he 'doesn't feel like this' – which, along with its usual meaning of not liking something, focuses our attention on his physical situation. Here, deep underground, visually completely isolated, with his hands outstretched like a blind man, he doesn't feel – in other words, can feel Nothing – like this.

The strange thing is that this poem, like all the other poems that go nowhere and end in a void, can in one sense be taken negatively, as an extreme of hopelessness, but at the same time – cautiously positive – seems to deny that everything really is finally over; or, to put it more strongly, to assert that in this total isolation there is also something desirable, perhaps even some kind of promise. In Faverey, as in the mystical tradition, words like 'emptiness', 'absence' and 'nothingness' also have a positive meaning. More than once they are used to describe a (mental) situation which is evidently desired. 'If I only consisted of nothing / else;' Or: 'I think of little, // of nothing in particular'. Or: 'How it has made itself nothing / utterly escapes me'. Or, quite explicitly: 'What it's all about is, / I repeat, / almost nothing.' As I said before, death can never be totally excluded from that 'nothing', and to that extent the longing for 'nothingness', or 'almost nothing', is in my view not a death-wish, far from it, it is in fact a longing to reconcile oneself with death while still alive. The poems contain indications, some of them fairly literal, which support that interpretation. 'Hunting / the insignificant reconciles me / with my disappearances / more than I'll ever care for.' The most succinct formulation of this attempt at reconciliation, paradoxical as always, runs: 'Nothing helps.' Yes, the situation is hopeless, there is no way out. But no, there actually is, at the same time, something that does help: nothing.

It seems to me rather significant that Faverey seldom or never treats 'nothing' as a void, a sort of existentialist metaphor for an empty world abandoned by God. Rather, Faverey's 'nothing' is – in so far as it can be imagined – a concrete thing, a tangible thing. It is the tangible, the concrete, in its most minimal form. It is also, and perhaps primarily, the condition of being nothing to anyone else, nothing in terms of or as a function of anything else, in short: of being nothing except oneself. It is impossible to describe that condition in poetic terms; as soon as words are involved there *is* something else, something more generalised, a linguistic (and therefore also a social) context. Faverey seeks to eliminate that context by his own, linguistic means. That explains the many paradoxes, shifts of meaning, and negations. And it is also the purpose of the frequent (ungrammatical) use of the reflexive pronoun: it strengthens the self-referential character of these poems.

I would regard this poetry, then, less as a series of exercises in dying than as exercises in lack of meaning or, rather, as exercises on the borderline of the meaninglessness of language. But such formulations really sound much too imposing; Faverey's exercises have no philosophical or linguistic solemnity, and are never unambiguously tragic in tone. The opposite is the case throughout, as in the following:

Hans Faverey (1933-1990)
(Photo by Lela Zečkovič).

This one bows himself

to where nothing is;
picks the rope up,
coils the rope up,
blows away the letters

and himself leaves.

True, the reader is left with empty hands, but in my reading at least there is nothing negative in that. As reader, I am witness to an exercise in emptiness as strange as it is fine. With each movement the expectation of meaning, of something meaningful to follow, is immediately erased. But this experience of Faverey's 'nothing' is of a pleasant kind of near-weightlessness; it is quite free of metaphysical pathos and in this resembles the late Paul van Ostaijen (who had influenced Faverey from the beginning, according to a couple of rare interviews). This little poem is also reminiscent of Van Ostaijen in its (implied) vaudeville-like setting. The performance of 'this one' – as usual with Faverey, the reference is at once concrete and abstract – bears no relation to what the circus audience expects by way of tricks or 'stories'; everything that is built up is demolished again in the same move-ment; but the laconic matter-of-factness with which it happens creates for a brief moment a wonderful sense of space, an indefinable feeling of excite-ment.

Faverey once said that he was 'terribly jealous' of composers because they work with meaningless material, with rhythm and sound. He would like to do the same with words. But Faverey's poetry is musical only in a strange and unruly way – not in the way of *poésie pure,* nor of painting in sound, nor of song. Rather, it suggests associations with the repetitions, shifts and minute variations of minimalist music; or – better – with the largely absent-minded humming or mumbling of someone trying to grasp something beyond his understanding, something too great for words.

What gives this poetry its motive force is the sense of contingency, of dis-cord, of being beside oneself, with the consequent longing to 'coincide with myself'. It is meditative, not philosophical. The denials of self serve to bring one closer to oneself; the halting, disjointed, self-contradictory repetitions serve 'ceaselessly to lead (what exists) back to itself' – and to perpetuate that situation. Hence that floating between being there and not there that we find in many of the poems, perhaps most impressively in the last poem but two of the last volume; 'Rosamund lies in her bath full length // and won't get out.' Hence, too, the (often) illogical but self-evident combination of action and passivity, of active and passive forms: 'To that I summon / and am sum-moned'. Or : 'As I approach I am // appraised.' The strange thing is that this poetry, which seemed at first defensive and enclosed, on closer inspection reveals an extreme openness. I know of no poetry which so disarmingly lays itself open to the emptiness and the insignificant in things and in ourselves, to 'all this being here for nothing', as Faverey's.

If this verse is comforting, as is often said, then it is because what it shows us is not that in the last resort there is something more between heaven and earth, a foundation on which everything rests, a guiding principle, but precisely that it is (on paper) possible to live without such a principle, that only the absence of such a principle enables us to avoid armouring ourselves in panic against all things greater than ourselves, and even to trust them.

It seems to me that the famous poem about the '8 rowers' can be read in this way; in slow motion they move 'with each stroke ever farther / from home', and eventually, without desire or resistance, as it were 'in accordance with their task', they disappear inland, into the land. Occasionally, as in the poem 'Very slowly the slug slides ', Faverey goes so far as to describe this being 'absorbed into a greater whole' as a completion, a consummation. Anyone with the courage to open themselves to the most uncertain of threshold experiences (or perhaps rather: to open themselves *during* the most uncertain of threshold experiences), will receive their reward. Disappearances are implicit in such experiences, and are associated with gifts. First comes the activity, a paradoxical activity since its object is to open oneself, and thus be passive – and then other, more powerful forces take over. Or, to end with the poet's own marvellous images:

As I approach I am

appraised. It is a flower
I do not recognise, which has
recognised me, brings me ashore,
lays me down gradually as
sometimes the sea does someone
who must have drowned.

CYRILLE OFFERMANS
Translated by Tanis Guest.

TRANSLATIONS *Against the Forgetting* (Tr. Francis R. Jones). London, 1994.

Six Poems by Hans Faverey

Very slowly the slug slides
across the path, and before
she knows it she is safe.

But in the undergrowth,

where the leaves are,
where it is cool,
her consummation awaits:
to be absorbed into a greater
whole, a quicker drier beast.

From *Collected Poems* (Verzamelde gedichten, 1993)
Translated by Tanis Guest.

Without desire, without hope
of reward, and not from fear of punishment,
to fix the reckless, the relentless beauty

in which nothingness communicates itself,
expresses itself in what exists.

May the god who lies concealed within me
grant me a hearing, let me have my say,
before he strikes me dumb and kills
me while I watch, while you watch too.

From *Collected Poems* (Verzamelde gedichten, 1993)
Translated by Tanis Guest.

The landscape around me, in me,
breathes attentively.

Without haste it consumes itself. These

are the roots of the wind
laid bare: the nerves
of my spinal cord. Here my heart

erodes, sand appears, at times
light swirls under my nails.

No other space than this
will I accept; I hardly

ever sing.

From *Collected Poems* (Verzamelde gedichten, 1993)
Translated by Tanis Guest.

I hear the wheel stop turning;

for there is
no wheel. I do
what I have told myself.

I stay where I am unmoving.

I must do what I shall

tell myself. The grass greens;
the blackbird sits on its nest;
the daybreak fingers its
rose-tinted twilight

with in-held breath.

From *Collected Poems* (Verzamelde gedichten, 1993)
Translated by Tanis Guest.

I have forgotten

what I came here to do.
That's why I'm staying.
Of all the things

that can be done, and that
will happen of themselves,
the odd one must, now and again,
go right for me:

a motionless green-gauze

dragonfly; a fish swimming backwards.
A circus artiste, fallen from
her ball, and then at once
climbing back on – Success:

there she stands: she opens her arms,
her legs are thin. I draw breath;

it works: the world stops still.

From *Collected Poems* (Verzamelde gedichten, 1993)
Translated by Tanis Guest.

Too often there is not much going on
in the transitory world the god allows
himself, and then some idle boredom

pervades his emptiness, and he,
turning for once from his most lucid
thoughts, just leaves it to itself, drawn back

once more for a moment by remnants of
memory: beloved dark god; fish of
manlike form, gone to sleep beneath
crucified tree; blind, deaf and dumb
bellringer; sea-cow, tolerant mistress
to always such utterly lost fishermen.

From *Collected Poems* (Verzamelde gedichten, 1993)
Translated by Tanis Guest.

Middle

Dutch Literature as a Mirror

of European Culture

The twelfth-century Latin source of Maerlant's *The Heroic Deeds of Alexander:* the *Alexandreis.* The fact that the Latin verses in this manuscript are surrounded by an abundance of glosses and comments is typical of a medieval school text.

The literature of the Middle Ages is a truly European literature, probably much more so than the literature of today. Paradoxically, the main reason for this was the omnipresence of a language and a literature which were not a natural environment for *anyone* in Medieval Europe. A situation the Esperanto movement could not even dream of – when was the last serious plea made for the implementation of their ideal in Europe? – actually existed in the Middle Ages. Common schooling in a language which was foreign to everyone, Latin, and the fact that this language was the universal medium of intellectual communication, gave medieval culture a far-reaching unity.

Dutch medieval literature, like its counterparts elsewhere, provides ample evidence of this fundamental medieval cultural unity. The number of Middle Dutch literary works not connected, either directly or indirectly, with the Latin of the Church, the arts and sciences, can be counted on the fingers of one hand. And even when Middle Dutch literature distances itself somewhat from this Latin well-spring and follows its own course – as in the romances of chivalry, for instance – this does not mean that it becomes detached; it is still part of the mainstream of European vernacular literatures.

One striking example of this is Jacob van Maerlant's *The Heroic Deeds of Alexander* (Alexanders geesten, c.1260). The source of Maerlant's work is the twelfth-century *Alexandreis,* one of the central texts of the Latin school tradition. This was written by the scholastic Gautier de Châtillon as a creative imitation of Virgil's *Aeneid* – only this time with Alexander the Great as its protagonist instead of Aeneas – and had quickly established itself as a *pièce de résistance* in the teaching of Latin grammar. It was probably at school, in these same Latin classes, that Maerlant himself became acquainted with the *Alexandreis,* increasing and refining his knowledge of Latin and the classics as he tried to interpret it. In doing so he must certainly have become familiar with the heroes to whom Alexander is repeatedly compared by Gautier: the main characters from the grand epics by Virgil, Statius and Lucan, with whom the *Alexandreis* is continuously and deliberately made to reverberate.

Of course, when Jacob van Maerlant decided to translate the *Alexandreis* into Middle Dutch, probably not long after finishing his education, he could not use such comparisons. Although he himself was quite at home in the world of the ancient epics, it was a closed book to the uneducated lay audience for whom *The Heroic Deeds of Alexander* was intended. But, as he did so often, Maerlant found a clever way out; where appropriate, the characters in *The Heroic Deeds of Alexander* are compared with Gawain, Charlemagne, Tristan, Parthonopeus, Perceval, and a host of other heroes from the vernacular romances of chivalry.

What makes Maerlant's comparisons even more interesting is the fact that only a small number of these works have come down to us in Middle Dutch versions. Of course, it is possible, and even likely, that some of them have been lost; but, for reasons I will not go into here because they would lead us too far from our main subject, there is at least as strong a case for saying that Jacob van Maerlant was able to refer just as easily to Middle Dutch, Old French and/or Middle High German romances – because the audience he was aiming at was familiar with works in all three languages. Maerlant moves from one literature to the other without commenting on the fact, which illustrates very clearly that to him and his audience Dutch literature (or French or German literature, for that matter) was not a distinct entity at all. Rather, it was part of the wideranging body of literary texts in the vernacular that the European aristocracy had had written for them by educated clerks from the twelfth century onward – a literature, therefore, which was tied up with a particular social class, rather than with a particular language or state.

It is all too easy to assume that Middle Dutch literature played only a minor part in this European concert of elite vernacular literatures. After all, Dutchmen are very fond of quoting Heine's apocryphal remark that he would go to Holland when the Apocalypse took place, since there everything happened fifty years later than in the rest of the world. But, without resorting to the opposite form of chauvinism, I would like to stress that the assumption that Middle Dutch literature merely played a supporting role on the European stage is true only up to a point.

There is one thing of which, on occasion, the Dutch really are prepared to be a little proud; and that is the fact that they are open to anything of quality from abroad – and it is true: more Penguin books are sold every year in the Netherlands than in Scotland and Wales together. This openness to foreign influences was already manifest in the Middle Ages. The eagerness with which certain European literary masterpieces were translated in the Low Countries speaks volumes; the fact that there were at least two Dutch translations of the enormous *Roman de la Rose,* and at least three of the even larger *Lancelot en prose* (both thirteenth century) indicates the intensity with which European literature was taken up in the Low Countries. In addition, works in foreign languages penetrated the Dutch language-area much more quickly than the pseudo-Heine factor might suggest. Often there was not more than a generation between a Latin or Old French original and its Middle Dutch translation; and as we approach the heyday of Middle Dutch literature, the decades shortly after 1250, the gap becomes even smaller.

European literary developments, then, were followed very closely in these parts; but there are also several important genres in which the Dutch language-area led the way. This is especially true for the field in which the Dutch feel particularly at home until this very day: moralising. Nowhere did the stream of moralistic literature, and especially that of an urban, bourgeois kind, rise as early as in the Low Countries. Another genre where the earliest vernacular representatives are found in the Low Countries is that of the *artes,* those writings on theoretical and practical knowledge which are so much valued by present-day researchers into the cultural history of the Middle Ages. Then there are the so-called *abele spelen* (noble or beautiful

Jan van Ruusbroec in the Zoniënwoud (Koninklijke Bibliotheek, Brussels)

qparaurg simpel en wise

Dur die mane ten goechsten es
charaurg es ten naesten des
et ay end achte dusintoth
end vl. dair toe leerh
end polij unleg mede
charaurg es dair i maesterstede

charaurg i tempate q phisrome bemuoly
et libet comitatur disposicoris illy planet
ou gaudet fine bono fine malo morg ed esout
mog et isout eu bonds by domies fraudes stupis
knes mog no magni corpis flaui color

plays), which are the earliest examples of serious secular drama in any European vernacular. Finally, there is the magnificent mystical literature produced, especially in Brabant, from the thirteenth century on: the mystics Ruusbroec, Beatrijs van Nazareth and Hadewijch are regarded as the *crème de la crème,* also from an international perspective.

In fact this international recognition of the Middle Dutch mystics continues a tradition of interest from abroad in Middle Dutch literature which already existed in the Middle Ages. Hadewijch's work was known in southern Germany possibly in the thirteenth century, and certainly in the fourteenth – an area hundreds of miles from the region in which it originated and originally functioned. Work by the most prominent fourteenth-century representative of the great Middle Dutch mystical tradition, Jan van Ruusbroec, was translated into Latin several times, and around 1350, during his own lifetime, his *The Adornment of the Spiritual Wedding* (Die chierheit der gheesteliker brulocht) was read as far away as Strasbourg; two generations later compilations of his work even appeared in English. Similarly, the lyrics of Duke John I of Brabant were recorded in a sumptuous manuscript made in Zürich around 1310, some ten years after his death.

A spectacular Middle Dutch *artes* manuscript: *Description of the Universe* (Natuurkunde van het geheelal) (Herzog August Bibliothek, Wolfenbüttel)

Duke John I of Brabant in the Manesse Codex (c.1310) (Universitätsbibliothek, Heidelberg).

In this famous Manesse Codex (often depicted on stamps and place-mats), the Brabantine duke-cum-singer takes his place among the international elite of medieval courtly lyricists: the *troubadours* from the Provence, the *trouvères* from northern France, and great poets from the German Empire such as Gottfried von Strassburg and Wolfram von Eschenbach. And the duke's lyrics were not, as one might suppose, translated from the Brabantine dialect into German especially for the occasion (which would be remarkable enough in itself); rather, all the indications are that John I actually composed and wrote his songs in the literary language of the Rhineland, precisely to bring about this cultural interplay on the European stage.

This illustrates once again how foolish it really is to adhere to modern language boundaries in the study of, for example, Middle Dutch lyrics – which in fact, means wrenching these lyrics from their European and historical context and forcing them into a completely anachronistic and, whether intentionally or not, a nationalistic framework. All in all, Middle Dutch literature is a European literature in the fullest sense.

Dutch literary history?

So far we have been discussing the European character of Middle Dutch literature in rather grand terms; but if one takes this view, what would be left of the concept of a Dutch literary history of the Middle Ages? Does this not become a foolish illusion, highly dubious from a scholarly point of view, and also a form of needless self-torture, considering the problems involved in writing such a history? To me this seems a perfectly fair question; which does not mean that the answer is equally self-evident. For all the international and European character of Middle Dutch literature, I think there is scope for discussing Middle Dutch literature as a phenomenon in itself, and there are several good reasons for doing so. The arguments for this are of two kinds. The first relates to the subject itself, and is therefore probably the weaker of the two. The better argument, to be quite honest, is primarily ideological, and reflects the way in which literary history and how it is taught are determined by culture and politics.

Before going into this, however, I would first like to approach the matter from the perspective of what may be called non-normative research. This shows that, while we ought to consider Middle Dutch literature in its European context, this does not mean that the concept of Middle Dutch literature is in itself a useless one. The fact that around 1330 Jan van Boendale describes Jacob van Maerlant as the 'vader der Dietse dichtren algader' (the father of all Dutch poets) at any rate suggests an awareness of some linguistic and literary community; and Middle Dutch literary practice provides sufficient evidence in support of Boendale's words to allow us to speak of a separate Middle Dutch literature. The influence of the patriarch Maerlant himself, for instance, is to be found everywhere in Middle Dutch literature, even in the romances of chivalry which he criticised so severely. Compared to the truly immeasurable influence of Maerlant on Middle Dutch literature, on the epic, moralistic literature, historiography and the *artes,* his influence 'abroad' is quite modest, even if we are willing to accept, on the authority of Maerlant's apocryphal epitaph, that his fame reached across the Alps. It is true that occasional striking traces have been found of the reception of Maerlant's work abroad, but these are not much more than flying sparks from a fire that reached virtually every Middle Dutch author, whether they found its heat pleasant or scorching.

Statue of Jacob van Maerlant at Damme (Photo by Martine Meuwese).

Of course there is nothing unexpected about this, if only because in the Middle Ages Dutch was no more a world language than it is today; and because of this simple fact it had to rely primarily on the small area where it was spoken. Its main natural opening to Europe was to the east, where there was no significant linguistic frontier. This led to innumerable examples of interaction between German and Dutch across the present border between the Netherlands and Germany. Also, of course, the southern part of the Dutch language-area had direct access to a great European literature, the French. It appears, though, that this cultural exchange was mainly a matter of French literature being imported, for however many small indications have been found for the multilingualism of prominent French literary circles like that of Gruuthuse, the counts of Flanders and of Guines, we have yet to discover any really significant evidence of an upstream movement, that is, from Middle Dutch into French.

Cultural and especially linguistic differences meant that Middle Dutch literary life had to rely mainly, and sometimes even exclusively, on its own resources. In this light, it is actually not so silly to describe Middle Dutch literature as a separate literary province, as long as one remains alert to its interaction with other linguistic and cultural systems. There are no scholarly reasons that should prevent anyone from writing a new literary history of Middle Dutch literature.

But while these may be sufficient reasons for studying Dutch literary history as a separate entity, they are not the only ones. Even if there were no scholarly justification for it, I would go so far as to say that we should find it very hard indeed to forswear such a subject or concept as 'Dutch literary history'. The fact of the matter is that notions such as this one go far beyond purely rational consideration; they are, so to speak (and I know it is a dangerous expression to use in this context), in our blood. In considering the culture of the past, we cannot fully rid ourselves of the way we have been shaped by our own culture and history, however hard we may seek for historical accuracy. Nowadays this cultural and historical influence implies a special bond with the Dutch nation – and I suspect this will continue to be the case even now, when since 1 January 1993 tomatoes and dentists seem to be freely traversing Europe.

One does not have to be a nationalist, nor a chauvinist, to be affected by that bond – as a result of the educational system, the legal system, the form of government and countless other factors that for more than a century have united the nation of the Netherlands in a way which, from a historical point of view, may be extremely relative and even somewhat coincidental, but which still provides a tie stronger than virtually any other, inside or outside its borders. Many of us will remember the lists we made as schoolchildren for cosmic self-aggrandisement, when we had nothing else to do: Frits van Oostrom – 25 Anna van Saksenstraat – Oranjewijk – Leiderdorp – South Holland – The Netherlands – Benelux – Europe – Earth – and then things turned into a shambles : The Solar System, The Milky Way, The Universe, and, for some, God. But whatever the exact content of the lists may have been, it was as clear as day that, then as now, the strongest supra-individual tie was with the nation of the Netherlands, not with one's neighbourhood or village, let alone with the somewhat tragicomic Benelux; and if ever such a national tie was in danger of slackening, then the Queen's Birthday would be just around the corner. Even on the moon it was America versus Russia; and while I am not a good judge of such things, I know of few multi-billion projects that look as chauvinistic as the European space programme. Thinking in terms of a national framework is a deep-rooted practice, among intellectuals, as well as other peoples, and especially among literary historians: after all, they owe most of their subject and their *raison d'être* as scholars to it. As we all know, the foundations of this way of thinking were laid in the nineteenth century; the same conviction with which we are now building our united Europe then stoked the fires of nationalism. As always when an attempt is made to legitimise political innovation, this could only be done by referring to the past: and therefore all over Europe national frameworks were projected into bygone days, and historiography was mobilised to reconstruct a development which would lead almost inevitably to the nineteenth-century situation. Belief in a national identity and national character – long before such notions became tainted by the horrors of our own century – played a major part in this, and literature in particular was a splendid medium for identifying them, for here national identity, or whatever passed for national identity, was spelt out in so many words.

As far as Dutch literary history was concerned, these beliefs led to a roll

of honour in which the baton of national awareness passed, in reverse chronological order, from E.J. Potgieter (1808-1875) to Willem Bilderdijk (1756-1831), and then to Betje Wolff (1738-1804) and Aagje Deken (1741-1804), to Justus van Effen (1684-1735) and Pieter Langendijk (1683-1756), and above all to our literary giants from the Golden Age: first and foremost, Bredero and Vondel, the pillars of Amsterdam Golden Age culture, but also the aristocrat P.C. Hooft, who had, after all, published the *Dutch History* (Neederlandsche Histoorien) in 1642, and Constantijn Huygens, who was presented as the ideal and typical son of the people of the Netherlands. In the Middle Ages, too, there were authors to be cherished by patriotic hearts: Jacob van Maerlant, of course, perhaps not a great artist, but a selfconfident burgher – and, it was also said, especially in Flanders, one with a healthy dislike of the French language and character –, Geert Grote and Thomas à Kempis, and, last but not least, the lively city girl Mariken van Nieumeghen, heroine of the Low Countries version of the Faust story. All these authors and characters make up the literary waxwork gallery of a nation which saw itself, as it still does, mainly in bourgeois terms – and that includes the brilliant gadfly Multatuli, who wiped the floor with the Dutch mercantile mentality in the nineteenth century, and even Queen Beatrix, who is esteemed above all in the Netherlands for being such a hard worker.

As we have already said, the foundations of this nationalist view of Dutch literature and culture were solidly laid in the nineteenth century; and the very terms I have just used to represent it show how far we are now moderating our faith in this kind of construction. Without doubt, these stereotypes have very often resulted in distorted views, especially when facts were forced to fit this self-image where they would not do so naturally. Many things that conflicted with this self-constructed image of people and nation were tucked away on the shelves of history, or even excluded altogether.

This meant, for instance, that the importance of the nobility to Dutch culture in the Golden Age and the Middle Ages was largely ignored, for the nobility was, after all, associated with the French. Purism also gained ground

Stylising the Dutch past: a historical painting by Ch. Rochussen (1864), depicting the presentation of the *Rhymed Chronicle of Holland* (Rijmkroniek van Holland) by Melis Stoke to Count William III.

Hendrik van Veldeke in the Manesse Codex (c.1310) (Universitätsbibliothek, Heidelberg).

in the field of philology: the lyrics of Duke John I were 'retranslated' into what was supposed to be the pure Brabant dialect in which one might have expected Brabant's founding father to express his inmost feelings, instead of the Rhineland gibberish in which his songs have come down to us. It was thought that the Rhineland (now German territory), as a border region, could not possibly be more than a hybrid backwater; only fairly recently have the Dutch begun to realise that this projection of present-day national borders has clouded their view, and that the Rhineland does indeed form part of their literary history. Especially where great literary figures were concerned, competition between the two or even three countries involved assumed grotesque proportions; the quarrel between the Netherlands and Belgium over Jacob van Maerlant still simmers even today, and the twelfth-century poet Hendrik van Veldeke, claimed by the Netherlands, Belgium and Germany, has often been dragged across the border from one country to the other in a positively embarrassing fashion.

All these are examples of how an anachronistic concept of nationhood has clouded our view of Middle Dutch literature; and the same can be said, *mutatis mutandis,* for the other literary histories of Europe, where similar processes took place. Ultimately, this way of thinking in terms of pure and hybrid culture, of indigenous and exogenous, of national character, and of nativeness and foreignness, may well have helped sow the seeds of the excesses that our century has had to suffer.

In this context, we should pay heed to Ernst Robert Curtius' *Europäische Literatur und lateinisches Mittelalter* (1948). As his passionate preface to the American translation makes quite plain, this great book was written

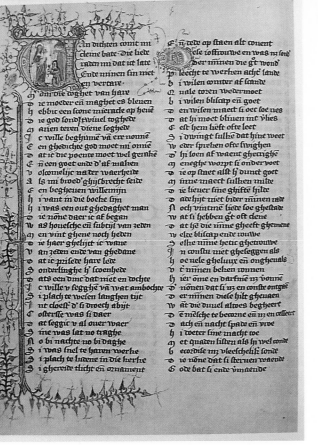

The beginning of the
Beatrijs (fourteenth century)
(Koninklijke Bibliotheek,
The Hague).

Ernst Robert Curtius
(1886-1956).

precisely in order to stem the tide of nationalism and of barbarism to which Curtius, who so greatly loved and valued the culture of the Occident, had seen Europe fall victim in the period around the Second World War. To this end, he stressed the far-reaching homogeneity of that culture; in other words, he used tradition as an antidote. (By the way, this shows very clearly that great scholarship need not necessarily seek to avoid value judgements; they can go together.) However impressive and influential his masterpiece may have proved to be, and however inescapable his thesis that European literature in essence formed a unity, what Curtius would most have liked to banish altogether, that is, the concept of literary histories based on one language and/or territory, has continued to exist. Since 1948 at least a hundred must have been written, and all by authors who knew Curtius' work well. The reasons why they, as well as the public whose needs they apparently cater for, are not prepared to face the ultimate consequences of his views, must be, firstly, that it is – to say the least – not totally meaningless to concentrate on the literary history of a particular language-area, and secondly, more importantly, that notions of language and nation are too deeply ingrained to be easily abandoned.

All the more reason then, I would say, to consider the medieval situation, and to confront ourselves and our young people with what is in my opinion the chief purpose of teaching history: the dialogue with what is different – a dialogue, in this case, with a cultural phase during which Dutch literature, for all its local fragmentation, probably had a stronger European character than it does now; and with a period, especially, in which translating, borrowing and adapting work written in another language was not regarded as a job on the side that a writer did in addition to his really creative work, or as an escape route for lesser writers, but, on the contrary, as an integral part of being a great artist. The Middle Dutch masterpieces *Reynard the Fox* (Van den Vos Reinaerde, twelfth / thirteenth century) and *Charlemagne and Elegast* (Karel ende Elegast, c.1300) were adapted from the French; there is not a single text by Maerlant which did not make use of sources in other languages; the *Beatrijs* poet (fourteenth century) based his text on a Latin exemplum; and Hadewijch draws on the treasure-house of French and Latin literature, and even on church music, to write poetry in Dutch which is still remarkably impressive. None of these would have been of any significance, none of them would have existed at all, without the European soil in which they were rooted; and, seen in this light, Middle Dutch literature is indeed an exemplary mirror of European culture.

FRITS VAN OOSTROM
Translated by Inge van Eijk and Frank van Meurs.

FURTHER READING

CURTIUS, ERNST ROBERT, *European Literature and the Latin Middle Ages*. New York, 1953.
OOSTROM, FRITS VAN, *Court and Culture: Dutch literature, 1350-1450*. Berkeley / Oxford, 1992.

'The finest painter in the whole Christian world'

Hans Memling and His Art

Hans Memling, *St Ursula Shrine*. Before 1489. Wood, gilt and painted, 87 x 33 x 91 cm. Memlingmuseum, Bruges.

Five hundred years ago, on 11 August 1494, the painter Hans Memling was buried in Bruges. The notary of the St Donaas Church noted in his diary that 'the finest painter in the whole Christian world' had died that day. Of the painters known collectively as the 'Flemish Primitives' (a name invented in the early nineteenth century to denote fifteenth-century painting in the Southern Netherlands), more work by Memling has come down to us than by anyone else. Almost one hundred paintings bear his name. On the occasion of the five hundredth anniversary of his death in Autumn 1994, some thirty of these are being brought together in Memling's own city for the first time since 1939.

We know nothing about Memling's personality, and the historical information available about his life is extremely sparse. The most important thing which is known about him with any certainty is that he was registered as a citizen in the 'poorterboek' (burgher book) of Bruges on 30 January 1465. The record refers to him as 'Jan van Mimmelinghe', and also gives his father's name (Herman) and his place of birth, Seligenstadt in Germany.

Seligenstadt is situated east of Frankfurt am Main, and to the south of that town there is a village called Mümling, from which the painter took his name. Although his baptismal name Johannes is given in the burgher book as 'Jan', he was also known in Flanders under his German first name, Hans. He must have been at least twenty-five years old at the time when he was registered as a burgher (citizen), so it is assumed that he was born between 1435 and 1440. Virtually nothing is known about his life in Bruges, either. We know that he owned a few houses there, married and took on apprentices. In 1467 he was Master of the Guild of St Luke, and in 1473 or 1474 he entered the elite 'Brotherhood of Our Lady of the Snow'. When he died he left three underage children.

Since Memling appeared in Bruges almost immediately after the death of Rogier van der Weyden in Brussels, it is generally assumed that Memling had until that time been a pupil of this master. It is not known when and by what route he found his way to Brussels. Art historians agree that Van der

Hans Memling, *Diptych with the Virgin and Maarten van Nieuwenhove*. 1487. Oak, 44 x 33 cm (per panel). Memlingmuseum, Bruges.

Weyden was an important influence on Memling's art, but he probably took his first painting lessons in the German Rhineland. One of the most famous works we have by him, and certainly the most unique, is the *St Ursula Shrine* which is now in the St John's Hospital (Memlingmuseum) in Bruges. The scene depicted on this shrine is set in Cologne, and the background to it is so realistic – with the famous Cathedral under construction – that it is concluded that Memling must have lived and worked in Cologne for some time.

Flemish painting in the fifteenth century was recognised even in its own time to be special and of high quality. Quite apart from the technical innovations which these painters introduced, they also succeeded in breathing a realism and warmth into their paintings which still gives their works the directness of photographs even today. The most significant innovation was that these painters no longer worked directly onto the walls of churches and other buildings, but painted on wooden panels. This meant that their works could be moved around and sold.

They also perfected their oil-based paints and the associated painting technique, which gave their work a special shine and durability. Among these Flemish Primitives the great names are the brothers Hubert and Jan van Eyck, Rogier van der Weyden, Dirc Bouts, and Hans Memling. Probably the best place to look for the roots of these painters' technique and their characteristic style is in the art of miniature painting (book illumination), which already by the end of the fourteenth century had reached a remarkably high level and taken on its own character in Flanders.

Among these painters, Hans Memling is known mainly as a master of bourgeois taste, which is probably why art historians often do not rate him as highly as, for example, Van Eyck or Van der Weyden. However, it is very

questionable whether this is a fair judgment (and it is to be hoped that this new exhibition will also result in a greater appreciation of his work). Perhaps the current view is partly determined by the fact that so much of Memling's work has come down to us. For of course he was a craftsman, working to commission and having to take into account his donors' wishes, which were not always very original.

For instance, the many paintings of the Madonna and Child which are ascribed to Memling are essentially a reflection of the fact that the fifteenth century saw the flowering of the veneration of the Virgin Mary, and particularly among the wealthy burghers in the cities. Fortunately a few of these Madonnas by Memling have come down to us in their original form, as part of a diptych or triptych. The best-known and certainly the most beautiful example is the diptych which is also to be found in the St John's Hospital in Bruges, where a total of seven of Memling's works are housed.

The left-hand panel of this diptych shows a representation of Mary with the Child on a cushion on the table in front of her. On the right-hand panel we see the young Maarten van Nieuwenhove in adoration before the Virgin. According to a note on the frame, the subject of the portrait is twenty-three years old, which dates the diptych to 1487. Maarten van Nieuwenhove was a member of one of the rich merchant families in Bruges, and a few years later became mayor of the city. The contrast between the serene detachment of Mary and the self-conscious but also affectionate admiration with which the young Van Nieuwenhove regards her, is like the contrast between heaven and earth. And yet the whole still forms a single painting.

To emphasise this unity, Memling has placed both figures in the same space, a room with open windows looking out onto a green landscape. The colourful tablecloth and the bright red material of Mary's cape continue into the right-hand panel, where Maarten is seated at the same table as the object of his adoration. The bright red cape also recurs strongly in the stained glass window on the right above Maarten, in which his patron saint is slicing his cape in two with a sword. Similarly, there is a stained glass version of the Van Nieuwenhove coat of arms on the left behind Mary. And as if to make the two panels completely inseparable, there is a round mirror hanging on a closed window below that family coat of arms, in which the whole tableau is repeated in silhouette.

There is a comparable diptych in Chicago, though this time the donor is unknown to us, as well as an equally comparable triptych from 1487, whose central Madonna is now in Berlin, while the two side panels are in the Uffizi in Florence. This triptych was probably commissioned by Benedetto Portinari, a member of a Florentine banking family which also did good business in Bruges. Here too we see the donor on the right-hand panel, while the left-hand panel depicts his patron saint *(Sanctvs Benedictvs)*.

Paintings of this kind were first and foremost an expression of devotion. By having himself immortalised in this way, the donor would henceforth be constantly in worship before the Holy Virgin, and under the protection of his or her patron.

The same applies to the larger triptychs, on which donors had themselves portrayed with their whole family, such as the famous *Moreel Triptych* dating from 1484. Here the left-hand panel shows the donor, Willem Moreel, who was twice in succession mayor, bailiff and treasurer of the city of Bruges. The Moreel family originally came from Italy, and were among the city's most distinguished and richest burghers. On the panel, Willem is portrayed with his five sons and his patron saint Guillaume de Maleval. On the

Hans Memling, *Moreel Triptych.* 1484. Oak, 120.7 x 69; 121.1 x 153.4; 121 x 68.6 cm. Groeningemuseum, Bruges.

Hans Memling, *John Donne Triptych*. c. 1480. Oak, 71.1 x 30.5; 70.8 x 70.5; 71.1 x 30.5 cm. National Gallery, London.

right-hand panel kneels his wife, Barbara van Vlaenderberghe, protected by St Barbara and accompanied by her eleven daughters. It was extremely important for the religious efficacy of such a portrait that none of the children should be omitted.

An important painting for the present-day reception of Memling's œuvre is the so-called *Donne Triptych* (or *Chatsworth Altarpiece*), which provides also a good example of the close cultural relations between the Low Countries and the British Isles during this period. This work was commissioned by John Donne of Kidwelly, a Welsh nobleman who had, among other things, spent some time in Calais in the service of the English King. For years art historians have been convinced that the triptych dates from 1466, which is incorrect. As a result of this mistake it became one of the key pieces in the interpretation of Memling's artistic development. In fact, the triptych was painted around 1480.

It was the rich burghers who could also afford to have 'ordinary' portraits painted of themselves. Hence we have a double portrait of the same Willem and Barbara Moreel on two panels, the backs proudly bearing their names and coats of arms. Since many panels which used to be part of diptychs or triptychs have gone their own separate ways as time has passed, it is no longer always clear how a portrait originally worked. In the Metropolitan Museum of Art in New York there is a double portrait of the banker Tommaso Portinari and his young wife Maria Maddalena. In this case the two portraits are almost certainly the two side panels to a central panel, since lost, which would have depicted a Madonna or some other religious scene.

The most fascinating portrait by Memling is of an unknown young woman, dated 1480 on the frame. The woman is looking out of the panel as if through a window. Her hands are folded and seem to be resting on the frame of the painting – a *trompe l'oeil* effect which was to become very popular among later portrait painters. She is dressed in stylish earthy colours, interrupted by a broad, white collar, above which part of a bright red bodice

Hans Memling, *Portrait of a Woman or the 'Sybilla Sambetha'*. 1480. Oak, 38 x 26.5 cm. Memlingmuseum, Bruges.

can be seen. Her evident wealth is further emphasised by the seven gold rings with precious stones on her fingers and the golden chain with a cruciform gold pendant set with green stones and pearls.

The totally impassive serenity with which she looks at the observer must have made a deep impression soon after this portrait was created, even though that impression may have been different from what we now perceive. In the sixteenth century someone added a cartouche in the black background at the top left bearing the words *Sibylla Sambetha quae et Persica, An: ante Christ: Nat: 2040* (The sibyl Sambetha, the Persian, in the year 2040 BC). And to emphasise that this was not just a Persian beauty, a long text was added at the bottom of the frame, probably by the same person, explaining that she is a 'wicked monster'. Fortunately, when it comes to art everyone is free to judge for themselves.

LAURAN TOORIANS
Translated by Steve Judd.

Memlingmuseum
Mariastraat 38 / 8000 Bruges / Belgium
tel. +32 (0) 50 33 99 11
Opening hours: 9.30 a.m. – 5 p.m. (closed on Wednesdays)

The special exhibition runs at the Groeningemuseum (Dijver 12 / 8000 Bruges, same opening hours and telephone number) from 12 August to 15 November 1994.

The

Unfinished Work of Art

The Paintings of René Daniëls

In 1979, René Daniëls (1950-) painted a series of works which he called *The Corruptible Muse* (La muse vénale), the title of a poem by Baudelaire. The painting depicts an eel and some mussels. Daniëls saw this as 'a reference to the contemporary artist's compulsion to produce'. The painting was a comment.

René Daniëls, *The Corruptible Muse*. 1979. Canvas, 150 x 210 cm. Stedelijk Van Abbemuseum, Eindhoven (Photo courtesy Paul Andriesse, Amsterdam).

In an interview in *De Haagse Post* in 1983, Daniëls said:
'*What is new art? Every archetype has had its turn. In that respect there is nothing more to be achieved. I think that commerce has to a great extent killed off art. After all, what do you see nowadays? Someone invents some little thing and it's taken up, exploited. Even by the artists themselves. As soon as that sort of serial work makes an appearance, you can bet your life that commerce will be involved. And that's when it becomes production in the economic sense. I have always resisted serial production of that type. It means the death of art. I think you should keep fighting all the time.*'

René Daniëls, *Untitled (gramophone record).* 1977. Canvas, 200 x 150 cm. Stedelijk Van Abbemuseum, Eindhoven (Photo courtesy Paul Andriesse, Amsterdam).

In 1982 he painted *Dutch Herring,* depicting young artists devouring each other like herrings. The idea came to him one day when he was eating herring. It flashed through his mind all at once: what if they discovered how tasty they are themselves? 'Then they might gobble each other up and we would have nothing left!'

It reminded him of *The Cannibal,* the manifesto written by Francis Picabia, an artist he greatly admired. Picabia, too, wanted to laugh the notions attached to traditional painting out of court. Daniëls admires in him 'a freedom, a playfulness and vitality you seldom encounter'. Certainly not in the Netherlands. That's probably why his early paintings were such a sensation when they were first exhibited. They were greeted with enthusiasm; this was 'new painting'.

There is a certain trend in painting that has been crystallising ever since the seventies: a sort of 'new image painting'. In the Netherlands people speak of the 'young Dutchmen' and the 'new painting'. It is a reaction to an art that was primarily formalist, abstract or conceptual in nature.

Painters started using traditional painting materials again; they even started to paint in a traditional way again. They returned to figurative work, in all sorts of ways; and in doing so they borrowed a great deal from tradition. They appropriated and 'quoted from' that tradition.

Daniëls says, however:

'It's my feeling that in most cases it has to do with a certain immaturity, a search for a starting point. It's also a sign of the times. We're in an art book

era. Everyone's looking things up in books and making "works of art" on the basis of what they find. That's why there are so many quotations from the great masters. But in most of these works the individual idea is too feeble to support the form. All those quotations seem to me more a sign of weakness than of vitality. Appearances seem to contradict this, but it's my view that art is currently at a standstill.'

Daniëls introduced an entirely different way of painting. His fiercely painted canvasses at first resembled eruptions of punk-like violence. In one of the paintings from the *Historia Mysteria* series he shows, in allegorical form, what he thinks of the Dutch art world. It depicts a figure under an umbrella in a gloomy wood, accompanied by a tortoise or a snail.

Daniëls' key work *Untitled (gramophone record)* from 1977 was a reply to the 'new painting'. It was, as it were, a 'physical manifesto', a painting in which the emphasis lay on painting itself. It is painted with broad brushstrokes, with large, powerful gestures. It was quite simply a sensation, and a clear plea for the art of painting.

In that painting you could see the beginnings of the myriad forms of the 'new painting': the highly personal and subjective next to the more universal. Daniëls' great merit lies in exactly this combination of the conceptual or fundamental tradition in painting with expressiveness and an extremely personal lyricism.

Daniëls says:

'That 1977 painting of the gramophone record was no still-life, but a surrealist image that suddenly looms up in front of you. All in all it was actually a very surrealist painting. It was also expressively painted, which was particularly important to me at the beginning. Real expressionism has more to do with the doing, and arises from very strong motivations. That became slightly less important to me, later on. I can't summon up artificial emotions again and again, and I think that's also the reason I'm always trying something different.'

Daniëls has a great admiration for the work of Magritte, Polke and Picabia. He imbued his own painting with the 'tradition of Picabia', who once remarked: 'If you want pure ideas, you have to change ideas as often as you change your shirt.'

Daniëls' work is concerned with the 'constantly changing meaning of things'. Do I really see what I see? Nothing is fixed. It reminds us of Magritte: 'ceci n'est pas une pipe' ('this is not a pipe'). What is it then, a pipe that looks like a pipe, but isn't one?

The French philosopher Michel Foucault saw this phrase, which Magritte wrote in an elegant hand under a carefully drawn pipe, as destabilising the concept of representation. 'Things have matching qualities', Magritte wrote in a letter to Foucault, 'Interrelationships between peas, for example, show matching qualities, both visibly (their colour, shape and size) and invisibly (their nature, taste and weight). This is also true of what is false and what is genuine. Things are not similar to each other, they have, or do not have, matching qualities.'

The recurring motif of the bow-tie in Daniëls' work can thus be inter-

René Daniëls, *Under Review*. 1982. Canvas, 130 x 190 cm. Museum Boymans-van Beuningen, Rotterdam (Photo courtesy Paul Andriesse, Amsterdam).

preted in various ways: as a flat decorative motif, in short an illustration of a bow-tie, or as a spatial motif, as in *Zebra Fine Exhibitions* or *Messebild* (both 1985), an exhibition area made up of two side walls and a back wall. Image shifts and image rhymes are the elements he uses.

The power of imagination plays an important part in Daniëls' paintings. In his work he has surrounded himself with a deliberate fairy-tale aura of magic and mystery. He is humorous, and has a light touch. The colours of his paintings are clear and transparent because he always applies the paint very thinly. This way of working in thin layers increases the uncanny intensity of his work.

His work used to be called 'meta-painting', because Daniëls was constantly referring to the art of painting. His comments were ironic. In *The Spray Army* he made fun of the art of graffiti. In another painting a group of elegant ladies and gentlemen are pictured in the pinkish atmosphere of a bar, scene of a 'conversation about painting'.

Under Review (1982) is probably one of his most forceful paintings. There is an internal struggle taking place on the canvas, between the figures and the pictorial quality. Two figures are carrying on a dialogue with each other, but also with the stray areas of colour, yellow, orange, red and blue around them. Many of his paintings can be seen as both figurative and abstract; this is 'impassioned' painting: its intentions often remain unclear, but it grips you, it gnaws at you. Paintings like *Painting on Bullfight* and *Painting about Bosch's Missing Flood Painting*, both from 1985, are almost abstract works. True, the familiar bowtie motif is there, the exhibition hall, but at the same time they seem like paintings without an image, no more than a composition with areas of colour.

At the beginning of 1986 Els Hoek, who knows his work particularly well, wrote an article about Daniëls in the art magazine *Metropolis M* entitled 'Past Imperfect'. These two words went to the heart of the matter: a painting, drawing or gouache by René Daniëls is never finished. 'Even if he did it years ago and hasn't laid a finger on it since, his work remains open to new meanings.'

This œuvre will literally remain unfinished, as the result of a brain haemorrhage Daniëls suffered at the end of 1987 and from which he has not completely recovered. Since then he has been incapable of continuing his work as an artist.

Seven years after her article in *Metropolis M*, Hoek wrote in *De Volkskrant:*

'This imperfection is different, powerless and sad: what might not still have been produced in the then 37-year-old artist's studio! His art is alive, it forms an important point of reference for colleagues, young and old, and can regularly be seen not only in the Netherlands but also abroad. The title of the 1986 article was wrong; it should have been: Present Imperfect.'

Daniëls attracted international interest very early in his career. He participated in exhibitions like *Zeitgeist* in Berlin, a plea for the art of painting, and Documenta in Kassel. At Documenta one of his paintings was part of the 'collective memory' that the curator Jan Hoet gathered together in the tower of the Fridericianum, among masters like David, Gauguin, Ensor and Beuys. In 1992 he received the David Roëll Prize for his entire œuvre. He had already been awarded the Sandberg Prize in 1988. He was given the prize because, as the jury report said, 'he creates space, in his paintings literally, and in our heads metaphorically'. At the end of 1993 a selection of his work was exhibited at the Arts Club of Chicago.

Daniëls' work, or at least the incomplete quality of that work, reminds us, writes Hoek, of something the literary critic Kees Fens said:

'What does complete mean? Definitively drained, emptied; the work no longer fills itself. What does incomplete mean? Filling up after every emptying. Incompleteness implies the possibility of metamorphosis; it is the very nature of art.'

PAUL DEPONDT
Translated by Gregory Ball.

René Daniëls, *Messebild.* 1985. Canvas, 100 x 140 cm. Private collection, Amsterdam (Photo courtesy Paul Andriesse, Amsterdam).

Babel

behind the Dikes

Living in the Bijlmermeer

The Bijlmermeer is new. That in itself is enough to put many people off. Anything new is bound to be *hated* by an Amsterdammer. How often have I had to listen to the argument: 'That sort of place is *artificial,* designed on the drawing board. It hasn't grown organically, like Amsterdam. Look at the way the canals grew, like a living organism, naturally, one after another like the skins of an onion.'

I look at the canals. They are magnificent. And artificial. Every chair, table, house, street, town is artificial. Anyone who wants to live naturally should crawl into a cave. Art is artificial. And so is Amsterdam. The dam on the River Amstel was well-placed for the pursuit of certain trades and commercial activities. Just as there were and are various factors which make a particular place a suitable site for a settlement: clean air, clear water, a natural harbour, fertile ground, good means of transport, climatological conditions, etc.

No, the Bijlmer is no more artificial than so many other, older towns and suburbs. The only difference is that they were there before we were. We were already used to them even before we were conscious of them. And apparently we cannot stop ourselves from wanting something that we are used to in an entirely new place. But how *can* something new be old? Moaning about the absence, in the Bijlmer, of quaint half-timbered pubs or cafés, of untidy old secondhand bookshops, or those darling little Jewish textile shops is a surefire way of making yourself unhappy. They are just not there.

There is something in their place: space. But many residents of Amsterdam (and also of the provinces) would seem to suffer collectively from agoraphobia: the space here, created, accentuated, given shape, and made *tangible* by those huge trailing buildings evidently frightens people. Not until my guests look down from the stronghold of my balcony on all that green, on the metro train gliding quietly by, the rustling foliage, and the towers of Amsterdam in the hazy distance, will they admit that it is really quite a nice view – even though most of them hasten to add that of course they would never be able to live here. They would go round the bend.

Well, people don't go round the bend that fast, but I sometimes wonder

In 1966 the construction of a residential area was started by the Bijlmermeer-polder in the South East of Amsterdam. It was loosely inspired on principles set out in Le Corbusier's *Charte d'Athènes,* in which he summarised the conclusions of CIAM 4 (Fourth International Conference on Modern Architecture, 1933). Residential areas were to be developed in those parts of towns most favourably situated from a geographical and climatological point of view. Green zones should be designed to shield the residential areas from the industrial zones. The strict separation of various means of transportation and the provision of sufficient recreational facilities were also considered of great importance.

The CIAM conferences brought together architects who often espoused different approaches to architecture. Yet they were united by what Gerrit Rietveld described as 'seeking what architecture can do to allow society to function well'. They were looking for rational and often outspokenly anti-artistic solutions to the great housing shortage that followed the First World War.

The Bijlmer became a peripheral area with high rise blocks arranged in a uniform pattern, cut through by two metro lines and surrounded by elevated roads that guide traffic over bicycle paths and walkways on ground level. The residential blocks themselves were interspersed with green zones. The strict separation of functions, together with the idea of a community, defined the construction of the Bijlmer: the green zones were intended for communal use, to be sure, but so were the garages, the workshops, the inner streets, and more.

Built on the basis of an idealistic architectonic and

what is wrong with me that I like living in the Bijlmer? What the heck, there is nothing wrong with me – or at least not *that*. Not that I idealise the Bijlmer, I've been living here too long to do that. I can see quite well that it is just as much a prey to vandalism, thuggery, pollution and neglect as Amsterdam which has the image of being such a wonderful city. No, in that respect I am not naïve. But does that mean that I want to proclaim the beauty of the Bijlmer?

'Beauty' is an awkward word. It cannot be measured, it is at the mercy of taste: of personal taste which can be changed by experience or education, and even be influenced by mood; and of collective taste, which exercises power. You can be told what you must find beautiful, and it is very difficult to resist that pressure (the tyranny of the phenomenon 'fashion'). Beauty can also, almost as a reaction to what other people think, be a question of will: you can sometimes *decide* to find something beautiful, in the absence of an objective criterion. I often look outside and see those massive, long horizontal lines, which make the buildings seem lower than they are, I see the austere shapes which, if nature and civilisation are placed in opposite camps, form a symbolic contrast with the jumble of luxuriant green below them, or with apocalyptic cloud formations above, and I ask myself: 'Why, if Mondrian is beautiful, would this not be?' I sit and ponder, but cannot find a proper answer. Not that everything is beautiful here; however, not everything Mondrian ever did is considered beautiful either. But all this is really beside the point. I am fairly indifferent to the look of my surroundings. A Belgian friend once asked me: 'Living here, where do you get the inspiration for those marvellous translations?' *Touché!* I did do one translation in the idyllic hills to the south of Carcassonne, but I challenge anyone to prove that that had anything to do with the result. All the others were done in the Bijlmer, not because I find it 'beautiful' here, but because I find the conditions here agreeable and conducive to the way I wish to live and work.

Sometimes, irritated by my own hair-splitting, I decide: 'Dammit, it *is* beautiful, because *I* think so!' – but I really couldn't care less. What is

High-rise building in the Bijlmermeer (Photo Gemeentearchief Amsterdam).

social vision, the Bijlmer was soon considered by many people to be a failure. These critical voices often refer to the failure of the community concept in a multicultural society and to the increasing deterioration of the area, with the attendant decrease in security. Isolated arguments have even been heard for a partial demolition of the high rises as a solution to the area's social problems. In 1993 the Bijlmer was the subject of world-wide media attention when an Israeli freight plane crashed into an apartment block there.

Communal walkway in the Daalwijk building (Photo Gemeentearchief Amsterdam).

important to me is that it is *different,* and that difference is exactly what I want. But the difference also demands a certain way of life, of looking, of occupying space; it demands a deconditioned view of things. And for some mysterious reason or other people still refuse to accept that something different really is genuinely different, and not the same as something from the past that happens to be still stuck in their head. The fact is that the Bijlmer is an architectural adventure of such un-Dutch proportions, vision and allure, that the whole of the clod-hopping Dutch art world takes umbrage at it.

A phobia for the new? Quite likely. But it was as long ago as 1928 that Le Corbusier said: '*Imagine you are walking through a new city. You are beneath trees, between big lawns, huge green spaces, breathing fresh air, hearing almost no noise. You don't see any more houses, how is it possible! Through the branches of the trees you will glimpse, silhouetted against the sky, and far removed from one another, enormous towers of crystal, higher than any building in the world. And not a stone to be seen on these enormous buildings, only crystal and proportions.*'

Eureka! That is my Bijlmermeer! Hardly anyone realises it, but the Bijlmer is unique in character. When I came to live here in October 1971 the area was still a complete mess (waste land, site huts, mud, debris). Since then the services have improved, but the unique character was there from the beginning. I smelled it, I drank it in, I saw the space, the light, the proportions, I liked it – and I like it still. What pleases me here is not only the intermingling of lots of green with modern building materials in full accord with Le Corbusier's principles, but even more the combination of on the one hand an unconventional, cosmopolitan atmosphere stretching over a vast area, and on the other peace and quiet and an almost village-like intimacy. This intimacy arises from the easy contact between neighbours, either from balcony to balcony, or on the walkways, at the market, on the small enclosed greens and lawns near the ponds and playgrounds within the hexagons of the high-rise buildings.

The spaciousness, the cosmopolitan atmosphere, the imaginativeness are all part and parcel of the daring architectural design and the wide variety of ethnic groups. Some people who do not wish to deny the Bijlmer a certain appeal but are still unhappy about it, say that it 'was built in the wrong country'. They've got a point there. Only I blame the country. And the city – even though I'm an Amsterdammer myself. For I do believe that a suburb like this (I'm only referring to its architecture), outside Rotterdam for example, would have caused far less commotion than here near Amsterdam, where the artistic and intellectual climate is the most nitpicking, intolerant, dictatorial, unadventurous, self-satisfied and prejudiced that I've ever encountered. In one of the many discussions about the Bijlmer someone once said: 'An Amsterdammer doesn't want space, an Amsterdammer wants a street.' He was probably right, but then I only think: 'Too bad for the Amsterdammer, but just dandy for me.' If there's one place I never ever want to live again it is in a street – or in an area where only 'whites' live.

I also believe that it is because of the wide variety of ethnic groups that racial tolerance is, in my opinion, greater than in most other parts of Amsterdam and in other Dutch cities – and that tolerance is for me, lacking in illusions as I am, one of my few genuine illusions. For instance, it is to my mind utterly unthinkable that a dark looking (Dutch) colleague of mine should undergo the same experience here as he recently did on the Amsterdam canal where he lives, where his (Dutch) neighbours called him a 'filthy Turk', adding that he should 'sod off to his Sahara'.

With about fifty different ethnic groups it would, moreover, be simply too much trouble to get into a lather about any one of them. There would be no end to it, should you be so inclined. Not that the different ethnic groups

Market on the Fazantenhof
(Photo Gemeentearchief
Amsterdam).

always have a lot to do with one another, but even if they do not live *with* each other, they certainly live peacefully alongside one another. When we see that in some parts of the Netherlands the arrival of one single group of refugees or asylum-seekers can almost unleash a riot, then the Bijlmer is a miracle of racial integration. And moreover, when we consider that the Netherlands is no longer a purely white nation and never will be again, then it is not strange that the Bijlmer is often held up as an example.

Be that as it may, in the flat I have been living in since 1987 I may be one of a white majority, but I have long been used to belonging to an ethnic minority the moment I set foot in the shopping centre a hundred meters away. In the café on the square, where I sometimes read the paper or have a drink, and which is a true microcosm of the Bijlmer, that is abundantly clear. When I see the white-haired grandmother-with-her-shopping-bag-and-grand-daughter talking there to the alcoholic with-a-stinger-to-take-away-the-sting, or the little Moroccan dancing with the voluptuous West Indian woman, I can't help thinking: 'That's how it ought to be.' After all, what Queen Beatrix, the then Prime Minister Ruud Lubbers and the then Mayor of Amsterdam Ed van Thijn said about 'solidarity' and 'multi-coloured community', after the disaster of 4 October 1992, when an El Al freight plane destroyed a whole block of high-rise flats, expressed something we, Bijlmer residents, had known for a long time.

This too is something that few people realise: that there is a sense of neighbourliness, especially among those who are old-timers here. In that respect this neighbourhood does not differ from other neighbourhoods, even though in all other ways it is an untypical corner of the Netherlands, a Babel behind the dikes where 'anything goes'. Crap and roses. Everyone who lives here is aware of this, or at least that's how it seems. And that is at the core

Green zone in the Bijlmermeer (Photo Gemeente-
archief Amsterdam).

of the community spirit. I, for one, can no longer do without the diversity of colours and clothing. And equally the peace and quiet and the space I have here. And I know that I am not the only one to think that way.

In the eyes of the outsider the Bijlmermeer is doomed. The media have consistently done a hatchet job on the area, stigmatising it as a cesspool of criminality, a place where no one in his right mind lives – certainly not writers or artists (although I know a few). The press has used such terms as 'social garbage chute for Amsterdam', with a 'condemnation-order future'; an alderman for public housing, would you believe it, has spoken of 'those goddam flats' and the American professor Oscar Newman, who was brought in in 1979 and for 25,000 guilders was willing to tell us how to deal with a ghetto, made a hit with his pronouncement: 'All those poor, black people with children in those anonymous buildings, that can only lead to disaster.'

A hit? That depends; For such phrases as I have cited above are only to be heard from the mouths of those who don't live here. I have been accused of being an idealist, (even though I've been living here for twenty-three years), of wearing blinkers. Let me tell you, two robberies and the scales fall from your eyes. But when others bewail everything that is wrong here, I do not necessarily have to follow suit. It seems to me only appropriate that a dissenting voice should now and then be heard. It doesn't help much. People are very attached to their prejudices. But that only strengthens our community spirit: Bijlmer residents are not ashamed to be nonconformists.

AUGUST WILLEMSEN
Translated by Elizabeth Mollison.

Myth

and Reality in the Human Geography

of the Netherlands

External perceptions of a country are frequently only partially correct and, at worst, may be highly inaccurate. Influences such as hearsay and media reports can distort images to a degree that is often not realised and may be difficult to rectify. In many ways it is arguable that this is particularly true with respect to the Netherlands. Some features of this country are firmly imprinted on the mental maps of many foreigners: the architectural attractions of Amsterdam; bulbfields and the pasture landscapes of the western provinces; the IJsselmeer Polders; and perhaps the Afsluitdijk, the enclosing embankment of the IJsselmeer. Beyond this, however, external images are normally extremely vague. There is little appreciation of the diversity and tensions to be found throughout the country in terms of, for example, agricultural systems, urban development or political and religious affiliations. This can be readily demonstrated in the context of landscape: external perceptions are dominated by canals, dikes and the western pasture lands, yet the fascinating *Atlas of Dutch Landscapes* (Atlas van Nederlandse Landschappen) recognises no less than twenty-three distinct landscape regions of varying sizes.

Against this background the main theme of this contribution is the importance of encouraging more accurate perceptions of the intricate human geography of the Netherlands. What cannot be claimed, however, is that this can be effectively achieved in the space of one short article; indeed, an entire book would scarcely do justice to the subject. All that can be attempted is to demonstrate the potential for progress in this direction by focusing on a range of topics. Those selected – regional economic diversity, rural development challenges and urban environmental quality – have been chosen to highlight for the reader the considerable gap between myth and reality which can exist across a broad spectrum of Dutch life.

Regional diversity

One of the most important perceptions is that of widespread prosperity within Dutch society. In many respects, quality-of-life indices show that this

Fig. 1.
The Netherlands:
an orientation map.

perception is justified, especially when broad European comparisons are made. Yet it is also true that significant regional economic contrasts have been recognised for many decades. Since 1945, those parts of the country most consistently causing concern have been the North (the provinces of Groningen, Friesland and Drenthe) and the deltaic province of Zeeland, south of Rotterdam (fig. 1). More than anything else, in the early postwar years this concern reflected unemployment in these areas. In 1958, for example, national unemployment was only 2.8%, yet in Zeeland it was 4.9%, in Groningen 6.3%, in Friesland 6.9% and in Drenthe 11.2%. Such contrasts have had an important long-term influence on national regional policy even though, compared with recent experience, unemployment on this scale may not seem severe.

On one level, long-standing economic problems in both the North and the delta are explicable in terms of a weak resource base. These are regions that have not had the benefit of large-scale resources able to act as the basis for impressive economic take-off. This is the case even though the North has long been the Netherlands' prime source of natural gas. Vital though this resource is to the country as a whole, its extraction in Groningen and other northern locations is a largely automated process which generates little employment or other form of regional income. The efficiency of pipeline technologies, which distribute the gas throughout the national economy and to other European markets, ensures that almost no economic activity need be attracted to the energy source itself.

At a deeper level, however, lagging economic development has reflected less tangible factors. In the delta the most important of these was inaccessibility. Even though this region lies between two of Western Europe's most dynamic industrial conurbations – Rotterdam and Antwerp – historically this mosaic of estuaries and islands repelled economic activity because of a lack of good fixed road communications. In the North, meanwhile, a fundamental problem has been a perception of inaccessibility. Despite the fact that all the northern provincial capitals are less than 200 km from the heart of the national economy in the western provinces, in the minds of many investors (and, for that matter, ordinary individuals) the North has an undesirable image of remoteness.

While the North and the delta were the primary problem regions in the past, an important feature of the Dutch regional economic system is that it has been very dynamic. This is most graphically demonstrated by recent experience in the delta, where isolation has been thoroughly broken down by major road improvements. New employment has followed, especially around Middelburg and Vlissingen in the southern delta. Equally importantly, it has become possible for workers living in the delta to commute to jobs in Rotterdam to the north, North Brabant province to the east and, indeed, Belgium to the south. The benefits of this new integration are immediately apparent from regional unemployment trends. In the late 1950s, unemployment in Zeeland was almost twice the national average and more than double the levels prevailing in neighbouring prosperous provinces. Today Zeeland has the best provincial unemployment record in the country: significantly lower than any other province, and only two-thirds the national average.

Other regions have fared less well, as two further examples demonstrate. Limburg, once literally the powerhouse of the Netherlands, lost the last vestiges of its all-important South Limburg coalfield twenty years ago because of heavy financial losses and irresistible competition from natural gas. Whereas this province had long enjoyed the most stable provincial economy and the lowest unemployment in the country, its labour market rapidly deteriorated to rank among the worst in the country. More recently, Limburg's location close to the economic heart of Europe, and the effects of various government policies, have produced a partial recovery. But it is most unlikely that there will be a return to the very favourable economic circumstances of the past.

Similarly, conditions in three economically vital western provinces – North Holland, South Holland and Utrecht – have tended to destabilise over the last two decades. Although this region remains the heart of the Dutch economy, industrial automation, the swing from secondary to tertiary activities and the decentralisation of business to new locations have all had far-reaching implications for the labour markets of the western cities. These days the western provinces' unemployment rates are typically close to or above the national average, a sharp contrast to earlier times when they were consistently much lower.

Further examples could be cited, but two things are evident from this brief review. On the one hand, the regional economic system in the Netherlands is substantially more diverse than is frequently assumed. On the other, this system is in a state of constant evolution in response to a diverse range of forces. Here it may be added that these forces – for example, industrial restructuring and multinational investment – increasingly emanate from outside the country. This poses major challenges for economic and physical planners on a variety of scales, from local to national.

Rural development challenges

A second popular image is that of the inherent efficiency of Dutch agriculture. This may well spring from the reputation enjoyed by the country's horticultural industry, and from the advanced farming economy established in the IJsselmeer Polders in the postwar period, but it is in fact based on an extremely incomplete picture. For a more balanced view it is necessary to draw into the frame the farming systems typical of mainland rural areas, rather than those of the IJsselmeer Polders. These systems are in general concerned with dairy farming in the western provinces, and with more mixed arable / animal husbandry in the slightly elevated southern, eastern and northern regions. Largely because of land pressure and inheritance laws which subdivided the land, agriculture in all these districts has been characterised by small and fragmented farms. Farms larger than 30 hectares have been rare, while almost all holdings have comprised several parcels of land, widely distributed throughout the local area.

For many reasons, farm structures of this type are highly inefficient, and to deal with them a nationwide programme of land consolidation (*ruilverkaveling*) has been in progress since the mid-1950s. This has achieved impressive results with respect to reducing the fragmentation problem (fig. 2). Also, by pursuing a range of additional goals, it has done much to improve social and economic conditions in rural communities. This was considered essential to maintain the well-being of these communities and prevent the development of an unacceptable socio-economic divide between rural and urban societies.

Although the land consolidation programme has been far reaching, however, it has posed problems. One is that, while land fragmentation has been greatly ameliorated, success with farm enlargement has been very variable from district to district. This is one reason why only a fifth of all holdings as yet have more than 30 hectares of land. Secondly, the programme has generated strong environmental opposition, largely because on many occasions it has literally required the reconstruction of rural landscapes. This has meant the loss of, for example, hedges, ditches, ponds and belts of woodland, all with their attendant flora and fauna. Approaches to land consolidation have been substantially modified since the mid-1980s to reduce this environmental impact, but it will be some time before the full effect can be assessed.

Thirdly, given the European Union's problem of surplus farmland, it is arguable that consolidation may benefit individual farming families but is not essential for society. Instead it may be that the latter's interests would be

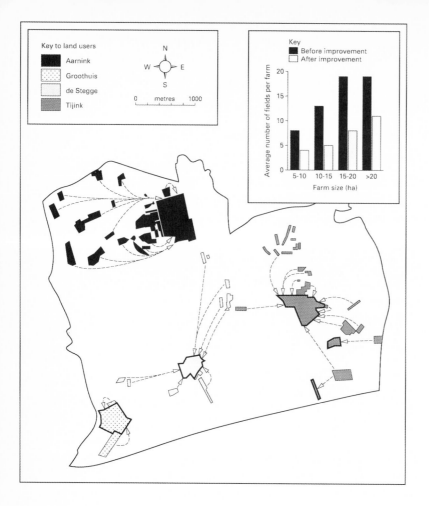

Fig. 2.
Farm fragmentation and consolidation: examples from Genemuiden.

better served by the transfer of agricultural land to other purposes. In much of the country the effects of this argument are as yet limited. However, in the congested western provinces of North Holland, South Holland and Utrecht it has encouraged important shifts in physical planning. Outstanding among these has been the creation of extensive recreation areas on former farmland. These developments usually comprise new woodlands, lakes, cycle paths, training circuits, etc, and their immediate function is to enhance outdoor opportunities for an increasingly prosperous and leisured society that is extremely short of natural recreation space. In addition, several of these parks have been strategically sited between neighbouring towns and cities, where they function as green wedges helping to maintain the separate identity of centres which might otherwise merge. Meanwhile, this changed attitude to agricultural land is now readily observable even in the IJsselmeer Polders. As fig. 3 demonstrates, while the majority of this new land remains in agricultural use, significant areas have been devoted to recreation facilities. Many of these are intended to ease the recreational pressures felt in the western provinces; as such, they are an important tool of national spatial planning. In this respect, the Northern provinces, too, provide an important and much needed open area for recreational activities.

Perhaps encouraged by the renowned heritage core of Amsterdam, a third image of the Netherlands is one of quality in the urban environment. There is certainly more than a grain of truth in this. Quite apart from Amsterdam's finer architectural features, much renovation has been undertaken in the hearts of the country's towns and cities over the last twenty or thirty years, often by private investors, but also by local and national public bodies. Under the *Monumentenzorg* provisions, for example, houses and churches – predominantly in the towns and cities – account for three quarters of the state's investment in heritage conservation. In some instances, projects have been confined to single buildings, or even parts of buildings; in others, individual streets or districts have provided the focus. Whatever the scale, the tendency has been for the quality spiral to move upwards. In suburban development also, concern for design quality has a distinguished history. In both Rotterdam and Amsterdam, the city planning departments have been responsible for suburban expansion schemes which have gained world-wide reputations. More generally, postwar private and public suburban developments have typically emphasised landscaping through, for example, extensive and often imaginative use of greenery and water.

Especially since the 1970s, however, the other side of the urban develop-

Fig. 3.
Recreation facilities on the East Flevoland Polder.

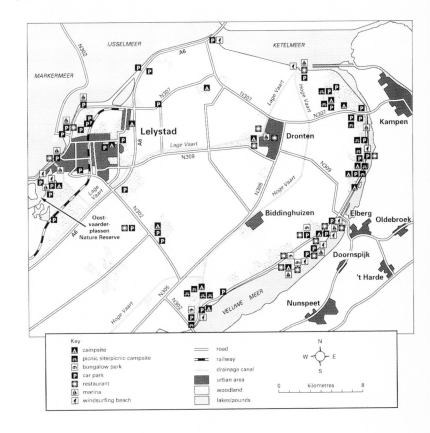

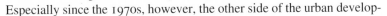

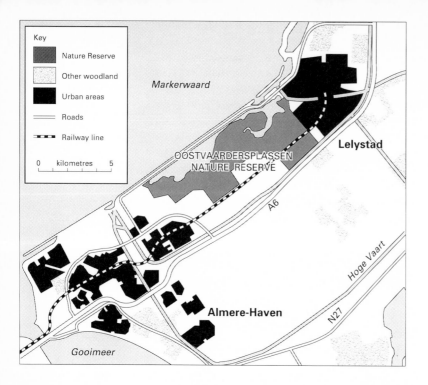

Fig. 4.
From industrial zone to
nature reserve: Oostvaardersplassen, South Flevoland.

ment coin has been recognised. Suburban public housing development, once
executed with great confidence and often to great acclaim, received a severe
setback when the scale and monolithic design of Amsterdam's Bijlmermeer
scheme led to widespread rejection by its intended residents. Similarly, the
new town movement has suffered from publicity given to experiences such
as those of Lelystad in the IJsselmeer Polders. Although it lies only 50 km
from Amsterdam, Lelystad's image is all too often that of an isolated city,
distant from high-order amenities and therefore far from attractive to potential new employers. Perhaps the most graphic demonstration of this failure
to draw in anticipated employment is to be found in the Oostvaardersplassen
nature reserve, south west of Lelystad (fig. 4). Far from being the outcome
of a deep-seated commitment to nature conservation, as might easily be
assumed, this area was originally earmarked for incoming industry which
would have provided many employment opportunities for Lelystad.
Successive plans produced by the State Service for the IJsselmeerpolders
testify to long-standing official commitment to this. But commitment without investment was unable to meet the employment needs of Lelystad,
which has now become a large-scale out-commuting centre and a source of
return migration to the mainland. Nor was it able to hold back the natural
development of a major wilderness area in the Oostvaardersplassen which
ironically became, through Dutch support for environmental protection, one
of Western Europe's largest nature reserves.

One effect of problematic new development has been to foster concern for
the well-being of existing cities and, especially, for those districts where
urban decline problems are severe. Often overlooked by the outside
observer, these areas are extensive and in general are tenement districts built
as the economy rapidly developed between about 1860 and the First World

War. Most lie outside historic urban cores (the natural focus of preservation and rehabilitation efforts) and therefore have extensive dilapidation problems. These are exacerbated by the fact that late-nineteenth-century development normally took place swiftly, with lax controls and with costs to the investor being minimised.

Planning concerns for these run-down districts gained momentum in the 1960s, the initial preference of the authorities being for widespread demolition followed by redevelopment which drew its design philosophy from suburban expansion schemes. Old street patterns were to disappear, to be replaced by an entirely new urban morphology; greenery, space and pedestrianisation would be central to the replacement residential environments; 'non-conforming' businesses – the source of a good deal of employment – would be discouraged; and the new housing stock would be designed to attract a broader cross-section of society than did the decaying tenements, in which the poor, immigrants, the elderly and young adults often tended to predominate. But before it could become firmly established on the ground, this approach to the problems of inner-city decline was challenged and rejected, forcing urban planners to adopt a radically different stance.

Above all, this policy reversal was the result of intense and sustained public protest in a single inner-city district, Amsterdam's Dapperbuurt. Here protestors argued throughout much of the 1970s that the price to be paid for redevelopment was too high. Social disruption, local employment losses and the elimination of a distinctive urban environment were unacceptable. Eventually the beleaguered city planners and council capitulated, allowing rehabilitation (not redevelopment) to become the norm throughout Amsterdam's nineteenth-century belt. Before long this was also the preferred strategy in other major cities, not least because of their planning authorities' reluctance to become involved in similar environmental conflicts. Thus townscapes, local economies and communities are safeguarded while living conditions are radically improved. By any standards this represents a substantial shift in favour of urban conservation.

This does not mean that inner-urban areas are devoid of redevelopment. Some tenements are too decayed to save and, as in other Western European countries, redundant space has been created by the decline of inner-urban industry. In addition, the Dutch have not escaped the common problem of the abandonment of old port areas, chiefly in response to technological change in the shipping industry (particularly containerisation) and the increasing size of ships. To some extent the solutions found for these types of urban decline are essentially those adopted in most developed countries. For example, with its blocks of offices and private apartments, the north bank of Rotterdam's Nieuwe Maas river bears a strong resemblance to major North American port redevelopment schemes. Further plans, for the overspill of the city's central business district functions to the south bank of the river, serve to underline this trend. Yet away from the immediate city core, the planners' preferred strategy for land released by port decline is entirely different. Here emphasis is placed on social housing aimed at the needs of local communities (fig. 5). In this context an important link with the policy of inner-city rehabilitation can be identified. In many instances this rehabilitation entails reducing the number of dwellings per hectare in order to achieve desirable living standards. But any new housing in the

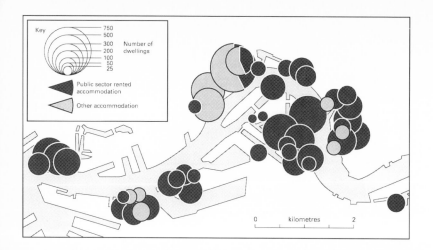

Fig. 5.
Housing development on
the Rotterdam waterfront.

vicinity – such as that built on disused dockland – provides the opportunity to accommodate displaced families locally, helping to reduce an aspect of social disruption that urban improvement schemes cannot avoid entirely.

Conclusion

Little need be said by way of conclusion, because the intention of this article has not been to distil into one dense survey a comprehensive assessment of the Netherlands' human geography. Instead, an overriding aim has been to expose levels of complexity and diversity that are commonly overlooked by most observers. Space constraints have meant that important topics have had to be left undiscussed, but it is hoped that enough has been said to encourage the reader to apply to other aspects of Dutch life and society the approach adopted above. Deeper insights for the individual can only come from a more probing, critical approach, and there is as yet much to learn from this compact yet fascinating country.

DAVID A. PINDER

For the English-speaking reader wishing to pursue this approach, a number of up-to-date information sources can be suggested. One is the journal *Tijdschrift voor Economische en Sociale Geografie,* which regularly publishes short articles under the heading 'Window on the Netherlands'. The subjects chosen for these articles are very varied, while their coverage is usually admirably detailed. In addition the IDG (Information and Documentation Centre for the Geography of the Netherlands) publishes an excellent annual *Bulletin* plus special reports and is also able to respond to specific requests for information. A particularly valuable feature of the *Bulletin* is its bibliography of recent publications on the Netherlands. The address of the IDG is: Department of Geography, Utrecht University / P.O. Box 80 115 / 3508 TC Utrecht / The Netherlands. Those seeking insights into current approaches to national physical planning will find useful the report *On the Road to 2015,* published by the Ministry of Housing, Physical Planning and Environment (P.O. Box 20951 / 2500 EL The Hague / The Netherlands). Annual statistical volumes well worth consulting for information on an exceptionally wide range of subjects include *Jaarcijfers voor Nederland* (in which much is translated into English); the smaller *Statistisch Zakboek;* and the *Regionaal Statistisch Zakboek.* All are published by the CBS (Central Bureau of Statistics): P.O. Box 959 / 2270 AZ Voorburg / The Netherlands. Finally, a valuable external overview of the Dutch economy is provided at intervals of approximately two years by the OECD in its economic report *The Netherlands.*

The Wadden Sea:

A Special Area – Specially Protected?

After years of comparative peace and quiet there is once again a threat to the environment of the Wadden Sea. In December 1993 the Dutch cabinet decided that, after a ten-year moratorium, from 1994 onwards it is permissible to drill for gas in the Wadden Sea. From the purely economic point of view, that can really be taken for granted: it is estimated that the value of the gas which can be extracted from under the Wadden Sea amounts to some 15 thousand million Dutch guilders. This makes the economic importance of the operation only too clear. But from the environmental viewpoint, drilling for gas in the Wadden Sea seems like ecological vandalism: the Wadden Sea area is after all an exceptional nature reserve, protected by both national and international regulations, and the protection and development of the area is the prime objective of dozens of policy documents and memoranda. It is by no means certain that economic and ecological aims can be reconciled in such an area.

The Frisian Islands in the Wadden Sea. The bottom of the picture shows part of the mainland, with the naval port of Den Helder on the left, the Great Dike and the IJsselmeer in the middle, and Leeuwarden and environs on the right (Photo from the ESA-satellite ERS-1, received in Fucino, Italy, 27-28 July 1991).

The Wadden Sea as a special area

The Wadden Sea area extends from the coast of the province of North Holland, via Friesland and Groningen, along the German coast and right into Danish waters. The Dutch section, with the mainland of Friesland and Groningen on its southern edge, is bordered to the north by five inhabited islands, from Texel to Schiermonnikoog, and several uninhabited ones. Its special character lies in the fact that it is a very tidal area. At high tide the water of the North Sea flows into the area through various larger and smaller channels between the islands; at low tide a large part of the area, especially the numerous sand bars, becomes dry land. Mud flats form the boundary between wet and dry.

These special circumstances make the Wadden Sea far and away the largest nature reserve in the Netherlands, and the most important area in Europe for water birds. The special conditions of ebb and flow, wet and dry, of channels and sand bars lying just below or just above the water line, have resulted in a unique flora and fauna – not only the area's characteristic vegetation, but also its exceptional marine life. On every high tide large quantities of food flow into the Wadden area. This abundance of food and the comparative peace of the area make the Wadden Sea literally a nursery for salt-water fish, and especially for seals. At the same time the abundance of food and the extent of the area make it very attractive to birds: for migratory birds in particular the Wadden Sea is an important feeding and resting area.

Threats

Of course nature reserves, even when they are as extensive as the Wadden Sea, are not hermetically sealed off from the outside world. Influences from without can quickly pose a threat to the precarious and vulnerable ecological balance of such an area. Water pollution is a particularly important fac-

Seals sunbathing (Photo by Jan van de Kam).

The Wadden Sea at low tide: mussel bed with seaweed (Photo by Jan van de Kam).

tor for the Wadden Sea. It does not come only from local sources such as households, industry and agriculture, which are responsible for pollution direct from the land. In this case the polluted state of the Rhine also plays a major role. Some of the water of the Rhine flows from its mouth at Rotterdam via the North Sea into the Wadden Sea; some also ends up in the Wadden Sea via the River IJssel. It has already been established on a number of occasions that dangerous substances discharged into the Rhine in Switzerland, France or Germany, can after a time be traced in the Wadden Sea. This happened, for instance, after the Sandoz fire in Basle in November 1986, when large quantities of pesticide were swept into the Rhine. Apart from this pollution from the land, recreational use, water sports and tourism, and in particular the international shipping passing on the North Sea, constitute a continual risk to the Wadden Sea. The disaster of the oil tanker Braer in 1993, with the resultant pollution of the Shetlands, demonstrated the risk yet again. It is true that international shipping routes have been agreed for the Wadden Sea and that these should in principle provide adequate security. But the question is whether these agreements are always respected and, above all, what happens in an emergency.

Apart from pollution, from whatever source, and industrial overfishing, a further significant threat to the environment of the Wadden Sea is disturbance. It is mainly a question of noise nuisance, again partly caused by recreation and tourism, but also by military practice flights over the area. In its function as a resting place for birds the Wadden Sea needs quiet above all else.

Mud flats by the Wadden Sea (Photo by Jan van de Kam).

Special policy

The number and diversity of the threats means that a large number of policy areas and thus also a great many organisations are involved in the protection of the Wadden Sea. Up until the mid-seventies, policy could only be described as fragmented: various ministries and a large number of provincial and municipal services and bodies each had their own views, tasks and competencies. However, between 1976 and 1980 the Principal Planological Ruling for the Wadden Sea came into being. A Principal Planological Ruling is an extraordinary ruling under the Dutch Physical Planning Act, a ruling which is implemented by means of a special procedure. To put it in a nutshell, this Ruling for the Wadden Sea makes it possible to formulate an integral and coherent policy for the whole area. In fact it means that the numerous activities in the area and its various contradictory functions can be reconciled to one another, with a view to maintaining its international significance as a nature reserve. The administrative organisation and the division of tasks in the area has also been modified with this in mind. The latter has led amongst other things to coordination both horizontally (between different ministries) and vertically (between state, provinces and municipalities). The creation of a variety of consultative and advisory bodies was soon found to be an inadequate, but nonetheless necessary step towards comprehensive and effective policy making. After these consultative bodies had formulated the broad outlines of the policy, in the eighties work was concentrated on various plans to implement it. In the meantime, in 1981 part of the Wadden Sea area was designated a nature reserve; this designation will soon cover almost 90% of the area and should guarantee it special protection. Furthermore, since 1984 the Wadden Sea has been a so-called 'Wetland' according to the International Ramsar Convention. Finally, the area is also covered by the more recent European Bird Directive.

Protection enough, it would seem. In any case the Netherlands government has taken considerable pains, both at home and internationally, to give the Wadden Sea area the status of a nature reserve and to establish the protective measures in as many policy documents and agreements as possible. Moreover, this policy has been advocated and stimulated to a considerable extent by Dutch environmental and nature conservation organisations in general, and by the National Association for the Preservation of the Wadden Sea in particular. This latter organisation was established as long ago as 1965 and has fought from the outset against the impairment of the Wadden Sea area, amongst other things by opposing industrialisation on its shores, plans for land reclamation, etc.

The future: gas under the Wadden Sea

It has been known for some time that there is natural gas in the bed of the Wadden Sea. These fields link up with the extensive oil and natural gas fields further offshore in the North Sea. Since the price of oil went up by leaps and bounds in the seventies, these latter fields have been extensively exploited, as have the natural gas fields near Slochteren in the north of the Netherlands, which produce large quantities of natural gas, partly for domestic use, partly for export.

Nevertheless, in view of the special character of the Wadden Sea and the special status of the area, as laid down in a variety of policy papers, it was decided in the early eighties to declare a ten-year moratorium on the extraction of natural gas from the Wadden Sea. For some time it looked as though the natural gas companies, the NAM (Netherlands Petroleum Company) and the large petroleum companies involved with it, were going to regard this moratorium less as a postponement than an abandonment. But the relatively easy, and thus inexpensive extractability of the natural gas under the Wadden Sea now makes it an attractive proposition after all. For the Dutch state the extra income from natural gas is a welcome supplement to the lower than expected national income. Indeed, a not insignificant part of Dutch government income comes from the profits from natural gas.

Among other things, in December 1993 the Dutch cabinet decided on a compromise. As yet drilling for gas in the Wadden Sea itself is still prohibited. Drilling towers and drill shafts, plus all the accompanying transportation activities, would cause far too much disturbance to the 'Wadden Sea quiet area'. But drilling for gas from the shore, so-called high angle or directional drilling, will be permissible on certain conditions. Those carrying out this high angle drilling must ensure that disturbance to the marine area itself remains within acceptable limits, and that possible accidents have no immediate disastrous consequences for the precarious environmental balance. A significant economic disadvantage of this method is that in this way it is not possible to extract the whole of the gas.

The more militant sections of the environmental movement have in the meantime protested vociferously against the plans. They view the extraction of natural gas in the Wadden Sea as confirmation of a slogan from the early days of environmental awareness: 'If we had to poison our wombs for the sake of our economy' ran the biting text of that time, 'then we'd do it'. Other environmental groups appear to have bowed to the inevitable. These groups want to devote their energies to exacting the most stringent environmental conditions for the drilling as both the Environmental Impact Statement and the permit procedures are still to come. This point of view, which in principle has also been adopted by the government, will result in further extensive study being carried out on how to drill for natural gas with the maximum care for the environment and the minimum of risk. Before the first gas has been extracted from the Wadden Sea in 1999, a great many reports will undoubtedly have been written on the environmental effects. Nevertheless, the question arises as to whether this decision does not mean that the internationally accepted precautionary principle has been trampled under foot. But more important than this discussion of principle is the question of whether the Wadden Sea area will actually survive this environmental interference. The answer will probably only emerge in fifty years' time.

PIETER LEROY
Translated by Rachel van der Wilden.

Platform for the extraction of natural gas, with feeding gulls and terns in the foreground (Photo by Jan van de Kam).

Gardening

in the Netherlands

Farmhouse garden (Photo Stichting 'Tuinen Mien Ruys').

What are the differences between Dutch and English gardening? Well, the Dutch don't have as many greenhouses as the English do, nor do they approach deadheading with the religious zeal of the English (in fact there isn't even a word for it in Dutch), and they spell 'camellia' with only one 'l'.

One does not even see many camellias here, owing to a persistent belief that they are not hardy in the Netherlands, and that is another difference between Dutch and English gardens: the plants. The Netherlands is colder than England, not much colder but just enough to make a difference in the choice of plants (not as great as that between the Netherlands and Ireland, but noticeable enough). I live in a coastal region of the Netherlands and my garden is in the centre of a town and surrounded by walls, which makes it rather milder in winter than areas further inland. Not so very long ago I simply could not find many of the enticing plants described in English gardening books; nurserymen would say, dismissively, 'that isn't hardy here', or, more irritatingly, 'you found that in an English book, didn't you?' But more and more of them are available now, which, as the Dutch winters have not become noticeably milder, would seem to indicate either that people have become more willing to go to the trouble of protecting plants in winter, or that they have been so affected by the prevailing gardening wind from England that they feel they have a right to these goodies too.

For there can be no doubt that the English influence is enormous. In the Netherlands, just as in England, gardening is becoming ever more popular; also, as in England, it is *English* gardening, taken over bodily, that is popular. The innocent 'boerderijtuin', the farmhouse garden, an authentically Dutch form with its row of espaliered trees, its neat gravel and symmetrically placed hortensias, is being swept away by a flood of English cottage gardens, a form alien to Dutch tradition which sits rather awkwardly in the broad and open Dutch landscape.

The English landscape, since the Romantics anyway, is at its best when wild and untouched by human hand; what is beautiful about the Dutch landscape is precisely that it has been touched, worked over and in some cases entirely created by the human hand. The symmetry of dikes, ditches and fields, flat as far as the eye can see and presided over by a vast and usually cloudy sky, could not be more different from the cosy English patchwork of rolling hills, high hedgerows and irregular shapes. There is no mystery in the Dutch landscape, nothing hidden or enclosed, no follies or other eccentricities, and even those farmhouse gardens lie there openly on display to the outside world. The English garden on the other hand is a refuge, hedged or fenced about, part of one's castle, a place, sometimes literally, of retirement.

The English dream of retirement to the country and cultivation of one's garden awakes no corresponding echo in the Dutch soul: 'I can't think where people did retire to,' said a Dutch friend of mine, 'but it wasn't to a garden in the country'. Nor was gardening an acceptable pastime for the

Modern farmhouse garden: a combination of vegetable beds and ornamental flowers (Photo Stichting 'Tuinen Mien Ruys').

middle classes, and certainly not for the male of that species. This is even more noticeable in France, where the great houses had their gardens and the working classes grew vegetables in their allotments but a university professor or a lawyer would never dream of devoting any time to so demeaning an activity as gardening.

But things are changing now; gardening has become fashionable, everybody is doing it. And one glance at the gardening section in any bookshop is enough to see where the impetus comes from. The number of English gardening books translated into Dutch is phenomenal, although a great many of them are, it must be said, of the coffee table variety: lovely pictures with a trickle of text, sometimes slightly mistranslated. On the other hand one of the greatest classics of gardening writing, *The Well-Tempered Garden* by Christopher Lloyd, has inexplicably never appeared in Dutch, although some of his later books, more adaptable to the coffee table format, are available. Then again a writer whom one would oneself perhaps not have gone to much trouble to publish in a foreign language, Beverley Nichols, does exist in Dutch: a translation of *Down the Garden Path,* minus many of its purplest passages and all its breathless dots, came out here recently.

Dutch gardening literature is practical and deadly serious: the tradition of the discursive gardening book does not exist here. There is no E.A. Bowles, no Canon Ellacombe, no Sir Arthur Hort, none of those gardening vicars of the English world. Older books had titles like *Your Garden an Arcadia* (Uw tuin een lusthof) or *Directions for Meaningful Gardening* (Een aansporing tot het zinvol tuinieren) and were very different in both style and spirit from *The Unconventional Garden* or *The Garden of Ignorance.* Nowadays the titles are less pedestrian but the books themselves, with one or two exceptions, are still rather more meaningful than light-hearted.

However, a great many Dutch people – and all Dutch gardeners, I sometimes think – read English; perhaps nobody needs a translation of *The Well-Tempered Garden.* And then there is television: having BBC on the cable seems to have dispensed Dutch television from the need to produce its own regular gardening programme: why bother when there is *Gardeners' World?* This programme can sometimes be extremely frustrating for the foreign viewer, mainly because of all the wonderful gadgets and accessories that are brandished on it and which are not to be found here. You end up with an idea of the English garden centre as a cornucopia of the most wonderful and inaccessible objects, without which gardening is almost impossible. Still, we are resourceful, in our way: a friend of mine who became fired with enthusiasm by some tip about cuttings went to a great deal of trouble to get hold of the sterilising medium that was required. Having abandoned the search in garden centres she ended up with a friendly chemist who was willing to listen to her problem (others seemed shocked by the idea that there might be something among their wares that would serve to sterilise a cutting) and who provided her with a kind of denture powder, which did the trick.

Going directly to the source of gardening supplies, the growers, one also comes across the English influence; there one does sometimes find some lively gardening writing. Unlike gardening books, which often resemble catalogues, the nursery catalogues do tend towards the discursive, and scattered among the references to English authorities there are occasional flour-

Modern garden with a pond (Photo Stichting 'Tuinen Mien Ruys').

ishes, like Rob Leopold's description of the smell of *Ambrosinia mexicana* 'Jerusalem Oak'. Not having smelled it myself I cannot confirm this but it has made me extremely curious: 'This reminds me of the smell in the school playground when, with small magnifying glasses, we used to concentrate the sun's rays onto pieces of mica.'

'The garden which lay around it would be a lady water-colourist's heaven, herbaceous borders, rockeries, and water-gardens were carried to a perfection of vulgarity, and flaunted a riot of huge and hideous flowers, each individual bloom appearing twice as large, three times as brilliant as it ought to have been and if possible of a different colour from that which nature intended. (...) You could hardly see any beautiful, pale, bright, yellow-green of spring, every tree appeared to be entirely covered with a waving mass of pink or mauve tissue-paper. The daffodils were so thick on the ground that they too obscured the green, they were new varieties of a terrifying size, either dead white or dark yellow, thick and fleshy; they did not look at all like the fragile friends of one's childhood.'

I am always reminded of this description when I visit Boskoop, the nursery town of the Netherlands, where every second house seems to run a nursery in its back garden. The soil must be tremendously fertile there: every garden brims over with flowering shrubs of the most glaring hue and each one is more hideous than its neighbour. Although this passage is actually about an English garden (it is from *The Pursuit of Love* by Nancy Mitford), it applies beautifully to the kind of garden that corresponds to those Dutch interiors you sometimes get a glimpse into from the street: carpets on the tables, potplants on the window-sills and a mass of objects on every horizontal surface – china cats, tiny brass windmills, biscuit tins with geese on them.

The other kind of Dutch interior is resolutely modern and uncluttered: white walls, one abstract painting, three black leather chairs and sometimes one cup on the glass coffee table to indicate that living people have been there. The kind of garden corresponding to this interior consists largely of architectural elements: there is lots of paving, sometimes of several different kinds, an overdose of railway sleepers, many differences in level and masses of *Alchemilla mollis* blurring all the corners. These gardens look as though they had all been designed by the same person; in fact they are all inspired by Mien Ruys, the Netherlands' most influential modern garden designer. She was the first in Holland to adopt the idea of 'een wilde beplanting in een strakke vormgeving' (wild planting within a strict layout) – strict but not symmetrical – differing from the English proponents of this view in her use of modern materials, which blend in well with the average Dutch suburban or semirural villa type of architecture. But in the wrong hands, or without interesting plants, such gardens can be sometimes dull – and have given poor *Alchemilla mollis* a bad name.

In recent years the planting has become yet wilder, after a little side step in the seventies towards the idea of really wild plants in no layout at all, which wouldn't suit the Dutch (or many other gardeners, come to that); and now the most influential Dutch garden writer is Elisabeth de Lestrieux, who has produced a series of books with beautiful photographs advocating a return to symmetrical layouts with box and yew hedges and her own prefer-

Experimental roof terrace garden (Photo Stichting 'Tuinen Mien Ruys').

ence for restrained, pastel, colour schemes. This is most definitely the opposite of the cottage garden, there is no question of jumbling everything in together; on the contrary the plants, and other ingredients like old terracotta pots and faded wrought-iron garden furniture, are extremely carefully disposed (and prices in antique shops have rocketed in consequence).

This is sometimes more like interior decoration than gardening, and some people may find it a little too precious for their taste. However, its influence cannot be denied, especially on the roof terrace garden, a specifically Dutch form which is unfortunately invisible to the outsider. An aerial photograph of Amsterdam or any other big city would certainly reveal hundreds of hidden green eyries, burgeoning with potted plants and tenderly protected against the ferocious Dutch winds.

Allotment garden.

Another interesting phenomenon is the Dutch allotment: many a frustrated gardener living in the city bicycles off a couple of times a week to a little garden in an allotment complex. Unlike the rooftop variety, these gardens are extremely visible, particularly from trains, and some of them display a dogged kind of eccentricity that is lacking in the grander sort of gardening. Some are just plain vegetable gardens but many are real ornamental gardens, with patios and little houses where their owners can go and stay in summer. These complexes are usually surrounded by water, in the form of ditches, and they often have a network of other ditches running through them, with little bridges at strategic intervals. However hideous the gardens may be, and some of them are indescribably awful, there are few more pleasant sights in the Netherlands than a row of pollarded willows leaning over one of these ditches: timeless – Clusius and Boerhaave would have seen them thus – and unchanging.

SARAH HART

Park for Modern Art

The Middelheim Open-Air Sculpture Museum in Antwerp

Henry Moore, *King and Queen* (1952) (Photo Middelheim Museum, Antwerp).

Sculptures like the open air. They decorate the gardens of royal palaces and stand in squares in city centres. The idea that modern sculpture comes into its own when in contact with nature gained acceptance after the Second World War. 'Sculpture is an art for open spaces', said the British sculptor Henry Moore. 'It needs daylight and sunlight. I'd rather put my sculpture in a landscape, any landscape, than in the most beautiful building I know.'

In 1950 the then burgomaster of Antwerp, Lode Craeybeckx, taking advantage of the keen interest aroused by the much publicised open-air exhibitions in Battersea Park in London and in the Sonsbeek Park in Arnhem in the Netherlands, had sculptures erected in the lovely gardens of Middelheim Park on the outskirts of the city. Craeybeckx, the eloquent and inspiring champion of an ambitious cultural policy, felt that as a 'land of painters' Flanders attached too little importance to sculpture. That same year the exhibition in the park drew 125,000 visitors, and its success led to the foundation of the Middelheim Open-Air Sculpture Museum in Antwerp.

For many centuries there had been a number of *hoven van plaisantie* or pleasure grounds just outside the city. These were small country houses surrounded by delightful parks, which were used as summer residences by well-to-do Antwerp families. Many of these properties fell prey to urban expansion, but in 1910 three of them were purchased by the City Council to save them from redevelopment and were opened to the public as parks. Middelheim is by far the most beautiful of the three.

Records dating back to 1342 refer to 'a stead known as Middelheim'. From the sixteenth century on, a succession of Antwerp families used it as their summer residence. A painting in the collection in the Broodhuis Museum in Brussels shows a small castle in Flemish-Renaissance style on the land. In the eighteenth century this was rebuilt in Louis XVI-style, probably in accordance with plans drawn up by the Parisian architect Guimard. Though the castle was damaged during the Second World War when both the German and the Allied armies used it as a depot, it still retains its elegant eighteenth-century appearance.

It has always been the aim of Middelheim to provide a broad international overview of modern sculpture, from precursors like Rodin to our own times.

A series of biennials was launched, each devoted to a single country or a specific theme. As time passed the cycle lost momentum, but the first biennials in the fifties were a true revelation. For the first time the public could experience the power of modern sculptors from Italy, France, Germany and Great Britain through the extensive, high quality ensembles that were presented year after year. These biennials have clearly left their mark on the collection in the open-air museum.

The Middelheim collection does not offer an exhaustive overview of twentieth-century sculpture, but it certainly includes more than enough exquisite pieces to make a walk through the park an exciting experience. The museum can be compared to the sculpture gardens of foreign institutions like the Kröller-Müller Museum in Otterlo (The Netherlands) or the Louisiana Museum near Copenhagen (Denmark). It includes powerful female sculptures by Aristide Maillol as well as carefully-studied abstract work by Max Bill, a serene *Flautist* by the German expressionist Ernst Barlach as well as a fanciful *Dog* cut from sheet iron by the American master Alexander Calder. Two eminent sculptors, Henry Moore and Ossip Zadkine, advised the museum during the early years when it was putting together the collection. The City of Antwerp bought the bronze sculpture *King and Queen* from Moore in 1952, and this is one of the highlights of the collection to this day. The works by Ossip Zadkine in Middelheim's possession

Marino Marini, *Miracolo* (1951-1952) (Photo Middelheim Museum, Antwerp).

Rik Wouters, *Crazy Girl* (1912).

include a bronze *Orpheus* whose torso represents the structure of a lyre.

The picture of twentieth-century sculpture which Middelheim provides gives the visitor a good idea of the diversity of the language of shapes which modern artists have developed. Their pursuit of originality and their desire to express their own personality led to a hitherto unknown individualism. This can be seen in Middelheim in, for example, the highly-diverse emphases brought to the human figure by powerful personalities like Alexander Archipenko, Alberto Giacometti, Käthe Kollwitz and Pablo Gargallo; so that visitors walking in the green stillness of the park find themselves musing on the complexity of contemporary man.

Among the open-air museum's finest assets is the attractive ensemble of work by Italian sculptors assembled largely as a result of purchases made in the fifties. Giacomo Manzù is represented by his best-known theme, a serene *Cardinal,* but also by a graceful female dancer and two bronze high reliefs, one of which depicts the *Crucifixion* and the other the *Entombment.* In his representation of Christ's Passion, Manzù achieved a power of expression which conveys the – still very real – drama of the world war. To represent Marino Marini's work the museum has the sitting nude *Judith* and the equestrian statue *Miracolo.* The latter recalls the conversion of St Paul on his way to Damascus: blinded by a heavenly light, the rearing horse throws its rider. We should also mention five fine sculptures in terracotta produced by Arturo Martini in the thirties and the seductive *Faun* by Marcello Mascherini which was inspired by Claude Debussy's well-known prelude. There is also by Mascherini a *St Francis* stretching out his hands towards the sky in ecstasy, of which a second copy embellishes the sculptor's grave.

A visit to Middelheim is a good opportunity for foreign art-lovers to get to know the Flemish sculptors. One of the most dynamic sculptures in the garden and a favourite with the public is *Crazy Girl* by the painter and sculptor Rik Wouters (1882-1916). One of the Brabantine fauvists, his paintings and aquarelles are an ode to colour and light. Some of his most intense works were produced near the end of his life when, suffering from cancer, he felt the approach of death. The freshness of his palette can be admired in the Royal Museums of Fine Arts in Brussels and Antwerp. Middelheim has a subdued self-portrait by him in bronze as well as two sculptures of his wife Nel, whom he immortalised many times and in many different positions. She was his model for the above-mentioned *Crazy Girl* in 1912. The exuberant movement of the figure was inspired by a performance by the American dancer Isadora Duncan which had made an enormous impression on the artist. A year later, Nel posed for the second large sculpture, *Domestic Concerns.* In this larger-than-life depiction, Wouters captures his wife as she interrupts her household chores to listen to him, her arms crossed over her apron.

A leading sculptor of the Belgian avant-garde was Oscar Jespers (1887-1970). He made his debut as an impressionist and arrived via cubism and expressionism at a sober realism with solid volumes, as his monumental female figure *In the Sun* in Middelheim attests. As an example of the work of the sculptor and graphic artist Jozef Cantré (1890-1957), a representative of Flemish expressionism, the open-air museum has the studied composition

Oscar Jespers, *In the Sun* (1947) (Photo Middelheim Museum, Antwerp).

in wood *Two People,* in which a man and a woman, Hero and Leander, are diagonally opposed.

An eventful history is attached to the sculpture *Jan de Lichte* by Roel D'Haese (1921-). Jan de Lichte was an eighteenth-century highwayman who was sentenced to death when still a young man and executed in Aalst. He inspired the Flemish writer Louis-Paul Boon to write a remarkable novel, *The Gang of Jan de Lichte* (De bende van Jan de Lichte, 1957), in which he described the conduct of the highwaymen as a struggle of simple people against the economic powers which oppressed them, as a portent of the French Revolution. Roel D'Haese's statue, a bronze monument three metres high, was intended first and foremost as a homage to Louis-Paul Boon. The sculptor dreamed of having the work erected in the main square in Aalst, Boon's town, but the plan met with opposition from the local Catholic party which was reluctant to honour a 'scoundrel' in the heart of the town. Neither was he successful in his attempt to find it a place in the village of Velzeke where Jan de Lichte was born. Eventually, and very much against the wishes of the artist, the sculpture came to rest among the trees in Middelheim. Thus, after a long-drawn-out struggle, the open-air museum was enriched with a splendid piece thanks to the efforts of some friends of the arts who feared that Roel D'Haese might otherwise destroy his work. *Jan de Lichte* can be seen as a high point of post-war sculpture in Flanders. The young gang leader is depicted with rebellious pride; the rope he is holding hints at his death on the scaffold, his face is hidden behind a mask. Despite the violent subject, the sculpture expresses great tenderness.

The smallest and most vulnerable sculptures in the Middelheim collection are shown in a pavilion designed by the architect Renaat Braem. Braem, a pupil of Le Corbusier, was not only an extraordinarily active craftsman but also a pugnacious advocate of modern architecture who did not shun public debate in what he once called 'the ugliest country in the world'. Daylight gently streams into the sober and yet elegant white building he designed for the open-air museum. The centrepiece of this pavilion is *The Great Game of Chess* by Vic Gentils (1919-). The pieces of the game of chess were constructed by Gentils using table legs, parts of a grand piano, balusters, oars and other everyday objects to form larger than life-size figures and were then burned black or sprayed white.

Roel D'Haese, *Jan de Lichte* (1979-1987) (Photo Middelheim Museum, Antwerp).

In the eighties it became clear that Middelheim needed a new impetus. Because of the City of Antwerp's financial difficulties, the open-air museum no longer received a grant for purchasing new work. Consequently, a balanced acquisitions policy became impossible, and embarrassing gaps began to appear in the collection. Important trends from the sixties, seventies and eighties like *arte povera* and minimal art were not represented at all. Sculptures were regularly added, thanks to donations, but as a result the stretches of grass housing the collection became 'overpopulated', while another part of the park went unused.

In 1993 Antwerp became Cultural Capital of Europe. The organisers made it known at the outset that they favoured long-term investments rather than short-lived, prestige projects. Consequently they decided to use the event as an opportunity to expand the open-air museum, rearrange the existing collection and purchase ten new works from living artists.

The intention is that this core of new sculptures shall eventually expand to provide an overview of late twentieth-century sculpture. The works were selected by 'Antwerp 93' Project Manager Bart Cassiman. He turned the area that had previously been used for Middelheim biennials into a permanent section for contemporary sculpture. Cassiman emphasised the fundamental change in attitude of the artists, who no longer make a monument for an arbitrary stretch of grass but design their work for a specific spot, bringing the characteristics of the surroundings into play.

An intriguing presence among the new sculptures is *Never Mind,* a work by the British artist Richard Deacon. He presents an egg-shaped wooden structure supported on a steel base. In its shining perfection the form creates a theatrical effect in the midst of nature and seems to underline its own 'unnaturalness'. The Danish artist Per Kirkeby was also invited to create a work and he set about the task with great thoroughness. With the help of a builder he built a monumental brick sculpture resembling an abstract temple that can be used as a pavillion in which to exhibit works of art. Kirkeby's work can be seen as architecture as well as sculpture. The inside of this building looks like a brick labyrinth in which the contrast between the open sky and the narrow passageways jolts the visitor's observations. The new ensemble also comprises a series of pictograms by the American artist Matt Mullican; a tree with a thousand tongues by the German Thomas Schütte; two 'windows' by the German Isa Genzken; a double sculpture consisting of stacked-up letters by the German Harald Klingelhöller; two bronze figures hanging from trees on either side of an avenue and desperately reaching out to each other by the Spaniard Juan Muñoz; an empty pedestal by the Belgian artist Didier Vermeiren; an installation with gigantic beams by Bernd Lohaus who lives in Antwerp.

Vic Gentils, *The Great Game of Chess* (1966-1967, detail) (Photo Middelheim Museum, Antwerp).

Richard Deacon, *Never Mind* (1993) (Photo Middelheim Museum, Antwerp).

There is no doubt that the most talked-about acquisition is the reconstruction of a prehistoric bird, the *Archaeopteryx* by Panamarenko (1940-). Panamarenko made a name for himself as a builder of aeroplanes which do not fly and cars which cannot be driven. His best sculptures radiate the lightness of dragonflies and the poetry of handiwork and represent the age-old dream of man, who wants to soar high above the earth under his own steam. Panamarenko is fascinated by science and technology, but he is not satisfied with book learning: he wants to experiment for himself and try out what the laws of nature teach him. This has resulted in all sorts of bizarre inventions, including a flying rucksack. The *Archaeopteryx* is a solar-powered bakelite robot in the form of a moving prehistoric chicken. Panamarenko's dancing free-range chicken has a fragile charm that immediately won it a position of honour in the Middelheim collection. However, you do need a spot of luck when you visit because the chicken does not work every day.

JAN VAN HOVE
Translated by Alison Mouthaan-Gwillim.

ADDRESS

Middelheim Open-Air Sculpture Museum
Middelheimlaan 59-61 / 2020 Antwerp / Belgium
tel. +32 (0) 3 827 15 34
Opening Hours: June / July: 10 a.m. – 9 p.m.
August: 10 a.m. – 8 p.m.
September: 10 a.m. – 7 p.m.
October – May: 10 a.m. – 5 p.m.

Panamarenko,
Archaeopteryx (1993)
(Photo Middelheim
Museum, Antwerp).

'An

Utrecht lady's charms'

Belle van Zuylen / Isabelle de Charrière

'And yet just now a lady's charms / Make my gay bosom beat with love's alarms / (…) But she from whom my heart has caught the flame, / Has nothing Dutch about her but the name.'

Thus wrote James Boswell in 1763 about the eighteenth-century Dutchwoman who has in recent years been the subject of two biographies, one in Dutch and one in English, as well as studies and dissertations in America and Europe, and about whom there have been plays and a film, – undoubtedly therefore a remarkable person. So remarkable in fact, that the Institute of Womens' Studies in Amsterdam is named after her.

Belle van Zuylen was born into the nobility on 20 October 1740 at Zuylen Castle outside Utrecht. Her full name was Isabella Agneta Elisabeth van Tuyll van Serooskerken, known in the Netherlands as Belle van Zuylen and elsewhere as Isabelle de Charrière after the man she married, the Swiss Charles-Emmanuel de Charrière de Penthaz. She owes her reputation to her writing, her character, her ideas and her emancipated personality.

The discovery – or rather rediscovery – of this exceptional woman at this time is no unexpected coincidence. In 1974 the Dutch took the initiative of commissioning the publication of her complete works and correspondence, prepared by an international team of English, Swiss, Belgian, French and Dutch scholars in close co-operation. It appeared between 1979 and 1984 in ten india-paper volumes. It is this first complete, scholarly edition, written in French, the language in which she herself wrote, that established the basis for her rapidly growing acclaim.

Belle's father presided over the knights of the province of Utrecht and was a member of the States-General. Her mother, Helena de Vicq, the daughter of a well-to-do Amsterdam patrician family, was a wealthy orphan who married Baron Van Tuyll at the age of fifteen. Belle was the first of seven children and received a sound education under the guidance of a Swiss francophone governess. French was widely spoken at that time in European – and Dutch – society; it was the international language of culture, learning, finance and trade. A great deal of correspondence was then written in French, so that it is not surprising that Belle also wrote in that language. When she was ten, she was sent with her governess to stay for some time in Geneva to further her intellectual education. On the return journey she stayed for a time in Paris. What we know about her life between her tenth and eighteenth years comes from her governess, Jeanne-Louise Prevost, who returned to Switzerland in 1753 but maintained a correspondence with her pupil, of which only Prevost's letters have survived.

The first letter in Belle's hand dates from 1760, a letter written to Baron Constant d'Hermenches, a Swiss colonel in the service of the States-General in the Netherlands. He was a cultured gentleman, a friend of Voltaire and the Prince de Ligne, a welcome guest at the courts of Paris, London, Vienna, Brussels and The Hague. She met him at a ball given by the Duke of Brunswick, guardian to the young stadholder, Prince William V of Orange. Because d'Hermenches had the reputation of being a Don Juan and was living apart from his wife, their meeting created a sensation, the more so since Belle flouted etiquette by asking him to dance with her. Her parents left the ball, taking their daughter with them. But the contact had been made and an exchange of letters followed, secretly at first of course, but ultimately lasting fifteen years. During that time they only saw one another occasionally, and there was never any question of there being an affair between them. But there is not the slightest doubt that they were very much in love with each other; or rather with the impression that they had of one another. They exchanged hundreds of letters, which literary critics consider to be among the finest and most exceptional epistolary literature in Europe. The sincerity, intelligent subtlety, sensitivity and depth with which Belle portrays and analyses herself in these letters is quite unique – not only as a remarkable contribution to cultural history in the eighteenth century, but especially as an unparalleled psychological account of the modern European woman. Her most famous predecessor in epistolary literature, Madame de Sévigné, provides in her letters a superb description of society and morals at the French court in the seventeenth century. Belle gives an introspective account of feminine reality in such a fascinating manner as never before. Moreover, her reflections on this are so broad in their scope that they embrace not only womanhood of the eighteenth century, but womankind of all time.

So apart from her brilliant and direct style, which rivals that of the leading authors of the Enlightenment, Voltaire and above all Diderot, it is her

Drawing of Zuylen Castle by L. Ph. Serrurier. Rijksarchief, Utrecht.

modern and universal appeal that accounts for the present interest in her. In the captivating honesty with which she reveals her thoughts and feelings, she expresses the essence of femininity in its present-day perspective. There are therefore many reasons for her widespread appeal: in literature because of her stylistic qualities, in cultural history through her intimate concerns with various aspects of the Enlightenment, and in sociology through her aura of emancipation. At a time and in an environment in which that was unusual, she exhibited an emancipated character and an autonomous personality. We now have access to this in the twentieth century through the publication of her complete works, a great deal of which had been hitherto unknown, since only fragments or unreliable texts were available.

Something more about her life was first published in 1906 by the Swiss professor Philippe Godet in his *Madame de Charrière and Her Friends,* (Madame de Charrière et ses amis). In this biography he provided an attractive portrait of her, based on letters and documents that he had unearthed, and of which he included substantial fragments. It appears from this that Belle's opinions and feelings had not always made life easy for her, despite her privileged surroundings and the fact that her parents were reasonable and broadminded. Her correspondence with Constant d'Hermenches had been prompted by her irresistible need for a sympathetic hearing.

From an early age, under the guidance of her well-educated governess, Belle had read a lot. She knew the classics and the French seventeenth century. She read contemporary writers in French and English, in which she was fluent, and she had lessons in mathematics and physics. Religion was something of a problem for her. Her parents were Protestants, but Belle could not go along with the doctrine of predestination, and her spirit was too sceptical to accept dogmas easily. Early on in her life she abandoned religion.

She was no less critical in her observation of other institutions, particularly social norms. For instance, the privileges of the aristocracy, to which she herself belonged, in her view frequently gave rise to a vacuity filled with

Portrait of Isabelle de Charrière. Jens Juel, 1777. Canvas. Bibliothèque Publique et Universitaire, Neuchâtel.

Le Pontet, the house of Belle and her husband in Colombier (Neuchâtel), as drawn by Léon Berthoud in 1867 (Musée Neuchâtelois).

pride of ancestry and the pleasures of the chase. When she was twenty she wrote a satire on this, *Le Noble (1763),* her first known literary work, which caused a scandal and was withdrawn by her parents.

She soon realised that she would not be able to air her independent opinions in public writings, and so for the time being she expressed them in letters and other writings which were circulated unobtrusively, with the result that most of them have failed to survive. But this added to her awareness of the precarious and inferior situation of women. To achieve some measure of freedom it was essential to be married. But here too she registered a socially unacceptable situation: marriage was after all not a matter of free choice; such factors as social class, wealth, business or hereditary considerations were the guiding principles. Love was incidental or entirely irrelevant. Such a marriage was not for her.

There was certainly no lack of suitors. She was a 'suitable' match, wealthy, of good family, handsome according to witnesses and portraits, very intelligent and loveable to boot. In her twenties marriage is one of the dominant themes in her biography. Several candidates crop up during that time both from home and abroad, but without success. If they do not back off of their own accord because Belle is too intelligent or too independent, she turns them down because she does not find them interesting and cannot feel anything for them. Moreover, as she wrote to Boswell, *'I am wealthy enough not to need the fortune of a husband, my temperament is lively enough and I have sufficient mental ability to manage without a husband and without a household; I do not need, as they say, to be looked after'* (17 Jan. 1768). Not until her thirty-first year does she decide to embark on marriage with the one-time governor of her brothers, who loves her, of whom she is fond and who is prepared to allow her all the freedom she wants – a *mariage de convenance.*

Laus Steenbeke as Benjamin Constant and Will van Kralingen as Isabelle de Charrière in Digna Sinke's film *Belle van Zuylen* (1993).

The second part of her life was spent mainly in Switzerland, in her husband's manor Le Pontet; his two unmarried sisters also lived there permanently, even surviving Belle. She would have liked to have children, but that was not to be. During the first ten years of her marriage she did her best to adapt herself to the role of a conventional housewife. She did not succeed.

Her husband's benign temperament was not particularly ardent and the atmosphere was not stimulating. In 1783 Isabelle began to accept the situation; she withdrew more and more into herself and stayed, sometimes completely alone, in Chexbres, Payerne and Paris. From that time on she also used her freedom to write and publish. Until her death on 26 December 1805 there was a stream of novels, short stories, plays, essays, pamphlets, poetry, on a wide range of themes: morality, culture, politics, social conditions, marriage, education, the position of women and so on. In addition there were various musical compositions and her extensive correspondence.

One of her most prominent correspondents at that time was the future statesman and author Benjamin Constant. She met him in 1787, shortly before the outbreak of the French Revolution, in the Paris salons which she then frequented. He was nineteen, she forty-six. He worshipped her because she was beautiful, charming and free, completely accepting and understanding him, just as his uncle Constant d'Hermenches had done when the roles were reversed. The relationship between Isabelle and Benjamin was a passionate affair hovering between love and motherly affection. Their correspondence is brilliant and fascinating. The association lasted until her death, though there was a break in their intimacy when Constant began an intimate affair with the young writer and ambassador's wife, Germaine de Staël, for whom Isabelle even before her acquaintance with Constant had felt little sympathy.

Madame de Charrière left her papers to a friend who knew and appreciated her work, but the friend died soon after the birth of her first child. This son, Eusèbe-Henri Gaullieur, inherited the literary legacy. It was from him that Sainte-Beuve, the renowned nineteenth-century French critic, acquired some of Belle's letters. He published two extensive studies on her, in which he expressed the hope that her work would be collected since in his view it constituted some of the best French literature produced outside France.

Her first biographer was Godet, who also had a number of her works reprinted as well as publishing part of the d'Hermenches correspondence. This meant that she was rescued from obscurity, which was quite an achievement. But there was no follow-up, and no further research until three quarters of a century later when the collected works and the new biographies were published. Everything written about her between 1900 and 1970 was based on Godet, and did her scant justice. The material from and about her was much more extensive than Godet knew, and his account failed to appreciate her originality and the modern and universal quality of her insight.

It was also due to Godet that attention was first paid to her in England. The English author Geoffrey Scott and his wife Sybil were staying at Ouchy on Lake Geneva, when he noticed, one foggy November day, a copy of Godet's forgotten book in a Lausanne bookshop. He and his wife were so struck by Belle's character that they went round all the bookshops in the days that followed, looking for more information about her. Three days later Scott began his own biography, based on Godet, but revitalised by his own enthusiasm. The book appeared in 1925 under the title *The Portrait of Zélide* and it immediately had a far greater success than Godet's original work, running to seven impressions within the first year. Scott wrote his book because Godet's work was only available second-hand and because he wanted to divest Isabelle de Charrière's life of local biographical details of no interest to many readers. Moreover he felt a personal bond with her and he declared: *'All I have here done is to catch an image of her in a single light, and to make from a single angle the best drawing I can of Zélide, as I believe her to have been. I have sought to give her the reality of a fiction; but my material is fact.'* His wife Sybil meanwhile translated four of Madame Charrière's short stories *(Le Noble, Lettres de Mistriss Henley, Lettres de Lausanne* and *Caliste)* into English, under the title *Four tales by Zélide* (1925).

Scott called Isabelle Zélide because this was the name she gave herself in a written self-portrait. It was also the name given her by the Scottish writer James Boswell, who went to Utrecht as a law student in 1763 and there met the Van Tuyll family. He fell in love with Belle, and an account of this can be found in his humorous and entertaining correspondence with her, quoted by Scott and included in the collected works and letters. An amusing description of their relationship occurs in 'Boswell in Holland', part of the publication of the Boswell papers, on which Scott also collaborated. Boswell wanted to get Belle to admit that she was also in love with him. In

reality she felt a warm affection for him, but realised that marriage to him would place her in a dependent and subservient position. One of her letters contains the well-known comment 'I have no talent for subordination!'

England always had a considerable attraction for Belle and evidence of this is clearly given in her correspondence and her writings. Having learned the language at a young age, she spoke and wrote it fluently. She read the English authors of her day and was familiar with Pope, Richardson, Sterne, Fielding, Defoe and Godwin. Together with a young friend she translated Fanny Inchbald's novel *Nature and Art,* and she studied such philosophers as Smith, Locke and Hume. She stayed for some time in London and elsewhere in England, visited David Hume and dined with him, and was presented at court. In her novels *Lettres de Mistriss Henley (1784), Lettres écrites de Lausanne (1785), Sir Walter Finch et son fils (1806),* England and the English often play an important part, and she shows her keen powers of observation in her descriptions of the country, its inhabitants and customs, individual places and peculiarities. She went to the theatre, saw Shakespeare plays and admired the famous actor Garrick. She knew English history and praised the British parliamentary system, which she offered as a model for the Netherlands.

It is therefore not surprising that English scholars have recently shown a keen interest in Belle. Two of them, C.P. Courtney at Cambridge and Dennis M. Wood in Birmingham, were members of the editing board of the Collected Works. Courtney recently published one of the two new biographies of Isabelle de Charrière, and Wood published a biography of Benjamin Constant, in which he focused attention on his relationship with Isabelle de Charrière, and revealed the results of new research. It is to be hoped that new translations of the writings themselves will soon follow. For we may confidently expect that interest in the work of this remarkable woman will increase as rapidly in Great Britain and America as it has done in Europe; and not only among specialists in eighteenth-century literature, but also in the much wider circle of those with an interest in literature and in culture.

PIERRE H. DUBOIS
Translated by Peter King.

FURTHER READING

COURTNEY, C.P., *Isabelle de Charrière (Belle de Zuylen).* Oxford, 1993.

DUBOIS, PIERRE H. and SIMONE DUBOIS, *Zonder vaandel. Belle van Zuylen, een biografie.* Amsterdam, 1993.

GODET, PHILIPPE, *Madame de Charrière et ses amis.* Geneva, 1906, 2 vols.

SCOTT, GEOFFREY, *The Portrait of Zélide.* London, 1925.

WOOD, DENNIS, *Benjamin Constant.* London / New York, 1993.

Œuvres complètes, I-X. Amsterdam, 1979-1984.

riting

as an Act of Revolt and Emancipation

The Work of Monika van Paemel

Monika van Paemel was born on 4 May 1945, and because of the war she was delivered on her grandmother's farm in the country village of Poesele in East Flanders, where she also spent her childhood years. It was only later that she was taken from there, against her will, to her parents' house in the city of Antwerp. These circumstances were later to play an important part in her literary work, whose material and themes she derives largely from her own life, with very close links binding real life and writing. Her debut came in 1971 with the short novel *Amazone with the Blue Forehead* (Amazone met het blauwe voorhoofd), and anyone looking back at that work today can see that it already shows virtually all the thematic, formal and stylistic characteristics of her later work. In this sense it could even be said that she has been writing the same book for the last twenty years, extending and deepening her themes and gaining an increasingly firm hold on the structure and style of her novels, but always concerned with what is, for her, the essence and purpose of writing: the conquest, defence and justification of her independent personal existence as a woman and an artist in a world dominated by men and the violence of war. The trauma of her birth at the end of the Second World War lies at the heart of this: an unwanted child to parents who had wanted a son, a girl whose mother pronounced the verdict on her that 'it would have been better if she had never existed', and also the daughter of a father who had fought as an ss soldier in Russia and then gone underground.

Writing therefore becomes first and foremost the secret weapon with which she tries to free herself from her origins, and it remains – for the rest of her life – the perfect tool for giving expression and form to the development of her individuality, hard-won from history and society. In *Amazone with the Blue Forehead* she tells how as a child she marked trees with her own signs – an early form of writing – as proof that she *existed*. Elsewhere in the same book she defines writing as 'an essential form of disloyalty – breaking out – setting free'. The theme of curtailed freedom is symbolised even in the title by the Brazilian parrot, which is caged up in a town house and filled with a homesick longing for the vastness of the forests. This whole first novel is uninhibitedly dominated by the rebellious desire to 'be herself as a woman, in other words: free'. As one sign of this, the author also gives herself a new name in the book, 'Gisela', just as she is to give herself a different name in each of her following works. Beyond doubt, all these names should not be seen primarily as (transparent) disguises for a novelist who wants to conceal herself, but rather as indications of the changing forms in which she depicts herself in successive stages of her life.

One fact associated with this central theme is that, as early as *Amazone with the Blue Forehead,* the two different worlds in which Monika van Paemel spent her childhood years take on the sharply contrasted symbolic meaning which they will retain through all her later works. On the one side is the carefree outdoor life in the still unspoiled landscape of the Leie valley, and as she looks back on this life with nostalgia, it takes on the significance of a paradise forever lost. It is emotionally described as the place of the warm nest, the domain of caring mothers and a life of unthreatened communion with animals and plants. Opposed to this is the city, the place where her parents and grandparents live – and where grandmother Marguerite is the central figure – the feared and detested domain of the conservative bourgeoisie with its oppressive rules of behaviour and Catholic morality. For Gisela, this is where misery begins. She arrives in a man's world of dominant, unimaginative 'fathers', for whom bricks and mortar seem to represent the greatest good. Her fierce rebellion against this forms the sarcastic exposé element in the book.

When Monika van Paemel wrote this book, she was a young woman in her mid-twenties, married and the mother of two daughters. Her marriage itself, which she no doubt did experience as oppressive, remains in the shadows, but her personal, mostly internalised view of life stands out all the more clearly. The main theme is an exuberant longing for love which is very closely associated with the longing for freedom. In general this means a love of the uninhibited pleasures of earthly life, but in more concrete terms it is love as the highest rule of conduct, as lusty erotic intimacy, as moral and emotional involvement in what is going on in the world. Each of her later books contains wonderful evocations of the sensual pleasure provided by her amorous lover, or the lack of it. These feelings are experienced in a quite physical, sensual way, and they include motherhood and in a broader sense concern and care for animals, for everything which arouses the writer's inclination to protect and defend: her 'herderscomplex' (shepherd complex) as she calls it in the essay *Experience* (Het wedervaren, 1993).

At the very beginning, Monika van Paemel found the form and style which were to remain her permanent trademark, and these are within the modernist tradition. The structure of her novels is fragmentary and mosaic-like, the narrative lyrical, associative, contemplative and dramatic rather than epic; her way of writing is spontaneous, emotional but controlled by the power of form, dynamic, in turn staccato and measured. Her second novel, *The Confrontation* (De confrontatie, 1974), is the dramatised depiction of two opposing personalities within herself, in the form of Mirjam, who is forceful, ruthless and bitterly rebellious, and Zoë, who needs security, gentleness and harmony. It is not until the end of the book that the two come together again in an unstable equilibrium. Her third novel, *Marguerite* (1976) is an attempt to settle accounts with the figure of her grandmother, who is grippingly portrayed as a brisk businesswoman whose independence she identifies with, while at the same time she finds her mocking and narrow-minded bourgeois mentality repulsive.

It was not until nine years later, in 1985, that the substantial novel *The Accursed Fathers* (De vermaledijde vaders) appeared. This book caused a considerable stir among Dutch and Flemish critics, and was proclaimed a masterpiece. It can be read as a synthesis and at the same time as a monumental expansion of the triptych which preceded it. The author, this time in the form of Pamela, draws up a balance-sheet of the first half of her life. The self-portrait which emerges from this is illuminated from many different angles, and as well as the themes of the earlier novels it also includes a pointillistic picture of her own generation in the riotous emancipation movements of the 1960s and 1970s, together with the critical rethinking and disillusionment which followed them.

A whole gallery of family portraits is constructed around this picture, painted in lively brush-strokes and contained within the still larger framework of a period of Flemish history which is in turn linked with world history. The key theme here is war, which is associated with the figures of the father and grandfather. Hence these two take on a symbolic significance: the sons of the Flemish soldiers on the IJzer Front in the First World War fought on the Eastern Front in The Second World War. The sharp and violently emotional consciousness of the writer Pamela is always at the centre of all the events she evokes and the father functions as her greatest opponent. He is not only Pamela's own personal father, he also stands for the whole caste of 'gentlemen', authoritarian rulers and cynical exploiters of all kinds, from generals to industrialists, who control and subjugate the world at will and plunder it like an occupied territory. In one of the fiercest, most bitter and most poignant parts of the novel, she finally settles accounts with him and his whole world in the form of a long, furious 'letter to the father'. In these virulent pages, the personal struggle for liberation which runs right through Van Paemel's works reaches its climax. Here again, the remembered images of her childhood years, surrounded by nature and caring foster mothers, form a positive counterbalance. When these contrasts are generalised, they broaden out into an archetypal conflict between the 'feminine' and the 'masculine' principles; coloured by the psychological motifs and emotional impulses of the author, the result is little less than the primordial struggle between Good and Evil which rules the world. This view certainly forms part of the female perspective from which the entire novel is written, but that by no means makes Pamela's story susceptible to appropriation by the doctrinaire feminist movement. It is both too complex and too personal for this, too much the work of an obstinate writer who 'doesn't want to belong anywhere any more', and who consciously sees isolation as her artistic vocation: she writes what she is, and that is a woman.

Van Paemel has won many prizes for her work, particularly for *The Accursed Fathers,* which gained one of the highest literary awards in the Low Countries, the Triennial State Prize for narrative prose, in 1987. Translations into Swedish *(Fäders Förbannelse,* 1989), French *(Les pères maudits,* 1990) and German *(Verfluchte Väter,* 1993), mean that this novel is also well-known abroad, particularly in Germany, where it has been well received by the authoritative journals.

It was not until 1992 that another large-scale novel, *The First Stone* (De eerste steen), appeared, again showing a close thematic link with the previous books, but clearly springing from other tragic events in the author's life.

At the beginning of the story, her alter ego May, in a state of deep desperation and feeling that she is all alone in the world, flees from her home to
Israel, the Promised Land of the Bible. However, in this foreign land where
she had hoped to find forgetfulness and healing she is overwhelmed by
obsessive memories. The direct cause of her sorrow, the suicide of her sev-
enteen-year-old daughter, is revealed to the reader only gradually by a subtly applied narrative technique of suggestive delay. This theme is projected
against the background of the whole of May's known past, and her own birth
under the auspices of death and violence is seen as the remote cause of the
tragedy. A feeling of impotent guilt convinces her that it really would have
been better if she had never lived, and the individual freedom which she had
so prized turns out not to exist at all – since what could she do to prevent the
fatal events anyway? This whole woeful story of a personal tragedy, told in
a poignant style with a sense of controlled pathos, is elevated to a higher,
suprapersonal level by May's account of her experiences in modern-day
Israel. After all, this country has also been born of a collective tragedy, and
because of its past it is now subject to war and terrorism every day. The
Jewish women with whom May temporarily lodges in a Jerusalem basement, and from whom she seeks protection and comfort, all turn out to have
uprooted and divided lives behind them as well. This and other parallels,
further enriched and reinforced by a number of symbolic motifs so that individual human destinies become interwoven with the destinies of others and
a whole political situation, make it clear that with *The First Stone* Monika
van Paemel has written a novel with a universal dimension.

PAUL DE WISPELAERE
Translated by Steve Judd.

Monika van Paemel (1945-)
(Photo by Paul van den
Abeele).

Extract from *The First Stone*
by Monika van Paemel

On one of their trips relations between them had become very strained.
Hagar had been reluctant to come in the first place and refused to go anywhere off the beaten track. May felt as if she had been put in quarantine and
suspected that there was another, modern world out there behind the Biblical
facade. Hagar and May often seemed to be talking about two conflicting real-
ities. 'Where are the people?' May had asked. 'Everywhere,' Hagar replied.
'I can't see them,' said May. 'Perhaps they don't want to see you either,'
laughed Hagar. 'I wouldn't want to live in the kingdom of the blind,' May had
observed acidly. 'No one is asking you to,' retorted Hagar. 'I suppose my
nose isn't the right size,' said May. Hagar grinned. 'Much too long, and you're
determined to stick it in everywhere.' 'Buy yourself a pug dog,' May advised
her. And so on and so forth. At night everything had to be put right with
kisses.

They had driven in silence through barren hills. A hot desert wind was
blowing. The car was like an oven on wheels. Suddenly May had caught

sight of a herd of black goats, with white faces. As the car approached, the animals skipped up the slope and stood there looking down at them, motionless and out of reach. May wanted to clamber up after them. Hagar shouted that it was pointless. 'They're stupid creatures!' She went on shouting even after May had started the climb: the echo of her voice seemed to be trying to block May's path upwards. The goats had disappeared from view, but the pebbles rolling down betrayed their presence. May cut her hands. On closer inspection the rocks turned out to be covered in grey-green scrub. That's what they used to weave the crown of thorns, thought May. 'Who are they?' asked the echo in her head. The goats stood there bleating at her in mockery. They had been stripping the land bare since the time of Abraham. The dust from the eroded soil stung May's eyes. She was about to give up the chase, when she saw a goat within striking distance. Perfectly balanced on the loose stones. It was chewing on a length of something indefinable. Its black eyes gleamed as though swimming in oil. The blaze on its elongated forehead was like a brand. A swollen udder hung down between its hind legs. 'Hello, Daisy,' said May. The goat did not move a muscle; it looked right through her. May slid cautiously back down, aware that she risked being butted in the small of her back. 'Well?' Hagar's gesture seemed to ask. 'I couldn't get close enough to them,' May had mumbled. 'What did I tell you?' Hagar was satisfied. But if she thought that May had given up trying to get better acquainted with both goats and people, she did not yet know her travelling companion.

In the middle of nowhere, heading in no particular direction, an old blind man had come towards them, led by a boy. 'They have lots of eye disease,' said Hagar, as though it were some genetic peculiarity. 'Malnutrition and dust, lack of hygiene, vitamin deficiency.' May rattled off what she had learned. Sympathetic whites are well-informed about the wretchedness of the deprived. The old man looked as wise as he was helpless. A gaunt face with sharp features. The typically hesitant gait, groping his way forward. Hagar had slowed down in order to make less dust. The boy had said something to the old man. Was it his grandfather? Then he raised a clenched fist. May saw the man and the boy disappearing in the wing-mirror as though they were a mirage. 'The lame leading the blind,' May had said. 'There was nothing the matter with the boy,' replied Hagar. 'I mean us.' May had realised just in time that it would be better to leave Brueghel out of it.

Almost back in civilisation, they were held up by a flock of sheep which were blocking the road and were in no hurry. All Hagar's beeping did nothing but provoke hilarity in the children who surrounded the car in an instant. May looked at the golden yellow houses with their green-painted door frames and remembered the watercolours that they had painted at school. These were the same houses. She had learned to draw this country without knowing it, the antique version at least. The house in Nazareth. Joseph and Mary. Baby Jesus.

A girl and a woman emerged from an underground oven. They had been baking bread on the hot stones. The leaven to make the dough rise had come from the previous batch. For thousands of years. The same leaven. The same bread. The same stones. The girl wore a lilac dress and blue plastic sandals. Her white scarf was tied in a knot at the neck. She crossed her arms and smiled. For no reason. Good-naturedly. The mother walked behind her daughter with a dish of round loaves. Her black dress had an embroidered bodice and an embroidered strip in the same pattern running from top to bottom on either side. The ends of her veil had been crossed under her chin and thrown back over her shoulders. A knitted lilac cardigan completed her outfit. The woman was smiling, proud of her bread, proud of her daughter. If Hagar had not restrained her, May would have gone straight off to have a cup of coffee with them. In frustration she took a petit beurre biscuit from the packet that Hagar carried round with her everywhere. In bed the crumbs chafed May's back like gravel. A little girl pressed her nose against the car window. May wound it down to give the child a biscuit. The packet was snatched out of her hands with such force that May was thankful not to have lost a finger. Even the sheep realised that Hagar's patience was at an end: they scattered in all directions. The moment Hagar opened her mouth May had cried 'What did I tell you?!' on her behalf. But she thought: Something's wrong. The palms of her hands were burning. Her skin was full of splinter-like thorns. It took her a whole evening to extract the wretched things with a pair of tweezers, the tears running down her cheeks. For days afterwards black tips kept appearing. She held a thorn under a magnifying glass and saw that there were barbs along its length. 'Your hands are going to get infected,' Hagar had said. May bought disinfectant from the chemist's and sat soaking her hands three times a day. 'I'm washing my hands of the whole thing,' she would say to deflect her friends' solicitude. She dreamed that she had got lost in the Negev, and as happens in dreams she knew in advance that she would not escape from the desert alive. A black billy-goat barred her way. She tried to skirt around it, but it leaped from left to right until May stopped to face her doom. The monster maintained that it could transform stones into bread, but that what it was really after was her soul. It was a large, hairy billy-goat with curled horns and its distinguishing feature was a long woolly tail. Its coat was shot through with silver threads. It did not need to leap on her, its eyes were enough to make May wake with a scream. 'I dreamed of the devil,' she said. Hagar had looked at her as though she was insane.

Hands trembling, May had gone to the kitchen to make herself a glass of warm milk and honey. The old sorcerer had given her quite a fright. Ruth had brought ointment to help May get rid of the last few thorns. She studied May's hands like a fortune-teller and shook her head. It's lucky your sins are not written in your hands, May had thought. Ruth had been evacuated from London to Wales during the blitz. In a village school the children had stared at her. 'Where are your horns?' They had never seen a Jewish child but were firmly convinced that Jews had horns and goat's feet. They were devils incarnate. 'Can you believe it? Children. They knew nothing about anything. And yet there It was,' Ruth had said, still astonished. In Ruth May recognised the girl with the baggy socks and a name-and-address tag pinned to her coat. Ruth had been lucky. On the continent devils went to hell to burn forever. Your dreams don't count, thought May. Not really. You couldn't help it. When she saw May sitting hunched up Ruth had put her arm around her. 'Come on, sweetie.' 'She hasn't even got hair on her legs,' Hagar had exclaimed.' 'I'm going to let mine grow from now on, nice and sexy,' said Alida. 'I don't want goat's legs,' moaned Dina. Mischa had stuck his two extended forefingers above his head. 'Just you wait till you've got a wife,' Ruth had observed, grimacing. Even Hagar admitted that she no longer shaved her armpits since

Omar Sharif had said in a television interview that he found a woman's hairy armpits a turn-on. 'Chassez le naturel, il revient au galop,' Davy had said. He had run his fingertips up May's leg from ankle to knee. With his eyes closed, as if reading braille. 'You've got smooth legs.' May had not been sure if that was a compliment, but it was certainly a turn-on. Since then she had not touched the stubble under her armpits. Mathilde had a thing about excess hair. Beards, moustaches, pubic hair. She had even shaved the expectant mothers so that after giving birth they were as smooth as inflatable dolls. May had been given a sleeveless nightgown by Leonce. Mathilde disapproved. She made May put on a bed jacket at visiting times. May protested because the wool itched, but it was no good. 'Big girls keep their necks and shoulders covered,' was Mathilde's dictum. One hair had escaped her passion for pruning; it curled out of a mole located like a courtesan's beauty spot under Mathilde's left nostril. When Mathilde bent over her May had to exercise great self-control not to pluck it out. She was also troubled by the question whether or not Mathilde was aware that her nun's face had a certain attraction, and if so, why she left that solitary hair like a lonely stalk in a field of stubble.

May has been so lost in thought that she realises too late that someone is banging on the door of the basement. Hagar is dragged away from the decisive climax of the baseball game. The lady from upstairs is at the door. Angry or upset. May cannot make out what is wrong. Hagar slams the door and strides over to the television to turn down the sound. 'Always making a fuss!' The lady from upstairs is palefaced and timid. If she is hanging out washing on the balcony and sees May in the garden she quickly ducks back inside. While she is chatting to the boy who does the gardening May has seen her peering through the blinds. Her husband does the shopping. He looks as though he can walk through walls. Thin and white, with everything sagging. An elderly couple that one would not suspect of outrageous behaviour. True, one mustn't take a bath after ten in the evening because the water gurgles in the pipes. No cycles in the hall. No wet newspapers in the letterbox. No loud music on the Sabbath. And no pets of any kind: they belong out of doors. 'They are difficult people,' grumbles Hagar. Obviously her husband was not home when the lady upstairs was getting worked up over the noisy television. He comes later. 'It was as if there was a war going on', his wife had told him. He also wished to take the opportunity to say that no climbing plants must be trained up the walls. The vermin climb up the foliage like a ladder. His wife has found another salamander in the kitchen, and she was completely beside herself. 'Salamanders are part of this country,' growls Hagar. When May heard the faint 'plop' for the first time she did not know what it was, but Hagar immediately grabbed the broom. A frantic chase had ensued until May managed to trap the salamander under a newspaper and carry it outside in a rolled-up ball. 'Careful, they bite!' shouted Hagar. Ten minutes later May had seen a salamander sitting motionless on the bedroom ceiling. As though it had spirited itself in by magic. She slid under the sheets in the fervent hope that the creature would not parachute into bed. Between half-closed eyelids she saw Hagar looking from the salamander to her but feigned sleep. They both had good reason to pretend there was nothing hanging over their heads.

In a village in Flanders a five year-old girl had seen her father and grandfather shot. The men were taken to the main street with their fellow-villagers and made to run forward ten at a time. 1940. The first row of soldiers were on one knee, the second row stood behind them so that there was a double line of rifles to face. The men's clogs had clattered on the cobbles. Some men staggered to their deaths with sprained ankles. The officer in command gave the order to fire and the same time dropped his raised arm. The men stumbled, fell on top of each other, crawled a few yards further. Before those watching could recover from the shock the next ten men were ordered off at the double. The few who refused were immediately shot in the back of the neck. The little girl had always sat on grandfather's lap at table. He dipped his bread in lukewarm milk and fed her. In the large family, where everyone was busy, the old man and the youngest child had been inseparable. After the war the girl suffered nervous attacks. Loud voices startled her. She had an inexplicable fear of the stationmaster who gave the signal for the trains to leave with an orange-and-white disc. The village doctor said it would pass when the girl started her periods. The fears redoubled. She should marry as soon as possible, then. Next the woman became aggressive. A child would put things right. She completely ignored it, and the grandmother had to look after it. The houses, which had been built hurriedly after the war, had paper-thin walls. You could hear the neighbours arguing, and the woman could not stand it. The doctor kept telling her not to make a fuss over nothing. One evening there was a war film on TV. The family had not been watching, being frightened to death of such things. It was as if their neighbour was hard of hearing, the set was on so loud. 'It was as if the tanks were thundering through the room,' the grandmother was to testify later. And then there were those German commands. On the mantlepiece there was an antique iron decorated with a bunch of dried flowers. The woman had grabbed it, gone round the back to the house next door and smashed the neighbour's skull in. The village doctor had written a note recommending her committal to a lunatic asylum. May remembers the modified heavy flat irons which were heated on the stove and later on the gas. Margarethe would spit on the sole-plate. If the drops of spittle sizzled, the iron was too hot. In the summer Margarethe wore a sleeveless jacket while she did the ironing. When she placed the iron on the linen it was as though her breasts swelled under the pressure of her arms. Margarethe had always grumbled while ironing. The smell of stale sweat released from the armpit of the shirt when it was heated particularly upset her. As though all her washing and scrubbing had been for nothing. The son of the village doctor had also become a doctor, but soon left for a developing country. 'That one is even crazier than his father,' Margarethe had said.

From *The First Stone* (De eerste steen. Amsterdam: Meulenhoff, 1992, pp. 84-91).
Translated by Paul Vincent.

esert

Island Dutch

Imaginary Voyages,

Adventures and Robinsonades in the Low Countries

Imagine the dilemma of a man whose wife, maid servant, horse and dog have all fallen into the river at the same time, and who realises he can save only one of them. Does he choose his wife, who is old and is soon to go to Heaven anyway, or his maid, who gave him so much pleasure, although there are others like her? What about his horse, a highly prized animal, but not as loyal as his dog? Should animals take precedence over human beings? Not an easy choice. It so happened that the man we are talking about hesitated, causing all four of them to drown. The public outcry that followed made the man flee his village and travel to a country ruled by monkeys. A strange story, but it befell the protagonist of *Voyage through Monkey Land* (Reize door het Aapenland, 1788). This was one of the novels in a long tradition of journals, travel accounts, adventures, imaginary voyages and robinsonades published in the Low Countries in the eighteenth century. In previous centuries, to please their patrons, the gentlemen of the East and West India Companies, Dutch sailors and explorers had brought back information about foreign lands in standardised formats. Occasionally their logs would be published, and these 'journals' would gain in popularity when personal notes were added. They became 'descriptions of travels' and keen publishers quickly saw the potential of these accounts. Most Dutchmen have heard of Willem Ysbrantszoon Bontekoe's description of his travels to the East Indies, which, first published in 1646, has gone through some hundred editions to date. Accounts like these could be used as a framework for the stories that emerged when the seventeenth turned into the eighteenth century. Fiction made its way into these descriptions and new ideas and adventures, such as the Spanish picaresque novels, influenced writers' imaginations; and they didn't even have to leave their homes.

It was in this literary climate that a remarkable work reached the book shops in Amsterdam in 1708: *The Description of the Mighty Kingdom of Krinke Kesmes. (…) by H[enrik] Smeeks* (Beschryvinge van het magtig koningryk Krinke Kesmes). The story tells of a trading voyage to Panama and 'the unknown Southland', but it also speaks of the new philosophy of Descartes and gives a realistic depiction of scurvy. Observant readers may have noticed that Henrik Smeeks is an anagram of Krinke Kesmes, and there are more such word plays in the description of this utopian kingdom: there is an island called 'Nemnan' (Dutch 'mannen' = men) and one called 'Wonvure' (Dutch 'vrouwen' = women). One part of the story is of particular interest: the account of a Dutch cabin boy. Stranded on a desert island, he survives hardship through his own ingenuity and his good luck in finding the contents of a stranded wreck. After a while he is captured by savages, who in turn are taken prisoner by soldiers of Krinke Kesmes. There he decides to stay, teaching Dutch to the natives. The story achieved international notoriety in the twentieth century when scholars claimed it to be the source for none other than Defoe's *Robinson Crusoe,* published eleven years later in 1719! However, the similarities don't prove plagiarism, and although Defoe possessed a few Dutch books and supported the Dutch King William III, it is very doubtful whether he could read Dutch. Still, *Krinke Kesmes* was successful, as five contemporary editions show. Most interesting is the fact that a German translation was published in 1721, entitled *Der Holländische Robinson*! This ragout of Utopia, Crusoe and Gulliver in a sauce Hollandaise of Newtonian and Cartesian philosophy had become a

Frontispiece of *The Description of the Mighty Kingdom of Krinke Kesmes* (1708).

Robinson Crusoe, as portrayed by Bernard Picart in the Dutch edition of the novel.

'robinsonade', a story after *Robinson Crusoe*. Indeed, Defoe's masterpiece had been an immediate international success, in the Low Countries as well as elsewhere. A translation appeared within a year and the prolific Dutch writer Justus van Effen made the first translation into French (Amsterdam 1720-1721). Imitations and adaptations followed in rapid order and 'Robinsons' emerged from many cities and provinces in several languages.

'All adventures in which one finds unusual sea journeys, shipwrecks and a stay on remote and desert islands, one is used to call Adventures of Robinson, following the first part of Robinson Crusoe's adventures (I am not speaking of parts two and three), so beautifully written in English, and that is not a bad habit, because one knows immediately what the author's intentions are and what his work is all about.' These are the opening lines of the anonymous author of *The Adventures of the Old and the Young Robinson* (Gevallen van den ouden en jongen Robinson), which appeared in print in Amsterdam in 1753, and they indicate that 'Robinson' had become a household name among the reading public. Yet it is not easy to define the

The old and young Robinsons, stranded on their island (from *The Adventures of the Old and the Young Robinson*, 1766 edition).

'robinsonade'. The Dutch scholar W.H. Staverman, author of *Robinson Crusoe in the Netherlands (*Robinson Crusoe in Nederland, 1907), follows Herman Ullrich, the first Robinson-bibliographer, in including all stories that bear the name Robinson, or involve a stay on a desert island. However, many stories should be qualified as 'adventure story' or 'imaginary voyage', since shrewd publishers sometimes just changed titles, to improve their sales. *The Reckless Robinson* (De wispelturige Robinson) was added to *The Miraculous Adventures of the Unhappy Florentine* (De wonderlijke levens-gevallen van den ongelukkigen Florentyner, Leiden 1730). *The Memorable Voyages of Captain Robert Boyle* (De gedenkwaardige reizen en zeldtzame gevallen van kapitein Robert Boyle, Amsterdam 1739) became *The New English Robinson* (De nieuwe Engelsche Robinson, 1761) in a second edition and later *The New and Present-Day English Robinson* (De nieuwe en hedendaagsche Engelsche Robinson, Amsterdam 1794). *The Ball of Fortune* (De Bal van 't fortuin, Utrecht 1746) was 'robinsonised' to *The Rare and Miraculous Case-Histories of the Brandenburg Robinson* (De zonderlinge en wonderbare lotgevallen van den Brandenburgsche Robinson) four years later. Several of these stories were translated into Dutch (often from German) and one finds Robinsons from Saxony (1730), Sweden (1733), Silesia (1754) and Lebanon (1757).

Title page of *The Walcheren Robinson* (1752).

Original tales in Dutch were also produced. *The Holland Robinson* (De Hollandsche Robinson) was published anonymously in Gouda in 1743 and tells of the amorous adventures of Mr **** in France and Portugal, his capture and enslavement by pirates (led by a Frisian (!) muslim Ismael Reys aka Ubbo Penninga). Our hero escapes, but new misfortunes land him on a desert island, from which he is liberated after twenty-eight years. He returns to the Netherlands after having spent some time with an Indian tribe in California. The similarities with Robinson Crusoe are striking, but where the Englishman remorsefully returns home, the Dutchman adds more adventures, and his stay on the island is only one of them.

A different story is found in *The Walcheren Robinson* (De Walchersche Robinson) – Walcheren is an island in the Dutch province of Zeeland – 'written by himself' and published in Amsterdam in 1752. Nineteen-year-old Sofia flees her home with her lover Eduard and they embark on a ship to the West Indies. A storm casts them up, together with a teacher, Filopater, on a desert island. A boy Robinson is born, but his parents die and Filopater is taken prisoner by pirates. A lion cares for the young boy, protects him against evil, and Robinson survives with fortune and God's providence on his side. Filopater returns to the island and takes Robinson back to Walcheren, where his grandfather's inheritance provides him with enough money to live happily ever after. Detailed geographical descriptions and the involuntary stay on the island are a few of the many similarities with Robinson Crusoe. One may also detect the influence of the Arabic novel *Hay Ebn Yokdhan* (1150) by Ibn Tophail, translated into Dutch in 1672. While in the Dutch story the religious reflections are definitely Dutch Reformed, both stories show that human beings, even when they grow up in solitude, can know God through nature.

Benjamin Knobbel is the hero in the anonymous story *The Changeling* (Het verruilde kindt, 1755), which describes the trials and tribulations of a student / teacher in England. After years of teaching young noblemen he is sent on a mission to the Bermudas, but a storm wrecks the ship and he lands on an island, together with a sailor. They build a ship and leave for England, are separated, but find each other later, after it is discovered that they were exchanged as foundlings.

The title *The Female Cartouche* (De vrouwelijke Cartouche) – Cartouche was a famous French highwayman – suggests a different story, and indeed, rascally deeds and banditry form a substantial part of this novel, which was written by Petrus Lievens Kersteman and published in Den Bosch in 1756. Our heroine is Charlotta, who, after being chosen by pirates to be their captain, is unable to suppress a mutiny and is marooned on a desert island. There she has to stay for six years to repent of her sinful life. A Spanish captain rescues her eventually and the story ends when she enters a convent in Spain.

'The nicest spot in Europe, and I mean Lively and Elegant THE HAGUE, was the charming place, where my eyes first saw daylight', are the first lines of *The Hague Robinson* (De Haagsche Robinson, Alkmaar 1758). The anonymous writer refers with disdain to the chicaneries in Dutch politics in The Hague and he presents an alternative: the island Tirevas (an anagram of 'veritas'?), where he had been stranded after many adventures. Here he found the ideal society, where neither money nor noble birth are important and only one God is recognised. However, after four years, he feels homesick and he travels home to write the story of his life.

Alexander, the hero of *The Hague Robinson,* tells his readers that he had been constrained by 'het geval', which in Dutch means 'fate' as well as 'coincidence', and even 'adventure' (as in Robinson Crusoe's case). The same combination of fortune and providence can be found in a story published a year later in Harlingen: *The Miraculous Adventures of Maria Kinkons* (De wonderlyke reisgevallen van Maria Kinkons). The (female?) author A.G.l.m. portrays Maria in his / her opening lines: *'It is seldom that one sees Daughters trying to do things that fit Men and that are male enterprises; on the contrary one sees them quietly staying at home and occupying themselves with household chores. However, it was different with me, who had more interest in male than in female affairs, which sometimes brought me in the greatest difficulties, but, fortunately, I always got out of them again.'* These difficulties started when, dressed as a man, she signed on as a sailor, but was taken prisoner by Arab pirates. After escaping from slavery in a ship, she ends up on a desert island. There she is raped by a baboon and meets her man Wednesday (!). With him she travels back to the Low Countries, after having met Patagonian giants and people bearing their heads on their chests.

Another Maria, last name Ter Meetelen, had similar experiences: adventures in men's clothes, an unfortunate sea voyage and years of captivity in Northern Africa. But there is a striking difference: this Maria was for real. Archival records show that a ransom was paid by the Dutch, and that she was set free following twelve years of slavery. She returned to Amsterdam in 1743 and her story was published in Medemblik in 1748: *Miraculous and Remarkable Adventures of a Twelve Year Slavery* (Wonderbaarlyke en merkwaardige gevallen van een twaalfjarige slavernij, van een vroupersoon. Genaemt Maria ter Meetelen, woonagtig tot Medenblik).

The reading public must have had a difficult time separating fact from fiction, certainly when novelists used proper names of ships, captains, places, countries, and assured their readers in the introduction that is was all truth: the manuscript was found, strange creatures do exist, the style is typical of a sailor's narrative (i.e. simple, the content is more important), the story is not like all those novels that give improbable events or unbelievable falsehoods etc.

Charlotte, who is the person behind *The English Female Robinson* (De Engelsche vrouwelijke Robinson, Amsterdam 1760), claims that she has no intention 'to write a novel and does not want to hold up the reader with fictitious stories'. But her title is very misleading, because there is no similarity whatsoever to Defoe's work, no one in the book is called Robinson and no one even reaches an island!

Other stories also depart from the original Robinson Crusoe. Sometimes the island episode is just one among many other adventures and in a few cases the main character does land on an island, but it turns out not to be deserted at all. The island itself can remain very vague: one is bound to find a cave, albeit with great difficulty; the unmistakable pond is there and so is the lovely valley. But it is hard to find a description of the beautiful spot as poetical as in the original Robinson. The protagonists are different too: later Robinsons are seldom hard workers or handymen. Certainly, they all thank God for saving their lives, most of them find provisions from the ship, build a house, go hunting, fall ill, and leave the island better men and women. Almost as predictable are the adventures of the hero(ine) away from the island: many Robinsons are either taken by pirates or captured by the Turks with subsequent enslavement. Various stories begin with a duel over a woman, robberies by highwaymen en route, followed by a life as a sailor. Although erotic elements do appear, love or romance is dealt with in a superficial way, and Robinson Crusoe, who himself does not ever seem to miss women, could not have been the example.

It was the translator of Richardson's *Clarissa* (1752-1755), Johannes Stinstra, who in his introduction readily admitted that the story was fiction, but that this was balanced by its other excellences, which were true to life and which kept probability intact. The novel was slowly making its way into moral acceptance, was becoming 'sensible' and 'proper', and, unlike in the past, authors identified themselves. The voices of pedagogues and moralists began to be heard: Rousseau recommended Robinson Crusoe for his pupil Emile, and Johan Heinrich Campe's *Young Robinson* (Robinson der Jüngere, 1779-1780) broke all booksellers' records. The Dutch translation of this German remake of Robinson was called *Manual for a Natural Education or Robinson for the Young* (Handleiding tot de natuurlijke opvoeding, of Robinson Crusoe ten dienste der jeugd), and went through eight different editions between 1780 and 1836. The story is written in the form of a dialogue between a parent and his children. To make Robinson's task more difficult and to impress on children the great necessity for self-reliance, the author does not provide our hero with tools, instruments or food saved from the wreck.

Adventure stories, robinsonades and imaginary voyages did not immediately and completely vanish at the end of the eighteenth century in favour of novels with a moral lesson, suitable emotions or more sentimental self-expression. Revolutionary times proved useful for satirical and political travels to utopian islands, back to nature and away from the western world. W.E. de Perponcher's *Rhapsodies or Life of Altamont* (Rhapsodieën of het Leeven van Altamont, Utrecht 1775) describes a settlement on a desert island and propagates the idea that 'the closer to nature, the closer to happiness'. Dr Schasz is the mysterious author of such exciting titles as *Voyage through Wonderland* (Reize door Wonderland, Amsterdam 1780), *Voyage through Monkey Land* and *Voyage through the Land of Voluntary Slaves* (Reize door het land der vrywillige slaaven, 1790). Gerrit Paape's *The Happy Emigrants, or the Small Colony of the South* (De gelukkige emigranten of de kleine volksplanting van het Zuiden, Antwerp 1788) discusses, in the form of an allegorical epistolary novel, political ambition, slavery, freedom of religion and 'freedom for women to show their emotions'. Similar feelings can be found in *The Colonists* (De kolonisten, Amsterdam 1826) and *The Frisian Robinson Crusoe* (De Friesche Robinson Crusoe, Sneek 1834). However, when Willem Bilderdijk sent his characters up, up and away in a balloon in his *Remarkable Air Voyage and Planet Discovery* (Kort verhaal van eene aanmerkelijke luchtreis en nieuwe

A Robinson Crusoe board game in German, French, Italian and Dutch (Germany, c.1840).

planeetontdekking, 1813), the heyday of robinsonades and imaginary voyages was over. Readers had to wait for Jules Verne to pick up where his predecessors left off.

The story of the Dutch robinsonades is not yet complete: we lack a comprehensive bibliography and a clear picture of authors and reading public. However, it demonstrates that the presence of Dutchmen in colonial conquests around the globe was reflected in a literature not yet carved into modern literary conventions. It also shows how closely interconnected the North-West European literature of the time was. In addition to the interesting encounters of western-minded man (and woman) with other races and cultures, it has all the excitement of adventure and imagination in it. Prose had become an instrument for launching ideas, aggressive opinions and powerful fantasies. Travel in the eighteenth century was not just a tourist's adventure with many inconveniences; it was still in an exploratory phase in a world that had not yet given up all its secrets. Together these elements formed a strong formula for success.

Scenes from the Life of Robinson Crusoe, a catchpenny print (wood engraving, probably by Alexander Cranendoncq, Gorinchem, c.1820).

Robinson Crusoe stands for the human being as economic individualist, looking for the basics in an unspoiled world, investigating the essentials of religion and relying on his energy, determination and ingenuity. He has survived the ages and crossed geographical and language boundaries, in the most imaginative forms and shapes: in theatre, cartoons, films, advertising and business (in the fifties Dutch shoe shops sold Robinson sandals). Even though the original three-volume book is seldom read, young and old readers still share Robinson's despair during his lonely first days, or his fear when seeing the footprint in the sand, and many people have fantasised about life on a desert island, with their ten favourite books or pieces of music.

And what happened in Monkey Land, the story I mentioned at the beginning? The monkeys all came together in one grandiose effort to become humans. They chopped off their tails and bled to death. Fortunately, dear readers, this all happened in a dream.

TON J. BROOS

FURTHER READING

BROOS, TON, 'Robinson Crusoe in the Low Countries', *Dutch Crossing,* 23, 1984, pp. 32-45.

BROOS, TON (ed.), *De wonderlyke reisgevallen van Maria Kinkons ... door A.G.l.m..* Amsterdam, 1986.

BROOS, TON, ANTON BOSSERS and JELLE KINGMA (eds.), *Robinson in the Old and New Worlds.* The Hague, 1992.

BROOS, TON, 'De oudste neerlandicus extra muros: Nederlands op Krinke Kesmes en andere merkwaardige gevallen', *Neerlandica extra muros,* XXXI, 2 (May 1993), pp 20-31.

BUIJNSTERS, P.J., 'Imaginaire reisverhalen in Nederland gedurende de 18e eeuw', in: *Nederlandse literatuur van de achttiende eeuw. Veertien verkenningen.* Utrecht, 1984, pp. 7-35.

DEKKER, RUDOLF M. and LOTTE C. VAN DE POL, *The Tradition of Female Transvestism in Early Modern Europe.* New York, 1989.

GOVE, P.B., *The Imaginary Voyage in Prose Fiction.* London, 1961.

GREEN, MARTIN, *The Robinson Crusoe Story.* London, 1990.

HUBBARD, L.L., *A Dutch Source for Robinson Crusoe. The Narrative of the El-Ho 'Sjouke Gabbes' (also known as Henrich Texel). An Episode from the Description of the Mighty Kingdom of Krinke Kesmes, Et cetera by Hendrik Smeeks 1708 – translated from the Dutch and compared with the story of Robinson Crusoe.* Ann Arbor / The Hague , 1921.

ROGERS, PAT, *Robinson Crusoe.* London, 1979.

SMEEKS, HENDRIK, *Beschryvinge van het magtig koningryk Krinke Kesmes* (ed. P.J. Buijnsters). Zutphen, 1976.

STAVERMAN, W.H., *Robinson Crusoe in Nederland.* Groningen, 1907.

ULLRICH, HERMAN, *Robinson und die Robinsonaden. Bibliographie, Geschichte, Kritik.* Weimar, 1898.

he

Art of Evocation

The Symbolist Movement in Belgium

Symbolism as a literary movement was inaugurated in France by Jean Moréas in his 1886 manifesto. In it he paid tribute to Charles Baudelaire as 'the true precursor', but the further course of the movement was determined by very diverse poets like Verlaine and Mallarmé and Rimbaud – the *poètes maudits* – together with Corbière, Villiers de l'Isle-Adam, Lautréamont, Laforgue and many others. The symbolist artists turned away from realism and naturalism and their underlying positivist or materialist values; the new movement went in search of the reality behind the outward forms, probing into the inner essence of things, into the Ideas. Consequently, in its craving for the spiritual, symbolism is essentially an idealistic, etherealising art, the 'revealer of the Infinite'. The perfect form of expression for this Idea – the ineffable or Absolute – was the symbol, since a symbol always offers an indirect, approximate evocation of the essence of things.

The means available to the poets to suggest the unsayable brought them closer to music, the abstract, ideal art *par excellence*. From now on music will be regarded as the highest art form, displacing the Horatian 'ut pictura poesis'. 'All art constantly aspires towards the condition of music', wrote Walter Pater in his *Studies in the History of Renaissance* (1877). In France Paul Verlaine formulated the new creed in his poem 'Art poétique' (1874), advocating 'Music before all else' – a condition which could be achieved by a highly suggestive, subtle, hazy and drifting reproduction of sensations and moods: 'Nothing more precious than the grey song in which the Undefinable and the Distinct meet' (in *Long Ago and Not So Long Ago* – Jadis et naguère, 1885). And for Mallarmé, too, evoking or suggesting was more important than precise designation: 'to *name* an object is to suppress three-quarters of the pleasure of the poem, the pleasure that derives from the joy of gradually guessing; to *suggest* the object, that is the ideal.'

Symbolism soon developed many ramifications and variations; it also quickly spread across Europe and pervaded art forms other than literature. More than a style, it also became an attitude to life, an art form which expressed a 'state of mind', drawing on an internationally recognisable arsenal of recurring themes and motifs (such as fate and death; the bride, the lily or the swan as symbols of innocence). The lyrical 'I' of the artist also liked to hide behind the personae of myths and legends. Thus, the sphinx and the *femme fatale* are present as typical symbolist clichés which illustrate the mystery of life, intrinsically linked to the conflict between good and evil and the struggle between man and woman.

In Belgium, the flowering of symbolism coincided with the rise of avant-garde art in the final years of the nineteenth century, a period which produced an amalgamation of artists and art forms such as had never been seen before (nor has ever been seen since): as well as the intense cooperation between poets and visual artists so characteristic of symbolism, at that time the cultures of the country's two main languages – Dutch and French – showed a remarkable unity. We have to remember that, for historical reasons, between 1880 and 1900 French culture had become dominant even in Dutch-speaking Flanders.

It seems almost inconceivable today, with the institutionalised federalisation of the Belgian state, but a hundred years ago artistic life in Belgium formed part of one common culture and literature, which was French. The most important Belgian symbolist poets – Maurice Maeterlinck, Emile Verhaeren, Max Elskamp, Charles van Lerberghe and Grégoire Le Roy – were Flemings who wrote in French. The most prominent Dutch-speaking symbolist writer, Karel van de Woestijne, found the roots of his art in French literature. However, in a portrait of Verhaeren that developed into a picture of his generation, Van de Woestijne also pointed out that the Flemings writing in French were actually 'uprooted': French 'has grafted a Latin culture onto our primal Flemish being, onto our Flemish tongue and our Flemish mentality, turning us into hesitant double beings.' And Van de Woestijne was one of these 'double beings'; because in direct opposition to his links with French culture was the fact that as a poet he was part of the Van Nu en Straks (Today and the Day After) movement. And while this movement deliberately cultivated an international image, it also gave new impetus to Flemish consciousness. Karel van de Woestijne and August Vermeylen, the spiritual leader of Van Nu en Straks, were not the only ones who made a conscious effort to establish their Flemish identity in the broader European context. Even those who wrote in French were conscious of their Flemish identity or of their roots in Flemish tradition. The Antwerp writer, wood engraver and folklorist Max Elskamp, a childhood friend of Henry van de Velde, put it like this: 'I see in Flemish and I write in French.' The same applies, broadly speaking, to Verhaeren and Maeterlinck.

The far-reaching assimilation of French culture and art in Belgium can be seen as one aspect of a much broader symbiosis of art forms at the end of the nineteenth century. Was not the idea of the synthesis of all arts or of *Gesamtkunstwerk* the origin of Wagner's success and of the 'Wagnerism' that was rapidly taking hold? Here too, however, a slight distinction needs to be drawn. Though Belgian symbolism was part of an international movement, the richly-varied œuvre of each of the various artists – writers as well as painters and sculptors – expressed individual nuances and characteristics which seemed to constitute a typical Belgian form of symbolism.

The inextricable connection between literature and the visual arts is typical of the Belgian situation: artists and writers often treated the same subjects, collections of poems appeared with illustrations, paintings produced a graphic evocation of literary works. Even more striking perhaps is the fact

Cover by Henry van de Velde for the magazine *Van Nu en Straks* (1892-1893).

that the Belgian symbolists based their work not so much on the mysterious, unreal dream landscapes peopled with swans and princesses that were so typical of the French, as on the actual landscape, a real – often also historical – space around which a suggestive and enigmatic portrayal of mood was built up. Verhaeren summed it up in 1887 in an article in *L'art moderne*: 'One starts with the thing seen, heard, felt, touched or tasted, and then goes on to create the evocation.' Thus in the work of Maurice Maeterlinck (for example, in the collection of poems *Hothouses* – Serres chaudes, 1889) and of Georges Rodenbach (in the novel *Bruges the Dead* – Bruges-la-morte, 1892) the actual cities of Ghent and Bruges only served to evoke an oppressive and melancholy atmosphere of death, decay and suffocation. It is certainly no coincidence that *Bruges the Dead* appeared with a title page illustration by Fernand Khnopff, or that *Hothouses* was illustrated by George Minne, who like Maeterlinck was from Ghent and unmistakably a kindred spirit. The picture of the seemingly dead city, just like the image of the 'octopus city' (from the 1895 collection of the same name) introduced by Verhaeren, was to win international acclaim.

Innovation in Belgian art at the end of the nineteenth century was concentrated in two centres: in Brussels, where the most progressive artists got together in Les Vingt (or Les XX) in 1884, and in the immediate vicinity of Ghent, where the brothers Karel and Gustave van de Woestijne gathered around them a number of artists in the artists' village of Sint-Martens-Latem.

Jean Delvin, James Ensor, Fernand Khnopff and Théo van Rysselberghe were among the original members of Les XX (when there were 13 of them); others soon joined the group, including Alfred W. Finch, Georges Lemmen, George Minne, Félicien Rops, Jan Toorop (from 1885) and Henry van de Velde (from 1889).

Van Rysselberghe, who was the main advisor to the group's Secretary and central figure, Octave Maus, looked very much to France. The group presented the work of its own members in annual salons, and each member could also present work by other Belgian artists or foreign guests with whom

Frontispiece by Fernand Khnopff for George Rodenbach's *Bruges the Dead* (Bruges-la-morte, 1892).

Jean Delville, *The Treasures of Satan.* 1895. Canvas, 258 x 268 cm. Museum voor Moderne Kunst, Brussels.

Théo van Rysselberghe, *The Reading by Emile Verhaeren.* 1903. Canvas, 181 x 241 cm. Museum voor Schone Kunsten, Ghent.

he felt an affinity. In this way Brussels became a crucible of international avant-garde art. The leading contemporary artists – Paul Cézanne, Walter Crane, Paul Gauguin, Georges Seurat, Vincent van Gogh and James McNeil Whistler – were introduced to the public of the time, but there were also literary evenings and concerts of chamber music. A number of members of the group – not least among them Henry van de Velde, a French-speaking Fleming from Antwerp – concentrated on the decorative arts. They gave shape to their ideas in prints, posters, book illustrations and numerous works of art, pursuing a broader social role for the art which they wanted to bring to a wider public.

When the cultural activities of Les xx were taken over by La Libre Esthétique ten years later, they were past their innovative peak; but together with the French-speaking writers who joined forces in magazines like *La jeune Belgique* (1881-1897), *L'art moderne* (1881-1914) and *La société nouvelle* (1884-1914) they had succeeded in thoroughly changing the face of Belgian art.

The literary symbolism which emerged in Belgium at the same time as naturalism was mainly propagated in *La jeune Belgique.* Under the management of Max Waller, the paper became the mouthpiece of the formalistic *l'art-pour-l'art* aesthetic, while in *L'art moderne* and particularly in *La société nouvelle,* the emphasis was on the social responsibility of the artist.

George Minne, *The Small Kneeling Boy.* 1896. Bronze, H 46.6 cm. Private Collection.

These – contrasting – ideas served as a direct source of inspiration for the Dutch-language magazine *Van Nu en Straks* (1893-1894; new series 1896 – 1901), which set itself up as the independent mouthpiece for all current and new art movements, both at home and abroad. However, in an article on 'Art in the free community' (1894) August Vermeylen, then a (Dutch-speaking) student at the (French-language) Free University in Brussels, defended a concept of art which was in line with the symbolist aesthetic. In his 'Notes on a Modern-Day Movement' (1893), written under the pseudonym A.V. de Meere, he had already stated that 'art today' is more concerned with 'the mystery' that 'is all around us and in us', and that artists try to let 'the central idea, the unchanging mystery shine through the transience of the visible forms'. And for him also it is the Flemings who write in French, particularly Maeterlinck and Elskamp, who foreshadow a whole new future for the Flemings.

The Art Nouveau design of the first volume of the magazine *Van Nu en Straks* was itself an emanation of the syncretism of the new artistic trends of the time. The journal appeared with a cover design by Henry van de Velde and was lavishly illustrated by Van de Velde himself, by Toorop, Thorn-Prikker, Van Rysselberghe, Baseleer and others; moreover it included inserted plates by Xavier Mellery, Vincent van Gogh (the entire third issue was devoted to him), George Minne, Ch. Ricketts, Jan Veth, Lucien Pissaro and James Ensor.

It was largely because of its attention to 'social issues' and to anarchism that the much more soberly presented second series of *Van Nu en Straks,* launched in 1896, marked a definite change of direction. Nevertheless, it gave prominence to Karel van de Woestijne as the poet who could be called a symbolist in all respects. Van de Woestijne became a symbolist prose writer and a discerning, sharply analytical art critic. In 1900 he settled in Latem, the village on the River Leie, with his brother Gustave who was two

The first so-called 'Latem group', c.1902. From left to right: Hector van Houtte, George Minne, Gustave van de Woestijne, Valerius de Saedeleer, Karel van de Woestijne and Albijn van den Abeele.

Gustave van de Woestijne, *Peasant in His Sunday Best.* 1910. Canvas, 65 x 48 cm. Private Collection.

years younger and with his friend Julius de Praetere, a typographer, painter and decorator. Together with George Minne, Albijn van den Abeele and Valerius de Saedeleer, who were already living there, and Albert Servaes, who arrived later, they formed the first so-called 'Latem group' (the second Latem group of artists – Frits van den Berghe, Constant Permeke and Gustave de Smet – were representatives of expressionism).

The poet Van de Woestijne, who was well read in contemporary French literature but also thoroughly familiar – through self-study – with classical and renaissance art, was a charismatic leader. In a journalistic article written in 1924, he confirmed that he read aloud from Plato and the work of the fourteenth-century Flemish mystic Jan van Ruusbroec, as well as from Shakespeare and the latest works by Maeterlinck and Ibsen.

Like their interest in the art of the Flemish Primitives (which they had discovered at an exhibition in Bruges in 1902), the hankering after mysticism is a common feature of this first Latem group of artists. They were almost all mystics at heart; they practised a sort of evangelical symbolism and sought to deepen their inner life through an intimate alliance with nature and the simple human being. Here, too, they linked up with literary symbolism, which itself reveals a pastiche of medieval art and folk art, manifested among other things in a conscious hankering for the archaic. Yet another striking similarity is the fact that Maeterlinck even translated one of Ruusbroec's main works into French and provided an introductory commentary *(The Ornaments of the Spiritual Nuptials* – L'ornement des noces spirituelles, 1908).

Karel van de Woestijne, whose own early poetry and prose (including *The Latem Letters about Spring* – De Laethemse brieven over de lente, 1902) are

Fernand Khnopff, *Secret-Reflet*. 1902. Pastel and colour pencil on paper, d 49.5 cm and 27.8 x 49 cm. Groeningemuseum, Bruges.

characterised by melancholy and an autumnal sombreness and by numerous other typically symbolist motifs of decline, expressed his admiration for symbolist art on various occasions. Like George Minne, Van de Woestijne had grown out of the naïve or primitive inclinations of the Latem group and become part of a much broader – but also much more sombre and more disturbing – European movement. Van de Woestijne considered Minne one of the greatest artists of his time and wrote several articles and essays on his work. In 1920 he noted these striking characteristics of Minne's sculptures: *'fragile figures, monumentally large, close, overflowing with ripe emotion, with profound suffering, peaceful contemplation – firm in their simplification of form and full of rich composition. It is as if nature has been simplified and the human body looks protracted and ungainly. But what an unusu-*

ally rich rhythm of surfaces and lines (even in the distorted positions of the body); what new heights expression achieves! (...) These figures (...) are surrounded by an atmosphere of delicate incorporeity and, what is more, they are the honest work of an artist who has lived life.'

The inward-turning movement that characterises many of Minne's figures and is an expression of the decadent-symbolistic tendency towards hyper-individualistic introspection and self-analysis – an attitude which typifies Karel Van de Woestijne's work as well – is also found in the much more picturesque characters who people the paintings of Gustave van de Woestijne. Gustave starts with the very specific reality of simple rural life, but succeeds in adding an immaterial, enigmatic element to this material world. Thus the repeated portrayal of the Latem farmer, Deeske, is the personification of Man in his alliance with nature, with the earth, the plants and the animals, but he is also (for example, in *The Bad Sower,* 1908) set free from the earth and spiritualised. Another key figure with Gustave as with Karel van de Woestijne is the blind man, who in the visual language of symbolism stands for being detached from earthliness, for contemplation, for looking towards the superterrestrial, the metaphysical: here the blind man becomes a Seer with supernatural gifts.

In his artistic criticism of his brother's work, the poet Karel van de Woestijne particularly emphasised modest piety as the constant factor: not the outward, objective reality, but the inward emotion of his own inner life forms the basis of this art.

Yet not all symbolist art shows the same 'primitive' piety or consecration. With Fernand Khnopff, for example – perhaps the greatest of the symbolist painters and an enthusiastic admirer of Delacroix and Gustave Moreau while in Paris, though he also felt a very strong affinity with the Pre-Raphaelite Burne-Jones and Rossetti – the idealistic element is not so much pious as influenced by the occultism of Joséphin Péladan. 'Sâr' Péladan's Rosicrucian order enjoyed considerable prestige in Belgium (and indeed in the Netherlands, too). Khnopff was one of the first followers of Péladan, and they became friends. For Khnopff as for Péladan's disciples, art was a religion, but this meant a special manneristic, strongly allegorical reproduction of reality, excluding all forms of realism. The narcissistic, aristocratically-refined art of Khnopff – a Belgian of German origin – combines pretty well all the leitmotifs of French and British symbolism. It thus confirms the remarkably international character of the symbolist conceptual universe.

ANNE MARIE MUSSCHOOT
Translated by Alison Mouthaan-Gwillim.

FURTHER READING

BOYENS, PIET, *Flemish Art: Symbolism to Expressionism.* Tielt, 1992.

GODDARD, STEPHEN H. (ed.), *Les XX and the Belgian Avant-Garde: Prints, Drawings and Books ca 1890.* Lawrence / Ghent, 1992.

LEGRAND, FRANCINE-CLAIRE, *Le symbolisme en Belgique.* Brussels, 1971.

NACHTERGAELE, VIC, *La réception du symbolisme franco-belge en Flandre.* Oeuvres et Critiques (ed. Damblemont), XVII, 2, 1992, pp. 19-39.

ames

Ensor, Pioneer

of Modern European Art

James Ensor (1860-1949) was a European painter of considerable stature and along with Gauguin, Van Gogh and Munch a pioneer of modern European art. He left behind an œuvre of paintings, drawings and etchings which in their modern expressiveness are proof of his brilliant creative powers and almost unlimited technical ability.

The story of this 'prince of painters' began in Ostend, where James Sidney Ensor was born on 13 April 1860. His British father, an eccentric intellectual, could not adapt to the mentality of this provincial town, was unable to find work and eventually turned to drink. His mother, who came from Ostend, ran a souvenir shop. Her mother and sister lived with them, as did Ensor's sister Mariette, a year younger than himself. Ensor grew up among these dominating women, who 'worked like slaves in the summer and dozed through the winter'. The maid used to tell him bizarre stories in the kitchen. We can imagine the lad wandering round in the shop enthralled by the fantastic shells, carnival masks and Chinese souvenirs with their mysterious images.

School did not suit Ensor, and in 1873 he was given painting lessons by two local watercolourists, Eduard Dubar and Michel van Kuyck. Ensor was not very impressed by their teaching and at the age of fifteen was painting landscapes of the surrounding area on little pieces of cardboard, the so-called 'cartons roses', still hesitantly drawn but revealing an unmistakable talent and feel for three-dimensionality and light.

In 1876 Ensor took drawing lessons at the Academy in Ostend and from 1877 he studied at the Royal Academy of Fine Arts in Brussels. The contacts which Ensor established in Brussels later proved to be of greater significance than his training at the Academy. He met a number of young progressive artists: Fernand Khnopff, Willy Finch, Willem Vogels, the critic-painter Theo Hannon and Eugène Demolder who was to publish the first monograph about Ensor in 1892. Theo Hannon introduced Ensor to his botanist sister Mariette Rousseau-Hannon and her older husband Ernest Rousseau Sr., a professor at the Free University of Brussels. The atmosphere in this free-thinking, art-loving family, where scholars, men and women of letters and artists were regular visitors, certainly sharpened Ensor's keen mind and perhaps also his anarchic tendencies.

James Ensor, *Rooftops of Ostend.* 1884.
Canvas, 157 x 209 cm.
Koninklijk Museum voor Schone Kunsten, Antwerp.

James Ensor, *Woman Eating Oysters.* 1882.
Canvas, 207 x 150 cm.
Koninklijk Museum voor Schone Kunsten, Antwerp.

Describing the time of his debut, Ensor spoke of 'the blazing epoch of the struggle for art'. Never before had artistic trends in Europe followed each other with such speed. Impressionism had reached its peak and symbolism, with the artist taking a subjective standpoint, was in the air. Ensor made his debut in 1881 at La Chrysalide in Brussels and in 1884 co-founded the avant-garde group known as Le Cercle des Vingts (or: Les xx) which would later become famous.

The realist-impressionist period: 1879-1885

During this period Ensor was looking attentively at the things that surrounded him and the people with whom he shared his life, as is apparent from the hundreds of precise sketches as well as the paintings dating from that period.

In 1880 he painted *The Vlaanderenstraat in the Snow* and *The Vlaanderenstraat in the Rain,* and in 1881 *The Vlaanderenstraat in the Sun,* all in impressionist style with vibrant brush strokes. These are bird's-eye views of the town, seen from the studio window on the fourth floor of the corner house in the Vlaanderenstraat, a motif also beloved of the French Impressionists. However, Ensor did not go so far as Claude Monet in *The Cathedral of Rouen* (1894) who allowed the shapes to be corroded by the light into suggestive spots. Like Willem Vogels, Ensor kept to dark tones and made no use of pure, unmixed colours on his impressionist palette. In another painting, *Rooftops of Ostend* (1884), which also derives from the view from the attic window, three-quarters of the panoramic painting is filled with a bank of hazy clouds above a narrow band of houses. Ensor's concern was not with topographical information, but with a mosaic of colours overhung by a cloudy sky.[1]

Ensor, who lived near the sea, painted near-monochrome blue and grey seascapes using a palette knife. Marvellous white clouds sometimes tower over the sea, or a bank of clouds full of grey nuances gathers, threatening as the clouds above the North Sea often are. In *After the Storm* (1880) Ensor takes his talent for colour and masterly use of the palette technique to the verge of the unreal.

It is as if his sensitivity to delicate colours and light-modelling predestined Ensor to paint still lifes during this period of fascination with 'the reality of things'.[2]

At this stage his composition is characterised by straightforwardness. A slippery flatfish is shown on a little bed of straw next to a wicker basket and a copper kettle. Elsewhere vegetables and poultry or flowers have been deposited carelessly. Oysters and porcelain rest on a white tablecloth, chinoiserie from the souvenir shop is displayed on a wool table cover with busy motifs. Bottles, dishes, linen and oysters are almost tangible.

The characteristics of the still lifes, 'the reality of things', modelling with light and masterly palette knife technique are also found in the portraits. In the realistic drawings the parts densely shaded in soft black chalk introduce a sort of quiet melancholy. This can also be seen in the painted portraits for which fishermen, members of the family and friends acted as models. *The Boy with the Lamp* (1880), a dark silhouette against a smooth background, shows that the young Ensor did not hesitate to use a palette knife and thick gooey paint to paint figures that contrast with the rest of the picture. The lad looks in fascination at the light playing on the fishing lamp. The so-called 'salon pictures' like *Afternoon at Ostend* (1881), *The Bourgeois Salon* (1881) and *Russian Music* (1882) are set in the drawing room of his parents' home. It is the typical nineteenth-century bourgeois drawing room with table and chair coverings in busy patterns, stereotyped ornaments in front of the mirror on the mantelpiece, and high windows with heavy curtains. The typical rituals of the day unfold within this interior: ladies drink coffee, play the piano, embroider, chat, await a visitor or feel terribly bored. Filtered light and shadow create a sort of 'unheimlichkeit' or uncanniness, in complete contrast to the objectifying light of the French Impressionists. In *Woman Eating Oysters* (1882) the act of eating is almost incidental. The woman, the bottles , the flowers, the porcelain and the white table cloth are most marvellously shown in their own 'reality of things'. It is the first painting in which Ensor's palette becomes lighter, which was also the reason it was refused for exhibition at L'Essor salon in Brussels in 1883; though he was able to show it in 1886 at the third salon of the artists of Le Cercle des Vingts, of which he was one of the most talented members. The critics were certainly not negative about his entry for the first salon in 1884. They praised his coloration, the atmosphere, the colour harmony and his innate talent, but in their view the drawing was awkward and in need of improve-

James Ensor, *The Entry of Christ into Jerusalem.* 1885. Black and brown crayon on paper, 206 x 150.3 cm. Museum voor Schone Kunsten, Ghent.

James Ensor, *Self-Portrait with Flowered Hat.* 1883. Canvas, 75 x 61.5 cm. Museum voor Schone Kunsten, Ostend.

ment. Their censure became scathing when they noticed that Ensor, who like Delacroix took colour and not line as his starting point, ignored their advice and was imitated by a number of young artists.

From realistic to symbolic light: 1885-1887

In 1885 Ensor the painter became considerably less productive. Was he perhaps offended by the criticism and looking for alternative paths for his creativity? Or was he simply searching for an outlet for his intensely active imagination? Rembrandt's symbolic treatment of light, chiaroscuro and transparent, incorporeal figures certainly inspired the new style Ensor developed, for which he could draw on the whole wealth of visual observations from his realistic period. He made a number of copies based on etchings and drawings by Rembrandt. *The Death of the Blessed Virgin* and *The Three Crosses,* as well as a number of other works which draw attention to the light question, could have been copied from the 1885 publications of the magazine *l'Art.*

Between 1885 and 1886 Ensor produced remarkable large-format drawings which he then showed in 1887 under the title *Visions,* later grouping them under *The Halos of Christ or the Sensitivity of Light.* Ensor described light as 'merry', 'harsh', 'alive and radiant', 'sad and broken', 'tranquil and serene', 'intense'. So light was given a set of human emotional values.

James Ensor, *Adam and Eve Expelled from Paradise.* 1887. Canvas, 205 x 245 cm. Koninklijk Museum voor Schone Kunsten, Antwerp.

Turner had also expressed this by means of double titles in a number of his Bible scenes.[3] He equated 'shadow and darkness' with *The Evening of the Deluge,* in which the sun has disappeared and the world has come to an end. He used 'light and colour' for *The Morning after the Deluge – Moses Writing the Book of Genesis,* when sun and hope return. Ensor associated harsh light with *Jesus Presented to the People* (1885), the alive and radiant with *The Entry into Jerusalem* (1885) and the sad and broken with *Satan and the Phantastic Legions Tormenting the Crucified* (1886). In the earliest of these works, *Jesus Presented to the People,* Ensor no longer reined in his imagination. It is a strange scene, built up of light that annihilates form so that out of squiggling little pieces of arabesque and nervous fragments of line dematerialised human figures appear in droves. It is a web of dream creating the drama in Rembrandtian chiaroscuro. Christ is standing on the axis of the drawing but in the sultry atmosphere no one pays any heed to his presence. Ensor illustrated a deadly form of repudiation, the inner affront of being ignored, of not being accepted. He himself knew these feelings, and it is here that the Christ-Ensor identification in his œuvre starts. It was to last throughout his creative period; after that it no longer had any point and disappeared.

Ensor brought his personal problems very directly into another crayon drawing, *The Entry of Christ into Jerusalem* (1885). Here the monogram of Les xx – some of whose members were hostile to him – appears on a banner, and is later found as an identifying sign on people's backs and on balconies. The drawing of the head of the French politician-philosopher Emile Littré, which is clearly stuck on, must certainly also have had some significance. In 1852 Littré had written a French adaptation of the positivistic views of the German David Strauss, which Ernest Renan also discussed in *The Life of Jesus* (1863). Christ is presented as a sort of social anarchist whose life ended in the failure of death. Ensor the anarchist could scarcely have identified with that. He was anti-clerical, like many in the 1880s, and inclined to liberalism politically, but he was religious. He identified with

Christ the Messiah who was stronger than death and became the inspiring force behind Christianity. In the same way, Ensor wanted to become the leading figure in modern art.

Ensor's etchings are closely related to his drawings. Some 140 etchings were produced between 1885 and 1893. They have the same subject matter, the same light quality and marvellous technique as the drawings, of which Marcel de Maeyer used the word 'licht-weven' ('weaving light').

But it is not only in Ensor's drawings that alienation from reality breaks through. Marcel de Maeyer discovered with the aid of lateral light and infrared photography that both the *Skeleton Studying Chinoiseries* (1885) and *The Children Dressing* (1885) were touched up once the paint was dry, thus making the intimate, realistic character of the paintings unrealistic. He also described the hybrid character of a number of realistic paintings and drawings to which Ensor added fantastic motifs around or after 1887, without changing the original date, such as the masks in *Masks Studying a Black Conjurer* (1879), the alienating hat in *Self-Portrait with Flowered Hat* (1883), and the dematerialised, transparent groups of people in the realistic drawing, *The Mystical Death of a Theologian* (1880).

Several paintings by Ensor from this period of unrealistic light also reveal the influence of 'Turner the brilliant' as Ensor described him in his writings. His seascape *Sunset over the Sea* (1885) is much closer to the visionary light of Turner than the optical light of the French Impressionists. The composition of the etching *Christ Calming the Tempest* (1886) is inspired by Turner's *Ulysses Deriding Polyphemus,* a line illustration of which he probably copied in or soon after 1884 from *English Painting* (La peinture anglaise, c.1882) by Ernest Chesneau. Ensor's painting entitled *Christ Calming the Tempest* of five years later (1891) has the same rolling clouds and surging water as *Snow Storm. Hannibal and His Army Crossing the Alps* and, to an even greater extent, *Snow Storm. Steamboat off a Harbour's Mouth.* Both Turner paintings belong to the Tate Gallery collection in London.

Walther Vanbeselaere noted the affinity between Turner and Ensor in *Children Dressing* (1886): 'realised in a subtle range worthy of Turner'. Herman T. Piron drew a comparison between its golden-white light and Turner's *Music Party, Petworth;* the ethereal atmosphere is even clearer in *A Bedroom, Petworth* where golden light filters through the drawn curtains.

Adam and Eve Expelled from Paradise (1887) leads us to suspect that Ensor, who called the painting 'a study of light', had very likely seen actual paintings by Turner before 1887, perhaps on a visit to Mrs J.F. Ensor-Andrew who lived in Fulham in London. Here we have the same swirling light as in *The Angel Standing in the Sun.* But there are other elements in Ensor's painting which are so similar to Turner that it is hard to believe they are accidental. The earthly paradise has become a stretch of burnt earth with two nude figures running away, the same nude figures who in *The Angel,* pursued by death, run into the foreground. Turner produced several paintings with the lower foreground in burnt-earth colours showing puny animals and people, among them *Shadow and Darkness – Evening of the Deluge.* The marvellous sky with blue, yellow and pink against the earth in dark ochres is highly expressive and typical of Turner's late work.

In Ensor's *Fall of the Rebellious Angels* (1889) we again see the typical

domed light with an angel in the centre and underneath a vision of aggressive colour and conflicting movements evoking the apocalyptic vision of God's rejection. After 1885 the paintings are less frequently painted with a palette knife because the application of fluid transparent paint better conveys the vision's lack of substance. The *Fall of the Rebellious Angels* is of a grandiose abstract expressionism, gestural painting of the highest quality fifty years before 'action painting' came into being. Yet Ensor did not abandon reality altogether. Some small, naked women move in the foreground, giving the vision a sense of realism.

There was an abortive attempt in 1971 to show the paintings of Turner and Ensor together; this would certainly be worth doing, so that an in-depth study can be made of influences and affinities.

The masked universe: 1887-1895

The start of the second great creative period in Ensor's career as a painter began as early as 1887. Many of the brilliant works he produced are masks for his fear.

Ensor was afraid of death in all its many senses: afraid of the physical death which had taken his father in 1887; afraid of the death that would result from abandoning his own identity either voluntarily or involuntarily by joining the masses; afraid of losing his own identity as an artist by no longer being creative. At the same time, there was also the fear of women which can perhaps be explained by the dominant women of his childhood and the sad decline of his 'superior' father to whom he bore a strong physi-

James Ensor, *Fall of the Rebellious Angels*. 1889. Canvas, 108 x 132 cm. Koninklijk Museum voor Schone Kunsten, Antwerp.

James Ensor, *Skeletons Fighting for the Body of a Hanged Man*. 1891. Canvas, 59 x 74 cm. Koninklijk Museum voor Schone Kunsten, Antwerp.

cal resemblance and whose extravagance he also shared. With his thin countenance and black clothes he resembled death; in Ostend he was called 'Pietje de dood' ('grim reaper').

Christ and demons were part of the normal symbolist vocabulary, as were death and Pierrot, the sad clown. Death hovers in the air in the form of a skeleton with a scythe in *The Triumph of Death* (1887), a tiny drawing in which insect-like monsters are inscribed in flowing writing in the burning air. Between the sort of high buildings in a narrow street which Gustave Doré so often drew, flees a crowd composed of fantastic arabesques, splendidly contrasting with the vertical lines of the houses. There is no escape, neither for the wench, nor for the judge, nor for the clergyman with his aureole. Love, power, doctrine, clericalism, death – they all seemed to threaten Ensor's own identity and he ridiculed them with increasing sarcasm.

In the drawing *Demons Taunting Me* (1887) there does not seem to be much left of the self-assured artist who painted the famous *Self-Portrait with Flowered Hat* in 1883 and drew an equally confident *Self-Portrait* in 1884. Here Ensor appears as a fearful man attacked by a group of demons. Three of them are women, one of whom has the features of Mariette Rousseau and another those of Augusta Boogaerts, Ensor's intimate friend from 1888 to his death. But his feelings for Mariette Rousseau, the unattainable love, are unmistakably apparent in drawings, paintings and etchings. Ensor remained a bachelor, and his relationship with the women who flattered him and whom he flattered was ambiguous: he was attracted by them while at the same time they alarmed him, as is apparent from a gem of

James Ensor, *The Entry of Christ into Brussels.* 1888. Canvas, 258 x 431 cm. The J.-Paul Getty Museum, Malibu.

a painting with bright red and blue on a pearly-white background: *Skeletons Fighting for the Body of a Hanged Man* (1891), an absurd scene. Ensor is strung up between two groups of jeering spectators standing in doorways on either side. He looks in horror at the two richly attired skeleton female rivals pitching into each other, one with a brush and one with a mop; inset is his body that will be served up as a stew.

In 1888, the same year that Gauguin painted *Jacob's Struggle,* Ensor produced his symbolist manifesto, a painting of enormous dimensions entitled *The Entry of Christ into Brussels.* Stephen McGough wrote his doctoral thesis on the subject. It is his hypothesis that the Ensor-Messiah of art, confronted by Seurat's image of society in *Sunday Afternoon on the Island of La Grande-Jatte,* wanted to make an even more striking picture of Belgian society. The painting is a grandiose and very personal censure of society by the fearful Ensor-Christ, who realised he was not accepted as a great artist, and never would be because he was too much himself to keep step with the others. Consequently, before his creativity is dealt a mortal blow, he rides upon an ass into Brussels, the Mecca of art, to triumphant acclaim. In front of him a chaotic group of masked people follows the grotesque drum major, while behind him members of Les XX, consumed by envy, hang over a balcony vomiting. The orderly fanfare seems to form a stage which draws the lone Christ-Ensor figure out of the crowd and into the foreground. The meaning of the writing on the banners and flags is clear: 'Vive la sociale' (Long live the 'Sociale'!), 'Fanfares doctrinaires toujours réussi' (Doctrinal fanfares always effective) and 'Vive Jésus roi de Bruxelles' (Long live Jesus King of Brussels!).

Such interesting events as processions, political marches and carnivals lose their identity in this painting. They are merged and consequently ridiculed in a grotesque fashion. The whole scene bathes in an orgy of light and unadulterated colour: venomous yellow, spiteful green, aggressive red are laid directly on the canvas one against the other so that each achieves its maximum intensity. Is the grotesque vision that censures society symbolist expressionism or expressionist symbolism? The interest in the Christ figure, the unreal atmosphere and the subjective involvement which becomes visualised reality in the tradition of Bosch and Brueghel are symbolist. The direct translation of Ensor's uncontainable emotions into raw colours and distorted figures is expressionist.

The *Man of Sorrows* (1891) may be said to mark the final stage of the Christ identification. Ensor employed two media to shout out his dread, anger and fear: the No mask of oriental drama with puckered brow and wide, open mouth; and a theme from Christian iconography, the crown of thorns with the blood that flowed through Christ's hair and down his face. Painted in flesh-coloured carmine and reseda green, this gruesome cry resulted in an expressionist masterpiece almost without parallel.

After the *Entry,* Ensor's unique creative invention of the masked individual whose mask relates to the whole human being, appears again in a whole new universe of splendid mask paintings. Though they are not as numerous as is usually thought, their titles are telling: *Old Woman with Masks* (1889), *Astonishment of the Mask Wouse* (1889), *Grotesque Singers* (1891), *The Rare Masks* (1892) and *Masks and Death* (1897).

The Intrigue (1890) is a masterpiece that puts Ensor on a par with Gauguin, Van Gogh and Munch. A group of masked people and a skeleton cluster around an amorous couple – some writers say Mariette Ensor and the Chinese friend whom she married two years later. The faces of the masks against the subtle blue-grey air reflect secret pleasure, venom and falsehood. The brutal, unadulterated yellow, green, blue and red of the still sensually handled mass of paint heightens the intriguing, emotional atmosphere and turns it into an almost clownish event. But above all the painting is a feast of colour, resonant light and expression.

In 1892 Ensor created a remarkable little painting entitled *Consoling Virgin,* its lines executed with refinement and beautiful pastel tints. Ensor is kneeling humbly before the muse. Is he appealing for inspiration? He is holding an unusable, misshapen brush. That is also the case in *Kermis* (1901) and in *Skeleton Painter in His Atelier* (1896). Ensor, a tall man, stands like a dwarf with a feverish, cadaverous face in front of an easel bearing a tiny canvas. The brushes in his hand and in his jacket pocket are all so misshapen that they are no longer usable. And what is a painter without a brush? 'For him [Ensor] identity revolved literally and figuratively around his brush. With the brush and what he could realise with it, his self-assurance would stand or fall, he himself would stand or fall.' We will not go further into Herman T. Piron's psychoanalytical explanation, but it is clear that the Ensor of the nineties was beginning to doubt himself. He wrote to Pol de Mont that initially criticism had spurred him on to produce better and better work, but that he could no longer cope with it. He lacked not only the creativity but even the desire to paint.

The decline of creativeness: after 1896

Suddenly in the nineties Ensor developed an interest in historical facts which he treated in a fictitious way, notably in line drawings and etchings.

James Ensor, *The Intrigue.* 1890. Canvas, 90 x 150 cm. Koninklijk Museum voor Schone Kunsten, Antwerp.

He was certainly familiar with the book, *The Political, Dramatic and Grotesque History of Holy Russia* (Histoire politique, dramatique et caricaturale de la Sainte Russie, 1854) by Gustave Doré. Libby Tannenbaum has already pointed out the transfiguration of Jacques Callot's *Le Pisseur* into Ensor's *The Pisser* (1887). He put modern graffiti on the wall and above them wrote 'Ensor est un fou' ('Ensor is a madman'). He used the etching again as a wall decoration in the painting *The Droll Smokers* (1920), in which the painter Willem Paerels offers a cigar-smoking skull on a dish to Ensor's cigarette-smoking woman friend. Grandville also provided Ensor with 'transfiguration material'. The affinity between Ensor's *Self-Portrait Surrounded by Masks* (1899) and *Les célébrités du jour* is too great to be accidental. Ensor used these works, and probably also Kawanabé Kiosa's smoking, music-playing, fighting, naked skeletons, reproduced in volume 15 of the 1899 issue of *The Studio,* as a starting-point, as he had done earlier with oysters, fruit, fish, porcelain and people. He transformed them completely. This was in line with the spirit of the time; Manet transfigured existing works of art, as did Gauguin and many others. So the term 'transfiguration' has no pejorative connotation whatsoever; reference to the sources can only lead to a better understanding of the artist's technique and subject matter.

From 1910 Ensor began to copy his own paintings from his realistic period in bright colours: *Woman Eating Oysters, The Bourgeois Salon, Still-Life with Duck.* For *The Domain of Arnheim* (1890) he took his inspiration from Edgar Allen Poe's *Fantastic Tales,* while *The Black Cat and other Horror Stories* provided the inspiration for a number of drawings. The etching *Hop Frog's Revenge* (1898), a collection of people who hang burning in a kind of chandelier while a circle of people below gape up at them, is inspired by Poe's perverted character and his 'sometimes lugubrious nihilistic game of death and decay'.[4] The sarcasm is of a totally different order than in *Devils Give Angels and Archangels a Thrashing* (1888) made in the spirit of Hieronymus Bosch.

It is certainly not the case that Ensor produced no successful paintings, etchings or drawings in this period. He painted landscapes and still lifes in pastel colours that are full of wondrous poetry; *The Artist's Mother in Death* (1915); mythological scenes with sensual little nudes in almost transparent, light colours such as *The Abduction of Andromeda*, (1925); and a number of paintings with the portrait of his girlfriend: the *Double Portrait* (1905), *The Droll Smokers* (1920) and *Portrait of Augusta Boogaerts* (1915). Dorine Cardyn has drawn attention to a small portrait of a later girlfriend, Emma Lambotte, in one of the lively scenery paintings for *Love's Gamut* (1912). The little portrait goes back to a painting executed in 1907. Lambotte and Ensor stand out clearly as a patch of colour amid a large crowd of marionettes. The sidelong glance of Emma, who looked after Ensor's business interests, is telling. The rather older Ensor leans towards her, a misshapen brush protruding from his hat; he is holding a little marionette with outspread arms and legs between the two of them, a hyphen accentuated by the sunshade in dazzling vermilion red. And a number of Watteau-like drawings in pastel or sanguine still betray his talent for colour, inspiration and masterly drawing skills.

But these works cannot really be said to enrich Ensor's œuvre. That was already complete by the end of the great mask period. Ensor, who lived close to the sea, knew the pattern of high and low tide better than anyone. He also knew that in his life's tide the ebb lasted many evenings; and the deserved fame which was at last conferred upon him after 1900, could do nothing to change that.

LYDIA M.A. SCHOONBAERT
Translated by Alison Mouthaan-Gwillim.

James Ensor, *The Droll Smokers*. 1920.
Canvas, 77 x 66 cm.
Private Collection.

REFERENCES

1. HOSTYN, N., *Exhibition catalogue James Ensor.*
Musée du Petit Palais, 1990, p. 140;
H. Todts, *Exhibition catalogue James Ensor.*
Central Museum Utrecht, 1993, p. 73.
2. MAINGON, CH., *Emile Verhaeren, Critique d'Art.*
Paris, 1984, p. 144.
3. KITSON, M., *Turner.* Deventer, 1964.
4. BORRE, J., 'Edgar Allan Poe's imago ongeschonden',
De Nieuwe, 22.8.1980.

FURTHER READING

DELEVOY, ROBERT, *Ensor.* Antwerp, 1981.
ELESH, JAMES N., *James Ensor. The Complete Graphic Work.*
New York, 1982.
LESKO, DIANE, *James Ensor. The Creative Years.*
Princeton, 1985.
HOOZEE, ROBERT, SABINE BOWN-TAEVERNIER and
J.F. HEIJBROEK, *James Ensor. Drawings and Prints.*
Antwerp, 1987.
TRICOT, X., *James Ensor. Catalogue raisonné des peintures.*
Antwerp, 1992, 2 vols.

Master of Word and Image

Marten Toonder and the Bumble Comic Strips

Marten Toonder (1912-) is an extremely popular author in the Netherlands. He owes this popularity primarily to the 177 adventures of Tom Puss and Mr Bumble, in form a series of comic strips but in content much closer to illustrated short stories, with recurring characters and a very specific mythological universe. The stories appeared as daily strips in the *NRC-Handelsblad* newspaper before being published as collections. The first story appeared in 1941, the last in 1986, when the writer / draughtsman brought the series to a decisive end by having the main character marry and settle for a comfortable future devoid of adventure. The publishing house De Bezige Bij has been publishing the comic strips in book form since 1967, though this did not stop *NRC-Handelsblad* reprinting the earlier stories, to the great delight of their readers.

The earliest stories were intended for children. The main character in these stories is Tom Puss, a small cat who has all the necessary qualities to occupy the central role in an adventure story: he is fearless, level-headed and intelligent, a true problem-solver, James Bond in cat's clothing. He has no need for macho antics, no pathos, and keeps a low profile – in fact, he has everything needed to be sure of winning the sympathies of a Dutch readership which does not care for humbug. And yet after only three instalments Tom Puss was displaced in the reader's sympathies by another figure who entered the stories, Mr Bumble. He is a bear with a pot belly and all the characteristics of a gentleman. A gentleman of standing, as he himself says. He walks around with a jovial expression – and with good reason, for he is comfortably off ('Money is no object') – has a healthy appetite and is attended by his faithful manservant Joseph, who performs his role of gentleman's gentleman with true dedication.

The fact that Bumble is a rather 'un-Dutch' gentleman is apparent from his impatient lack of understanding of sober facts and material issues. Toonder explored the narrative possibilities of this anachronistic anti-hero with unerring skill, and turned Bumble into the real main character of the stories. True, Bumble always appears in partnership with his 'young friend' Tom Puss, but alongside this artful problem-solver he plays the role of someone who, while in his own mind he always brings the adventure to a satisfactory end, is actually the person who creates the problems in the first place.

The most important change was that the comic strip became aimed less and less at children, and more and more at adults. The drawings became more refined, and this applied even more to the written text. The stories were no longer purely about adventures for their own sake; they now focused mainly on the theme, and especially the humour, which was particularly bound up in the use of language. What was originally called *The Adventures of Tom Puss* later came to be known by Dutch readers simply as the 'Bumble comic strip'. This short collective term describes an œuvre of author-illustrated stories which are characterised by a highly literary prose style.

As the individual stories were threaded together, the narrative context gradually acquired a more coherent character; readers got to know and recognise the secondary characters. The actions of Mr Bumble often originate in his home, Bumblestone Castle; this is located in the little town of Rumbledon, whose inhabitants feature regularly in the stories. Bumble has dealings with a mayor who likes the easy life, a snobbish aristocrat, a bigoted police chief, an obsessive scientist, a charlatan of a psychotherapist, a petty civil servant, a zealous grocer, a pathetic idiot, a tea-drinking woman neighbour, and a couple of rogues. Their names are known to virtually every reader in the Low Countries: Mayor Dickerdack, the Marquess de Canticleer, Chief Constable Burly Bull, Dr Sickbock, Soulpincher, Dryknot, Mr Goodspice, Zackary Heep, Miss Dingle, and the villains Wal Super and Wally Woddle. They are all regular characters who became familiar and much-loved figures to faithful readers of the Bumble stories because of their predictable reactions to situations and their linguistic specificity. The linguistic idiosyncrasies created by Toonder are so spot on that they have become widely known and been lovingly adopted as general currency in the national lexicon: 'If you understand what I mean', 'I didn't know I had it in me', 'Money is no object', 'A gentleman of standing', etc. Expressions borrowed from the Bumble strip are used frequently by many Dutch-speakers, usually with a knowing wink.

The Bumble stories can be read separately as humorous adventure stories, with references to the problems of people and the world, and with an implicit philosophical purport. And yet when you have read one story, you want to read more. And you must do so, if you are to gain an insight into the consistency of the themes and of the fictitious world of Bumble.

In that world, the characters are real people in their way of thinking and their behaviour – despite the fact that they are predominantly portrayed as animals. In addition to Bumble and Tom Puss, bear and cat, the mayor is a hippopotamus, the idiot a goose, the aristocrat a cock. But there are also characters who live in a parallel world. These characters, drawn with human faces, include the wicked magician Hocus Pas, who tries to wield power, and diligent 'little people' such as Knowit and Pete Pastinake, who try to protect nature. And precisely because of their intensive interaction with nature, they have an esoteric knowledge of the magic powers which those who live in the human world have long forgotten. It is striking how frequently these 'dwarves / little people' from the parallel world come to Bumble's aid when he gets into trouble.

A good example is provided by the story *The Top Dogs* (De bovenbazen,

1968). Bumble wins a wager with Tom Puss. As a result of this small addition to his already considerable wealth, that wealth suddenly increases enormously. It passes a critical point, beyond which money only attracts more money. Bumble becomes so rich that he cannot do other than enter the circle of the super-rich – the 'Top Dogs'. This has far-reaching consequences; he can no longer mix with those of limited means, such as his young friend Tom Puss. He also has to uphold the principle that nature must be destroyed as much as possible; 'Exterminate nature', he is told, 'Nature is our biggest enemy. Nature renews itself.' Completely in keeping with this ideological principle, liberal quantities of DDT are sprayed on the crops to control a plague of pests – so much so that even the spiders disappear, which are then replaced by robot-weed-killers. These mechanical spiders maintain the production process but cannot take over the useful work of the spiders. The balance of nature is thoroughly disturbed, and an ecological disaster threatens. Initially, Bumble is tempted to take up with the Top Dogs, to trust them and to let himself be impressed by their lifestyle and their views. When he sees the consequences of those views, however, he changes his mind and wishes to end his collaboration. With the help of his friends from the parallel world, he succeeds, using magical means. For magic plays just as big a role in the adult Bumble comic strips as in the children's stories, when Tom Puss was still the hero. The main difference is in the hostile forces and characters with which the later hero Bumble comes into contact. Although explicit references to the real world are never made, the similarities enable the reader to see through the magicians, gurus, miracle-workers, cheats, raving academics and entrepreneurs, and to recognise in them, without any difficulty, people and situations from the real world.

This gives the stories an element of social and cultural criticism; allusions to youth culture, addiction, sectarianism, intolerance, consumerism, xenophobia – all are to be found hiding behind ironic metaphors. And yet they always remain relatively secondary elements, because the fundamental theme is not related to the 'here and now', but to man's place in the cosmos, to the inadequacy of human endeavour, particularly when that is too exclusively rational and focused on self-interest.

The narrative strength of Bumble as a main character is that the reader can identify with him easily, especially because of the weak aspects of his personality. He is gullible, naïve, vain, moody, always looking for an easy life, easily influenced, short-tempered, a snob and a boaster. He is also a coward; except when he 'flips' and throws caution to the wind, for he is a hothead whose passion is particularly aroused when two things coincide: when his assessment of his own worth is impugned, and when he is confronted by injustice. For inside Bumble the well-to-do gentleman there also lurks Bumble the noble knight, who is quick to believe that he is destined for a high calling. In short, every reader finds something of himself in this imperfect but good-hearted and generous character.

Bumble's task in life is to undergo adventures by tackling the injustice in the world – something he always does with success, though usually in spite of himself and only with the help of Tom Puss. Bumble always takes the credit for that success in a closing commentary at a banquet, which he modestly calls 'a simple but nutritious meal', served by his faithful manservant. In spite of his human weaknesses, his spiritual qualities raise Bumble above

Mr Bumble and his spiritual father, Marten Toonder (1912-).

the notables from his social milieu, for whom *homo homini lupus* (dog eats dog) is an unwritten rule of life.

The humour in the characters, in the situations and, above all, in the language take away any trace of didactism or 'labouring the point' from the stories. Through these stories, with their fairy-tale-like plots, Toonder offers his readers much food for thought, but much more to smile at. His style is filled with a mixture of archaic language and neologisms. The stories contain his own highly original creations, but also virtually all the figures from the classical art of *Rhetoric* – all used to great effect in the service of mild irony.

Toonder also wrote and drew other, less well-known comic strips, such as *Kappie, Panda* and *King Hollewijn*. He created short, poetic animated films and later, in 1983, also a full-length animation with Bumble as the main character, entitled *If You Understand What I Mean* (Als je begrijpt wat ik bedoel). In 1965 Toonder settled in Ireland, inspired both by the rural beauty of the country and by the local mythology which came to him both from the mouths of the inhabitants and from the many folk tales, and which fitted in perfectly with his sensitivity to a parallel world such as that evoked by his own imagination. In 1992 the eighty-year-old Toonder received his first ever literary prize, the Tollens Prize for Dutch literature. In the same year he published the first part of his autobiography, *When the World Was Flat* (Vroeger was de aarde plat); this was followed in 1993 by the second part, *The Sound of Flowers* (Het geluid van bloemen), which deals with events during the Second World War, when his studio remained open and served as a cover for anti-German counterfeit work.

In Bumble, Toonder created a cult figure, a fact which is apparent from the existence of the Hague Bumble Society. There is also a publishing house, Panda, in The Hague, which specialises in Toonder's work; in 1990 Panda began publishing all the Bumble newspaper strips in their original form. Bumble strips have been translated into Danish, Swedish, Norwegian, Finnish, German, French, English, Spanish, Papiamento and Indonesian. The stories have for a long time appeared as comic strips in a number of English-language newspapers, including *The Irish Independent, The Birmingham Gazette, The Bristol Evening Post, The Evening Advertiser, The Evening Citizen, Kensley Newspapers, The Lancashire Evening Post, The Manchester Evening News* and *The Sunday News*. In 1993 Toonder's prose occupied centre stage in the Translation Project of Story International in Rotterdam. The refined quality of Toonder's prose makes its translation a creative adventure, a very special challenge. On the basis of an English translation, focusing particularly on *The Trull-Keepster* (De trullenhoedster), authors from fifteen countries translated his work into Slovak, Turkish, Italian, Chinese, Arabic, Afrikaans, Hungarian, Farsi, Rumanian, French, Russian, Sranang and a number of African languages. Earlier translations have appeared in English under titles such as *The Flatteners* (Het platmaken) and *The Kookle* (Het kukel).

AART VAN ZOEST
Translated by Julian Ross.

Mr Steinhacker realised he was facing one of the unin-formed, so he went into great detail explaining the prin-ciples of being a Top Dog. 'When money exceeds a crit-ical mass', he said, 'it starts attracting money. The result is a so-called fusion. Is that clear?'

'Yes, of course', said Mr Ollie blankly. 'A fushion'.

'Very well', resumed the other. 'This fusion must, of course, be guided, or else we'd have grave difficulties. Isolation, O.B.! Our group must work in isolation in order to keep control.'

'Oh yes', Mr Bumble muttered dazedly, and the mag-nate tried another tack, seeing his visitor understood nothing.

'You belong to the Upper Ten now, old man', he said, raising his voice. 'We possess everything. Everything, understand? It's a hard job, and so you've got to stick to the rules.'

'Rules?' repeated Mr Ollie with a start.

'Exactly', A.S. confirmed. 'Never give money away. Always say you have too many commitments, that you need all you have. Promote wastage; it benefits produc-tion. Promote boredom; it creates the desire for new things. Exterminate nature; nature is our biggest enemy. Nature renews itself – and we can't have that ...' He stopped, noticing the blank expression on Mr Ollie's face. 'We'll keep an eye on you', he concluded. 'We'll give you advice; but here's a prepared guide which describes everything. And here's a bundle of shares, which gives you all DDT to start with, O.B., just to start with. Use them well! Follow the manual – and don't mix with any of the, er, impecunious!' With these words, he led his deflated guest to the door and showed him out.

After dinner, Mr Bumble went for a stroll, in order to com-pose his thoughts. Evening was falling, and a soft breeze cooled his forehead. 'Strange, really, to be a gentleman', he thought, 'Here I am, inconspicuous and modest. And yet I own all the DDT in the world, and I intend to do many good things with it. Tom Puss is in for a surprise. It's a pity he left in anger, but once I've done something noble ...' He fell silent and frowned. 'Hm,' he mused. 'It's easy to talk, but what *am* I going to do with the DDT? Hm. I could, of course ... No, I'd better ... what if ... er, or if I ... or, hm ... better not?' After a while, the worried businessman reached the Dark Forest, and his troubled gaze fell upon a little fellow who was bending over a plant with much concern. 'Good evening', he said kindly. 'Aren't the plants growing well? Oh well, life isn't easy. Sometimes we Top Dogs think we're alone in our troubles, but it's consoling to see that a humble peasant has his problems, too.'

'I'm not a humble peasant', the little fellow said coolly. 'I'm Pete Pastinake and I can hear the plants growing.'

'That's er, nice', Mr Ollie remarked, a bit abashed. 'Pleasant sound?'

'It depends', Pastinake said. 'Sometimes it sounds like honey, and sometimes as fuskus. But this is a bad sum-mer. I can't hear anything.'

'I can't either,' muttered Mr. Bumble, listening atten-tively. 'Why is that?'

'That's because of the yellow gnawer', the little fellow exclaimed angrily. 'Look, all the plants have been gnawed at!'

Mr Bumble and Pete Pastinake walked through the ravaged twilit meadow. The former was pleased, for he had found an excellent object for his good works; but the other wasn't so sure. 'What is deedeetee?' he asked suspiciously.

'Ah', Mr Ollie exclaimed, 'that's the stuff that exterminates insects – cockroaches and beetles and gnats and spiders – and everything! Helps immediately, you'll see. Just spray it around – and they're taken care of.'

'Impossible', said the little fellow. 'Spiders and gnats can't be sprayed at the same time.'

'But they can', maintained Mr Bumble, a bit put off. 'I'll prove to you that I can rid this meadow of vermin within a few moments.'

'No', the other insisted obstinately. 'It can't be done. The only way to fight the yellow gnawer is with what I've got here. Look.' He stopped by a low stone hutch and opened a little door.

Mr Ollie bent forward to see, and leaped back immediately. 'Aggh!' he exclaimed with disgust. 'Spiders! Big ugly spiders! Do you breed them, Mr Pastinake?'

'Yes', said the little fellow proudly. 'These are brown sneakers. They're hatched just in time. Now they can put an end to the gnawer plague before it becomes too bad. These sneakers are the yellow gnawers' biggest enemy.'

The spiders quickly spread out over the plants, in search of the beetles, and soon the meadow seemed still again. But, on the plants, a grim war was being waged. 'The battle is on', muttered Pete Pastinake with satisfaction. 'The brown sneakers always win, but they need some time …'

'Brown sneakers', Mr Bumble repeated in disgust. 'Dirty spiders! And if they win, we might very well be in for a spider plague! Bumblestone Castle will become full of cobwebs, and a gentleman won't be able to go for a stroll without getting creepy threads in his face. No, this is old-fashioned and unhygienic, if you understand what I mean. I've got something better.'

'There is nothing better', the little fellow said.

But Mr Ollie was already on his way. 'This matter must be left to me', he said to himself. 'This is my big chance to show what a Bumble can do with DDT.' With this in mind, he entered his house and marched up to the telephone.

'Good evening, Mr Oliver', said Joseph, looking up from his newspaper. 'There's a beetle plague in the plants, by your leave, sir. The Rumbledon City Courier says we're threatened by a crop failure. This is very deplorable, sir.'

'Nonsense!' Mr. Ollie exclaimed. 'I have the matter in hand! Let me get to the telephone, Joseph.'

Mr Bumble took the beetle plague firmly in hand. That same evening he gave his orders by telephone, and the next morning the results could be seen. When Pete Pastinake went to make his morning rounds to see if the brown sneakers were making progress, he was startled by the roaring of an airplane engine. It was a plane from the General Insect Extermination Service, and was leaving a thick mist of DDT in its wake. The dwarf covered his mouth with his hand and shrank back. 'What kind of gas is this?' he muttered palely. 'It makes the sound of bone grass … and I think I can also detect some skeleton herb.'

'Magnificent', Mr Bumble said, watching the sky not far from there. 'This shows what modern technology can do.'

'May I disturb you for a moment, if I may be so bold, sir', said his servant, Joseph. He looked hesitantly at the roaring plane and shouted over their noise. 'It's about the insects, by your leave, sir!'

'Yes!' Mr Ollie exclaimed. 'We've inexorably stopped the vermin in their tracks! Er, what is it you want, Joseph?'

'It's about the gnats', the faithful servant explained. 'In your bedroom, if you will allow me, sir. It's full of them – and they've become immune to my spray. Haven't you something better than DDT?'

Mr Ollie started wandering around aimlessly. The wind rustled through the dead plants, and the earth was covered with dead insects, their legs in the air. 'How horrible', Mr Ollie muttered. 'This once flourishing landscape has become a desert. Oh, what have I done?'

'You've disturbed the balance of nature', Tom Puss said.

'Disturbed the balance?' Mr Ollie repeated dully. 'It's much worse than that, young friend. I've exterminated the Brown Sneakers. The spiders, you know. They were the only ones who could destroy the beetles, if you understand what I mean.'

'But that's exactly what I mean', Tom Puss explained patiently. 'The only thing you can do now is to bring spiders here from an undevastated region.'

Mr Bumble pondered this. 'Hm. Bring in fresh spiders?'

he repeated. 'But that's it!' His face brightened. 'Of course!' he beamed. 'I could have thought of it myself if I hadn't been so preoccupied. I'm ready to do anything to remove all this barren misery!'

Just then they heard the roar of an automobile and the screeching of brakes. Mr Ollie turned with a start and saw Mr Amos Steinhacker wave to him from a large limousine. 'Hello, O.B.!' the oil king called heartily. 'Excellent work, old man! You've created a fine stretch of fallow land here! Ripe for industrialisation! My compliments! Can I do anything for you? Help me, and I'll help you. But first send away that little nobody over there.'

From the work of Marten Toonder (Translation courtesy of Toonder Studio's BV, Nederhorst den Berg).

oman

in Blue Reading a Letter

An Approach to Viewing Vermeer

A 'Vermeer', like a 'Rembrandt' or a 'Van Gogh', is something more than a painting. A 'Vermeer', whether it be a painting of a young girl in a turban, a woman with a watering can, a lady with a balance, or a music lesson, will bring associations with it that transcend any of these specific images. Hidden somewhere within an appreciation of it are memories of other impressions: the quiescence of a woman – deep in thoughts – reading a letter, the soft light effects that play across a woman adjusting her pearl necklace, or the delicate nuances of blues and yellows that transmit the serenity of a woman writing a letter.

Although the individual paintings are well-known, their cumulative impact is all the greater because the relationships underlying them reinforce and enhance such work. Vermeer's images, whether of a single figure lost in thought or of a quiet street scene, are intimate ones that remind us of moments or experiences in our lives so fleeting that we were hardly aware of their existence. Vermeer's genius was to capture their beauty and to transmit it to us in a way that we can relate to our own experiences.

Despite the intimacy of Vermeer's poetry, he does not seem to insert himself into his paintings. Unlike viewing a 'Rembrandt' or a 'Van Gogh', we are unaware of any personal struggles that may have affected his life or art. Part of the reason is certainly that Vermeer's life story is not well known, but the biographical questions that spring to mind when we look at a 'Rembrandt' or 'Van Gogh' do not even occur to us before a 'Vermeer'. We accept the strong, sturdy milkmaid as a figure who embodies the wholesomeness of Dutch life without asking who she was. Likewise, it does not seem crucial to know if the beautifully serene woman holding a balance is Catharina, Vermeer's wife. But, as with all abstract concepts, the reality of Vermeer's œuvre is somewhat more complex than the image of a 'Vermeer' would suggest. Paintings at either end of his œuvre do not fit into this comfortable niche, and a few well-known masterpieces like the *View of Delft* and the *Allegory of the Art of Painting* likewise have to be considered apart. In some of these exceptional paintings, moreover, Vermeer reveals aspects of his personality and character that are otherwise muted.

Trying to discover the essence of a Vermeer painting is akin to describ-

Johannes Vermeer, *The Milkmaid.* c.1658-1660. Canvas, 45.5 x 41 cm. Rijksmuseum, Amsterdam.

ing a sunset or reflections off a sparkling body of water; the description works only when it also takes into account the viewer's emotional relationship to the scene. While such discussions are by necessity subjective, they are nevertheless important in any analysis of Vermeer's works precisely because his paintings elicit such a response from the viewer.

In trying to find a framework within which to judge such reactions it is good to look more closely at the information Vermeer has provided for us in his paintings. He was an extraordinary craftsman who carefully conceived and structured his compositions to achieve the purity of expression he sought to convey. He had great sensitivity to optical effects found in the world about him, and translated these in his paintings through his use of light and colour. He mastered a wide range of painting techniques to allow his vision to take visual form. The mechanics of his painting techniques are, in fact, there to be assessed and analysed. It is also possible to examine the kind of changes in style and subject matter that occurred over the course of his career, as well as those more constant threads that he maintained within his approach to painting.

A particularly fascinating painting to approach in this way is one of Vermeer's most beautiful works from the mid-1660s, *Woman in Blue Reading a Letter.* In this painting we encounter an image so radiantly pure and simple in its elements, and so familiar in its subject, that we immediately empathise with the woman and accept her world as completely as our own. Yet we are also aware that this woman and her world are not exactly like reality. We approach the work with a certain reverence, partly because it was painted by Vermeer, but also partly because the image demands that response. It is a quiet world, without sound and without movement. We are drawn to the painting by the warmth of the light and the serenity of the image, but we are kept at a distance as well. The woman is so totally

Johannes Vermeer, *Girl with Pearl Earring.* c.1665. Canvas 46.5 x 40 cm. Mauritshuis, The Hague.

absorbed in her letter that she has no awareness that anyone has intruded upon her privacy. Seen in pure profile against a flat wall decorated only with a map of the seventeen provinces, neither she nor her environment welcome us into her physical or psychological space. Her pyramidal form, which is centrally placed in the composition, is partially concealed by the dark form of a table on the left and by a chair, turned slightly away from us, on the right. The physical barriers thus created effectively isolate her even though she is quite close to the viewer. A subtle tension exists in our relationship to the scene, one that pulls us back and forth as we subconsciously try to reconcile these conflicting signals.

By creating this psychological tension within the viewer Vermeer emotionally involves him in the painting and prepares him for the central focus of his work, the emotional response of the woman to the letter she is reading. He suggests her intense concentration subtly, without dramatic gesture or expression. The depth of her response, however, is clear in the way she draws her arms up tightly against her body, clasps the letter, and reads it with slightly parted lips. Vermeer is not interested in revealing the contents of the letter, or its origin, merely in that quiet moment when communication between the writer and the woman is at its fullest.

Vermeer captures that moment by creating an environment that echoes and reinforces it. A subtle light plays across the woman and the objects surrounding her, a light whose very presence helps establish the fullness of her privacy in the corner of a room for, by falling most sharply in the upper left, it implies the presence of a wall and window just outside the picture plane.

Johannes Vermeer, *Woman in Blue Reading a Letter.* c.1662-1664. Canvas, 46.5 x 39 cm. Rijksmuseum, Amsterdam.

The horizontal and vertical shapes of the table, chairs, and map surrounding her, their colours of blue and ochre, and their inner design patterns, both complement the static nature of the woman's pose and act as a foil for her intense concentration on the letter. The blue-black rod at the bottom of the map that passes directly behind the woman's hands, for example, provides a visual accent to the letter she is holding. The map, its muted ochre tonalities echoing the flesh tones of the woman's head and the browns of her hair, forms a field against which her emotions are allowed to expand. Although Vermeer separates the head from the map by juxtaposing the woman's highlighted forehead with the dark tones of the cartouche, the patterns of rivers and inlets seem to flow from, and respond to, her own form.

Finally, the shapes of the white wall, the clearly articulated areas defined by the objects in the painting, visually bind together the various compositional elements. Vermeer has established three basic blocks of wall, balanced though not symmetrical: the one in the upper left, the one just in front of the woman, and the one behind her. These quite distinct shapes play an active role in the composition; they read as positive elements that help provide a framework for the figure. Their bold and simple shapes enhance the quality of stillness and tranquillity that pervades the scene.

Vermeer's *Woman in Blue Reading a Letter* seems so right in colour, theme and mood that it is hard to imagine any other compositional solution. Indeed, as in other of his paintings, one has difficulty imagining Vermeer at work, as an artist who somehow had to compose and make tangible an idea

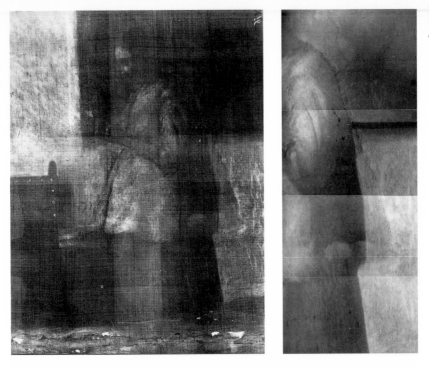

Infra-red reflectograph of *Woman in Blue Reading a Letter.*

X-ray of *Woman in Blue Reading a Letter.*

he had conceived in his mind. Part of our problem in visualising Vermeer's working procedure stems from a lack of available information. No drawings, prints, or unfinished paintings, indeed, no records of commissions offer clues to his intent or to aspects of his working process. No contemporary accounts comment on his work or his ideas. Our entire appreciation of Vermeer's achievement is focused on the end results of his extant paintings.

In recent years, however, it has been possible to look far more closely at the artist behind these paintings than ever before. Much information has come from the careful archival studies of John Michael Montias, who has unearthed a wealth of material about the relationships within Vermeer's extended family. New information about Vermeer's artistic procedure has also been gathered through a variety of technical examinations of the works themselves.

An x-ray of the *Woman in Blue Reading a Letter,* for example, reveals that the woman's jacket once flared out at the back, and perhaps also slightly at the front. The shape of the earlier design is visible in the x-ray because Vermeer started painting the white wall with a lead-bearing paint (lead white) around the blocked-in form of the jacket. An infra-red reflectograph shows many of these same changes, but also gives added information. The reflectograph works on the principle of heat absorption and picks up patterns of black or grey applied over a light ground. Thus the underlying jacket seen in the reflectogram must have been blocked-in in greys over the light ochre ground. In the reflectograph we can see that this original jacket had a fur trim along its bottom edge. He almost certainly changed the shape of the jacket to simplify the woman's profile and to enhance her statuesque character as she stands silhouetted against the back wall. Microscopic examinations give added information about the jacket. Vermeer used natural ultra-

179

marine for the blue of the jacket, which he painted very thinly. In the microscope it is thus easy to see the underlying paint layer. No additional colours underlie the woman's jacket, which means that the shape visible in the x-ray and reflectogram must represent a preliminary compositional stage before Vermeer began introducing local colour.

Vermeer's sensitivity to the optical effects of light and colour and his ability to transmit them in paint is one of the primary reasons why his images have the visual impact they do. Light effects in his paintings, however, are often not totally consistent. He used light and shade selectively for compositional reasons. In the *Woman in Blue Reading a Letter,* for example, the chair near the wall casts a shadow, or, more accurately, two shadows. A pronounced shadow also falls just below the map. The woman, however, who also stands near the wall, casts no shadow at all. Indeed, Vermeer emphasised her separateness by giving the wall immediately behind her a brighter tonality, as though her being radiated light rather than obstructed it. He even accentuated this effect by purposely softening the juncture of her form and the wall: he diffused the contour of her jacket with a light blue colour.

The woman, by not casting a shadow, exists in a different spatial and temporal framework than the objects surrounding her. While we can more or less determine where she is standing, we cannot measure her precise location. By casting no shadow she appears timeless, even though she exists within a recognisable interior space where shadows of objects in the room will change as the sun moves in its orbit. Though Vermeer has represented a moment in the woman's life, a moment of great privacy and intense concentration, the moment does not appear fleeting. It has a permanence that strengthens the psychological impact of the woman as she gazes at her letter. We are drawn to her image and held by it in ways that are not totally explicable, but that clearly have much to do with the way Vermeer has handled light, colour, and composition.

ARTHUR K. WHEELOCK, JR.

FURTHER READING

BLANKERT, ALBERT, *Vermeer.* New York, 1988.

MONTIAS, JOHN MICHAEL, *Vermeer and His Milieu: A Web of Social History.* Princeton, 1989.

NASH, JOHN, *Vermeer.* London / Amsterdam, 1991.

SLATKES, LEONARD J., *Vermeer and His Contemporaries.* New York, 1981.

SNOW, EDWARD A., *A Study of Vermeer.* Berkeley, 1979.

WHEELOCK, ARTHUR K., JR., *Jan Vermeer.* New York, 1988 (2nd ed. revised).

WRIGHT, CHRISTOPHER, *Vermeer,* London, 1976.

A special exhibition of Vermeer's paintings will be held at the Mauritshuis (The Hague) during the spring of 1996.

A

Naïve Engineer

Panamarenko's Art

Panamarenko is the Belgian who makes aeroplanes. Or are they works of art as well? If you ask him this question, he will give various answers or, more probably, no answer at all. He would like to be regarded as a 'savant'. Being an artist means nothing to him. Quite the contrary, in fact.

A perusal of his output – he has been working for about thirty years now – reveals fully-fledged machines, prototypes, test models and hordes of drawings. His creations cannot be categorised. With his own hands he pieced together an *Aeroplane (Six-Rotor Helicopter)* driven by means of bicycle pedals worked by the pilot himself. Then came the *Portable Air Transport* project: a portable, one-man flying system with internal combustion engine and propellers; various models were tested with limited results. He began a series of investigations into a closed system for accelerating matter, based on the movement of an electron around the atomic nucleus. Some sixteen scale models – the *Accelerators* – serve to illustrate the principle. Then there was the *Piewan:* a small, one-man, boomerang-shaped aeroplane, built entirely of aluminium and studded with propellers arranged in a swallow formation from its nose to the tips of its wings.

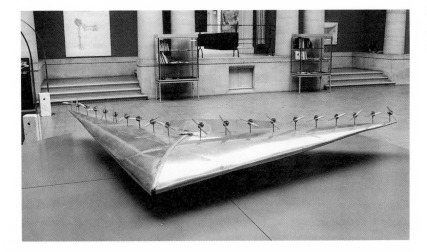

Panamarenko, *Piewan.*
1975. Museum van Hedendaagse Kunst, Ghent (Photo Heirman Graphics).

Panamarenko,
Meganeudon III. 1973.
Private Collection
(Photo Heirman Graphics).

Or perhaps you would prefer a giant dragonfly? The tail of the *Meganeudon II* can be folded up like a harmonica and the machine runs on large bicycle wheels. The wings, made of Japanese silk and balsa wood, are feathery and strong; they vibrate at very high speed because of a spring mechanism copied from the flight of the actual insect. Again it is propelled by means of pedals. A more recent series is based on the theme of a 'Journey to the Stars': a *Flying Carpet* – which floats above the surface on the Earth's magnetic field –, the *Flying Cigar Called Flying Tiger I*, and an *Adamski Saucer* for your interstellar travels.

Another recent design, the *Rucksack Helicopter*, is now available in various models, each equipped with the specially-designed *Pastille Engine.* Here you put your arms through the armholes, slip the harness over your back and fasten the safety buckle. Your are propelled into the air by means of blades and two mouth-like heads (made of transparent polyester). It is a perfect fit for the human body.

Work after work hovers between persuasiveness (because of the many details) and dream. Some are phantasmagorical structures, some absurd ideas, some are as light as a feather. But each of them leaves you with misgivings: could this machine lift a person into the air? – yes perhaps, but it would have to be someone very slight in build. And if this one can't, could one of the others? The misgivings do not leave you, they creep up the wires and ropes, steal across bicycle pedals and saddles, over adhesive tape and ribbon and along endless hinges and joints. Until they become irrelevant.

They say that Panamarenko's aeroplanes do not fly. But he couldn't care less what others say. For him they fly. Project after project is committed to paper, is built and rebuilt in test models or prototypes that result in even more new designs. Drawing and calculating come easily to him. He even produced a book: *The Mechanism of Gravity, Closed Systems of Speed Alterations; Insect Flight, Seen from inside the Body of the Insect; The Helicopter as a Potential Winner; 'U-Kontroll III', An Improved Airplane driven by Human Power; 'Polistes', Rubber Car with Jet Propulsion; 'Scotch-Gambit', The Design of a Large Fast Flying Boat.* In it Panamarenko draws and comments on the development of all these various projects.

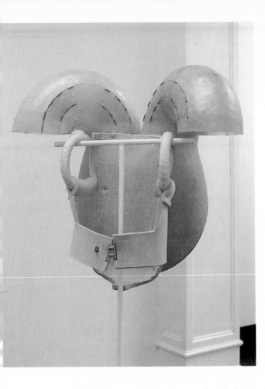

Panamarenko, *Rucksack Helicopter*. 1987. Museum van hedendaagse Kunst, Ghent.

Panamarenko, *Snow*. 1966. Museum van Hedendaagse Kunst, Ghent.

It brought together years of activity and appeared simultaneously in English and German.

Born in Antwerp in 1940, Panamarenko was first heard of in the company of a handful of artist friends who were involved in street campaigns which they themselves described as *Happenings*. That was back in the sixties when ideas blew over from America to Amsterdam, and from there drifted down to Antwerp. They took the form, for example, of Jasper Grootveld, of anti-advertising campaigns on the streets and the 'Provos'. The artists tried to make their activities 'more artistic and also more poetic' by incorporating snippets of poetry by the expressionistic poet Paul Van Ostaijen, but to no avail. The end result of the many *Happenings* was 'disruptive' groups of Provos and continual police intervention.

According to Panamarenko, these were no more than a series of 'fringe events', to which he contributed episodes like driving round in a Cadillac in a thick cloud of smoke, a seat of piled-up blocks of ice on the Henri Conscienceplein in the city centre, gigantic spinning tops made of bamboo and transparent plastic and powered by a motor, etc. Just as important, and dating from the same period, is the description of his profession in his passport: balloonist (because multimillionaire was not accepted), and a plan to cover the whole Palace of Fine Arts in Brussels with artificial snow during its occupation.

Out of all this – and above all 'to get shot of those problems with the police' – came the foundation of the Wide White Space gallery in Antwerp in 1966. It was to draw the international elite of visual art to Antwerp in the years that followed. Panamarenko and Marcel Broodthaers (though from Brussels) spent a good deal of their time here. It was also here that Panamarenko and Joseph Beuys met.

An indoor space. For Panamarenko that meant a place where he could develop the 'new materials' that so attracted him, and above all exploit their 'special potential', in a series of objects which left little doubt as to their status as works of art. A tree covered in artificial snow was taken into the gallery: that did not work. Then add a pair of Wellington boots, a leather school bag, a small pile of papers and *Snow* was created. Panamarenko had long ago lost interest in making 'sculptures'. He had discovered plastic, foam rubber, engines, processes, movements and forces and the relationships between forces and material.

At that time he made mainly wasters or replicas. He reconstructed *Crocodiles* – with a tank like the one in Antwerp Zoo – made of plastic stitched together, filled with sand and covered with net. The tank was made of tiles and cardboard. *Ducks* was made out of wax and linen. Battery-operated fluffs of cotton wool – *Moths in Cane* – hurtle around inside a little upright stack of straw. *Bags* are no more than cotton bags with seaweed soaked in polyester. The sprinkling system used at the royal greenhouses in Laken had served as the model for the wooden platform and rubber hosepipes above the bags.

Panamarenko's experiments with materials continue. He is still busy with their 'special properties', with what they can do. By combining those materials and those forms and principles to produce something like, let's say, an aeroplane, he succeeds in distancing himself from everything that one might expect from art and from other areas of social activity. In exactly the same way as exponents of pop art were fascinated by what was new, Panamarenko adopted a new graphic vocabulary from the world of advertising. And by borrowing from it, it proved possible to avoid what one might expect of a painting (paint, touch, emotion, etc.).

It was because of his 'derivations' from subjects and concepts from

Panamarenko, *Crocodiles.* 1967. Museum van Hedendaagse Kunst, Ghent.

Panamarenko, *Aeromodeller*. 1969-1971. Museum van Hedendaagse Kunst, Ghent.

science and technology that the German artist Joseph Beuys came to describe him as a 'naïve engineer'. It is an expression which serves as the perfect alibi for Panamarenko. He need answer no further questions.

Panamarenko showed his first aeroplane to friends (not to the public) on Monday 21 July 1969 at 5.30 in the morning during a champagne breakfast organised by the group to mark the televised moon landing of Apollo II. The venue was a rented house in the Beeldhouwersstraat in Antwerp which they used for activities which could not take place in the gallery 'simply because they were not commercial'.

The same house in the Beeldhouwersstraat, which closed its doors to the group a few months later, served as the first construction site for what was till then Panamarenko's most ambitious project: the airship *Aeromodeller*. Its construction was completed in 1971, in style: as a contribution to the open-air statuary exhibition *Sonsbeek-buiten-de-perken* in Arnhem in the Netherlands, Panamarenko undertook to fly the more than 11 meter-long zeppelin to the exhibition park. The attempt was abandoned because the airship proved impossible to steer. Then there was the competition organised by the Englishman Henry Kremer. To qualify, candidates had to cover a distance of 800 m. at a height of 3 m. with a flying machine driven by human power, describing a figure of eight in the air between two points. In 1972 Panamarenko tried his luck with the *U-Kontrol III:* grass-green, pedal-driven, bicycle chain, featherweight and made of balsa wood, metal and plastic. Problems of humidity prevented the machine from leaving the ground.

ILSE KUIJKEN
Translated by Alison Mouthaan-Gwillim.

FURTHER READING

THEYS, HANS, *Panamarenko*. Tervuren, 1992.

'A

sacred duty'

The Holocaust in Dutch Historiography

The 'Final Solution' hit Jews in the Netherlands particularly hard: 100,000 of the 140,000 Jews living in the Netherlands were murdered. Expressed as a percentage, over 70% became victims of the German extermination machine. The percentage was markedly lower in other Western European countries – in Norway and Belgium about 40%, in France 25%, while in Denmark nearly all the 8,000 Jews managed to escape deportation.

In the light of the markedly high Dutch percentage it is interesting to consider how historiography has reacted to the murder of the Jews. This article is confined to the work of three historians, Abel Herzberg (1893-1989), Loe de Jong (1914-) and Jacques Presser (1899-1970), all of them Dutch Jews who survived the Holocaust.

Herzberg initially went into hiding, but was later deported via the Wester-

Departure from Westerbork to Auschwitz (Photo Rijksinstituut voor Oorlogsdocumentatie, Amsterdam).

bork transit camp to Bergen-Belsen. He and his wife survived the war there. Returning to the Netherlands they were reunited with their three children, who had stayed in hiding. De Jong and his wife managed to escape to England in 1940. There, cut off from the rest of his family, who remained in occupied Holland, he spent the war years working for *Radio Oranje,* the broadcasting service of the Dutch government in exile. When he returned to the continent he found that nearly all of his family had been murdered. Presser went into hiding just in time, but his wife was picked up when she ventured out of the house. She was murdered in Sobibor.

Herzberg, De Jong and Presser have made important contributions to the historiography of the murder of the Dutch Jews during the Second World War. How did they approach this complex and overpowering subject? What follows is a broad brush impression of their historical writing about the Holocaust and also discusses the way in which they dealt with the activities of the Jewish Council. How did these three historians handle their emotional and moral involvement in the subject? And finally, what contribution have they made to helping the Dutch to come to terms with the full horror of what actually happened during the war?

In 1950 the first scholarly study of the murder of the Jews appeared. It was entitled *Chronicle of the Persecution of the Jews 1940-1945* (Kroniek der Jodenvervolging 1940-1945) and its author was Abel Herzberg. In the same year the Netherlands State Institute for War Documentation, which had been set up in 1945, commissioned the historian Jacques Presser to write a history of the persecution of the Jews in the Netherlands. Then five years later, in 1955, the then Minister for Education and Science asked Loe de Jong to write the history of the Kingdom of the Netherlands in the Second World War.

Herzberg's *Chronicle* is held by some to be the first historical work of literary merit on this subject in the Netherlands. It was among the earliest historiography on the Holocaust both nationally and internationally. The commissions given to Presser and de Jong are unique. In no other Western European country were such works commissioned. How can we explain this exceptional situation? It seems probable that Dutch society was shocked in a different way or more fundamentally than other Western European countries by the results of the German occupation. The extermination of more than 70% of Dutch Jews was a severe loss for the Netherlands, both in moral and physical terms. The shock to the Netherlands may have been all the greater because the Jewish population was relatively closely integrated into prewar Dutch society. Anti-semitism was not unknown in the Netherlands, but there was certainly no question of the kind of strong antisemitic tendencies to be found for example in France.

Abel Herzberg (1893-1989) (Photo by Bert Nienhuis).

In his *Chronicle* Herzberg gives a good overview of the vicissitudes of the Jews in the Netherlands during the war years, using a sober but harrowing style. This *Chronicle* has stood the test of time remarkably well; in 1978 the work was republished virtually in its original format 'because the general picture it gives of the persecution of Jews in this country corresponds to the reality'.

Herzberg defended the Jewish Council, just as he had spoken in defence of Bram Asscher, one of its two Presidents, when he and his co-President, David Cohen, were prosecuted by the Dutch legal authorities in 1947. The

Jewish Council had been set up in the Netherlands in 1941 under the German occupation as an organisation whose function was to implement the regulations laid down by the Germans. Herzberg stressed the need to understand the position in which the Jews found themselves in the war years. In his opinion, at the time that the Jewish Council was set up the view that it might 'avoid something even worse' had some validity.

Herzberg, who had been active in the Zionist movement before the war (from 1934 to 1939 he was chairman of the Dutch Zionist League) set what happened during the war explicitly in the perspective of Jewish history. So he considered that the Jewish Council was necessary to set the Jewish population of the Netherlands 'firmly in its place in Jewish history'. He thought it a positive factor that the Jewish Council had addressed itself to spiritual values: *'a historic task, which in earlier times and in other countries had been done over and over again and had contributed to the survival of the Jewish people. (...) Inwardly there was no surrender and that is of the utmost importance when you come to pass judgment on the actual conduct of the Jewish Council.'* During the occupation Herzberg himself had contributed to the spiritual resistance of Jews in the Netherlands. He was one of five editors of the *Joodsche Weekblad* (Jewish Weekly), the successor to *De Joodsche Wachter* (The Jewish Guardian), the paper of the Dutch Zionist League. In Bergen-Belsen, where in an attempt to maintain a minimum of order the inmates set up a court, he filled the role of public prosecutor.

Despite the huge number of Jewish victims, Herzberg thought that Judaism had not been defeated. 'To draw conclusions', he wrote, 'you need to do more than just count the corpses'. Herzberg saw in the foundation of the state of Israel not just the proof of unbroken Jewish vitality and the perpetuation of a principle, but also a condition for the Jewish fighting spirit. He closed his *Chronicle* with a reference to the state of Israel, founded in 1948: 'Here beginneth a new book of chronicles.'

The next milestone in Dutch historiography on the murder of the Jews was the publication in 1965 of *Ashes in the Wind. The Destruction of Dutch Jewry.* (Ondergang. De vervolging en verdelging van het Nederlandse Jodendom 1940-1945), commissioned by the Netherlands State Institute for War Documentation and written by the historian Jacques Presser. *Ashes in the Wind* is the title of the English translation, which was published in 1968. A year later the same translation also appeared in the USA under the title *The Destruction of the Dutch Jews.* Twenty years had passed since the end of the war. In 1961 the trial of Adolf Eichmann had taken place, and had attracted much attention in the Netherlands as well as elsewhere; Abel Herzberg was among those who went to Jerusalem to cover the trial as a journalist. An additional factor was that in the years leading up to the publication of Presser's book television had confronted many Dutch people with the murder of the Jews, for Loe de Jong had produced and presented a 21 part series entitled *The Occupation* (De bezetting, 1960-1965).

After the Eichmann trial and the TV series, *Ashes in the Wind* fell on fertile soil. It is no exaggeration to say that its two parts had the impact of a bomb. In a commemorative address after Presser's death in 1970 De Jong said: 'I don't believe that a historical work has ever appeared in our country whose dramatic *impact* can be compared to that of Jacques Presser's.' In eight months it sold 150,000 copies. For the first time the Dutch public appeared fully to realise the extent and the depth of the catastrophe wrought in the Netherlands by the destruction of the Jews.

Because Presser had chosen in his account to let the victims 'speak for themselves', the reader was mercilessly confronted by their suffering. In the foreword Presser spoke of *'a call to speak up for those who, doomed to eternal silence, could make themselves heard only here and now, this time only. The earth should reverberate with their lament, their complaint for one more time. (…) They had no one else but the historiographer to pass on their message. We think that we should not avoid speaking of a sacred duty.'* This was indeed no small task for a man who had himself emerged from the war so badly scathed.

Presser's work made a deep and indelible impression on many readers, among them members of a new generation which had in the meantime grown old enough to ask questions about the occupation period. The emotional way in which Presser told the story of the destruction of Dutch Jewry and the accusations in his book were not lost on the public. As De Jong rightly remarked in the commemoration address I have already mentioned, Presser held a mirror up to the reader: 'Behold, this happened in the Netherlands and, tacit reproach: This you have tolerated – you, Jewish leaders, you, Dutch authorities.' The reaction was an almost collective sense of at least passive guilt.

Portrait of Jacques Presser (1899-1970), taken from his identity card (Photo Rijksinstituut voor Oorlogsdocumentatie, Amsterdam).

Loe de Jong (1914-), working for *Radio Oranje* in London (Photo Rijksinstituut voor Oorlogsdocumentatie, Amsterdam).

While Herzberg had given an important place in his *Chronicle* to Jewish cultural and spiritual life, Presser placed more emphasis on the supposed class politics of the Jewish Council. Whereas Herzberg defended the formation of the Jewish Council and stressed its value as the representative body of the Jewish community itself, Presser saw it largely as the body which implemented German decisions. He spoke of 'collaboration' and compared the two chairmen to the captain of the Titanic: '*But if the Presidents liked to see themselves as captains of sinking ships, they should have remembered the captain of the Titanic who did not take to the boats – but perished in the waves. In May 1943 the Presidents of the Jewish Council agreed to supply the list the Germans had demanded of them – much against their own will and fully aware of the monstrous nature of their task. The writer must put on record that among the 7,000 names, two were conspicuous by their absence – those of Asscher and Cohen. Let that fact speak for itself.*'

Presser's book really touched the heart of the Dutch people. Reviews of it were marked by feelings of bewilderment, guilt and shame. Fellow historians however, were not unanimously enthusiastic about it. According to Presser's colleague I. Schöffer, who discussed the book in *Tijdschrift voor Geschiedenis* (Journal for History) in 1966, Presser tried too hard to distance the scientific side of his research from his history writing. Furthermore, he found the book too one-sided and too restricted both in its subject matter and its form. The crucial point of the criticism by Schöffer and others was that in his study Presser had chosen exclusively the perspective of the victims; as a result the systematic way in which the Nazis had conducted their programme of extermination was not clearly brought out. Also many critics thought that from a historiographical point of view Presser's book did not constitute an advance.

Criticism from Jewish circles concentrated on the central line of *Ondergang* (The title can be literally translated as 'downfall'). While Herzberg in conformity with Jewish history and tradition had made a clear connection with future events, everything in Presser's narrative led to the final destruction of the Jews. Herzberg was one of those Jewish critics who took exception to this pessimistic presentation of events.

In the twelve volumes of *The Kingdom of the Netherlands during the Second World War* (Het Koninkrijk der Nederlanden tijdens de Tweede Wereldoorlog), which appeared fairly regularly from 1969 on, Loe de Jong, Director of the Netherlands State Institute for War Documentation from its foundation in 1945 until 1979, paid considerable attention to the persecution of the Jews. In the first part, entitled *Prologue* (Voorspel), he began his discussion of the persecution of the Jews with Germany in the 1930s. In later parts, while reviewing the early history of the persecution and the origins of anti-semitism in both Europe and the Netherlands, he went back as far as the Middle Ages. He also looked at the prewar Jewish community in the Netherlands. Herzberg and Presser, on the other hand, both began their accounts with the German invasion. Furthermore, De Jong described at length and in painful detail what happened to the Jews who were deported after they arrived in the concentration camps. Presser had written relatively little about this aspect and De Jong wanted to remedy that. De Jong felt that Presser was just not capable of handling this aspect of the persecution.

As far as the Jewish council was concerned, De Jong left no one in any doubt that he thought this body 'was from the outset a tool in the hands of the Germans'. Contradicting Herzberg, he held that 'there was never any question of the Jews themselves really accepting the authority of the Jewish Council'. At various critical moments, wrote De Jong, large numbers of Jews disregarded the calls of the Jewish Council. So of the five to seven thousand people who were called up in May 1943 (De Jong is referring to the list which Presser used in his condemnation of the chairmen of the Jewish Council), only 500 actually obeyed that call. According to De Jong many Jews thought from the very beginning that the role of the Jewish Council was merely to help the occupying power in its work of persecution and deportation. Neither did De Jong think it just to pick out the two Presidents, Asscher and Cohen, as the only two guilty ones. De Jong's view was that Cohen had always been a more decisive influence than Asscher, and that the question of the collective responsibility of the Jewish Council as a whole also needed to be considered.

Herzberg had asserted in his *Chronicle* that the Jews needed the Jewish Council. De Jong thought that in making this assertion Herzberg had failed to take into account the reason why the Council had been founded in the first place. The fact that the Jews later turned to it in their despair was insufficient justification for its existence. De Jong's view was that the creation of the Jewish Council had made it easier to single out the Jews.

Interestingly, De Jong was prepared to tackle the question of whether or not things could have turned out differently. He thought that while giving a minimum of help to the enemy, the Jewish leaders could have tried to arrange for as many Jews as possible to go underground. Had they done so, his own parents – whom he does not actually mention here – might have accepted invitations to go into hiding. But the Jewish Council never considered a combination of legality and illegality. The Amsterdam leadership, wrote De Jong, lacked the necessary fighting spirit and nerve to take such risks.

According to the Israeli historian Saul Friedlander, who teaches history in both Tel Aviv and Los Angeles, the greatest problem facing the historian of the Holocaust is keeping a reasonable balance between strong emotional involvement and the intellectual objectivity required by this research. This was certainly true of Herzberg, De Jong and Presser; the more so in their case because they were themselves 'survivors'. Of the three authors it is Presser who is by far the most emotional in his writings. His work has been criticised for this but, steeped in emotion though it may be, it affects the reader as none of the others does. Despite the fact that it is never really possible to measure suffering one might nonetheless venture to suggest that of the three historians it was Presser for whom writing a history of the murder of the Jews was most difficult. Herzberg drew hope from his Zionist convictions and the formation of the state of Israel, where two of his children settled shortly after the end of the war. And De Jong, although he has devoted all of his working life to writing the history of the Second World War, was still able to stand back from his subject to some extent, since he was outside the Netherlands during the war years. He said during an interview about this: *'Had I as a Jew been in the Netherlands during the occupation and had to endure all that terror and misery I could never, given my character, have devoted the rest of my life to dealing with it. But I fled to*

England in fear for my life and the detachment that gave me enabled me to work on it.'

In the same article Friedlander warns against a premature closure of this subject, with attention paid to exclusively political decisions and administrative decrees, playing down the actuality of despair and the deaths of the victims. As it happens, you rarely find such a neutralising approach in the writing of Herzberg, De Jong and Presser. Because they regularly quote eyewitness accounts and do not shrink from describing what happened to them and their families, they have avoided writing a 'normal' historical account, in which the voices of the victims themselves are silent.

Of the three historians it is Herzberg who has used his own personal experiences least explicitly in his work. The opening pages of *Chronicle,* in which Herzberg describes his experiences and feelings on 15 May 1940, the day on which the Dutch Army capitulated, are openly autobiographical. Later on, however, references to himself in *Chronicle* are infrequent. But anyone who knows his account of the war, for example from his diary from Bergen-Belsen, *Land of Two Streams* (Tweestromenland), which appeared in the same year as *Chronicle,* will know that Herzberg is speaking from personal experience when he writes about arriving in Bergen-Belsen: *'Externally Bergen-Belsen did not appear any different from other concentration camps and everyone has read descriptions of those. But the dismal atmosphere that hung about the place, even when nothing special was happening cannot be understood by anyone who was not there; nor in truth can it readily be comprehended by those who were there.'*

Presser's *Ondergang* on the other hand is so much a personal testimony that as a reviewer rightly remarked in *Tijdschrift voor Geschiedenis* 'even the reader who does not know the author (…) will automatically be able through the book to *see* him, so personal is its style and tone'. Presser's descriptions of his own experiences are dramatic high points of his book. Thus he devotes several pages to a description of the raid on 6 August 1942 in which he and his wife were picked up. The passage about the screening process in which he and his wife escaped being selected makes the reader's blood run cold. Presser also describes how in desperation he called at the Jewish Council in a vain attempt to save his wife, who at that point was still being held at Westerbork.

De Jong too, perhaps imitating his colleague Presser, finds room in various places in his work for what are mostly short and matter of fact descriptions of his personal experiences during the war years. For instance, he described his flight to England and recounted how in London he 'knew' what the 'Final Solution' meant ('When I subsequently heard in July that my parents and younger sister had been taken away after the raid on 26 May I knew what that meant'). At the end of a chapter about what was done to help the Jews De Jong engaged in some self-criticism. He described how, at a time when the Jews were being deported from the Netherlands, he thought that the most useful thing he could do was to make 'a modest contribution to the final victory' through his work at *Radio Oranje.* 'I now think', he concluded, 'that I concentrated too much on the final victory and too little on my fellow Jews. I now think that I neither felt nor showed a sufficient sense of solidarity with them.'

Strikingly enough, the inclusion of one's own wartime experiences in the historiography of the Holocaust is, as far as I can see, an exclusively Dutch phenomenon. While Herzberg, De Jong and Presser did it almost as a matter of course, foreign colleagues and approximate contemporaries of this Dutch threesome, such as Raul Hilberg *(The Destruction of the European Jews,* 1961) and Léon Poliakov *(Harvest of Hate,* 1951) did not make use of their own wartime experiences in their historical writing.

Finally, have Herzberg, De Jong and Presser contributed to the process of coming to terms with the trauma of the Holocaust? That Dutch writers and historians had at least not failed when it came to transmitting knowledge of the Holocaust became clear in 1978, when the American television drama *Holocaust* was shown on Dutch television. As the historian Jan Bank observed in his inaugural lecture in Rotterdam in 1983, the Dutch television viewer was markedly less shocked and surprised by what was presented to him than were American and German viewers. For many Dutch people, the persecution of the Jews was 'living history', not some unknown phenomenon. That this was the case was in part at least attributable to the historical – and other – work of Herzberg, De Jong and Presser.

In the process of coming to terms, however, knowledge is only a first step. Only when what happened is integrated into a people's consciousness and leads to changes in behaviour is the end in sight. I would be claiming too much here if I asserted that where the Netherlands is concerned that process is complete. Any such claim would require further research. But a few observations from foreign researchers are relevant. In 1992 *Pinkas,* a series published by Yad Vashem about Jewish communities in countries under German occupation during the Second World War, produced its volume on the Netherlands. The authors were Joseph Michman (who after the war left the Netherlands for Israel), Hartog Beem and Dan Michman. In the chapter entitled 'Traumatic Recovery' ('Traumatisch herstel') they wrote *inter alia* that the behaviour of Dutch people during the persecution of Jews in their country contained much that was reprehensible. But they thought that the

The fence around the Jewish district in Amsterdam, 1941 (Photo Rijksinstituut voor Oorlogsdocumentatie, Amsterdam).

Netherlands differed from other countries occupied by the Germans in that there they were conscious of the fact that they had let the Jews down. Furthermore, Debórah Dwork, an American researcher, and Robert-Jan van Pelt, a Dutch historian working in Canada, recently drew attention to the fact that the Dutch reaction to the Holocaust was exceptional in that the Dutch had 'come to recognise and accept responsibility for their accommodation, complicity and collusion' in the murder of the Jews. In so far as this is indeed the case, the three historians whose work has been central to this article have undoubtedly made a substantial contribution to the formation of this consciousness.

The work of Herzberg, De Jong and Presser brought to an end the writing of history about the Holocaust by people directly involved in the subject. The murder of the Jews however, even nearly fifty years after the end of the Second World War, still attracts the attention of many scholars. Since the late 1980s in particular, a number of studies dealing with the Holocaust have appeared in the Netherlands. Most researchers in this field have no personal experience of the German occupation, very few of them are Jewish, they concentrate on particular aspects and their studies are in general characterised by a more factual approach.

It is Herzberg, De Jong and Presser who through their outstanding historical writing have forcefully drawn the attention of many Dutch people, and not only scholars, to the murder of Dutch Jews. In doing so they have rendered the Netherlands a great service.

CONNIE KRISTEL
Translated by Michael Shaw.

FURTHER READING

DWORK, DEBORAH and ROBERT-JAN VAN PELT, 'The Netherlands: German Persecution and Dutch Accommodation. The Evolution of the Dutch National Consciousness of the Judeocide', in: David Wyman (ed.), *The World Reacts to the Holocaust*. Baltimore, forthcoming.

FRIEDLANDER, SAUL, *Memory, History, and the Extermination of the Jews of Europe*. Bloomington / Indianapolis, 1993.

JONG, LOE DE, *The Netherlands and Nazi Germany* (3 Erasmus lectures with a foreword by Simon Schama). Cambridge, MA, 1990.

PRESSER, JACQUES, *Ashes in the Wind. The Destruction of Dutch Jewry*. Detroit, 1988.

n

Unfinished Chapter

The Second World War and the Holocaust

in Dutch Literature

On 10 May 1940 the Germans invaded the Netherlands. The Netherlands had tried in vain to avoid being involved in the Second World War by pursuing a policy of neutrality. There followed several days of heavy fighting. The royal family and the government withdrew to London and Rotterdam was bombed. The Netherlands capitulated on 15 May, and an occupation administration led by Seys-Inquart was imposed. At first, daily life continued more or less as normal, but gradually the German occupation tightened its grip and repression increased as Dutch society was organised along German lines. Artists and writers were forced to join the *Kulturkammer* (Chamber of Culture) and those who did not were forbidden to publish their work or give performances. The reaction of the Dutch was mixed. A small group began an active resistance, of which the illegal press was a part. Another section of the population collaborated with the Germans. The title 'collaborator' hides a multitude of sins, ranging from treason through endorsement of fascist organisations, working for the Germans, to artists who – in order to survive – joined the Chamber of Cul-

The Second World War and the Holocaust are important themes in postwar Dutch literature, and form the main themes in the work of one particular group of writers. Interest in the theme of the Second World War has not diminished; literary works in which the war plays a role continue to be published, written by those who experienced the war and have only now begun to write. The so-called 'second generation', the children of victims, of the persecuted and of collaborators are writing about the war. Authors who were not personally involved have also chosen the war as a literary theme. In this article we shall discuss a number of well-known literary works from the Netherlands, taking literature in the broad sense: diaries and reminiscences as well as poetry, novels and stories. Flemish literature and literature dealing with the struggle in the Netherlands-Indies are outside the scope of this article.

In this literature, events which took place during and after the war are placed in a meaningful context. That context may be Christian, Jewish, communist, philosophical, humanist, national-socialist or psychological, or it may be that of personal myth or apparently objective realism. Within these contexts a trend is visible, one which shifts from positive to negative imagery, from the idealisation to the exposure of the resistance movement, from meaningful adaptation to relativisation. In the stories about the camps, the central theme is unspeakable suffering.

The Netherlands in wartime: resistance and collaboration

'It is the duty of every Dutch person to resist the Germans, however dangerous that may be.' Many resistance novels have been based on this thesis, among others those of Theun de Vries. In *The Girl with Red Hair* (Het meisje met het rode haar, 1956), De Vries portrays the law student Hanna Schaft, who joins a resistance group. Her heroism and patriotism is apparent in the way she carries out many dangerous missions, but shortly before liberation she is captured and executed. Hanna S. is the first-person narrator in the novel. She tells of her awakening communism and anti-fascism; she

ture. Resistance and collaboration have been referred to as being 'right' and 'wrong' respectively, but the sharp distinction expressed by those terms has subsequently been criticised. The majority of the population tried to make the best of the situation and, as far as possible, to lead normal lives. After September 1944 the South of the Netherlands was liberated by the Allies. It was not until 5 May 1945, after the hunger-winter in the west of the Netherlands, that the Germans capitulated and the rest of the country was liberated. Of all social groups the Jews suffered most. The implementation of German race laws isolated them and excluded them from everyday life until the deportations began in July 1942, which then continued until September 1943. The Jews were taken first to the transit camps of Westerbork and Vught, and from there to the extermination camps of Auschwitz-Birkenau and Sobibor or the internment camps at Bergen-Belsen or Theresienstadt. A small section of the Jewish population were able to save themselves by going into hiding. Of the 140,000 Dutch Jews, some 100,000 lost their lives.

Hendrik N. Werkman, *Prison Camp for Hostages, St Michelsgestel* II. 1942. Hand printed. 65.5 x 50 cm. Gemeentemuseum, The Hague.

joins a workers' resistance group and falls in love with Hugo. After his death her resistance against the Germans intensifies. Her thoughts just before her execution reflect the central idea of the novel: *'There can be nothing in common between my murderers and myself (...) I die, but the spring and the sun remain untarnished. The Netherlands will be liberated. (...) I cry out to you. To everyone. The fascists extinguish my eyes and my breath, and my feet will remain in the beach grass.'* Her very last thought is 'I was a communist'. *The Girl with Red Hair* was made into a film in 1980, as many other war novels have been. The film, with its dull, grey-green tints, accurately reflects the atmosphere of war (as Egbert Barten pointed out in an essay on the Second World War in Dutch cinema). In the film, however, the political aspect is toned down while the theme of personal conflict is given more emphasis:

Hanna S. is not driven by political motives, but by emotions, and De Vries' emphasis on Hanna S. as a communist was omitted from the film. In *February. A Novel from the Occupation in 1941* (Februari. Roman uit het bezettingsjaar 1941, 1968), De Vries gives a detailed picture of the rising against the Germans in Amsterdam in February 1941, in protest against their first anti-Jewish activities. De Vries, himself a former member of the Resistance, puts the Resistance in a communist perspective with Hanna Schaft's anti-fascism and the role of the communist party in the February strike.

The Resistance is not the only subject to be treated. In *For a Lost Soldier* (Voor een verloren soldaat, 1986) Rudi van Dantzig paints an autobiographical picture of a young boy placed with a fisherman's family in the country during the war. The novel is at the same time a novel of war and of psychological development, relating how the boy Jeroen adapts to his new surroundings, how lonely he remains, and how, gradually, another boy from Amsterdam comes to occupy his daydreams and fantasies. A Canadian soldier seduces Jeroen during the liberation. The novel closes with his confused feelings of shame and desire, a problematic return to his parents, an anxious search for the soldier in newly-liberated Amsterdam, and the subsequent suppression of his homo-erotic experiences.

Literature sometimes questions the idea of a universal Dutch resistance to the Germans during the Second World War. The most important examples are *Pastorale 1943. A Novel from the Time of the German Occupation* (Pastorale 1943. Roman uit de tijd van de Duitse overheersing, 1948) by Simon Vestdijk, and *The Dark Room of Damocles* (De donkere kamer van Damocles, 1958) by W.F. Hermans. Vestdijk portrays the members of a resistance group who murder a collaborating Dutchman wrongly suspected of setting fire to a safe house. The motives of the resistance workers are not very noble and they are portrayed as a bunch of amateurs. Coincidence rather than conscious choice determines who collaborates and who does not. In Hermans' novel the insignificant Osewoudt carries out resistance work under the orders of an invisible *doppelgänger*, the officer Dorbeck. After the war, however, when Osewoudt is accused of treason, he is unable to prove

The Girl with Red Hair, a film by Ben Verbong (1980).

that Dorbeck ever existed. Osewoudt represents Hermans' view of man and reality. A person's actions are determined by subconscious motives; the wartime situation of fighting and chaos is, in fact, the norm. Truth and ethical values are simply a veneer. The novel is considered to be a high-point of postwar literature and has been made into a film by Fons Rademakers under the title *Dead Ringer* (Twee druppels water, 1963).

The treatment of the theme of good and bad (i.e. non-collaborators and collaborators) is increasingly focusing on the collaborators: what motivated the collaborators, and how bad were they really? Literary writers tried to understand the collaborator long before historians attempted to do so. Literature is proving itself to be a medium within which painful aspects of the war, too, can be explored. *A Lamb to the Slaughter* (Montyn, 1982) is a documentary novel by the author Dirk Ayelt Kooiman, based on conversations with the visual artist Montyn. Montyn, wanting to escape his narrow middle-class environment, serves with the German army and navy and experiences unthinkable horrors. After the war he is unable to adapt to a normal life. He repeatedly gives in to irrepressible urges for adventure, whether it be in wartime Korea, or leading evacuations of children in Vietnam.

Repression, hiding and deportation

The depiction of the fate of those in hiding, and of the deportees, is an important aspect of the war in Dutch literature. Gerard Reve's novel *The Decline and Fall of the Boslowits Family* (De ondergang van de familie Boslowits, 1946) is well-known. Without ever mentioning the word 'Jew', the novel shows how, slowly, almost imperceptibly, but no less effectively, the net closes around a Jewish family. Simon, the first-person narrator, is a friend of the Boslowits family. When war breaks out he hopes it will be an exciting time, but his opinion is radically altered by what happens to the Boslowits family. He hears from Mother Boslowits that acquaintances have committed suicide, that her son is being harassed and that she is no longer allowed to visit her husband in hospital. In vain Simon tries to help by fetching a doctor's letter which states that Father Boslowits is seriously ill. The family is 'taken away' and the father is put in a safe house but commits suicide.

Marga Minco's *Bitter Herbs: A Little Chronicle* (Het bittere kruid, 1957) views events from a Jewish perspective. The central character soberly recounts how members of her family are forced to move house and wear the yellow star, how they receive guidelines for 'the departure' and are taken away. When this happens to her own parents she manages to escape, staying in a succession of safe houses. After the war her uncle waits every day at the tram-stop for the family to return, but she has no such hope. No one will return.

Gerard Reve (1923-) in his young days.

The theme of going into hiding has produced several moving literary works. In his volume of poems *Orpheus and Ahasuerus* (1945) the historian Presser gives an account of how he came to terms with the death of his beloved, who was taken by the Germans. His poetry is an unusually detailed examination of the emotions he experiences: guilt, desire, grief to the point of self-entreaty that it be over, and the deception of control.

The Diary of Anne Frank (Het achterhuis, 1946) became world famous. In it, Anne tells her imaginary friend Kitty of the claustrophobic atmosphere in their safe house, of the petty arguments, the happy moments; all against the background of the evil historical reality. Andreas Burnier chose a completely different mode of expression in *The Boys' Hour* (Het jongensuur, 1969). In short chapters in which the chronology is reversed, a girl tells of her experiences from the time of going into hiding until the liberation (in the text, the liberation comes first). The child is intellectually precocious, and this means that she has problems adapting. She is surprised by the environments in which she finds herself (traditional Christian and orthodox Marxist): how can they all claim to be right? In Burnier's novel, as in Van Dantzig and Anne Frank, an important sub-theme is developing sexuality, highlighted by the experience of war.

The camps

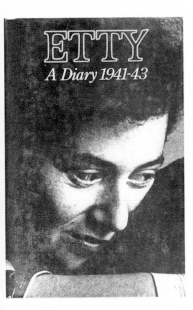

1981 saw the publication of the wartime diary of Etty Hillesum. Before this, *Two Letters from Westerbork* (Twee brieven uit Westerbork, 1962) had already been published; the complete letters and diaries followed. In her diary Hillesum, in the words of the author of the preface, develops a 'counter-scenario'. Against the background of persecution and destruction a mystical consciousness of the unity of God and man develops in Hillesum, and with it a love of her fellow men, which prompted her decision to heed the summons to Westerbork and to go with her people to their common fate. 'One would like to be a plaster on many wounds' is the last line of her diary. The letters from Westerbork give a disconcerting insight into the transit camp, where many Jews such as Etty Hillesum began their journey to the German death camps. 'Yes, it is true, our last human values are put to the test' she writes, after describing the degrading coagulation of so many human beings in a camp that is too small. In the midst of all the suffering we sometimes hear her mystical consciousness: 'I am not fighting against you, my God, my life is one long dialogue with you.' In September 1943 she and her family were deported to Auschwitz.

The novel *The Night of the Girondists* (De nacht der girondijnen, 1957) by Presser, is set in the Westerbork camp. A few years later, Presser went on to write the important historical account of the destruction of the Jews in the Netherlands, *Ashes in the Wind* (Ondergang, 1965). Here, in *The Night of the Girondists* a young man, Henriques, tells his story while incarcerated in the punishment hut. Via his pupil Georg Cohn, he reports to the Jewish camp supervisor, who is Cohn's father. Supervisor Cohn knows only one law: each week one thousand Jews must be selected for transportation. If he does not do this, someone else will. Henriques goes to work for Cohn, selling his soul to save his skin; he thus becomes familiar with the bewildering world of the camp where, after each week's transportation, a cabaret is performed. His acquaintance with Rabbi Hirsch leads him to realise his moral depravation and accept his Jewishness. As Hirsch is boarding the train, he stumbles. Henriques helps him, thereby revealing himself to Cohn as just like any other Jew and sealing his own fate. The novella contains a great many literary references: the departure of the train is described as a tragedy with five acts, and the camp as Dante's Inferno.

The charming title *A Childhood* (Kinderjaren, 1978) conceals the gruesome experiences of a child in Bergen-Belsen. Jona Oberski depicts deportation, life in a camp, and liberation through the eyes of a small child. A child egged on by the older children to stick out its tongue at the Germans, not realising the danger; a child who is put with the older children after his father's death and, with them, searches for the body of his father among the piles of corpses in the mortuary. It is normal for a child to fight for a place in its peer group, but not amid death and the threat of death. His exhausted mother dies from a contagious disease after the liberation of the camp. Will this child ever be able to lead a normal life again?

One of the poets who chose the Holocaust theme was Maurits Mok, in his collection *Background* (Achtergrond, 1965). In the poem 'Under the skin' ('Onderhuids') the poet tells how the suffering of the Jews haemorrhages inside him 'how they called out in vain, shrank from their own voices until they crawled worm-like over the ground', and how trees, clouds and stars hung silently over their despair.

After the war

Dutch literature and literary life are affected to a large extent not only by the Second World War itself, but also by its aftermath, the process of coming to terms with the trauma of the war, and the effect of this on postwar life. Sometimes controversies arise; as, for example, after the filming of *Bitter Herbs* in 1985. In the film the Jewish main character has a friend whose parents are collaborators. An improper dramatisation? In the eyes of Marga Minco most certainly, but not in the eyes of the filmmakers.

In the late sixties, Friedrich Weinreb caused a stir with his three-volume work *Collaboration and Resistance. An Attempt at Demythologisation* (Collaboratie en verzet. Een poging tot ontmythologisering, 1969). Weinreb is a Jew who, during the war, played what Presser has described as a 'strange and improbable game'. Weinreb compiled lists of Jews who should have been deported, but whose deportation could be avoided because they had a prospect of emigration. The Jewish Council accepted the lists. Weinreb's life is certainly full of improbabilities: arrest, liberation, collaboration with the Germans, and hiding. After the war he was arrested and sentenced for betraying innocent people to the Germans. The writer Renate Rubinstein encouraged him to publish his memoirs. She accepted Presser's interpretation that Weinreb served as a scapegoat for the shortcomings of countless non-Jews. W.F. Hermans argued the opposite case: he judged Weinreb guilty of treachery. The results of a government enquiry support his view. Nevertheless, the memoirs, which balance somewhere between fact and fiction, lies and truth, are an exceptional document.

In 'After 1945' (Na 1945), an autobiographical story in the anthology *Quarantine* (Quarantaine, 1993), Durlacher relates how, on returning to the Netherlands, he is confronted with a barrier of incomprehension on the part of his uncle and aunt, who survived the war. He is not allowed to talk about his experiences in the camps, only the experiences of his aunt and uncle are of interest. In others he senses embarrassment; they had thought him dead. With the help of an understanding notary he finds a room and returns to school. Only after some time does he dare to visit his parents' home, from which he and they were deported. He is not allowed to go inside. The next-door neighbour is wearing one of his father's suits. Grief and rage well up inside him. He must learn to live a normal life again, although his camp experiences have made complete adjustment impossible. In the title-story 'Quarantine', he is much older and able to revisit the Westerbork camp in an attempt to exorcise the past and be rid of his repressed emotions. The life and work of Durlacher are characterised by a number of Jewish experiences: childhood in Germany under the Hitler regime, escape to the Netherlands, deportation to Auschwitz via Westerbork, and the literary catharsis of those experiences. In the story 'Drowning' (De drenkeling) Durlacher tells how, while on holiday with his parents at Lake Garda, he sees two boys drowning as a storm is building up. He shouts for help but the adults are listening to the noisy loudspeakers. Only the waiter notices, and saves the boys. It is the day on which the Nazis murdered the Austrian Chancellor Dollfuss. The holiday ends in a menacing and threatening atmosphere. In the prologue to the book, 'We Knew Nothing' (Wij wisten van niets), the author goes in search of his former homes in Germany. The inhabitants claim that they knew nothing. The memories of Kristallnacht are still painfully real. But Durlacher concludes: the Germans should have known. They were seduced into barbarities, or watched indifferently. 'And a few courageous ones, such as the waiter Fritz at Lake Garda, save a drowning person from the waves'.

Marga Minco's short novel *The Fall* (De val, 1983) is extremely well written; coincidence and misunderstanding make up the tragedy of Frieda Borgstein. She is to escape with her family to Switzerland, but their helper betrays them: the family walk into a trap. Frieda herself manages to escape: she slips on the stairs while fetching a piece of clothing. For years she keeps the family alive in her imagination, thereby justifying to herself her own existence. When, on her eighty-fifth birthday, she wants to treat the residents of her old people's home, she falls into a hole which, coincidentally, has been left unguarded at that moment. At her funeral, by coincidence, a

Forged identity card of Marga Minco (with bleached hair!), issued in the name of 'Finkje Kooi'.

civil servant replaces his colleague: it is the helper, who turns out not to have been a traitor: he had himself been betrayed. The flashbacks to the past in Frieda's mind and the build-up of tension are important structural characteristics in this novel.

Neither can the younger generation escape the war. *Night Father* (Tralievader, 1991) is a collection of some forty-odd sketches from the life of a family. The father of that family has been in a concentration camp. Some of the stories are told by the father, talking about the camp. But the author Carl Friedman shows above all how incomprehensible these stories are to the children, how they are affected by them but nevertheless try to understand their father. When his son is spruced up and ready to go to his first dancing lesson, this is a cue for the father to tell another camp story; he had suffered from the cold, and that same son then sat for a long time with his feet in the refrigerator in an attempt to feel what his father had felt. The female narrator is not allowed to join the Guides, as her friend has done, because the Scouts and Guides mixed with members of the Hitler Youth before the war. The father tells stories of cowboys and Indians as if they were the ss acquiring *Lebensraum*. Father has 'got the camp'; that's the way it is and this dominates family life to such an extent that one of his sons exclaims that it would have been better if he had stayed there.

The (impossibility of coming to terms with the) Holocaust is placed in a broader perspective in Leon de Winter's novel *La Place de la Bastille* (1981). The main character Paul de Wit wrestles with his fate as the only surviving member of a Jewish family; one who, moreover, has never known his parents. In coming to terms with this, Paul passes through various phases: suppression of the past, curiosity, daydreams in which he meets his parents, involvement with Israel and psychological instability. A photograph taken in Paris, in which the vague image of someone resembling Paul can be seen, and the fact that Paul may perhaps have a twin brother, lead to strong emotions, desires, dreams and compulsive but unsuccessful attempts to find the twin brother. The failed attempt to give meaning to a past experienced as meaningless has a general application. For Paul it is impossible to place historical facts in a meaningful sequence. History is senseless and without purpose. Important historical facts, such as the founding of Israel, are due to insignificant and coincidental events. It seems impossible to discover the truth, even in one's own life. We are not sure whether Paul really does have a twin brother, or whether the Paris photograph actually shows what Paul sees in it. De Winter's method of continuously giving snippets of information to the reader makes for an exciting novel.

But there are other themes than the Holocaust and its devastating effects to be found in Dutch literature. Much of the work of the writer Armando, who is equally renowned as a visual artist, is devoted to the war. In *The Street and the Bushes* (De straat en het struikgewas, 1988), a boy relates his 'autobiography' in a sober and staccato style; he has clearly been influenced by the war in his youth and tries to discover what happened: why the landscape, that witnessed everything, is guilty; why one person is good and another bad; why evil can be so beautiful and fascinating, and what the enemy really looks like. Art provides the only opportunity to undo the forgetting of the past resulting from the advance of time, which destroys everything in its path. In 1967 Armando and Sleutelaar caused a sensation with

the publication of *The SS* (De ss-ers), a series of interviews with Dutch men and women who had voluntarily joined the Waffen-ss.

In Harry Mulisch's successful novel *The Assault* (De Aanslag, 1982) we encounter many themes; it is considered a high point in his work. Mulisch, too, focuses on the problem of guilt and innocence. During the war two resistance fighters kill a collaborating Dutch police officer in front of a certain Mr Korteweg's house. Korteweg is afraid that his reptile collection will be destroyed and moves the body, dragging it in front of the Steenwijk house. He does not put the body in front of his other neighbours's house, where there are Jews in hiding. The Steenwijk house is burned down by the Germans. Only the son, Anton, is eventually spared. On various occasions during his life Anton is confronted with the past. He meets the son of the murdered policeman, the resistance worker who shot the policeman, the girl Korteweg whose father committed suicide out of guilt. Anton is preoccupied with the question who is guilty and who is innocent. Immediately after the war, the answers to such questions were simple and obvious. In later war novels, however, matters are more complicated. There is no definitive and satisfying answer.

D.H. SCHRAM
Translated by Yvette Mead.

FURTHER READING

DRESDEN, S., *Vervolging, vernietiging, literatuur.* Amsterdam, 1991.
SCHRAM, D.H. and C. GELJON (eds.), *Overal sporen. De verwerking van de Tweede Wereldoorlog in literatuur en kunst.* Amsterdam, 1990.

LIST OF TRANSLATIONS

DANTZIG, RUDI VAN, *For a Lost Soldier* (Tr. Arnold J. Pomerans). London, 1991.
DURLACHER, G.L., *Stripes in the Sky* (Tr. Susan Massotty). London, 1991.
DURLACHER, G.L., *Drowning. Growing up in the Third Reich* (Tr. Susan Massotty). London, 1993.
FRANK, ANNE, *The Diary of Anne Frank* (Tr. B.M. Mooyaart-Doubleday). London, 1989.
FRIEDMAN, CARL, *Night Father* (Tr. Arnold J. Pomerans). New York, 1994.
HERMANS, W.F., *The Dark Room of Damocles* (Tr. Roy Edwards). London, 1962.
HILLESUM, ETTY, *Etty. A Diary 1941-1943* (Tr. Arnold J. Pomerans). London, 1983.
HILLESUM, ETTY, *Letters from Westerbork* (Tr. Arnold J. Pomerans). London, 1988.
KOOIMAN, DIRK AYELT, *A Lamb to the Slaughter* (Tr. Adrienne Dixon). New York, 1986.
MINCO, MARGA, *The Fall* (Tr. Jeannette Kalker Ringold). London, 1990.
MINCO, MARGA, *Bitter Herbs: A Little Chronicle* (Tr. Roy Edwards). London, 1991.
MULISCH, HARRY, *The Assault* (Tr. Claire Nicolas White). Harmondsworth, 1986.
OBERSKI, JONA, *A Childhood: A Novella* (Tr. Ralph Manheim). London, 1983.
PRESSER, JACQUES, *The Night of the Girondists* (Tr. Barrow Mussey). London, 1992.
REVE, GERARD, 'The Decline and Fall of the Boslowits Family' (Tr. J.S. Holmes & Hans van Marle). In: *Modern Stories from Holland and Flanders* (ed. Egbert Krispyn). New York, 1973.

A

Unity of Opposites

The Paradoxical Oeuvre of Harry Mulisch

In Dutch literature, the phrase 'the big three' has been used for the last twenty-five years to refer to the same three authors: W.F. Hermans, Gerard Reve and Harry Mulisch. Likewise, for a quarter of a century, the name of the Fleming Hugo Claus has been added when referring to 'the big four'. What the three Dutch authors have in common is that although they have been practitioners of virtually all genres, in the end it is their stories and novels to which they owe their reputation. It is also worth noting that Hermans has not lived in the Netherlands for some twenty years, and Reve too has spent long periods outside the country. Both have recently moved to Belgium. Mulisch, on the other hand, much the least Dutch of the three both in himself and in his work, has lived in Amsterdam for many years and shows no sign of exchanging his home city for any other.

Amsterdam is not where Harry Mulisch was born: he came into the world on 29 July 1927 in Haarlem, where he continued to live until he was thirty. His father, who came from the former Austria-Hungary, and his mother, daughter of a German Jewish banker, had met in Antwerp, and settled in Haarlem in 1926 after their marriage. With typical self-mockery, Mulisch calls himself a 'second-generation migrant worker'. Another much-quoted statement of Mulisch's on the subject of his international background can be found in his 'autobiography': *My Book of Hours* (Mijn getijdenboek, 1975). In it, alluding to the enormous difference during the war between his father's situation (he was a manager with a bank which had swindled Jewish Dutch people), and that of his mother's family, most of whom were deported to extermination camps, he says: 'More than having "lived through" the war, I *am* the Second World War.' It is no surprise then that the war plays a part in nearly all of Mulisch's books.

Mulisch is emphatically un-Dutch, not only as a person, but also in his work. The quotations above already demonstrate a form of irony which is used frequently by Mulisch, but seldom by the average Dutchman: self-irony, often in the form of hyperbole. Furthermore, and more significantly, there are connections to be made between Mulisch's individual works. Or, to put it more forcefully, Mulisch is consciously constructing an œuvre. His poetics are set down in the essay 'Self-portrait with Turban' ('Zelfportret

Harry Mulisch (1927-)
(Photo by Chris van Houts).

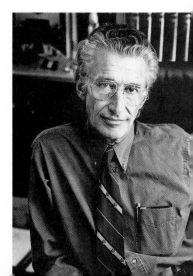

met tulband'), contained in the volume *Fodder for Psychologists* (Voer voor psychologen, 1961), from which the following passage has been taken:

'A writer's œuvre is, or should be, a totality, one large organism in which each component part is linked to all the others by countless threads, nerves, muscles, cords and canals, through which they remain in touch with one another and through which secret messages are sent back and forth. (...) This œuvre is the writer's new body, – a body which he has himself created, more tightly constructed, more lasting than the one his mother gave him. It is destined to outlive him when he departs this earth: not for eternity, but for some time. With this new body he will continue to breathe when he has long ceased breathing; long silent, he will yet speak through it.'

What are these 'threads, nerves, muscles, cords and canals', in other words, the constants in Mulisch's œuvre? The overarching constant is probably the 'unity of opposites'. Mulisch has indeed shown a great admiration for the fifteenth-century thinker, Nicholas of Cusa, whose name is linked with the concept of *coincidentia oppositorum*. This paradoxical unity can be captured in polarities such as extravert-introvert, exoteric-esoteric, clarity-obscurity, canonical-apocryphal. These polarities frequently occur in combination in Mulisch's work. To illustrate this, let us look at his two best-known novels: *The Stone Bridal Bed* (Het stenen bruidsbed, 1959) which earned him his place in the front rank of modern Dutch literature, and *The Assault* (De aanslag, 1982), his best-selling novel, much-translated and made into a much-acclaimed Oscar-winning film by Fons Rademakers.

The Stone Bridal Bed is a novel about ex-World-War-Two pilot Norman Corinth who, having taken part in the bombing of Dresden some ten years before, now returns to the town for a dentists' conference. During his stay in the rebuilt historic German town he has an erotic adventure with the attractive Hella Viebahn, the conference organiser, who had been an inmate of a concentration camp in the war years. At least as significant as Corinth's confrontation with Hella is that with his colleague Alexander Schneiderhahn, who passes himself off as a former camp tyrant and bully. But this is a deception, as Corinth later discovers. When Corinth beats him up, it is because of this lie. The novel ends with a Corinth who is evidently sliding into madness, setting fire to his own car after crashing it …

Summarised in this way, the book sounds like a 'classic' psychological novel with the theme of the (unsuccessful) working through of guilt feelings. This aspect has frequently been highlighted by commentators on Mulisch's work, and not wholly without reason, but the real theme of the novel is the paradoxical relationship between love and destruction (see the book's title). Mulisch stresses this relationship by reworking a multiplicity of literary and historical parallels in the novel. The most striking of these are the Homeric parallels: Dresden stands for Troy; Hella for Helen; Schneiderhahn, who is chased three times round a table, represents Hector. Corinth, then, is Achilles, but given his conquest of Hella, also a second Paris; and finally, Corinth has something of the archeologist Schliemann – Troy's treasure-hunter – about him. This series of parallels also has a counterpart on the stylistic level: at intervals in the text, there are three poetic fragments in Homeric style, complete with formulaic expressions and striking stock epithets. At first sight, these fragments contain flashbacks describing the bombing of Dresden; however, looked at more closely, they can also be read as a description of the sexual encounters between Corinth and Hella.

The Stone Bridal Bed is more than a psychological novel with multiple intertextuality: it is also a novel about poetics. This aspect is conveyed in the book through the use of symbols. The most emphatically poetical symbol is the house in Dresden where Corinth is staying: it is a labyrinthine entity, which does not appear to have been designed according to any specific plan, but to have grown up spontaneously. It is hardly surprising, then, that this extremely complex novel has in recent decades given rise to a large number of very divergent interpretations. There is even a word-by-word commentary on the novel: *The Key in the Cupboard* (De sleutel in de kast, 1989) compiled by J.A. Dautzenberg.

Compared with *The Stone Bridal Bed, The Assault* is at first sight a model of simplicity. Mulisch again takes as his starting-point a situation from the Second World War. The assault of the title takes place in Haarlem on a Dutch collaborator; it has particular consequences for the life of the main character, Anton Steenwijk. Through German reprisals, he loses his father, his mother and his brother, and the orphaned Anton is brought up by an uncle. It is years before he succeeds in working through the trauma of this early experience. Now for the majority of Dutch readers, and certainly those who remember the war, it is quite clear that in his novel, Mulisch is describing an attack which actually took place: the elimination of a traitor by the Haarlem resistance fighter, Hannie Schaft, who was shot for it by the Germans. Elsewhere in *The Assault,* Mulisch has worked other facts into his fiction, for example in the episode which takes place in the sixties. However, *The Assault* is not primarily about contemporary history, it is more a philosophical novel – one which deals with the question of guilt and atonement. In addition to this philosophical level, there are yet others: the psychological level (Anton is obviously an Oedipal type), and also, although it is well concealed, a poetical level. As in *The Stone Bridal Bed,* Mulisch uses symbols which refer to the making and understanding of his text. For example: Anton Steenwijk is an obsessive solver of crossword puzzles and cryptograms. This not only significant psychologically; it also tells us something of the way Mulisch wrote his novel, and how he would like it to be read – from both a horizontal and a vertical perspective, and with full awareness of the ambiguity of the language.

The symbolism which occurs throughout Mulisch's entire œuvre is taken in the main from two disciplines: alchemy and mythology. Mulisch himself commented on the principles of alchemy in *Fodder for Psychologists* mentioned above, and in the *magnum opus* of his essays: *The Composition of the World* (De compositie van de wereld, 1980). As for mythology, there are two figures from the ancient Greek world which we encounter remarkably frequently. Oedipus, of course, (a psychologist would immediately point out the writer's evident attachment to his mother) and Orpheus. These mythical figures have in common the fact that they have a special relationship to time: by marrying his mother, Oedipus has his life again – doubles it, as it were (note that the play which Mulisch dedicated to the Theban prince is called *Oidipous, Oidipous),* and Orpheus attempts with his Euridice to regain time past. Now it is also possible to view the creation of a work of art as a victory

Hugo Claus and Harry
Mulisch, posing as
SD officers (Photo © Ed van
der Elsken / Nederlands
Fotoarchief).

over all-annihilating time. A writer who, for example, produces a novel, wins a victory over oblivion, wins *his* Euridice out of the Underworld. The most obviously Orphic works in Mulisch's œuvre are the collection of stories *Paralipomena orphica* (1970) and the novel *Two Women* (Twee vrouwen, 1975), a lesbian variant of the myth. From among his essays, one should mention here a small book which is invaluable for a good grasp of this part of the œuvre: *Foundations of the Mythology of Authorship* (Grondslagen van de mythologie van het schrijverschap, 1987).

It is not only Greek myths to which Mulisch makes such frequent reference: the Egyptian world also finds its way into his work. Important motifs are those of the sphinx (always linked to the mother figure), the pyramid and hieroglyphics. Of the Egyptian gods, mention is made of Isis and Osiris for instance in *Last Call* (Hoogste tijd, 1985), a novel about the theatre, and in his substantial recent novel, *The Discovery of Heaven* (De ontdekking van de hemel, 1992), of Anubis, and above all of Thoth, the writer god, who even in antiquity was put on a par with Mulisch's 'patron saint' Hermes Trismegistus.

If it is primarily a picture of Mulisch the esoteric writer which emerges from the above, it must be said that a completely different side of Mulisch can be seen in the long essays from the 1960s. In *News for the Rat King* (Bericht aan de rattenkoning, 1966), in which he deals in detail with the origins of the anarchistic Amsterdam youth-movement of the time, and in his book on Cuba *Suit the Word to the Action* (Het woord bij de daad, 1968), as well as in the opera *Reconstruction* (Reconstructie, 1969), written in collaboration with Hugo Claus and others, Mulisch reveals himself as a left-wing anarchist writer. The striking thing is that he fiercely opposes dictatorship both at local and international level, but accepts the dictatorial leadership of Castro without any difficulty. This paradox provides yet another link between this politically engaged work and the rest of his œuvre.

RUDI VAN DER PAARDT
Translated by Jane Fenoulhet.

LIST OF TRANSLATIONS

'What Happened to Sergeant Masuro?' (Tr. Roy Edwards). *The Hudson Review,* XIV, 1961, 1, pp. 28-49.

'The Powers That Be' and 'Operating Garbage' (Tr. James Brockway). *The Literary Review,* V, 1961-62, 2, pp. 276-279 and 280-282.

The Stone Bridal Bed (Tr. Adrienne Dixon). London / New York / Toronto, 1962.

'The Death of My Father' (Tr. N.C. Clegg-Bruinwold Riedel). *Delta,* V, 1962, 2, pp. 86-97.

'Four Anecdotes on Death' (Tr. Ina Rilke). *Delta,* XI, 1968, 4, pp. 5-17.

'The Horses' Jump and the Fresh Sea' (Tr. Adrienne Dixon). In: *Modern Stories from Holland and Flanders* (ed. Egbert Krispyn), New York, 1973, pp. 95-117.

What Poetry Is (Tr. Claire Nicolas White). Merrick (NY), 1979.

Two Women (Tr. Els Early). London / New York, 1980.

Symmetry (Tr. Adrienne Dixon). London, 1982.

The Assault (Tr. Claire Nicolas White). London / New York, 1985; Harmondsworth, 1986.

Last Call (Tr. Adrienne Dixon). London, 1987; Harmondsworth, 1990.

A translation of *The Discovery of Heaven* will appear in the course of 1994.

Extract from *The Assault*

by Harry Mulisch

Far, far back during the Second World War, a certain Anton Steenwijk lived with his parents and his brother on the outskirts of Haarlem. There four houses stood close together along a quay that bordered the water for about a hundred metres. After a gentle curve, the quay straightened out and became an ordinary street. Each house was surrounded by a garden and had a little balcony, bay windows, and a steep roof, giving it the air of a modest villa. The rooms on the top floor all had slanted walls. The houses were somewhat dilapidated and in need of paint, for their upkeep had already been neglected during the thirties. Harking back to lighter-hearted days, each bore an honest sign with its name: Hideaway, Carefree, Home at Last, Bide-a-Wee.

Anton lived in the second house from the left, the one with the thatched roof. If it had not already been called Carefree when the family rented it shortly before the war, his father would have preferred to name it something like Eleutheria, written in Greek letters. Even before the catastrophe occurred, Anton used to think that Carefree meant a place where cares entered freely, not a place free from cares; just as someone could think priceless meant without cost, rather than beyond price.

The Beumers, an ailing retired confidential clerk and his wife, lived in Hideaway. Anton sometimes dropped in on them for a cup of tea and a biscuit, in the days when there were still such things as tea and biscuits – that is to say, long before the beginning of this story, which is the story of an incident. Sometimes Mr Beumer read him a chapter from *The Three Musketeers.* Mr Korteweg was the neighbour in Home at Last, on the other side of Anton's house. Formerly a second mate in the merchant marine, he was out of work now because of the war. After the death of his wife, his daughter Karin, a nurse, had moved back home. Anton sometimes dropped in here also, through an opening in the backyard hedge. Karin was always friendly, but her father paid no attention to him. There wasn't much socialising on that quay. The most aloof neighbours of all were the Aartses, who had lived in Bide-a-Wee since the beginning of the war. It was said that he worked for an insurance company, though no one was really sure.

Apparently these four houses had been intended as the beginning of a new development, but nothing more came of it. They were surrounded by fallow fields overgrown with weeds and bushes, and even some tall trees. It was on these undeveloped lots that Anton spent most of his time, playing with other children from a neighbourhood farther away. Occasionally in the late twilight when his mother forgot to call him in, a fragrant stillness would rise and fill him with expectations – of what, he didn't know. Something to do with later, when he'd be grown up – things that would happen then. The motionless earth, the leaves. Two sparrows that suddenly twittered and scratched about. Life would be like those evenings when he had been forgotten, mysterious and endless.

The cobblestones on the road in front of the house were laid in a herringbone pattern. The street did not have a pavement. It petered out into a grassy bank that sloped gently down to the towpath, where it was pleasant to lie on one's back. Across the wide canal – that only by its gentle winding showed that it once had been a river – stood a few farmhands' cottages and small farms; to the right, where the bank curved, was a windmill that never turned. Behind the farms, the meadows stretched out to the horizon. Still farther lay Amsterdam. Before the War, his father had told him, one could see the glow of city lights reflected against the clouds. Anton had been there a few times, to the zoo and the Rijksmuseum, and to his uncle's where he had spent one night.

Lying on the grassy bank and staring into the distance, he sometimes had to pull in his legs. A man who came straight from another century walked along the trampled towpath. The man was leaning square on a pole several yards long, while the other end was fastened to the prow of a barge. Walking with heavy steps, he moved the boat throught the water. Usually a woman wearing an apron, her hair in a knot, stood at the wheel, and a child played on deck. At other times the pole was used in a different way. Then the man remained on deck and walked forward along the side of the barge, dragging the pole behind him through the water. When he reached the bow, he planted the stick sideways in the bottom of the canal, grasped it firmly, and walked backwards, so that he pushed the boat forward beneath his feet. This specially pleased Anton: a man walking backwards to push something forward, while staying in the same place himself. There was something very strange about it, but it was his secret that he didn't mention to anyone. Not till later, when he described it to his children, did he realise what primitive times he had witnessed. Only in movies about Africa and Asia could one still see such things.

Several times a day barges, heavily laden colossi with dark-brown sails, appeared silently around the first bend and, driven solemnly onward by the invisible wind, disappeared around the next. The motorboats were different. Pitching, their prows would tear the water into a V shape that spread until it reached the bank on both sides. There the water would suddenly begin to lap up and down, even though the boat was already far away. Then the waves bounced back and formed an inverted V, a lambda that closed more and more, but now interfered with the original V, reached the opposite shore transformed, and bounced back again – until all across the water a complicated braiding of ripples developed which went on changing for several minutes, then finally smoothed out.

Each time, Anton tried to figure out exactly how this happened, but each time the pattern became so complex that he could no longer follow it.

ACKNOWLEDGEMENT

From *The Assault* by Harry Mulisch (Tr. Claire Nicolas White).

Copyright © 1985 by Random House, Inc. (USA and Canada).

Reprinted by permission of Pantheon Books, a division of Random House, Inc.

Copyright © 1985 by Harper Collins Publishers Ltd. (excl. USA and Canada).

Performing

Early Music in the Low Countries

During the last few decades musicologists have abandoned the general philosophical approach in favour of more scientific investigations. Research into archive material has been undertaken on a large scale. As well as the works of important but almost completely forgotten composers, there has been a good deal of interest in texts on organology, musical practice, musical rhetoric and instrumental techniques. All this has brought about a revolution in the interpretation of 'Early Music'.

The demand now is for appropriate performing standards. The score must be brought to life with the original subtleties of timbre. Playing early instruments or faithful reproductions of them according to the original techniques, and singing according to age-old principles (lyric-based, measured vibrato etc.) has opened the way for quite precise and authentic interpretations.

The Low Countries were involved at the very beginning of this renewal.

It all began in 1933 with Pro Musica Antiqua, the Belgian ensemble for Medieval Renaissance music founded by the pioneering American Safford Cape under the intellectual leadership of musicologist Charles van den Borren. A glance at the membership list shows that many of today's specialists in Early Music took their first exploratory steps with that company.

Then, from 1958 onwards, the Alarius Ensemble with Charles MacGuire (flute), Janine Rubinlicht (baroque violin), Wieland Kuijken (baroque cello, viola da gamba), Sigiswald Kuijken (baroque violin, viola da gamba) and Robert Kohnen (harpsichord) carried out some astonishing explorations into the chamber music repertoire of the seventeenth and eighteenth centuries.

But the real starting shot was fired in 1972. From that time onwards a large number of musicians began meticulously to follow the 'authentic' path to the music of the Middle Ages, the Renaissance and the Baroque. The movement remains unstoppable to this day, and has expanded further to include early Classical, Classicist, Romantic and Impressionist music.

The Alarius Ensemble ceased to exist in 1972. By that time, however, the Kuijken brothers (now including flautist Barthold as well) had already produced two offspring: the Kuijken Consort and the baroque orchestra La Petite Bande. The Kuijkens (often accompanied by other specialists) were

Jos van Immerseel (1945-)
(Photo BRTN).

soon to become Flanders' much-appreciated ambassadors of Early Music abroad. Those involved in the Kuijken String Quartet (founded in 1986) sought adventure and refreshment in the Classical and early Romantic string quartet repertoire. Sigiswald Kuijken expressed the essence of his search for authenticity as follows: *'You go back to the old technique, and by doing so you can eliminate a number of mistakes at a single stroke. You start again from scratch, from the same clean sheet as the people at the time. You begin with technical limitations, but these create new possibilities. You have to be convinced of the principle that limitations open up other possibilities – otherwise you should never start.'*

1972 was also a decisive year for the Flemish countertenor René Jacobs, who embarked on a singing career that year. Jacobs has always been attracted to the opera, in addition to solo parts in cantatas, oratorios and performances of vocal chamber music with his Concerto Vocale. In recent years he has mainly been known as a conductor of early Baroque operas.

In 1972 Paul Van Nevel started a group called the Huelgas Ensemble, which was to become an international authority on music from the Middle Ages and the Renaissance.

In the same year Philippe Herreweghe from Ghent decided to devote himself entirely to music. With his elite group, the Collegium Vocale, he skilfully hooked in to contemporary trends in interpretation and was the first to apply Baroque instrumental procedures to performances of choral music. He made some prestigious concert performances and recordings with Ton

Koopman, Gustav Leonhardt, Sigiswald Kuijken and Nikolaus Harnoncourt. Deftly taking advantage of the craze for Early Music in Paris, in 1977 he became leader of the Choir and Orchestra of the Chapelle Royale, which has now expanded to include the Ensemble Vocal Européen, a group of highly qualified vocalists. Herreweghe, along with a recently formed instrumental group, L'Orchestre des Champs Elysées, is now also focussing on the authentic approach to stylistic periods after the Baroque. The conductor sees the birth of this orchestra as another stage in his developing vision: *'I think it is unnatural to remain stuck on a single period. Partly because of our recordings, we are expected to come up with quality and a certain degree of originality. I want to approach the period from 1800 to about 1880 in the same way as I approached the Baroque.'*

The world of Early Music also contains a son of the City of Antwerp: Jos van Immerseel, who in 1972 won first prize in Harpsichord at the Royal Flemish Academy of Music in his home city. His reputation as a solo harpsichordist and pianist has carried him throughout Europe. The orchestra Anima Eterna was formed around him, and is exploring both Baroque and Classical music. Van Immerseel has recently been appointed Master of Piano at the Paris Academy.

Finally, 1972 was the year in which Paul Dombrecht graduated from the Brussels Royal Academy of Music as an oboist. Paul Dombrecht comes from the province of West Flanders, and since 1972 he has concentrated on the study of eighteenth- and nineteenth-century instruments. The unique wind ensemble Octophorus and the baroque orchestra Il Fondamento were established around this musician.

While the Flemish Early Music movement is maintaining itself in a modest

Harpsichord, made by Hans II or Andreas I Ruckers in Antwerp (1615) (Vleeshuis, Antwerp).

Eighteenth-century musical instruments, as painted by Peter Jacob Horemans (1700 -1776) (Germanisches Nationalmuseum, Nuremberg).

way on its home ground through a few public relations initiatives, the authenticity movement in the Netherlands, which was placed on a sound footing right from the beginning by educational and concert organisations, is now experiencing a period of great prosperity, thanks to the Utrecht Foundation for the Organisation of Early Music.

So far the authenticity movement in the Netherlands has crystallised principally around names associated with the recorder and the harpsichord. That the recorder has now become fully recognised as an instrument is due to a large number of Dutchmen, starting with Willem van Warmelo, who taught Kees Otten to play the instrument – which was much disparaged at the time – during the first half of this century.

In his turn, Frans Brüggen proved the value of the recorder as a concert instrument. Verve, spirit, dashing virtuoso technique and a faithful style of musical expression on historical instruments are all part of the armorial bearings of this man from Amsterdam, and are now also borne by the highly-respected 'Northern recorder school'. Together with harpsichordist Gustav Leonhardt and baroque cellist Anner Bijlsma, Brüggen has formed a masterful triumvirate of chamber music. He founded the Brüggen Consort in 1967, led Quadro Amsterdam and conducted Concerto Amsterdam and the Mozart Ensemble Amsterdam. He is currently working as conductor of the Orchestra of the Eighteenth Century (founded in 1980), with which he also brings us Romantic masters in their authentic sound and form.

What does the word 'authentic' mean to Frans Brüggen? *'It has no meaning at all. No, really none at all. There is of course a certain technical and*

Jan Brueghel, *Allegory of Hearing* (detail). c.1615. Panel, 65 x 107 cm. Prado, Madrid.

Gustav Leonhardt (1928-).

"seelisch" way of playing which has to fit the piece you are doing, but there are so many exceptions to those rules and the differences between composers and even between pieces are so great. Oh yes, it's a good thing the rules exist, and you do keep to them, but there are so many exceptions. It's just a basis, nothing more. It's amazing how we benefit from playing the old instruments. For example: there are absolutely no problems with balance. You don't have to talk about it – it's just there. Those instruments belong together – absolutely!'

The name of Gustav Leonhardt is associated with historical harpsichord- and organ-playing, both in solo repertoire and in basso continuo playing. In 1955 Leonhardt established the Leonhardt Consort, with his wife Marie Leonhardt as Konzertmeister. His interpretations of the Bach cantatas, which he recorded in full for Telefunken with Nikolaus Harnoncourt, are particularly impressive.

Leonhardt is known as the person who rediscovered articulation on the harpsichord: *'The harpsichord does of course have tremendous potential for articulation. The literature is enormously varied and it is such that you can certainly say it "speaks". Sometimes the music rather tends to "gesture", then again great tonal differences come to the fore. So speaking is only one element. In order to speak you need articulation, and also detailed dynamics … Everyone agrees that the harpsichord offers very little scope for dynamics. And this creates a tremendous challenge, because so much dynamic music was written for the instrument. So we can assume that there are ways of making us forget those limitations.'*

213

The Dutch harpsichord and organ school continued its illustrious progress with Ton Koopman, a student of Gustav Leonhardt. Koopman led the baroque orchestra Musica Antiqua Amsterdam until 1979, and in the same year he founded a new international baroque orchestra: The Amsterdam Baroque Orchestra. As a harpsichordist, organist and musicologist, Koopman was one of the first to see the importance of the old fingerings for rhetorical interpretation.

It would be impossible to give a complete summary of all the (young) Dutch ensembles and interpreters to be found in this exhilarating forum at present. However it would be irresponsible to fail to mention an ensemble like Camerata Trajectina, which brings to life sounds of the Netherlands' musical heritage from the sixteenth and seventeenth centuries. This company, which has been active since 1974 and is closely linked with the Institute of Musical Science at the University of Utrecht, shows how exciting and stimulating the integration of musical practice and musical science can be.

MARC PEIRE
Translated by Steve Judd.

SELECTIVE DISCOGRAPHY

RENE JACOBS (countertenor) / THE KUIJKEN CONSORT, *German Church Cantatas and Arias*, Accent Record Company, CD ACC 67912 D.

LA PETITE BANDE (Sigiswald Kuijken, René Jacobs, et al.), *Georg Friedrich Händel: Allessandro*, EMI (Deutsche Harmonia Mundi), 3 CDS 7 47910 8.

LA PETITE BANDE (Sigiswald Kuijken), *Haydn: Symphonies No. 26, No. 52, No. 53*, Virgin Classics Veritas, CD VC 790743-2.

COLLEGIUM VOCALE-GHENT / LA PETITE BANDE (Sigiswald Kuijken, Max van Egmond et al.), *Carl Philipp Emanuel Bach: Die letzten Leiden des Erlösers, Wq 233*, EMI (Deutsche Harmonia Mundi), 2 CDS 7 47753 8.

ENSEMBLE VOCAL ET ORCHESTRE DE LA CHAPELLE ROYALE / COLLEGIUM VOCALE-GHENT / IN DULCI JUBILO (directed by Philippe Herreweghe), *Johann Sebastian Bach: Matthäus Passion, BWV 244*, Harmonia Mundi France, 3 CDS 901155 57.

HUELGAS ENSEMBLE (Paul van Nevel), *Orlando di Lasso: lagrime di San Pietro*, Sony Classical Vivarte, SK 53 373.

RENE JACOBS (countertenor) / JOS VAN IMMERSEEL (pianoforte), *Ariette e Cavatine*, LP ACC 8017.

SIGISWALD KUIJKEN / GUSTAV LEONHARDT, *Johann Sebastian Bach: Sonatas for Violin and Harpsichord*, Deutsche Harmonia Mundi Editio Classica, 2 CDS GD 77170.

GUSTAV LEONHARDT (harpsichord), *Johann Sebastian Bach*, Philips, CD 416 141-2.

MONICA HUGGETT / TON KOOPMAN, *Johann Sebastian Bach: 6 Violin Sonatas BWV 1014-1019*, 2 CDS 410 401 2.

ORCHESTRA OF THE EIGHTEENTH CENTURY (Frans Brüggen), *Ludwig von Beethoven: Symphony No. 3 'Eroica'*, Philips, CD 422 052-2 (live recording).

Ger

van Elk Was Here

In the National Gallery in London there is a full-length double portrait of the Italian merchant Giovanni Arnolfini and his bride Giovanna Cenani, painted in 1434 by the Flemish artist Jan van Eyck. She has placed her hand in his; as they stand before the nuptial bed the two of them are entering into a pact. Between them hangs a convex mirror reflecting these two figures from behind and also two others facing the mirror, one of them probably the artist, for above the mirror is written 'Johannes de eyck fuit hic' (Jan van Eyck was here). These words not only give the panel a signature but make it into a document. This must have been the first time that an artist portrayed himself in a designated function.

The Dutch artist Ger van Elk (1941-) has frequently assigned himself a particular role in his work. In various interviews he has always explained this by saying that he himself was the cheapest model because he was always available. In Amsterdam he attended what is now known as the Gerrit Rietveld Academy from 1959 to 1961, when he left for Los Angeles. There he continued his training until 1963, but concentrated on studying history of art at the Immaculate Heart College. After travelling extensively through South and Central America he returned to the Netherlands in 1967. He still divides his time between the Netherlands and the New World.

Ger van Elk was twenty-two years old when the musician and designer George Maciunas explained in a manifesto the choice of the name 'fluxus' for his international and interdisciplinary movement. Fluxus was against expensive works of art, marketable art and commercial galleries. Fluxus rejected the attention given to individual artists, and as an antidote to this organised group activities of an unconventional nature. Cologne, Paris, London and Amsterdam were some of its centres in Europe. Among the participants were Wolf Vostell, Nam June Paik, Christo, Cage and Wim T. Schippers. It seemed as if the spirit of Dadaism had been reborn. Schippers and Ger van Elk worked together in 1962. Van Elk did not take part directly in the international fluxus movement but he felt drawn towards its informal collaborative way of thinking and acting. And some art critics rightly saw a

Ger van Elk, *Well Polished Floor Piece.* 1969, Photograph, 150 x 150 cm. Museum Boymans-van Beuningen, Rotterdam.

similarity between Marcel Duchamp, forerunner of the Dadaists, and Ger van Elk in their way of thinking and working; for both of them an unconventional theme was more important than the form.

An early example is the cactus that Ger van Elk lathered with shaving soap in 1969 and subsequently shaved clean with a safety razor. Two photos of *The Well Shaven Cactus* are evidence of this act. The first photo shows the lathered-up cactus with shaving tackle; in the second the tackle has been moved and the cactus stripped of its stubble. The photos do not make a documentary record of the action as a film or a series of photos would do, but by choosing the two important phases, before and after shaving, the emphasis is placed on the absurdist idea. The act itself, which for fluxus is always the main aim, remains, as does the performer, out of sight.

Yet this is not the case in the *Well Polished Floor Piece* dating from the same year. The photo that celebrates the floor-polishing shows a pair of male legs which tell us Ger van Elk was active here. They stand there like initials, a sign that the work has been completed and can be released, like a signature on a piece of sculpture or a painting. Unlike the group activities of fluxus, they attest to the individual artist's involvement in his work.

In Ger van Elk's œuvre the photo occupies a prominent, even central position. Originally the photo recorded a single act as in *The Well Shaven Cactus,* but eventually the medium was to lose its documentary character. Since a photo – however much it may be manipulated – records whatever is there to be observed, it can be said that, as Ger van Elk himself has said, his art aims at a realistic depiction of non-realistic situations.

The photos of *The Well Shaven Cactus* record a Dadaist-absurdist event, the photo of the *Well Polished Floor Piece* a domestic activity: the polishing of a parquet floor. In his later work Ger van Elk has often made use of the triangle as a composition form: always seeking to stimulate the viewer's visual faculty, he has developed a preference for unusual frames.

When Ger van Elk was in Los Angeles in 1971 he was confronted by the aftermath of an earthquake. Under a chunk of asphalt from a road that had been torn open he found a cigarette packet with some cigarettes still in it. This gave him the idea for the two photos of *The Discovery of the Sardines.* He replaced the cigarettes by sardines because he is crazy about sardines. Emerging from the cracks in the road, the small silver fish at first seem to be emerging from a dark underworld of human society, making a fascinating surrealistic image. In contrast with this enigma from another world, a fast car is speeding by whose chauffeur apparently has no eye for miracles.

The subtitle *Placerita Canyon, Newhall, California* indicates that the artist has not yet relinquished the documentary character of *The Discovery of the Sardines;* he is eager to convince us of the veracity of his vision.

So in addition to an affinity to Dadaism Ger van Elk's work has a bond with surrealism, the movement that was to succeed Dada historically. Van Elk's surrealism, however, has no Freudian overtones, nor is it in any way didactic, probably because wonder is its source of inspiration. What Van Elk offers us is not figments of the imagination but, like Picasso, finds and inventions.

In the series *The Missing Persons* (1976) Ger van Elk likewise presents us with a realistic depiction of a seemingly realistic situation. For example, in one photo from the series five statesmen are standing in a row for the official photographic record of their historic meeting, with an uncomfortable gap between two of them. In another three people are sitting together in overstuffed armchairs, all eyes directed towards an absent party. The photos allude to the way in which under dictatorial regimes figures are removed from official photos when people who have fallen from favour have to be expunged from the nation's memory. Ger van Elk constantly accentuates the

Ger van Elk, *The Discovery of the Sardines. Placerita Canyon, Newhall, California.* 1971. Two colour photographs (separately framed; 4th ed.), (2x) 65.5 x 55 cm. Collection Becht, Naarden.

Ger van Elk, *The Missing Persons. Conversation Piece.* 1976. Coloured photograph, 106 x 124 cm. Collection Nigel P. Greenwood, London.

artificiality of this kind of situation through, for instance, the poses the figures strike, their shiny pomaded hair or the garish nature of their surroundings. The photos are coloured in and sometimes rephotographed to bring home to the viewer how he has begun to take artificiality for granted.

In the series *The Adieu* (1974) the realism in a non-realistic situation is more complex. The artificiality is already anticipated in the title derived from two languages. A painting may be seen on an easel; on the painting is a path bordered by wintry-looking trees, a cliché for the romantic attitude to nature. The path leads the eye to the horizon as in Hobbema's famous *Avenue in Middelharnis* (1689), a painting that has been inspiring both professional and Sunday painters of the realistic-naturalistic type for over three hundred years now. On the path in *The Adieu* Ger van Elk is standing waving goodbye to the viewer, as if about to turn around, walk down the path and vanish. Relatively speaking, he is not much larger than Jan van Eyck in the National Gallery portrait but here he is the only figure doing anything, in fact he is the only figure in the 'painting' on the easel, which is foreshortened. If the canvas were to be turned further away from us the figure of Van Elk would also become invisible. The foreshortening emphasises the artist's gesture of farewell which gives the work its title. The 'canvas' on the easel also seems to be about to disappear through the heavy blue curtains that 'hang' behind it. The clichéd counterfeit of nature, not even painted in oils but a coloured-in photograph, is framed by luxurious textile. The one artificiality reinforces the other. Is art going to disappear together with Van Elk? In any event, with its incongruous frame *The Adieu* provides an ironic and whimsical commentary on the artificiality of traditional painting.

In a 1977 interview with the German art historian Antje von Graevenitz Ger van Elk said that he wanted to reconsider his point of view continually. To this he added: 'The only thing one can do is rebel.' These remarks clearly show that Ger van Elk has no intention of pursuing the same artistic course all the time. As his art is chiefly defined by its content, this, if it is to be innovative, requires shifts of view point. In the same spirit, the Flemish avant-garde poet and theoretician Paul van Ostaijen (1896-1928) wrote: 'I get up in the morning with the problem: what can I do now that hasn't been done before.' The problem of artistic renewal, crucial to every artist, is even more urgent for Ger van Elk because, preoccupied with the subject matter as he is, he is averse to an unchanging, recognisable style. His art, like his theoretics, is essentially dynamic.

In 1980 a large work, *Triangle Balance Pull,* came into being. Two figures appear to be pulling so hard on a rope that, with the soles of their feet set against each other, they and the rope form a horizontal diagonal. It is a trial of strength between two adult men, in which perspectival lengthening (of the legs) and foreshortening (of the trunk) give the viewer the sensation of witnessing a supreme effort. A formal balance is struck not only by the triangle, the various shades of red for the figure on the left also offset the violet-blue of the figure on the right. It is Ger van Elk who with his full length pits himself against Ger van Elk and in this way holds himself in balance.

By rejecting the support of a consistent style Ger van Elk frequently

Ger van Elk, *The Adieu.* 1974. Gouache and ink on colour photograph (in irregular quadrilateral frame), 132 x 84 cm. Stedelijk Museum, Amsterdam.

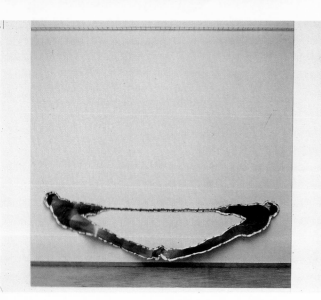

Ger van Elk, *Triangle Balance Pull.* 1980. Colour photographs and acrylic paint on canvas, 110 x 490 cm. Stedelijk Museum, Amsterdam.

Ger van Elk, *Paysage Saignant (Pressure Sandwich).* 1991. Oil on canvas / steel / paintings, 226 x 254 x 50 cm. Collection Liliane and Michel Durant-Dessert, Paris.

arrives at crossroads where he has to decide his direction without the help of a map. This is why he makes a figure of himself, or sometimes even two figures; Van Elk tussling with Van Elk in *Triangle Balance Pull* or Van Elk debating with Van Elk in *The Western Stylemasters* (1987). Furthermore, the title of the second work is in deliberate opposition to his desire not to be a stylemaster.

In 1971 in *The Return of Pierre Bonnard, 1917-1971* Ger van Elk displayed the back of a painting with stickers on it showing where and when it had been exhibited. And in 1975 in *The Last Adieu,* a work from the series *The Adieu,* he showed three paintings visible from the back only. If the artist was portrayed, the method of presentation made him invisible. In 1991 he took up the theme of the back that becomes the front once more by giving it the form of a sandwich. Since then he has employed the concept of the sandwich in a large number of variations.

The work created in 1991 has the half English, half French title of *Paysage Saignant (Pressure Sandwich).* As in *The Return of Pierre Bonnard, 1917-1971,* it is the back of a painting that is shown to us. Four canvasses have been screwed together, with a number of small landscape paintings wedged between them. Parts of these small paintings protrude out of the sandwich; the screws, one must assume, go right through some of them. The large splotches of paint around the screws create the impression, reinforced by the title, that the paint has been squeezed out of the small wedged-in paintings.

This drastic representation, which almost hurts the viewer physically, takes sides in the clash between serious artists and the numerous unoriginal producers of painted landscapes. The second-rate work is a wan reflection of the great movements and styles; it is the work of the imitators of the masters. There is no question of peaceful co-existence: great art crushes the rest, puts thumbscrews on it, reduces it to the garbage of art history. This is art's blood-stained battlefield.

In the spring of 1993 a large exhibition of new work by Ger van Elk was held in the Boymans-van Beuningen Museum in Rotterdam. The sandwich concept was so central to the exhibition that it was entitled *Sandwiches, Pressing, Pushing, and Pulling.* The tone was set by three-dimensional objects, varying in size from two to five metres. As early as 1968 Ger van Elk had made three-dimensional objects. In 1977 he told Antje von Graevenitz: 'I chose film in order to add moving parts to *sculpture'* (my italics).

At the Boymans-van Beuningen exhibition photographed and painted men's heads, already familiar to the viewer, were subjected to physical tor-

Ger van Elk, *Bitch.* 1992. Gloss paint and varnish on wood / framed photographs under glass, 74 x 452 x 63 cm (Photo: Museum Boymans-van Beuningen, Rotterdam, 1993 exhibition).

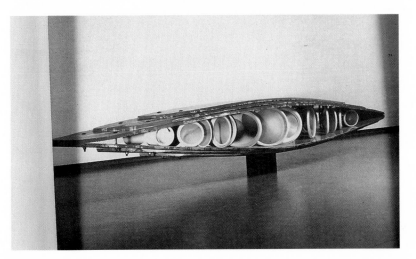

ture in various objects. In *Bitch* (1992) it is the turn of the female sex to be tormented. Photos of parts of female breasts and buttocks which, encased in circular pink frames, form an erotic ensemble, join forces to resist the pressure of the broad planks they are wedged between. The danger of being crushed makes the tension even greater than in *Triangle Balance Pull.* The 'jaws' that threaten to snap shut can, as the title suggests, also be seen as a vagina.

Exercise of Love, Hope and Faith from the same year is equally misogynistic. Stabbing red-, white- and black-lacquered women's fingernails protrude between the layers of a circular threedecker sandwich. On the top small pink noses poke through cracks in five places, suggesting that the rest of the bodies have been crushed. The size of the noses indicates that these men were no match for the super vamp. As in *Bitch,* deeply rooted fears are expressed here.

In his most recent work Ger van Elk depicts realistic situations surrealistically. Here he introduces a new theme: the battle between the sexes, its aggressivity and the traumas which result from it. While his early work already showed a remarkable amount of physical activity, violence has come to the fore since 1991.

In these latest works Ger van Elk is more present than ever. It can no longer be maintained, as he himself has done in various interviews, that he presents himself because he is the cheapest model. His own existence is now what is at stake. Presenting himself in his work has come to mean an almost physical resistance to threatening forces. With this, the rebellion which has been the guiding principle of his work down the years, has taken a dramatic turn.

JOSE BOYENS
Translated by Elizabeth Mollison.

Ger van Elk, *Exercise of Love, Hope and Faith.* 1992. Gloss paint and varnish on wood / ceramic / steel / photographs, 71 x 263 cm (Photo: Museum Boymans-van Beuningen, Rotterdam, 1993 exhibition).

The

Terrible Beauty of the Twentieth Century

A Portrait of Rem Koolhaas

'Funnily enough I have the feeling that it's not our imagination which is punished in the Netherlands but – much more alarmingly – our logic. It's one thing for them to dismiss us as a bunch of dreamers, but I think what they really can't bear to contemplate is the forbidding logic in our work, the Dutchness that lies behind it.'

This is how Rem Koolhaas (1944-), the Netherlands' most celebrated and most articulate architect, describes his relationship to his native country. While his fame is widespread there – to the point where even TV satirists have poked fun at his celebrity – and his views have dominated debate in recent years, his Office for Metropolitan Architecture (OMA) has built little in the Netherlands. On more than one occasion OMA has failed to secure a prestigious commission, and each time its design has given rise to a good deal of talk and controversy, with large sections of the architectural press accusing the client of timidly favouring mediocrity; so that the invisible shadow of an OMA alternative lies over the new building for the Lower House of Parliament in The Hague by Pi de Bruijn, the town hall for the same city by Richard Meier, and the Netherlands Architecture Institute in Rotterdam by Jo Coenen. Commissions such as the congress centre in Lille and, recently, the Jussieu university library in Paris suggest that the focus of OMA activities may be shifting to France, where Koolhaas has always been greatly admired.

Koolhaas has mixed feelings not only about his native country but also about his profession. Although architecture attracted great interest in the eighties, it became entangled in cosmetic debates where no real issues were at stake. 'Amid such an excess of good manners it is important not to go on being "cool", to become once more gauche, indigestible, impassioned.' With slightly pitying sympathy Koolhaas invokes the utopian architects of the past. We have lost the naïvety of that time, and with it their visionary élan: 'Great progress in sophistication, immense losses in commitment.' What Koolhaas would like to see is an architecture that is visionary without being naïve.

Koolhaas' passionate commitment is succinctly expressed in the name of his practice: Office for Metropolitan Architecture. The name is a statement of intentions. The concept of the metropolis brings together two elements, modernity and the city. The latter is a chaos of activities, the proximity of contrasts, density, conflict and congestion. The modern is what this age has that previous ages did not have: rapid traffic, telecommunications, endless masses of people. The modern is not a utopia with a superior, ideal order; the modern is what is unfinished, complex, uncontrollable.

The prevailing view at the end of the seventies was that modernity and the city were enemies, a view supported by the traumas inflicted on many historic town centres by the unrestrained pursuit of progress. But Koolhaas aims to overcome these traumas through a critical analysis of contemporary experience of the phenomenon of the city. He opposes a concept of the city which leaves no place for what is characteristic of modern life, for something as banal for example as a supermarket. By discussing Rotterdam, Berlin and Atlanta he questions the presumed universal validity of a historic, radial-concentric city plan. With compelling acuity he describes the Berlin Wall, the Les Halles shopping centre penetrating deep into the ground in Paris, the clustered tower blocks of La Défense constricted by urban motorways, the vast scale of the Bijlmer housing development on the edge of Amsterdam, the shapeless fringes of the urban territory: modern phenomena which have radically altered our perception of the city. Being characteristically provocative, he chooses precisely those examples which had been most reviled by the public at large: the beauty of the twentieth century is a 'terrible beauty'.

In 1978 Koolhaas published *Delirious New York,* a witty and lyrical ode to the modern city and to what he called 'the culture of congestion'. The book established his reputation but at the same time gave rise to the under-

OMA, *Panopticon Prison,* Arnhem (Axonometric drawing).

OMA, *Nederlands Dans Theater,* The Hague.

standable misconception that this proponent of metropolitan architecture wanted to transplant 'Manhattanism' to the Old World. That was not the case, however. For Koolhaas, the contemporary European metropolis was entirely different from Manhattan – less dense, less massive. In his view, in Europe today metropolitan potential is to be found less in the historic centres than in the peripheral areas. It is less a matter of the building volumes than of the empty gap. How to give that emptiness an urban significance? – that seems to him the most relevant town planning issue today.

Take for instance the Randstad conurbation in the Netherlands, where the so-called empty zones might as well be described as urbanised, encroached on as they are by haphazard and unplanned housing and industrial estates, expanses of glasshouses and shopping centres. The Randstad is in fact a carpet metropolis, as a former colleague of Koolhaas and kindred spirit, Willem-Jan Neutelings, puts it. Koolhaas himself says: *'If you add up the populations of Amsterdam, Rotterdam and The Hague you get 1.5 to 2 million people. The population of the Randstad as a whole is about 6 million. So there are 4.5 million people missing: they live "nowhere" and they represent a metropolitan potential that is only noticeable at present in the traffic jams and the tailbacks on the motorways (...). The Netherlands could achieve a different kind of metropolitanism, one which does not necessarily go with density of mass and as a result is pre-eminently modern.'*

As well as the theory, there is an impressive body of designs. Very often **Designs** they break away from the expected and predictable. There is a strong emphasis on the conceptual. Existing elements are rearranged, new connections are made, all leading to an entirely new interpretation of the situation. The design for the renovation of a prison in Arnhem*, in which the panopticon principle was neutralised by a few slight changes, is a good example.

Koolhaas' interest in the conceptual is accompanied by a certain distrust of form. Though there are frequent unobtrusive reminders of various modern masters, from Russian Constructivists to Team Ten, he remains sceptical about the futile coercion of form. The way in which he tries to escape from this is one of the most fascinating aspects of his work.

The bus station in Rotterdam, the police building in Almere, and the houses, supermarket and school for the IJ square in Amsterdam – all projects with a modest budget – draw on the formal vocabulary of modern trivia. They seem on the one hand to aim at blending in with the banal surroundings, while on the other they regain their original strangeness through minimal, disturbing touches.

The Nederlands Dans Theater and Byzantium in Amsterdam are buildings with no clearly delineated form. They fit into the city not as objects but as a collage. They are perceived as a discontinuity in the city silhouette, as an intensification of the continuous flow of visual stimuli.

At the same time there are designs with an a- or anti-architectural vision, defying tectonic description: the Zeebrugge terminal*, the patio houses built in Fukuoka, Japan. Finally, there is a long series of designs in which the architecture evaporates until it is on the point of disappearing: the Netherlands Architecture Institute*, the Bibliothèque de France* and the Zentrum für Kunst und Medientechnologie in Karlsruhe*. The fixed elements are kept to a minimum, walls are transparent, volumes disappear under the

OMA, *Biozentrum,* Frankfurt (Model, aerial view).

OMA, *Sea Trade Centre,* Zeebrugge (Model).

ground or behind a film of reflections. The Biozentrum in Frankfurt* is completely buried in the landscape. All that is visible of the Sport Museum for Flevohof* is a high fence of wire mesh: a tenuous block of air resting on the polder.

At one end of the spectrum lie the modest, 'trivial' designs, while at the other are the plans 'where the assignment completely coincides with the ambition of our name'. The Zentrum in Karlsruhe, the Bibliothèque de France and the Sea Trade Centre in Zeebrugge, three competition entries of 1989, are plans of this kind. These are all exceptionally large buildings, with a complex and varied design, which are completely accessible to the public; in other words, buildings for which there are no precedents. 'In each case what the client had in mind was more experimental than what we could have devised ourselves.' In the Zeebrugge terminal, for example, intended for ferry services across the Channel, all the conventional rules of architectural composition are turned upside down. Standing at the end of the jetty, it resembles a retort bubbling with the euphoria of sailing. Through glass floors and yawning voids the waiting passengers see at the same time a spirally ascending car park, a hotel, offices, a casino, a panoramic film screen

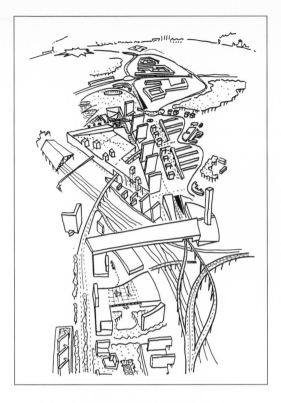

and a real panorama of the North Sea. The exterior is as enigmatically compact as the interior is confusingly open: a smooth, concrete shell constructed
like a cooling tower and crowned by a huge plastic bubble. It looks like a
monolith polished by the rough North Sea weather and lit by an internal
glow.

A comparable *mise-en-scène* of compressed activity and transport euphoria can be found in the plan for Euralille, the business district now under
construction in Lille next to the historic centre and around the station for the
high speed train. OMA is involved in this scheme not as the architect but as
the town planner. Although the notes to the plan stress the chaotic end result,
the compactness of the design is undeniable. It brings together the traffic
infrastructure – the high-speed rail link, the ring road, a car park – in a single linear element so that land is freed for urban use. This linear transport
combination then forms the base for a line of office blocks, a spine linking
the centre with the suburbs. This base itself is made transparent, so that the
passage of the high-speed train is visible everywhere, right up to the 'Parvis
de la Gare'. The train is embodied into the life of the city, becoming a source
of collective pride and excitement. Euralille never imitates the historic city,
but it has the qualities one wants from a city: an operational order, and at the
same time a variety of impressions, a stimulatingly vital appearance.

The end of 1992 saw the completion of the Kunsthal in Rotterdam, a
building for cultural events located in the Museumpark which Koolhaas also
designed, in cooperation with the French landscape architect Yves Brunier.
In this rich and complex work, his most important public building in the
Netherlands, many of the themes discussed are to be found. But it also draws

OMA, *Kunsthal,* Rotterdam
(Photo by Michiel Ibelings).

attention to one aspect that is often neglected or undervalued: Koolhaas' unconventional use of materials. He uses steel sections next to debarked tree trunks, yellow travertine next to roughly worked concrete. All materials are of equal value to the artist, wrote Adolf Loos in 1898, adding that the cladding was more important than the construction which held it in place, and that textiles are the common origin of both architecture and clothing. A particularly clear illustration of this thesis is the Kunsthal's auditorium, which is separated from the surrounding space by a thick curtain. When the auditorium is not in use, the curtain is kept open; when it is rolled up the rising hem gives it the elegance of an evening gown. The architect noted for his conceptual rigour has here produced an especially tactile building. Outside, the walls and roofs are covered with semi-transparent corrugated sheets. They reveal what usually remains unseen: the skeleton of the wall, the movement of the lift – but they conceal the windows. In the evening when artificial light projects the windows onto the corrugated sheets, the effect is unearthly.

PAUL VERMEULEN
Translated by John Rudge.

The designs marked with an asterisk have not been built.
An exhibition of the work of OMA will be held at the Museum of Modern Art in New York at the end of 1994. On this occasion the book *Small, Medium, Large, Extra Large* (a survey of the history of OMA) will be presented.

FURTHER READING   *Rem Koolhaas – Office for Metropolitan Architecture.* In: Architecture and Urbanism, 217, October 1988.
DIJK, HANS VAN, *Rem Koolhaas, Architect* (text in Dutch and English). Rotterdam, 1992.

From

Gazettiers to Newspaper Groups

The Press in Flanders

At the time of Belgium's independence in 1830, public life in Flanders was completely gallicised. The Flemish middle classes, those who could afford a daily newspaper, read mainly French publications. Flemish newspapers had a very small share of the market, and in any case appeared only one to three times a week. This weak position contrasts sharply with the flourishing beginnings of the Flemish press in the seventeenth century. In the Spanish Netherlands most publications were in Dutch, and the Flemish press set the standard for Europe.

The Flemish press before Belgian Independence

The development of the first Flemish newspapers during the rule of Albert and Isabella (1598-1631) had much to do with the fact that Flanders had many printers of renown. The first *gazettiers* were, after all, also printers. The first *gazettier* in the Southern Netherlands to be granted a licence to publish a newspaper was Abraham Verhoeven, with *Weekelycke Tydinghe* (Weekly News, 1629-1631). Two other Antwerp *gazettiers* were also given permission to publish newspapers. Other licences were granted to Flemish *gazettiers* in Ghent, Bruges and Brussels. At that time Dutch was a lively cultural language which was spoken in the highest circles. Naturally, there was no freedom of the press under the Ancien Regime. The press was subject to censorship and was the servant of those in power at the time.

The lead which the Flemish press had built up under Spanish rule (1555-1713) was lost during the Austrian period (1713-1792). Many 'enlightened' journalists of liberal ideas fled from France and came to Flanders, where they were able to resume their activities under the 'enlightened' Austrian rulers. The ideas of the French Enlightenment had enormous impact, and French became the language of culture. More and more French-language newspapers were launched in Brussels. During the period of French rule (1792-1814) French became the language of society and the upper classes abandoned Flemish for French. French-language newspapers increasingly drove out those in Flemish. During the Napoleonic period, a sort of linguistic compulsion was imposed on the remaining Flemish newspapers: they had to be published in French, but were allowed to include a Dutch translation!

By the time Belgium was incorporated into the Netherlands in 1815, the bourgeoisie was completely gallicised and only the lower classes in Flanders still spoke Flemish. King William I reacted against this with a deliberate policy of encouraging the use of Dutch. However, his regime was not popular with the majority because he opposed the Catholic Church. William I was faced with an insoluble dilemma: Catholic Flanders sided with the gallicised bourgeois opposition. The only support William received for his policy in Flanders came from the liberal – albeit gallicised – bourgeoisie. William I had made funds available for new Dutch-language newspapers, but these government newspapers received little support from the Catholic Flemish, most of whom were, moreover, illiterate. In the end William's language policy did little to help the Flemish press. The daily press remained the monopoly of the French-speaking elite.

Although William I abolished censorship, he passed a large number of repressive laws which restricted freedom of speech. The opposition press played a major role in the resistance to William I, and Belgium has never seen so many press lawsuits as during the short Dutch regime. When the revolution of 1830 erupted many journalists had already been exiled from Belgium. On their return to an independent Belgium many of these exiled journalists were politically active, and they were partly responsible for the very progressive press legislation introduced in Belgium in 1830.

The Flemish press and independent Belgium

After Belgium became independent in 1830 it had one of the most liberal press regimes in Europe. Many foreign journalists, mainly from France, were attracted by this liberal press climate and settled in Belgium. All political tendencies were represented, from unionist-oriented newspapers, which defended the new Belgium, to Orangist newspapers, which wanted to bring an end to the Belgian state and join up again with the Kingdom of the Netherlands!

The majority of publications were Catholic or liberal; but within each of these ideological pillars there were markedly different views, so that the press reflected a wide range of opinions. The French-language press in Flanders retained its dominant position and French now became the official language. The Flemish press had little opportunity to develop. Many Flemish people were illiterate; moreover, they were poor and could not afford the expensive dailies. Stamp duty kept the price of daily newspapers high, and the press thus continued to be the privilege of the wealthy bourgeoisie. Those newspapers which appeared in Dutch were only published one to three times per week, and their circulation was very small.

In 1844 a group of writers set up a Flemish newspaper, *Vlaemsch België* (Flemish Belgium). They had trouble raising the starting capital; in fact the largest sum came from a Walloon solicitor, Lucien Jottrand, a supporter of the new radical party. He gave the money not because he wanted to give the

MANDAG 18 APRIL 1994

BELGIE TREKT ZIJN ZONEN TERUG

A6

Het Nieuwsblad

Vlucht door wildpark

GENT OUDENAARDE EEKLO

DAGBLAD • PRIJS 26 Fr.

newspaper a radical flavour, but because he believed that the Belgian state would fall apart if the Flemish were not granted their rights. The Prussian embassy in Brussels also helped to finance this first Flemish newspaper; the ambassador immediately took out a number of subscriptions, and also requested official financial support from Prussia. Prussia was willing to support *Vlaemsch België* because the Germans expected the Flemish daily to support the controversial *Zollverein.* Such foreign support for newspapers was not unusual in the nineteenth century; France also supported French-language newspapers in Belgium. In its first quarter *Vlaemsch België* had quite a large number of subscribers. However, in subsequent quarters the number of subscribers fell sharply and after ten months the paper folded due to lack of funds. Only after the paper's disappearance did the Prussian embassy in Brussels receive permission from Prussia to provide financial support. Nevertheless, during its short existence, this first Flemish newspaper had taken up the struggle for Flemish rights, and made a conscious effort to inject new life into Flemish culture.

In 1848 stamp duty was abolished and the price of newspapers immediately fell. Initially this measure did little to help the Flemish press. It was mainly the French-language newspapers, with their larger potential readership, which benefited. The Flemish daily press did not develop fully until the last decades of the nineteenth century. A number of social factors stimulated its growth: a growing Flemish consciousness, the implementation of the first important language laws, universal plural suffrage and the decrease in illiteracy in Flanders. The fall in the price of daily newspapers was a further, very important factor. While the abolition of stamp duty had already paved the way for a price decrease, this was strongly reinforced by the fact that advertising was being developed as a new source of income. Thus the paper gained a second market, the advertisers, in addition to its readership. The third important factor in the development of cheap popular newspapers was technological advance. New typesetting and printing techniques meant that newspapers could be produced much more quickly and in greater quantities.

Towards the end of the nineteenth century, many 'penny-sheets' were launched in Flanders, all of them oriented towards the three main political parties: Catholics, Liberals and Socialists. Almost all of the major Flemish newspapers still published today were founded at the end of the nineteenth century; among them *De Gazet van Antwerpen* (Antwerp Gazette), *De Gentenaar* (The Ghent Citizen), *Het Volk* (The People), *Het Laatste Nieuws* (The Latest News) and *De Nieuwe Gazet* (The New Gazette).

If we look at the circulation figures for the Flemish press as a whole at the end of the nineteenth century, we see that these are still well below the figures for the French-language press. Nevertheless, the Flemish press had come a long way.

The aftermath of the First World War and political repression left their mark on the Flemish press. Newspapers which had actively collaborated with the Germans were banned, but the war courts were less severe with those newspaper publishers who had merely continued to publish. Most pre-war newspapers could thus resume publication after the Armistice, though a small number of newspapers which had not appeared during the war were, for various reasons, never published again. The first Flemish nationalist newspaper, *De Schelde* (The Scheldt), which changed its name in 1936 to

VANDAAG

De Standaard

DAGBLAD VOOR STAATKUNDIGE, MAATSCHAPPELIJKE EN EKONOMISCHE BELANGEN

Blauwhelmen klaar om zich weg te banen uit Ruanda

A
VVK
V
7iste jaargang — nr. 108
Maandag 18 april 1994
Prijs 28 fr.

Volk en Staat (People and State), was launched after the war as the mouth-piece of the Frontbeweging (This Front Movement grew up in the trenches to defend the rights of the Flemish soldiers). Not many newspapers were launched during the inter-war period. Two important Catholic dailies were set up, and are still in existence: *De Standaard* (The Standard) in 1918, and *Het Belang van Limburg* (The Interests of Limburg) in 1933. The same period saw establishment of a new socialist daily in Antwerp, *De Volksgazet* (People's Gazette, 1918-1976), as well as the first real Flemish tabloid *De Dag* (The Day, 1934-1944). The combined circulation of Flemish papers remained slightly lower than that of the French-language publications, but the enormous gap which had developed after 1830 had been almost closed. Also, fewer and fewer French-language dailies appeared in Flanders (there were now only five, and their circulation was gradually falling).

The Second World War had a greater impact on the development of the Flemish press than the First World War. Many dailies appeared in occupied Flanders. First there were the 'stolen' newspapers published against the will of their publisher-owners, such as *Het Laatste Nieuws* and *De Vooruit* (The Advance). Second, newspapers which wanted to continue publication, in preference to leaving their newspapers in the hands of opportunists: among others, *De Standaard, Het Nieuws van de Dag* (The Daily News) and *De Gentenaar*. Third, those which actively collaborated. In this third category only the pre-war daily *Volk en Staat* was politically active, in conjunction with the VNV (*Vlaamsch Nationaal Verbond;* Flemish National League) in Flanders. The other collaborationist papers were set up during the war itself, for example, the newspapers of DeVlag (*Deutsch-Vlämische Arbeits-gemeinschaft;* German-Flemish Labour League). After the war, however, political repression hit harder and all daily newspapers found themselves in the same situation, either permanently banned or temporarily suspended. This meant, for instance, that no major pre-war Flemish Catholic daily could resume publication in Brussels after the Second World War. *De Standaard – Het Nieuwsblad* was sequestered and *Het Nieuws van de Dag – Het Volksblad* was temporarily suspended. Only the 'stolen' dailies could be published again immediately (the liberal *Het Laatste Nieuws* in Brussels). All journalists who had worked during the occupation were prohibited from working. Some newspapers which had not appeared during the Second World War quietly died as a result of four years of inactivity. Among these was one of the oldest newspapers in Europe, *De Gazette van Gent* (The Ghent Gazette), which had been established back in the seventeenth century.

All these suspensions and disappearances did indeed provoke a consider-able number of new initiatives, although most of the resulting newspapers only enjoyed a very short life. Because Brussels no longer had a Catholic daily, a number of Catholic industrialists decided to launch a *Nieuwe Standaard* (New Standard). A few years later, however, when the family Sap (owners of *De Standaard*) bought *De Standaard* out of sequestration in 1947 for 25 million Belgian francs, the publishers had to change the title *Nieuwe Standaard* to *De Nieuwe Gids* (The New Guide). After the Second World War no more daily newspapers were launched in Flanders, with the exception of *De Nieuwe Gids* and *De Financieel Economische Tijd* (The Financial and Economic Times). This was a sign of new problems which would face the Flemish press.

The Flemish daily press today

Unlike many other European countries, concentration within the Flemish newspaper industry did not begin until after the Second World War. The number of daily titles in Flanders gradually decreased as a result of the many mergers. In 1993 there were eleven daily newspapers, controlled by only five groups. The stronger newspaper groups bought up papers, which they often continued to publish for a few years and then closed down. The surviving groups have thus established strong market positions and the weaker newspapers are unable to compete. In consequence, the pluralism of the Flemish press has decreased.

One of the worst shocks in the recent history of the Flemish press has been the failure of one of the most powerful Flemish newspaper groups, the *Standaard* group. The paper was declared bankrupt in 1976, partly as a result of bad management, but more particularly because of reckless non-media investments. The group was, however, able to resume its activities when a number of banks and Flemish industrialists financed a rescue operation. Their strategy has paid off: today the *Standaard* group is the market-leader of the Flemish press. With its daily titles *De Standaard, Het Nieuwsblad* (The News-Sheet) and *De Gentenaar,* the *Standaard* group has the largest market share in both sales and advertising.

With the exception of the liberal *Het Laatste Nieuws* group, the three remaining daily newspaper concerns belong, like the *Standaard* group, to the Catholic segment of society; these are *Het Volk* (The People) with *De Nieuwe Gids, De Gazet van Antwerpen* with *De Gazet van Mechelen* (The Mechlin Gazette) and *Het Belang van Limburg.* While all these papers lean towards the Catholic side, they have no ownership links with the Catholic party. Only *Het Volk* with *De Nieuwe Gids* is owned by a Christian syndicate. The fifth group, *Het Laatste Nieuws,* is liberal in orientation. This newspaper controls the liberal daily *De Nieuwe Gazet* (The New Gazette) and in 1986, for the symbolic sum of 1 franc, bought the only remaining left-wing publication, *De Morgen* (The Morning). *De Morgen* hoped that this takeover would enable it to make a fresh start after a long period of difficulty. *De Morgen,* started in 1976 as a result of a merger between the bankrupt Antwerp socialist daily *Volksgazet* and the Ghent *Vooruit,* continued to make a loss in spite of many efforts. In 1986 the Socialist party decided to stop all forms of financial support. The official explanation was that the financial 'hole' was too large, but the fact that the newspaper now and again criticised the party leadership undoubtedly contributed to the bankruptcy of *De Morgen.* Despite the fact that the support of its readership enabled it to be published again, *De Morgen* was unable to improve its circulation figures. Average circulation remained at around 30,000. Consequently the newspaper did not attract enough advertising, and its problems mounted once again. The new owners, *Het Laatste Nieuws,* are apparently now planning to dispose of the newspaper. If another group is not quickly found to take it over, this could be the end of *De Morgen.*

It must be emphasised that there is virtually no foreign involvement in the Flemish daily newspaper concerns (compare the French-language newspaper *Le Soir* (The Evening), which leads the Belgian market, in which the French newspaper magnate Robert Hersant owns 41% of the shares). The

DAGBLAD • UITGEVER: EGBERT HANS • MAANDAG 18 APRIL 1994 • 15de JAARGANG NR. 84 • 32 PAGINA'S • PRIJS 30 FRANK • EDITIE ALGEMEEN

DE MORGEN

Buitenland 12-16
Kultuur 26-27
Opinie 11
Sport 17-25
Service 28-29
Televisie 30-31

weekly press is a different matter: as the result of a merger, the Dutch group VNU controls all women's, family and television weeklies. In Flanders there is one major Flemish company competing with this Dutch group, namely Roularta. Roularta publishes mainly instructive periodicals.

Total circulation, which has for some time been ahead of the French-language press as a whole, has been declining during the last three years. Circulation gradually increased between the Second World War and the early 1970s but then fell to a low-point in 1975-1976, after which it rose slowly and then stagnated. In recent years, however, circulation has fallen to a lower level than the historic low-point of 1975-1976.

The Catholic press predominates, with 70% of the market. The liberals have 24% and the socialists 2% while 4% is neutral *(Financieel Economische Tijd)*. There is a notable discrepancy between readers and voters: in percentage terms the number of readers of Catholic publications is greater than the number voting for the Catholic party. With the socialist press, this situation is reversed.

After the Second World War the Flemish dailies increasingly focused their attention on various vexed questions which were to convulse political life in Flanders: the political repression, the Royal Question, the transfer to Wallonia of the French-language University of Louvain, the Brussels problem, the linguistic upheavals around Voeren (a place on the border of Flanders and Wallonia), the recent constitutional reform which offered Flanders more autonomy, etc. It is not possible to deal with these issues in detail here. Moreover, an analysis of the attitudes of the various newspapers towards such issues can only be based on scientifically proven, objective analyses of their content, and these are for the most part lacking.

The Flemish press is still a vehicle for political opinion, with the newspapers reflecting the opinions of those political parties towards which they lean. However, reporting of the recent constitutional reform often left much to be desired: the material was so complex that journalists either became entangled in jargon incomprehensible to the reader, or gave up. In recent years the press has totally failed to bridge the growing gap between the man in the street and the state. Moreover, intense competition and commercial reasons have led certain newspapers to abandon political and socio-economic reporting in favour of human interest stories and sensationalism.

In recent years, the publishers of daily newspapers have sounded the alarm more than once. Income from both sales and advertising is falling. The dailies are increasingly dependent on advertising and need to derive 55-70% of their income from this source if they are to remain financially viable. However, two of them, *De Morgen* and *Het Volk,* only derive 30% of their income from advertising. This is particularly dangerous for *De Morgen,* which also has a small circulation. In Flanders in 1988 only 25.1% of total media advertising was placed in daily newspapers; the figure for 1990 was 17.4%.

VTM, the new commercial television station which began broadcasting in Flanders in 1989, and BRTN radio, which began to broadcast advertisements in October 1990, are often blamed for this situation. Daily newspapers still derive a considerable income from classified advertisements (job vacancies, real estate etc.), but this market has also declined as a result of the economic recession.

Readers have also deserted the cause: between 1988 and 1992 the circulation of the Flemish press fell by 2.7%. Only *Het Laatste Nieuws* saw an increase in sales. This 'success' was due to a tabloid strategy: more gossip and sensationalism is apparently the only way to attract more readers. Many point to the commercialisation of the media – and in particular the commercial station VTM – as the root cause. It is often claimed that youngsters are in thrall to a visual culture and no longer read.

While revenue from advertising and sales is decreasing, costs are increasing. In Flanders between 1988 and 1992, the costs of the dailies rose by 31%, principally as a result of increasing wage bills and production costs. Increasing wage costs are certainly not due to increased employment because, with a few exceptions, all groups have trimmed down their operations. Moreover, many publishers complain about distribution costs, which are increasing while the quality of the distribution itself often leaves much to be desired.

In the past the publishers of the dailies have, naturally, sought strategies to improve their situation. A number of them became active in the weeklies market, with varying success. The commercial station VTM, in particular, ate into advertising revenue.

Initially all newspaper groups, with the exception of the *Standaard* group and *De Morgen*, were shareholders in the commercial station VTM (each to the tune of 11%). Media experts were highly critical of this merging of interests between the daily newspapers and commercial television, believing that it came frighteningly close to establishing a media monopoly.

In recent years the dailies have also tried to make themselves attractive to the reader: *Het Volk* has been given a face-lift, *De Standaard* has a new extra weekly magazine, *Het Laatste Nieuws* is pursuing a new content strategy and so on. Newspaper publishers will have to employ a deal of inventiveness and imagination if they are to diversify and find new market sectors for their companies.

But the problems persist, and the government is working out a new system of state support. Indirect supportive measures (among the most important of which are the zero-VAT rate, and reduced post and telephone rates etc.) have helped to keep the press going in the past. The principle of direct government support has been applied in Belgium since 1973, but there has been much criticism of the way in which that support is distributed and of the amount of the subsidy. The amount has become progressively smaller: in 1992 the Flemish press received 40 million Belgian francs. This 40 million had to be divided among four newspaper groups (The *Standaard* group rejected the support), and the resulting sums were a pittance which would not save any newspaper concern with financial difficulties. The Flemish government decided that an annual sum of 140 million Belgian francs is to be spent on government advertising. However, this means little when we consider that each year 2.3 *billion* Belgian francs' worth of classified advertising is published in the Flemish press alone. Proposed government expenditure of 44 million on the training of journalists also raises many questions, especially when we know that many newspapers are having to dismiss journalists. It is time for a serious press policy in Flanders.

ELS DE BENS
Translated by Yvette Mead.

FURTHER READING

BENS, E. DE, '*The Media in Belgium*'. In: *The Media in Western Europe*. London, 1992, pp. 16-33.

Dagblad, 104de jaargang nr. 90   26F

Maandag 18 april 1994

Het Volk

GENT

old

Leather and Lead Letters

Antwerp's Plantin-Moretus Museum

Is it the smell of freshly-waxed furniture, the creaking of the old small wooden staircases, the unique combination of industriousness and luxury? In any case the Plantin-Moretus Museum is not a museum where you just drop in casually on your way through the busy port city of Antwerp. Its exceptionally well-preserved interior and enviable typographical and art collections make it a place worth seeing in its own right, which more than holds its own with other Antwerp monuments such as Rubens' House or the Cathedral of Our Lady. The house known as *The Golden Compasses* (De Gulden Passer) was home to the successful enterprise run by Christophe Plantin (c.1520-1589) and his descendants. With them Antwerp developed into a typographical world centre to rank with Paris, Lyon, Cologne, and Venice. The house owes its name to Plantin's motto and his printer's mark, *Labore et Constantia* ('through work and perseverance'). The two concepts are combined in an open pair of compasses, the moving leg symbolising work and the fixed leg perseverance.

The Golden Compasses:
a family enterprise for three centuries

The *Constantia* expressed itself among other things in the fact that the *Officina Plantiniana* stayed in the hands of a single family for three centuries. Plantin's only son died when still very young, but the printer adroitly managed to bring some of his sons-in-law into the business. The Leiden branch office, about which more later, eventually ended up in the hands of his learned Calvinist son-in-law Franciscus Raphelengius and remained active as a humanistic-scientific publishing company until 1618. The main office in Antwerp was entrusted to the son-in-law he loved most, Jan Moerentorf, who latinised his name to Moretus. The provision in Jan I Moretus' will that after his death the enterprise should go to that descendant deemed most appropriate by the other members of the family proved of the utmost importance for the future of the enterprise. This clause was included in all subsequent Moretus wills until well into the nineteenth

CHRISTOPHORVS PLANTINVS,
TVRONENSIS.

Qui Plantine bonas hoc tempore iuſſerat artes
Creſcere, te iuſſit præla parare Deus.
Omnia χρόνω, inquit, doctorum ſcripta manebunt;
Hæc pius excudat dummodò Chriſtophorus.
E 4

The first known portrait of Christophe Plantin. A burin engraving by Filips Galle, included in his album *Virorum doctorum de disciplinis effigies XLIII* (Antwerp, 1572) (Museum Plantin-Moretus, Antwerp).

century. As a result the house remained undivided for three centuries and its history can be 'pegged' to a succession of individual names.

As is often the case with family histories of considerable length, the first generations of *The Golden Compasses* are the most interesting. Christophe Plantin, his son-in-law Jan I Moretus, and the latter's son Balthasar I Moretus combined intellectual aspirations, meticulous care for a book's formal qualities, and sound business sense, and these were to prove the foundation of an impressive fortune. Moreover Plantin, the patriarch, led a life which is often said to read like a novel. He was born around 1520 not far from the French city of Tours and as a child lived in poverty with his father, the only other member of the family to survive an epidemic of plague. He probably first came into contact with the world of books as apprentice to a Norman bookseller. In 1548 or 1549 he and his young wife established themselves in Antwerp, the trade metropolis that was then booming and offered excellent possibilities for dealing in luxury goods. It was in this field that Plantin was initially successful as a bookbinder. From 1555 onwards, however, he was given the chance to transfer his activities into the field of printing. The capital necessary to set up his enterprise was provided by the leader of the Family of Love *(Huis der Liefde)*, a new religious sect that was later to break through in England and America as well. In return, Plantin had to promise to publish the works of his financial backer in clandestine editions. This proved the beginning not only of the Plantin success story but also of Plantin's struggle with religion. The Family of Love, of which the printer became a committed disciple, preached love for one's neighbour and religious tolerance at a time when Western Christianity was torn apart by the deep rift between Catholics and followers of the Reformation. Publicly Plantin adhered to the Roman Catholic faith all his life, but this did not prevent him from cultivating sometimes extensive relationships with Calvinists. For a while he was the official printer of the Calvinist Antwerp City Council and of the rebellious Estates General. He also set up a subsidiary office in Leiden, which functioned from 1583 onward as the official provider of books to the recently founded university there. All this, however, did not prevent Plantin from signing excellent contracts with eminent representatives of the Catholic camp, among them the Spanish King Philip II, who also ruled the Low Countries, and whose stubbornness was to a large extent responsible for their eventual partition. King Philip acted as financial backer for Plantin's most impressive achievement: the new edition of the so-called Polyglot Bible of Alcalá, the greatest typographical achievement by a single printer in the sixteenth century. This was a scholarly edition of the Bible in Latin, Greek, Hebrew, Syriac and Chaldean, supplemented by an extensive critical apparatus. The King also appointed Plantin arch-printer *(architypographus)* of the Low Countries and – most important of all – he acquired the monopoly of the production of liturgical works for Spain and its overseas dependencies. No small matter, just when the Council of Trent had ordered a complete revision of all liturgical works.

This monopoly proved the real foundation of the family's wealth. Jan I Moretus succeeded in increasing the production of catholic polemical writings and religious works even more and so became the greatest printer of the Counter Reformation. Thanks to the Spanish (and therefore also the overseas) market *The Golden Compasses* remained a very profitable enterprise until well into the eighteenth century. The blow came in 1764 when the Spanish King Charles III rescinded all privileges enjoyed by foreign printers in Spain. But in the meantime the Moretus family had been ennobled and had secured its fortunes by means of successful diversification into other economic sectors. The publishing house had, in fact, become more the prestigious hobby of one of the richest families in Antwerp.

But let us return to the three great ones: Christophe, Jan and Balthasar. The story we have told so far might give the reader the impression that the *Officina Plantiniana* was an exclusively religious publishing house. Religious literature was, indeed, a powerful presence in the house's output from the very beginning. But alongside the famous Bible editions and editions of texts by the Church Fathers, scholarly and humanist works contributed just as much to *The Golden Compasses'* reputation for quality. Plantin printed works by such famous authors as the cartographer Abraham Ortelius, the mathematician Simon Stevin, the philologist and philosopher Justus Lipsius and the botanists Rembert Dodoens, Carolus Clusius and Mathias Lobelius. It is also worth mentioning that the first scientifically grounded dictionary of the Dutch language, the *Thesaurus Theutonicae linguae* (1573) by Cornelis Kiliaan, was printed by Plantin. Kiliaan was one of Plantin's regular proof-readers, and for a long time a lodger in his house.

In the scientific publications especially, layout and illustrations played an important part as well as the typography. The Plantin publishing house called on the best graphic artists of the time to illustrate its books. The lavishly illustrated baroque book reached its peak, never to be equalled again, under Balthasar I Moretus, who had shared his school benches with Pieter Paul Rubens. The friendship between the two resulted in some twenty unsurpassed title page designs.

The Museum

A detail of the Spanish gold leather on the walls of the Lipsius room (Museum Plantin-Moretus, Antwerp).

Anyone who wants to know more about Plantin and his descendants can choose from a rich selection of both specialised works and those written for a more general audience. But to experience what it really meant to make and sell books in the Renaissance and Baroque periods, that reading must be supplemented with a visit to the Plantin-Moretus Museum. When, in the nineteenth century, the *Officina* had sunk to the level of a third-rate enterprise, the Moretus family could not muster much enthusiasm for the sorely needed modernisation. The last book was printed in 1866. Ten years later Edward Moretus sold the buildings, the typographical collections, and the art collections to the city of Antwerp, which opened them all to the public in 1877.

Plantin had bought the house on the Vrijdagmarkt in 1579, when the company was already past its first peak. It did not look as fine then as it does now. Balthasar I Moretus was mainly responsible for rebuilding the unassuming dwelling into a grand patrician mansion. It was he who had the courtyard laid out in a restrained Renaissance style. The interior was luxuriously decorated with gold leather from Mechlin and Spain, and with tapestries from the Brussels and Oudenaarde workshops. Only a fraction of

the original furniture remains, but that fraction is enough to give us an idea
of the great wealth the family had achieved in the seventeenth century.
There is also a remarkable collection of paintings, again started by Balthasar
I Moretus. His friendship with Rubens resulted in a beautiful portrait gallery
of the family's ancestors, of Renaissance princes, and of the scholars
connected with *The Golden Compasses.* Balthasar's descendants also
amassed a particularly rich collection of furniture, and the building acquired
its present shape when Franciscus Joannes had a new facade built in Louis
xv style in 1761-1763.

No matter how beautiful the arrangement of the living quarters, no matter
how charming the courtyard, the unique feature of the Plantin-Moretus
Museum is that it gives the visitor an idea of the way in which books were
conceived, printed, and sold in the past. Until the nineteenth century the
book industry was an organic whole. In most cases one and the same person
acted as publisher, master-printer, and bookseller. The Plantin-Moretus
Museum is a splendid display case for this whole process of book production and distribution. It starts in the type-foundry, where master-type-
founders had been handling matrices and moulds ever since the time of
Balthasar I Moretus. The actual printshop is located in the biggest room in
the house, on the ground floor. Here texts were set by hand, line by line, in
the desired alphabets and founts, many specimens of which are still kept in
the letter room. Then the printers put the type under the printing presses, on
the other side of the same printing room. Two of the presses date back to the
time of Plantin or, at latest, his son-in-law; they are the oldest extant presses
in the world. After the texts had been approved by the proof-readers, whose
big table is installed in a quiet little room, the books were ready to be printed
in the numbers planned for each edition. Finally the books ended up in store
rooms or on the shelves of the bookshop. Clients could buy a single book

here, but large orders were also processed on the counter and sent to all corners of the world. In this way the products of the *Officina Plantiniana* took their place in thousands of libraries, among them the imposing private library of the Moretuses themselves.

The museum's impressive book collection goes back to Plantin, who wanted to put a working library at the disposal of his proof-readers. It only became a real private library with Balthasar I Moretus, who systematically integrated the products of his *Officina* into it, as well as manuscripts and the products of other printers, be they from Antwerp or not. When *The Golden Compasses* was handed over to the city of Antwerp, the collection encompassed about 500 manuscripts and 9,000 old volumes. The museum's curators saw to it that the library became the world's most complete collection of *Golden Compasses* editions. It is also very important for early book-production and publications, both from Antwerp and from other printing centres inside and outside the Low Countries. The museum possesses a copy of the so-called thirty-six-line Gutenberg Bible which Plantin bought to assist in the preparation of his own Polyglot Bible, and which has been given its own separate exhibition space. This rich collection later inspired other people to bequeath their own collections to the museum. The Max Horn Collection, for instance, consists of 1,447 beautifully bound French literary works spanning the period from the Renaissance to the Enlightenment. The *Golden Compasses'* rich typographical tradition also explains why in 1951 the founders of the Plantin Society selected the buildings on the Friday Market to house their series of courses on typographical craftsmanship, which will soon be reinstituted.

Finally, the Plantin-Moretus Museum is also unique because it contains the archives of the *Officina Plantiniana*. Detailed company archives of this kind are very rare; they therefore attract researchers from all over the world,

One of the two oldest presses (dating from the time of Jan I Moretus) (Museum Plantin-Moretus, Antwerp).

and often enhance the interesting exhibitions held in the museum. Research into the past of the Antwerp publishing-house has not been completed yet, and new monographs are being published all the time. In 1989 the editorial board of *De Gulden Passer,* the publication of the Society of Antwerp Bibliophiles, published a hefty volume to honour the arch-printer, which cast grave doubts on his membership of the Family of Love on the basis of typographical research. The last word on Plantin, let alone on Plantin and his descendants, will probably never be written. The reader has been warned.

PIERRE DELSAERDT
Translated by André Lefevere.

ADDRESS
Plantin-Moretus Museum
Vrijdagmarkt 22 / 2000 Antwerp / Belgium
tel. + 32 (0) 3 233 02 94 / fax + 32 (0) 3 226 25 16
Opening hours: 10 a.m. - 5 a.m. (except holidays)

FURTHER READING

NAVE, FRANCINE DE and LEON VOET, *Plantin-Moretus Museum.* Brussels, 1989.
VOET, LEON, *The Golden Compasses. A History and Evaluation of the Printing and Publishing Activities of the Officina Plantiniana at Antwerp.* Amsterdam / London / New York, 1969-1972, 2 vols.

LE BONHEUR
DE CE MONDE.

SONNET.

AVoir une maison commode, propre & belle,
Un jardin tapissé d'espaliers odorans,
Des fruits, d'excellent vin, peu de train, peu d'enfans,
Posseder seul, sans bruit, une femme fidéle.

N'avoir dettes, amour, ni procés, ni querelle,
Ni de partage à faire avecque ses parens,
Se contenter de peu, n'espérer rien des Grands,
Régler tous ses desseins sur un juste modéle.

Vivre avecque franchise & sans ambition,
S'adonner sans scrupule à la dévotion,
Domter ses passions, les rendre obéissantes.

Conserver l'esprit libre, & le jugement fort,
Dire son Chapelet en cultivant ses entes,
C'est attendre chez soi bien doucement la mort.

Sonnet composé par Christophe PLANTIN, imprimé avec le matériel de la célèbre Architypographie.

Le bonheur de ce monde

To possess a comely dwelling, neat and clean,
A garden lined with fragrant flowering trees,
Some fruits, fine wine, few bairns and little noise,
A wife to oneself alone, faithful, serene.

No debts, no amours, no lawyers, no disputes,
No need to share with kinsmen an estate,
To be content with little, expect nothing from the Great,
To order one's affairs as a just man suits,

To live with frankness and without ambition,
To be given without reserve to one's religion,
To tame one's passions, teach them obedience,

To preserve the mind unfettered, the judgment firm,
To say one's prayers while pricking out young plants,
Is to wait for death at peace in one's own home.

Christophe Plantin
Translated by James Brockway.

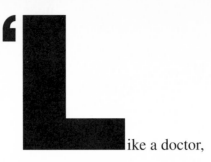

'Like a doctor,

without either love or loathing'

The Work of Henry van de Velde

In his standard work, *The World of Van de Velde* (De wereld van Van de Velde), written in 1967, A.M. Hammacher advances the view that the term 'Art Nouveau' ought to be suppressed as far as possible in writing about the Belgian master-of-all-trades Henry van de Velde (1863-1957). Hammacher himself seems to have had difficulty remaining within the bounds of his own stricture, however. At any rate, it shows clearly that Van de Velde's work around the turn of the century cannot be easily classified. He assimilated disparate influences. Inspired principally by the Anglo-Saxons, yearning in vain for recognition in Paris and enthusiastically received in Germany: Van de Velde could not be other than an eclectic. But Van de Velde was to become an eclectic in the manner of Raphael or Picasso: through the assimilation and unconventional confrontation of different traditions he evolved unmistakably from epigone to authentic innovator. In his earliest architectural creations he was certainly not the equal of his antagonist, Victor Horta. On the

The Bloemenwerf house (1895), Ukkel.

contrary; his own home Bloemenwerf in Ukkel, near Brussels, built in 1895, appears naïve and there is undoubtedly something amiss with its restless plan. Van de Velde was not in fact to develop into a fully-fledged architect, most particularly in Germany, until after 1900, the year of the final death throes of Art Nouveau.

Before the turn of the century his strengths lay elsewhere, his theoretical work being particularly important. This does not mean, however, that his didactic and discursive nature rendered his practical work sterile or second-rate, although, particularly in his early work, there is sometimes a discrepancy between the radical innovations propounded in his writings and the debt to English examples in that practical work.

Already during his first artistic career, as a painter, rationality and discussion link theory with practice. Not for nothing did the young Henry van de Velde opt for the cerebral pointillist techniques of neo-impressionism when he was a member of the avant-garde group Les XX. His great model, Georges Seurat, declared that there was little (romantic) poetry in his work, it was simply a matter of applying a method. As the American art historian Linda Nochlin has suggested, in this respect the divisional technique may even be interpreted as an artistic reflection of the industrial production process and its universal application. Van de Velde himself quickly concluded that 'Seurat's character displayed an extraordinary tendency to intellectualism; in everything that appeared new to his eye this tendency drove him to uncover the line of the engineer.'

This concern with the rational element in art can, of course, also be found in Van de Velde's concept of architecture and in his ideas about new design in general. *'Contemporary generations',* he believed, *'are composed rather of people of common sense than of people with feeling hearts. The moral crisis which Ruskin and Morris tried to bring about, sought to move the hearts of their contemporaries, … (whilst) I have constantly called on common sense and reason! Ruskin and Morris did their best to extirpate ugliness from people's hearts; I preach that it must be driven from their minds!'*

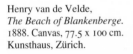

Henry van de Velde,
The Beach of Blankenberge.
1888. Canvas, 77.5 x 100 cm.
Kunsthaus, Zürich.

It is no coincidence that Van de Velde's switch to the applied arts came at the point when he had close contact with a number of prominent figures in the recently formed Belgian Workers' Party. For Van de Velde the artistic avant-garde could only develop by being a political avant-garde as well. But the opposite was also true, since for Van de Velde art undoubtedly encompassed a moralising aspect: more beautiful designs would change people for the better. Van de Velde declared, however, that he had no need for a religious morality (Ruskin) or a prior state of social justice (Morris). This somewhat naïve belief in the primacy of form not only distanced him from the historical materialism of his socialist comrades but also foreshadowed the later historical avant-garde who, on the basis of the laws of geometrical abstract painting, attempted to transform the whole environment. Morris and Ruskin's ideal of medieval craftsmanship was thus resolutely abandoned. The neo-gothic nostalgia of the English reformers was replaced by a utopian progressive optimism which saw in industrial mass production the means of improving the everyday surroundings of the proletariat. For Van de Velde, humanity should henceforth be accepted as it was; he would release it from ugliness 'like a doctor, without either love or loathing'. It is typical of Van de Velde that this fascination with the techniques of the engineer came to be intimately bound up with ornament derived from nature, which was to become the hallmark of Art Nouveau. A good example of this is the wooden Bloemenwerf chair of 1895, the decoratively curved slats of which are scarcely in keeping with the traditional view of an upright chair. On the one hand they recall the plant motifs of his paintings and the vignettes which he created for the periodical *Van Nu en Straks* (Today and the Day After), whilst on the other hand alluding to those skeletal steel constructions which so appeal to the imagination, such as the controversial Eiffel Tower, erected in Paris a few years before.

Bloemenwerf chair. 1895-1896. Oak. Henry van de Velde-Gesellschaft, Hagen.

Design for the 'Hoenderloo' museum (west side of the courtyard). 1923. Crayon on cardboard, 81.5 x 67.5 cm. Rijksmuseum Kröller-Müller, Otterlo.

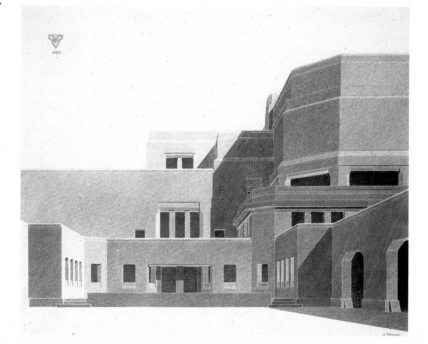

Ceiling light in Villa
Hohenhof.

This rationalist view of art did not lead Henry van de Velde merely to an endless flirtation with the latest whim of fashion. On the contrary, for him it meant a return to the roots of architectural history. Significantly, in 1903 he placed as a motto at the head of one of his texts a quotation from Hippolyte Taine in which the Greek temple is presented, not as the work of an over-heated imagination, but of cool reason. Twenty years before Le Corbusier juxtaposed photographs of the Parthenon and the temple at Paestum with illustrations of recent cars, Van de Velde declared that 'the creative process of construction (of the Greek temples) is exactly the same as that which serves to guide our engineers in the construction of machines, of metallic and transatlantic structures'. Indeed, 'classical' reminiscences come to the surface here and there throughout Van de Velde's work: certainly, in those instances where he marries geometrical simplicity with monumental design, as in the front sections of the tennis club in Chemnitz (1906-1908) and of the Cohen house (1929) in Brussels, as well as in the inner courtyard of Ghent University Library (1936). His archaism and the concept that pure organic form lies at the basis of civilisation are reflected not only in the Assyrian traits of his original design for the Kröller-Müller museum, which dates from the early 1920s, but also in the telluric forms of the houses which he built in Hagen between 1903 and 1906. Between the turn of the century and the outbreak of the First World War, Van de Velde assimilated an increasing number of classical elements into his design language. Moreover, his work from this period is generally regarded as the high point of his artistic career. His appointment in 1901 as artistic adviser for applied arts and industry to the court of the grand duke of Weimar marked the opening of this golden period, which included, among other buildings, the famous Kunstschule and Kunstgewerbeschule (1904-1911). Van de Velde's 'German period' reached its apogee, however, in the Werkbundtheater in Cologne (1914). The undulating concrete masses of this building illustrate his supreme mastery of form and his talent for marrying classical monu-mentality with fin-de-siècle elegance.

Past and future, tradition and renewal, these are not the only contradictions which make Van de Velde's work at once ambiguous and extremely interesting. Thus both Seurat and his great opposite Van Gogh were important for Van de Velde's development. Instead of Seurat's static serenity, devoid of all subjectivism, a number of Van de Velde's paintings from the early 1890s display an extremely enervated, restless touch, which suggests nature set in motion by cosmic forces. It may be said that, twenty years before Kandinsky, Van de Velde gave rise to the phenomenon of abstraction. The famous *Abstract Plant Composition* of 1893 is much more the representation of the idea of a plant than of a plant itself. Van de Velde's role as a pioneer of abstract art can scarcely be overestimated. His contribution was not only important for the subsequent development of painting, but was also and more importantly the motive for his switch, one hundred years ago, into the domain of applied art. It was precisely because he had arrived at an art which dissociated itself from the world that he was spurred on to create an art which was once again 'practical'. This did not mean that he attempted to produce socialist-realist painting but rather that, down to the last detail, he would transform everyday reality with the aid of a new design language. In his own home Bloemenwerf, living is itself transformed into a work of art. Not only the building, but also the furniture and wallpaper, the carpets, curtains, heating appliances, tableware, attire and ornaments were included in this *Gesamtkunstwerk*. Nevertheless, Adolf Loos later remarked scornfully that 'the time will come when the furnishing of a prison cell by Professor Van de Velde will be considered an aggravation of the prisoner's sentence'.

Seurat and Van Gogh, reason and emotion, straight and crooked line, Apollonian and Dionysian would therefore be harmonised at a higher level in the applied arts. We encounter this *Aufhebung,* for example, in Van de

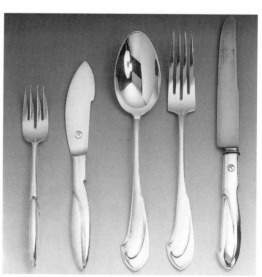

Henry van de Velde,
Abstract Plant Composition.
1893. Crayon on paper,
47.5 x 51 cm. Rijksmuseum
Kröller-Müller, Otterlo.

Cutlery for Karl Ernst
Osthaus. 1905-1906.
Silver. Karl Ernst Osthaus-
Museum, Hagen.

The Nouvelle Maison
(1927), Tervuren.

Henry van de Velde,
Summer Garden. c.1892.
Canvas, 172 x 67.5 cm.
Karl Ernst Osthaus-
Museum, Hagen.

Velde's view of ornament. Ornament functioned for him as the organic complement of form. The mutual connection can only be complementary and structural. *'The duty of the line',* he declared, *'consists in the suggestion of the application of a force at the point where the line of the design describes a curve, the cause of which does not appear to be necessary; at the point where the effects of the tension on the elasticity of the line of the design evoke an energetic thrust arising from the inherent quality of the design. Ornament so conceived completes the design; it is a continuation of it and we recognise the point and justification of ornament in its function. This function consists of the 'building up' of the design, not in embellishment.'* This definition of functional ornament was, of course, inextricably linked to the importance which Van de Velde came to attach to the line drawn by the hand as a gesture, which was the anthropomorphic relic of human creation. 'The line,' he wrote in 1902, 'contains the force and energy of the person who has drawn it.' The arabesque inspired by Van Gogh thus became the absolute principle of an inner framework of implements which have been designed in relation to the human body. Van de Velde therefore was not greatly impressed by Wilhelm Worringer's diametrical opposition of the concepts of *Abstraktion* and *Einfühlung,* of the tendency to abstraction and the expressionist projection of the creative Ego onto the art object. Function and the play of line dissolve into one another in Van de Velde's designs: the curved writing desk which Van de Velde designed in 1899 for Julius Meier-Graefe defines how far the user can reach, the ornamental design of the handle of a spoon differs clearly from that of a knife or fork and is obviously connected with the way in which we hold the cutlery. It is a question both of the elimination of and of the tension between opposites: Apollonian versus Dionysian, abstraction versus empathy, straight line versus rounded corner, functional severity versus ornamental play of line, modernity versus tradition, theory versus practice – opposites which can be found right up to Van de Velde's last work.

Even during his so-called 'second Belgian period' (1926-1946), when he sought links with a new generation of architects (who on the one hand had been influenced by him and other pioneers of the modern movement, but who on the other hand were also distancing themselves from them) there still remained something of these earlier oppositions. For example, Van de Velde was not satisfied with the pure force of volume in itself, in contrast to the most important innovators of the inter-war period. The building also had to be brought to life in various ways. In his Nouvelle Maison (1927) in Tervuren, in the Von Schinckel house in Hamburg (1928), in the polyclinic which he built for Dr Martens in Astene (1932) or in the old people's home for Jewish ladies in Hannover (1931) he made appreciative use of brown Dutch bricks. The subdued and expressive treatment in brick gives to these buildings a marked horizontal dynamic which, moreover, was strengthened by a typical Van de Velde trait: the rounded corners which, as in his very first furniture designs from before the turn of the century, bring about a fluent connection between orthogonal planes. Instead of a static composition of volumes, this brings about a plastic and dynamic continuum, the horizontal thrust of which is intensified by the indented edge of the roof, the design and positioning of the windows and awnings. In the contrapuntal disposition of rectangular and curved planes we also recognise Van de Velde's earlier fascination with linear ornament, whereby two lines of force, acting on each other, became the absolute principle of two natural forces stimulating one another. The rhythm of the curves, moreover, prompts the beholder not to consider the building statically, from a single vantage point, but to walk round the building – an effect which Van de Velde was already arriving at in some of his most important buildings from his German period, such as the Villa Hohenhof in Hagen (1907) and the Werkbundtheater in Cologne.

STEVEN JACOBS
Translated by Lesley Gilbert.

The hall of Villa Hohenhof
(1907), Hagen.

The Netherlands Antilles and Surinam, Treasure-Chests of Dutch-Language Literature

The Governor's House at
Fort Amsterdam
(Willemstad, Curaçao)

Dutch-language literature in the former colonial territories of the Netherlands Antilles, a group of islands in the Caribbean, did not flourish fully until 300 years after the Dutch West India Company first established itself on the islands. The Leeward Islands of Aruba, Bonaire and Curaçao, together with the three Windward Islands St Eustatius, Saba and St Maarten – the latter largely French-speaking – which are situated to the east of the mainland of Central South America, came into the possession of the Netherlands in 1634. Today, they form an autonomous constituent of the Kingdom of the Netherlands, with Aruba having a separate status since 1986. The population totals around 260,000 – Creoles and whites, Europeans and Chinese – of whom some 160,000 live on Curaçao. Although the official language of the islands is Dutch, the language of everyday use is Papiamento, with English and Spanish being widely used in commerce. Papiamento – a hybrid language which, as a result of the slave trade, contains not only Portuguese and Spanish elements, but also French, English and Dutch components – is a language which is still developing. The negroid component predominates in the island population, while on Aruba the Indian origins of many of the population can still be recognised.

In line with this mixed past, the spoken literature which has been handed down comprises popular songs, satirical rhymes and tales of Anansi the spider, of African origin. Written literature appeared on the scene only at the end of the nineteenth century, with the founding in 1886 of the Spanish-language periodical *Notas y Lettras,* under the leadership of the Hispanist Ernesto Römer and the best-known poet of the Netherlands Antilles, Joseph Sickman Corsen, whose descendants we shall meet again in the Dutch-language literature of the Antilles.

This first literature of the Netherlands Antilles was labelled 'art literature' by Colá Debrot, a phenomenon linked to the development of a spiritual awareness. Dutch-language literature – like literature in Papiamento – did not really develop until just before the Second World War – and in fact the main development came only after the War. Debrot, who was born on the island of Bonaire and who became both a lawyer and a doctor in the Netherlands, is regarded as the father of this literature. His novella *My Sister*

Cola Debrot (1902-1981) at
a political rally (Photo
Letterkundig Museum,
The Hague).

the Negro (Mijn zuster de negerin), which was first published in the Dutch
periodical *Forum* and which appeared in book form in 1935, focused attention on his compelling prose and the literary treatment of the issue of racism.
As an author, Debrot was able to distance himself from his subject, though
this is not to say that he did not hold strong views. The fact that *My Sister
the Negro* is a novella does not disguise its unadulterated opposition to the
racism which dominated the 1930s. A young white man returns from
Europe to Curaçao and tries to find love with a negress, oblivious to the hostile reactions from the community. He later discovers that the girl is his half-
sister. Debrot's novella *Pray for Camille Willocq* (Bid voor Camille
Willocq, 1946) can be seen as an expression of the duality which caused him
to seek 'unity', a synthesis. It is also this which he sought to bring to expression while in charge of the periodical *Criterium,* with his proclaimed
'romantic realism', a synthesis of rationalism and romanticism. The existentialist search for an existence which makes sense reached a peak in his novel
Clouded Existence (Bewolkt bestaan, 1948), and equally in his play *Goblet
to the lips* (Bokaal aan de lippen), in which it is once again the mixture of
races and cultures which occupies him. Debrot also wrote several novellas
and poetry collections, plus a number of penetrating, often witty essays, as
well as ballet articles. He was married to the American dancer Estelle Reed,
and in 1962 became the first governor of the Netherlands Antilles who was
Antillean by birth.

The second major Antillean author on Curaçao was Chris Engels – an
emigré from the Netherlands, in fact, where he had already published a number of poems. He was also a painter, composer and fencing champion, and
in addition founded the Curaçao Museum. He published his largely surreal-

ist and expressionist poetry under the pen-name Luc Tournier, which he also used as the editor of the periodical *De Stoep* (The Doorstep), which he founded in 1940 together with Frits van der Molen as a forum for Dutch writers living in exile as a result of the German occupation. But *De Stoep* also provided a home for a number of important Dutch-language Antillean poets such as Oda Blinder (pseudonym of Yolanda Corsen) and her brother Charles Corsen, who was also a painter and photographer, both of them grandchildren of Joseph Sickman Corsen. Oda Blinder, whose first poems lamented a lost love and whose work later embraced the theme of unattainable happiness, was the most important poet of those years, a writer whose wounded emotional life was expressed in moving lyric form.

Another writer whose work first appeared in *De Stoep* was Tip Marugg. Although he made his debut as a poet, however, his great strength and the source of his renown lay in his prose. His novels *Weekend Pilgrimage* (Weekendpelgrimage, 1957), *The Streets of Tepalka* (In de straten van Tepalka, 1967) and *Morning Blazes in Again* (De morgen loeit weer aan, 1988) deal with suicide, fear, loneliness and drunkenness in a way which was hitherto unknown in Dutch literature. Alienation, isolation, and an inability to achieve love created a link between Marugg and figures such as Albert Camus and Franz Kafka.

Frank Martinus Arion (1937-) (Photo by Chris van Houts).

Like Marugg, Boeli van Leeuwen is also an Antillean. His first novel, *The Stumbling Stone* (De rots der struikeling, 1959) received an immediate accolade. Both in this novel and in the two following works, *An Alien on Earth* (Een vreemdeling op aarde, 1962) and *The First Adam* (De eerste Adam, 1966), the inner conflict which characterises his work comes across to the reader as a portrait of a generation without roots and without prospects, a generation not unaffected by Christian existentialism.

A third generation of Dutch-speaking Antillean writers emerged with the debut of the Curaçao-born Frank Martinus Arion, who obtained a degree in Dutch from Leiden University, lived for a long period in Surinam and is attached to the Language Bureau on Curaçao. Following his debut with the poetry collection *Voices from Africa* (Stemmen uit Afrika) in 1957, he found his true form in the lengthy novel *Double Game* (Dubbelspel, 1973). The game of dominoes runs through the whole of this book as a *leitmotif*. The game is used to reflect a series of social relationships in matched pairs: poor versus rich, Dutch versus Antillean, white versus coloured, man versus woman, and so on. The term 'double game' is not restricted to its technical meaning within the game of dominoes, but is also a reference to the double standards of the male players. The ex-seaman Janchi and the former Shell employee Chamon join forces against the taxi-driver Boeboe Fiel and the bailiff Manchi. Janchi is having an affair with the bailiff's wife, while Chamon is a secret bedmate of Boeboe Fiel's other half. The game proves to be the literal downfall of the two cuckolded husbands: Boeboe Fiel is killed by Chamon in self-defence, while Manchi commits suicide. *Double Game* is a critical exposé of life on Curaçao, but is also a powerful and compelling narrative which achieved great success.

In a later novel, *Farewell to the Queen* (Afscheid van de koningin, 1975), Arion resumed the theme of the African origins of the Antillean people. As the first black writer on Curaçao after the white Antilleans Debrot, Van Leeuwen and Marugg, Arion wanted to be a writer with a message. *Farewell to the Queen* was dedicated to 'women with courage', his next novel, *Noble Savages* (Nobele wilden, 1979), to 'people with moral courage'. He was also the founder and editor of the periodical *Ruku* (1969).

Another Curaçao-born scholar of Dutch, who is also living in the Netherlands, was Jules de Palm. He made his debut in 1981, at the age of almost 60, with *Antiya,* a delightful collection of stories set on Curaçao. It was De Palm who, together with Pierre Lauffer – the most important Papiamento poet after 1940 – and René de Rooy, the bilingual Surinamese poet, stimulated (under the joint name Julio Perrenal) the re-emergence of Papiamento song, whose history he recounted in his first book. The Antillean guitarist Julian Coco worked with De Palm on reconstructing the music for these songs.

Jules de Palm (1922-)
(Photo by Jan van der Weerd).

Theatre is a much-loved activity in the Netherlands Antilles. Shakespeare (translated by Jules de Palm), Molière, Shaw and Sartre have all been successfully reworked and performed in Papiamento, and in Pacheco Domecassé the population has found a talented contemporary playwright and director. Originally a singer and guitarist, he is married to Diana Lebacs, who as well as being a singer and actress has also attained renown in the Netherlands as a writer of children's books in Dutch.

Both older and younger generations of writers have found their way into the many literary periodicals, which in turn have contributed to the liveliness of the literary scene and the development of critical opinion in the Netherlands Antilles. Although this small language area seems destined to retain a bilingual or trilingual national culture, the strong development of Papiamento is indicative of the need for its own cultural identity and of an increased distancing of Dutch, which is perceived as an alien language. How this phenomenon will develop in the future is by no means clear.

The former Dutch colony of Surinam, on the north coast of the South American sub-continent, enclosed to the east by French Guyana, to the south by Brazil and to the west by Guyana, gained independence on 25 November 1975. The Republic of Surinam then numbered 450,000 inhabitants: 20 years later, almost half have emigrated to the Netherlands. The Republic is financially bankrupt, economically and industrially paralysed and intellectually emasculated. The years of independence have resulted in maladministration, corruption, powerlessness and a military

View of the roadstead of Paramaribo (From J.G. Stedman's *Narrative of a Five Years' Expedition in Surinam: 1772-1777.* London, 1806, 2nd ed.).

coup, in addition to bloody civil disputes and, latterly, a high degree of dependence on the Netherlands and the European Community once again.

The country was acquired by the Spanish Crown 400 years ago, and later came into the hands of Amsterdam merchants; these in turn were followed by the English and in 1682 Surinam came into the possession of the Dutch West India Company. The population consists of descendants of African slaves, Hindustani contract workers, Javanese, Chinese and just two main groups of the original and oldest inhabitants, the Indians. Three languages are spoken: Dutch, Sranan Tongo – a creole language based mainly on English with words of African and Portuguese origin mixed in – and Sarnami-Hindustani.

After centuries of oral popular art, lyrical dramas and songs, the first collection of poetry in Dutch was the charming, pastoral *Surinamese Poetry Mixture* (Surinaamsche Mengelpoësij), written by P.F. Roos, planter and man of letters, and published in 1804 in Amsterdam. Later in the nineteenth century, the first prose written in Sranan was the work of Johannes King, whose diaries contained travel reports, visions, dreams and historical accounts. But it was the teacher J.G.A. ('Papa') Koenders who first consciously identified himself as a negro, and who accordingly set in motion cultural nationalism in Surinam. For ten years he published a pamphlet, *Foetoeboi* (1946-1956), in both Sranan and Dutch, in which he pursued his fight against colonialism. In 1934 this resistance was voiced much more forcefully by Anton de Kom in *We Slaves of Surinam* (Wij slaven van Suriname). Even before this, however, complaints about exploitation by the Dutch had appeared in Dutch-language literature, in two books by Albert Helman (pseudonym of L.A.M. Lichtveld): *South-South-West* (Zuid-Zuid-West, 1926) and *My Monkey Weeps* (Mijn aap schreit, 1928). Helman, born in the Surinam capital Paramaribo and of Indian extraction, left for the Netherlands at the age of eighteen to study for his teaching diploma and to take a course in music. He became a journalist and writer, worked as a composer and organist, travelled to Spain and Mexico, returned to the

Albert Helman (1903-), with his wife and daughter (Photo Letterkundig Museum, The Hague).

Netherlands in 1939 and played an active part in the resistance to the Nazi occupier. After the War he became a minister in Surinam and Auditor General, and later was made minister plenipotentiary in Washington. Disappointed by developments in his native country, he later withdrew, first to Tobago, then to the Netherlands once again.

In spite of all these activities, Helman remained a productive writer with a large œuvre of novels, novellas, poetry, historical works and translations to his name. His best-known novel, *The Silent Plantation* (De stille plantage, 1931), describes an idealistic plantation owner who sees his high ideals run aground on the rocks of colonial reality. Later novels such as *The Furious Silence* (De laaiende stilte, 1952) and *My Monkey Laughs* (Mijn aap lacht, 1953), once again show his disappointment and bitterness regarding the situation in the land of his birth. The narrator-poet-historian-polemist, former administrator and diplomat, journalist and musical critic, has not yet uttered his last word in his renewed exile. On his ninetieth birthday a new story collection appeared, *Neither Peace nor Quiet* (Peis noch vree, 1993), whose title illustrates how very much alive he still is.

With his first books, Helman was immediately given a place in Dutch literature – the first Surinamese to receive this accolade. To call him a Surinamese author would mean applying an exclusively geographical norm rather than a linguistic one. The day he would return to Surinam, so he wrote in 1946 'will be the day that I no longer feel a foreigner in my own country'. He did not return, and now refers to himself as the bad conscience of the Surinamese. As he put it in his poem 'Ahasuerus':

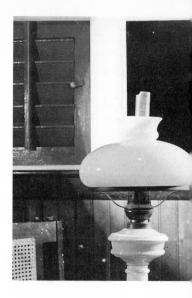

Bea Vianen (1934-).

So here I am now, alone and without a country
other than that dreamland that I
have renounced,
landless and everywhere, just like Ahasuerus.

Surinam was still a country without a written literature when Helman began publishing but, as in the Netherlands Antilles, Surinamese literature really began to flourish only after 1945. Theatre played a major role in this development. With his play *Usury* (Woeker), the writer, politician and painter Wim Verschuur had set the trend in 1936 with his denouncement – regarded as revolutionary at the time – of social conditions in Surinam. 1952 saw the appearance of *The Birth of Boni* (De geboorte van Boni), the debut of the radical politician Eddy Bruma, who spent the War years in prison on account of his nationalist activities (Boni was the name of a group of escaped negro slaves (marrons) who fought a guerilla war between 1765 and 1793). Bruma, who was to reach the positions of minister and of trade union leader, continued to publish, always in Sranan.

Also important was the work of the playwright and doctor Sophie Redmond, who had been coached by the Dutch director Paul Storm. The foremost poets of this generation published mainly in Sranan, with only a few publishing in Dutch as well. One of these few was Shrinivasi (M.H. Lutchman), who has outstanding works of lyric poetry to his name, mainly written in Dutch, though also in Hindi and Sarnami. For years on end a poem by Shrinivasi (with the opening line 'This is the country which I have chosen') was used as a kind of spoken 'theme tune' on Surinam television. The

Leo Ferrier (1940-) (Photo Letterkundig Museum, The Hague).

prolific prose-writer Edgar Cairo began writing in Sranan, but later switched to using his own idiom, a sort of 'surinamified' Dutch.

After Helman, Dutch-language prose did not really get under way until 1969 with the novels *Âtman* by Leo Ferrier and *Sarnami, hai* ('Surinam, I am') by Bea Vianen. With these two novels, wrote Hugo Pos – himself a gifted writer with several collections of delightful stories from and about Surinam to his name – 'Surinamese literature reached maturity'. Ferrier's *Âtman* (the word 'Âtman' means breath, the inner being, the self) uses realism as a vehicle to arrive at the core, the essence. His second novel, *El Sisilobi or the Basic Study* (El Sisilobi of het basisonderzoek, 1969), is situated among the intellectual elite and describes the quest for happiness in the struggle between a historically imposed and a self-assumed inferiority complex of the Creoles and Hindustanis.

In contrast to the work of Ferrier, which attacks the racial oppositions and lack of unity in his own country, the work of Bea Vianen contains almost no nationalist themes and can be considered as largely autobiographical. Her novels are an expression of the inner conflict felt by Hindustanis who have been to boarding school among the Sisters and who are therefore regarded as being Catholics. In *Punishment Cell* (Strafhok, 1971) the main character is a Hindustani teacher who has to choose between someone of his own race and a Javanese. And in *I eat, I eat until I can eat no more* (Ik eet, ik eet tot ik niet meer kan, 1972) the main character is tormented by his Creole grandmother because of his Indian father ('Indians are lazy'). Her fourth novel, *The Orange Paradise* (Het paradijs van Oranje, 1974) was the first to be situated in the Netherlands, and describes the flight from the unbearable atmosphere of Paramaribo.

In spite of research into its history (e.g. by Thea Doelwijt), Dutch-language literature appears to be dying out in Surinam more quickly than in the Netherlands Antilles. It seems likely that closer links will develop with the surrounding South American countries, though which language will then gain the upper hand is impossible to foresee at this time. All that can be said with certainty today is that the literature of both the Netherlands Antilles and Surinam has contributed a great deal to the enrichment of Dutch literature in general, and has come to form a permanent part of that literature.

MAX NORD
Translated by Julian Ross.

Not much Dutch literature from the Antilles and Surinam has been translated into English. Two exceptions are Cola Debrot's *Dagboekbladen uit Genève* and *Mijn zuster de negerin* (translated by Estelle Reed-Debrot as *Pages from a Diary in Geneva* and *My Sister the Negro* in *Antilliaanse Cahiers*, III, 2, June 1958).

There are also two pictorial surveys (in Dutch):
Schrijvers Prentenboek van Suriname (Compiled by Gerrit Borgers et al., with texts by Hugo Pos). Amsterdam / The Hague, 1979.
Schrijvers Prentenboek van de Nederlandse Antillen (Compiled by Anton Korteweg et al., with texts by Max Nord and Andries van der Wal). Amsterdam / The Hague, 1980.

The Art of Glass

Research carried out in recent years has shown that in the Middle Ages a considerable amount of glass was already being produced in the Low Countries, particularly in the southern, more wealthy part which today is Belgium. This was not high-quality glass; most of it was the so-called *Waldglas* (forest glass). The batch of which it was made contained a high proportion of impurities and it was usually greenish, yellowish or brownish in colour. The name derives from the glasshouses of that time, situated in the extensive German forests where sufficient fuel was available for the wood-hungry furnaces.

The development and prosperity of the Venetian glass industry at the end of the fifteenth and during the sixteenth and seventeenth centuries were important for Europe's glass industry. Despite the strict ban on emigration and the dire penalties they risked, many glassblowers left Venice and crossed the Alps to settle in the Low Countries and elsewhere. The first glassworks was established in 1549 in the flourishing mercantile city of Antwerp, where glass was made *à la façon de Venise* (in the Venetian manner). The workers and raw materials for the batch still came principally from Italy, the capital was provided by rich Antwerp merchants. Imports from Venice remained a constant threat, and therefore attempts to discourage them were made at regular intervals, with varying success.

It is difficult to tell the difference between a glass made in Venice and one made in the Low Countries *à la façon de Venise*. However, in the Low Countries a number of basically the same shapes developed differently from those in Venice; well-known are the *fluitglas* (flute) and the *slangenglas,* or as it is sometimes called *een glas met coppen als serpenten* (a serpent-head glass). These were shapes of Italian origin which acquired their own Dutch character.

During the Eighty Years' War (1568-1648) many glassblowers left the Southern Netherlands for economic, but also for religious reasons, and moved to the Northern Netherlands; and this led to a new period of pros-

Covered jar. The Netherlands, second half seventeenth century. *Façon de Venise,* filigree glass with alternating *a retorti* and *a fili* rods. Rijksmuseum, Amsterdam.

perity. In the north, in the Dutch Republic, the first glassworks to make glass *à la façon de Venise* was established in Middelburg in 1581. The local authorities welcomed this new type of industry within the city walls and offered a number of concessions. In 1597 in Amsterdam the city council concluded an agreement with Antonio Obizzo whereby the latter undertook to settle in the city with his family and to teach local glassblowers the art of blowing *Cristalleyne glaezen,* as glass *à la façon de Venise* was known. In return the city council provided Obizzo with a place to live, and exempted him from certain civic duties such as guard duty and the payment of taxes on beer. The latter was important because glassblowers drank a great deal of beer, the water being undrinkable! Glassblowers were notorious for their drinking capacity, and naturally this sometimes led to fights. During the seventeenth century glassworks were set up in many towns in the Dutch Republic, with varying success. The glassworks of the Hague, Haarlem, 's Hertogenbosch and Rotterdam were renowned.

From about 1675 lead crystal was made in England; this has a higher refractive index and greater clarity than the Italian soda glass. This discovery revolutionised glass production in Europe. English lead crystal conquered the market; not until the eighteenth century was lead crystal produced on the continent. In the second half of the eighteenth century Liège and Namur became important glass-producing centres. In the Dutch Republic production was confined to glass for everyday use, such as bottles, while more costly glassware was imported from England, Bohemia and the Southern Netherlands. In 1771 Le Francq van Berkhey remarked that, with the exception of 's Hertogenbosch, only coarse glass was made in the Dutch Republic.

Ancient decorative techniques

Diamond-point engraving dates from Roman times. In Venice the technique flourished again in the second half of the sixteenth century. North of the

Dish. Leiden, 1685. Diamond-point engraved by Willem Jacobsz van Heemskerk with an inscription in calligraphy. Rijksmuseum, Amsterdam.

Alps, diamond-point engraving in the Venetian manner began to be practised in the late sixteenth century. In the Dutch Republic in particular, the technique was developed to a standard not previously attained. The principle is very simple: scratches are made on the surface of the glass with a diamond point. However it takes a high degree of skill to achieve a good surface division on the curved surface of a glass. Details such as hands and faces reveal the hand of a master. The earliest examples date from the end of the sixteenth century. Although some diamond-point engraving was done by professionals, it was principally a pastime for the well-to-do. Famous engravers were: Anna Roemers Visscher (1583-1651) and Maria Tesselschade (1594-1649), daughters of the famous grain merchant and poet Roemer Visscher (1547-1620), and Anna Maria van Schuermann (1607-1678), a learned and – for her time – emancipated woman. The Leiden textile merchant and rhetorician Willem Jacobsz Van Heemskerk (1613-1693) decorated many bottles, goblets and bowls with diamond-point engraving and inscriptions in calligraphy. This was how he passed the time on his business trips by barge, as he tells us on one of his bottles.

Covered jar. The Netherlands, second quarter eighteenth century. Wheel engraved with the picture of a delivery room and the inscription 'Het, welvaaren, van, de, kraamvrouw, en, kintie' ('The well-being of the new mother and her child'). Rijksmuseum, Amsterdam.

Wheel engraving, like diamond-point engraving, was also known in Roman times. At the end of the sixteenth century a group of craftsmen and artists around Gaspar Lehman, a gem cutter to Emperor Rudolf II in Prague, developed wheel engraving. This technique flourished particularly in the glass centres of Germany and Bohemia; it became popular in the Dutch Republic during the second half of the seventeenth century and remained fashionable throughout the eighteenth century. In this process the glass is held with both hands against the edges of a rotating wheel, which cuts the image into the glass. It was not until the end of the seventeenth century that the technique superseded diamond-point engraving. Many wheel engravings with coats of arms, inscriptions, marriage tokens, erotic scenes, etc. have survived from the eighteenth century. Many glasses were engraved for one of the numerous societies which flourished at this time.

The most famous wheel engravers were without doubt Jacob and Simon Jacob Sang, both from Brunswick. They worked in Amsterdam from around 1750 until 1770, as newspaper advertisements of the time show.

Stipple engraving is a typically Dutch technique, in which minute specks are fractured from the surface of the glass with a diamond point to form a gossamer-like matt design. In the second half of the eighteenth century, stipple engraving became very popular in the Dutch Republic as a technique for decorating glasses. To stipple-engrave a glass was difficult and time-consuming; the result was a valuable object which cost a tidy sum. Frans Greenwood (1680-1763) is considered to be the inventor of the technique; he was probably inspired by mezzotints of the time. The most renowned stipple engraver is without doubt David Wolff, famous for his portraits of the stadholder's family and famous historical figures such as William of Orange and the patriot Daniel Hooft. Stipple engraving of glasses was still practised well into the nineteenth century by Andries Melort and Daniel H. de Castro, but the hey-day of Dutch glass craftsmanship was already over by this time, and the Netherlands did not achieve an international reputation again until the 1920s with the products of the Glasfabriek Leerdam (Leerdam Glassworks).

Covered jar. Glasfabriek Leerdam, 1925. Cut and engraved with the inscription 'den. nieuwen tijd, 1925' ('the new age, 1925'). After a design by H.P. Berlage. Rijksmuseum, Amsterdam.

Virtually no high-quality glass was produced in the Northern Netherlands during the second half of the eighteenth and the first quarter of the nineteenth century. It was not until after the Belgian Revolt of 1830-1832, when the Dutch borders were closed to Belgian imports, that Petrus Regout (until then a glass merchant) began to make glass tableware in Maastricht in 1836. In doing so he closely copied the work of his Belgian competitors, taking over their sales catalogues almost word for word. His products are therefore difficult to recognise. We know that his output must have been considerable from deliveries made to the courts of Kings William I and William II, and to the Royal Navy of the Netherlands, among others. He also exported a great deal to the Netherlands Indies and to North and South America.

Around 1890 a new arts movement developed in Europe and the United States, which was also represented in the Netherlands. Nieuwe Kunst was the Dutch contribution to the international Art Nouveau movement and the Dutch architects H.P. Berlage and K.P.C. de Bazel were its foremost exponents. In 1900 Berlage was the co-founder of 't Binnenhuis in Amsterdam, where objects designed by young artists in the Nieuwe Kunst style were sold. The glass factories in Leerdam and Maastricht initially took no part in these new developments.

Goblet. The Hague, last quarter eighteenth century. Stipple engraved by David Wolff with a picture of Caritas and three children. Rijksmuseum, Amsterdam.

The Glasfabriek Leerdam (formerly Jeekel, Mijnssen and Partners), set up in 1878, produced good-quality glass tableware, albeit in traditional designs in cut crystal, and for the less wealthy it produced pressed glass, an imitation of cut glass. In 1900 Berlage tried but failed to have a contemporary design for a set of glasses produced at Leerdam. He went instead to the Baccarat factory in France. However, this situation changed when P.H. Cochius became director of the Glasfabriek Leerdam in 1912. Cochius was not only an industrialist, he was also a theosophist and committed Christian with a strong social conscience. Working conditions in the factory were improved and he began to invite artists to design glassware that had to be not only beautiful, but priced for the mass market. The first artist to go to Leerdam, in 1916, was Cochius' kindred spirit De Bazel, mentioned earlier. 1921 saw the production of the first pressed glass tableware, designed by De Bazel. A number of other artists worked at Leerdam during this period, among them Chris Lanooy and the American architect Frank Lloyd Wright.

Meanwhile A.D. Copier, who had worked in the factory since he was thirteen, had become a designer in glass. In 1922 his first set of glasses, *Smeerwortel* (Comfrey) was produced, based on naturalistic forms. In 1927 the intelligent and artistic Copier was made artistic manager of the Glasfabriek Leerdam. His pressed glass *Graniver* pots from 1928 are well-known.

In 1923, following the Swedish example, the Glasfabriek Leerdam began to produce *Unica* glass, only one example of each piece being produced. Cochius supported the production of the *Unica* pieces. In addition to the *Unica* glass, from 1926 on *Serica* glass was produced. *Serica* glass designs were usually based on a successful *Unica* design, and were produced in varying quantities depending on their success. Between 1930 and 1950 Copier was the only designer of *Unica* glass, and indeed most of the everyday glassware from that period is his work.

In 1940 Glasfabriek Leerdam set up a course in glassmaking and glass cutting, the aim being to add new young talent to their existing generation of craftsmen. Floris Meydam and William Heesen Sr. were students at this Glass School.

The International Glass Movement

Until the mid-1960s, glass craftsmen in the Netherlands worked almost exclusively within the framework of the glass industry rather than independently and it was the industry which determined the style of glass objects. To many craftsmen this was a straitjacket.

In the United States, meanwhile, a movement was growing which favoured the production of glass objects using small, portable furnaces. This gave the craftsman more independence. Glass artists such as Willem Heesen Sr. and Sybren Valkema (who received the Lifetime Achievement Award from the American Glass Art Society in March 1994), inspired by what they had seen in America, soon began to work in this way in the Netherlands. Valkema started the Werkgroep Glas (Glass Workshop) at the Gerrit Rietveld Academy in Amsterdam where, in 1965, he built the first studio glass-furnace in Europe. Heesen experimented with glassblowing at the Leerdam factory, which he left in 1977 to set up his own studio, De Oude Horn (The Old Horn), in Acquoy near Leerdam. Many glass craftsmen went to work there for longer or shorter periods. The movement described above, which began in the United States and spread to Europe, was known as the International Glass Movement. The glassmaking course at the Gerrit Rietveld Academy and initiatives taken at the Oude Horn studio, among others, gave rise to a new generation of glass craftsmen, among them Durk Valkema, Sien van Meurs and Bert van Loo. Today there are two distinct trends in glass art. The first is sculptural, often in cast or pressed glass, and views a glass piece purely as an object. The second trend also incorporates a functional element into its designs, as was clearly the case with the early *Unica* glass of Leerdam.

Pressed glass service. Glasfabriek Leerdam, 1916-1922. Executed in several colours. After a design by K.P.C. de Bazel. Nationaal Glasmuseum, Leerdam (Photo by Tom Haartsen).

Numerous exhibitions, in museums as well as galleries, have helped to establish the Netherlands as one of the foremost producers of modern glass.

PIETER C. RITSEMA VAN ECK
Translated by Yvette Mead.

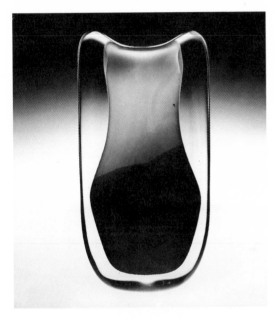

Unica glass vase. Glas-fabriek Leerdam, 1958. After a design by F. Mey-dam. Nationaal Glas-museum, Leerdam (Photo by E. Hesmerg).

Vase. De Oude Horn (Acquoy), 1989. After a design by Willem Heesen Sr. Nationaal Glasmuseum, Leerdam (Photo by Tom Haartsen).

Pressed glass *Graniver* pots. Glasfabriek Leerdam, 1929. After a design by A.D. Copier. Nationaal Glasmuseum, Leerdam.

Chronicle

Contents

An Impressive Home for Dutch Architecture

29 October 1993 saw the opening in Rotterdam of the Netherlands Architecture Institute, designed by Jo Coenen. It was the climax of a long history of attempts to establish an institution of this kind. 1988 was a crucial year for the Architecture Institute. In that year three institutions in the field of architecture merged: the *Stichting Wonen,* the *Nederlands Documentatiecentrum voor de Bouwkunst* and the *Stichting Architectuurmuseum;* and in the same year, 1988, the government and parliament were prepared to make funds available for an architectural museum. For political reasons, the Netherlands Architecture Institute was built in Rotterdam rather than Amsterdam, where the three merged organisations had their offices and would have preferred to stay. In contrast to Amsterdam and The Hague, Rotterdam had no national museum; it was therefore decided to establish the Institute there by way of compensation. The Architecture Institute in course of formation agreed, on condition that funds would be made available for a new building adjacent to the Boymans-van Beuningen Museum.

When firm commitments had been made regarding the site and the subsidies, six architectural practices were commissioned to submit plans: the Office for Metropolitan Architecture (Rem Koolhaas), Luigi Snozzi, Wim Quist, Hubert Jan Henket, Benthem / Crouwel and Jo Coenen, whose plan was eventually chosen. The funds available for the new building turned out to be considerably less than the estimated cost. It took almost two years to accumulate sufficient money to start building, during which time the plans were repeatedly adapted and rationalised.

Jo Coenen's design as it was executed reflects the various functions it houses. Archives, exhibition space and working areas are accommodated in three distinct structures. The stores which house the collection are located in a wing two hundred metres long. At the same time this part of the building forms a protective spine which screens the Institute from the bustle of the city. It marks the boundary of the Museum Park containing the Boymans-van Beuningen Museum, the Kunsthal, the Museum of Natural History and the Chabot Museum. Below the archives runs an arcade which is illuminated at night with a constantly changing pattern of computer-generated colours, a work of art by Peter Struycken. The core of the Netherlands Architecture Institute's extensive collection consists of the archives of a large number of major Dutch architects active from 1880 to 1940, such as Cuypers, Berlage, De Bazel, De Klerk, Dudok, Duiker, Rietveld, Van Eesteren and Berghoef. This means that the Architecture Institute administers a collection which, in its size and importance, is equalled by few other institutions in this field.

The second section is the brick box in which the exhibitions are held. As in the archive building, the facades here are for the most part blind. After all, the care and display of fragile drawings demands a relatively low light level. The exhibitions the Architecture Institute organises cover a broad area: architecture, interior design, town planning and landscape architecture. Its exhibition policy provides for a blend of historical and contemporary, Dutch and international themes. Material from its own collection is regularly shown, following the example of the *Documentatiecentrum* in the seventies. In addition, material from other sources is also exhibited. Three or four exhibitions are usually held simultaneously.

The Architecture Institute's third building is a disc of glass with, as canopy, a huge pergola. In the same way as Coenen designed the archive building as a protective boundary, the pergola was to be the Institute's landmark, comparable to the tower of the Boymans-van Beuningen Museum. The analogy between the two is further underlined by the light-green colour Coenen chose for the columns, the same as the copper roofs of the museum nearly opposite the Institute. The monumental effect of this huge pergola is reinforced even more by the pool that surrounds and reflects a large part of the building.

In this glass disc there are, as well as offices, the library, which is open to the public, and the reading room where the archives can be consulted. On the upper floors can be found a bookshop, an auditorium and a cafeteria.

The Architecture Institute's principal activities are collecting and making the collection available to the public, and the mounting of exhibitions. In addition, architectural knowledge is disseminated in other ways, such as the publication of catalogues and books, the *Archis* magazine, and the organisation of congresses, educational trips and courses.

HANS IBELINGS
Translated by Gregory Ball.

The Netherlands
Architecture Institute,
Rotterdam (Photo by Jannes
Linders).

ADDRESS

The Netherlands Architecture Institute
Museumpark 25 / 3015 CB Rotterdam / The Netherlands
tel. + 31 (0)10 4401200 / fax + 31 (0)10 4366975

Three Notable Restorations

When Antwerp was named 'Cultural Capital of Europe 1993', plans for a number of long-awaited restorations were pushed ahead. Suddenly there were the financial resources and the political will to set to work on a number of monuments. In the summer of 1993 many millions of tourists were able to admire the completed phase in the restoration of the cathedral. The central station, a nineteenth-century railway cathedral, was also thoroughly renovated. But the most crucial decision was to completely restore the nineteenth-century Bourla theatre, which had stood empty for many years, and to reintegrate it into Antwerp's cultural infrastructure.

This theatre is one of the few European buildings which bears the name of its architect. In 1819 the Parisian Pierre Bourla became Antwerp's city architect and in 1827, when the Netherlands and Belgium were still united under Dutch rule, he was commissioned to design the Théatre Royal Français, which was not officially opened until 1834. The freestanding building is of austere construction and is made up of two sections; an angular structure containing the auditorium and a semi-circular entrance hall with a massive foyer on the first floor. The auditorium is of the Italian type, with tiers of balconies one above the other.

For the interior, Bourla called in the French interior designers Humanité-René-Philastre and Charles Cambon, who had already made a name for themselves with theatre interiors in Strasbourg and Bordeaux.

In the 1960s a new theatre with great technical and scenic potential was built in the vicinity of the Bourla. The new building took over from the Bourla, which stood deserted for years. However, the people of Antwerp continued to love the Bourla, particularly since the new building looked so aggressive and awkward. From time to time there was talk of demolishing the Bourla, but luckily the tide turned.

The restoration included the installation of completely new stage machinery, though the unique original wooden machinery was retained because of its industrial-archaeological importance. In the entrance hall, architects De Winter and Van Hunsel have brilliantly incorporated a painting by the Antwerp artist Jan van Riet. The Bourla is now becoming the principal venue for theatre and ballet productions, especially since the other building is being remodelled to accommodate a wide range of events.

It is not only Antwerp and Brussels that possess a rich operatic and theatrical heritage; Ghent does too. Operatic performances took place there as early as the seventeenth century, and in 1698 the new municipal theatre near the Kouter opened its doors with Lully's opera *Thésée*. In 1835 the Ghent city council decided to build a new Grand Théâtre, virtually on the same site. This building was to be the visual expression of the wealth acquired by the bourgeoisie. The design was entrusted to the city architect Louis Roelandt, one of Belgium's most prominent neoclassical architects of the first half of the nineteenth century.

One of the most remarkable aspects of the Ghent Opera is the way it is designed to fit into its urban surroundings. Most theatres and opera houses in Europe were freestanding constructions, inserted into the fabric of the city in such a way as to make them an autonomous artefact of the modern city, but it was decided that this was not to be the case with the Ghent Opera. Instead of four facades, it has only two: a pronounced front facade and a rear facade; the same basic design as a city dwelling. This unusual construction makes for a unique ground-plan. The opera complex is L-shaped and, in addition to the actual auditorium on the first floor, has a sequence of three richly-decorated

The Bourla theatre, Antwerp.

The auditorium of the Ghent Opera (Photo by Bart Deseyn and Guy Oosterlinck).

halls: a foyer, an oval ballroom and a rectangular concert hall. The aim of Ghent's civic authorities was to build not just an opera house but a complete cultural infrastructure for the city, where concerts and festivities could also be held.

The U-shaped auditorium is surrounded by five galleries with balconies. Here Roelandt opted for a spatial design which was popular at the time. It is not only the interior decoration which gives the building a French feeling, but also the fact that the galleries are not divided into boxes, as in the so-called Italian style. For the interior, Roelandt called upon the French interior designers who had worked on the Bourla theatre. The rich polychrome decoration, with its abundance of gold leaf and stucco work, and the monumental chandelier, make this one of Europe's most beautiful auditoriums.

As was the case with the Bourla theatre, the authorities neglected for many years to modernise the technical infrastructure. The totally antiquated equipment of the Ghent Opera became more and more of a handicap. When, at the beginning of 1989, the civic authorities decided to close the Opera for safety reasons, the Flemish Opera Foundation (VLOS – Vlaamse Opera Stichting) was confronted with an acute renovation problem. The task of the VLOS, established in 1988, is to draw up a new common policy for the opera houses of Ghent and Antwerp; a policy concerning both the infrastructure and the organisation of events. Thanks to the efforts of many people, and of the manager Marc Clémeur in particular, the auditorium and technical equipment of the Ghent Opera have been completely renovated, and Flanders now possesses two full-scale opera complexes. The organisation of cultural events is being approached with a new dynamism which has already earned international praise.

The reopening of the Ghent Opera was officially celebrated on 2 September 1993 with a performance of Mahler's Second Symphony, the *Auferstehung*. It is to be hoped that the VLOS will be able to find the resources for the second phase of restoration, namely that of the neighbouring reception halls and the facade. The target date is 1998, three hundred years after the first performance of *Thésée*.

The Royal Dutch Theatre of Ghent was modernised at about the same time as the Opera House. This complex, built in 1897-1898 and designed by the architect Edmond de Vigne, lies between the Cathedral of St Bavo and the Belfry. This, like the Opera House, is not a freestanding entity within the fabric of the city. Its only public aspect is the beautiful neo-renaissance facade bearing a large mosaic by Constant Montald, which has been restored to its former splendour. As with the Bourla theatre the covered entrance, originally intended for horse-drawn carriages, has been incorporated into the vestibule. The restoration has greatly improved standards of comfort and safety in the theatre, as well as its technical capabilities; and this thorough-going treatment also involved a completely new layout for the square in front of the theatre.

MARC DUBOIS
Translated by Yvette Mead.

FURTHER READING

DECAVELE, J., B. DOUCET, et al., *De Opera van Ghent – Het Grand Théâtre van Roelandt, Philastre en Cambon.* Tielt, 1993. (Sommaire Français & English Summary)
MANDERDYCK, M., H. VAN HUNSEL, et al., *De Bourla Schouwburg: een tempel voor de muzen.* Tielt, 1993. (Sommaire Français & English Summary)

The Royal Dutch Theatre, Ghent (Photo by Luk Monsaert).

Cultural Policy

Dutch and English Ears

What has a writer to do with a university? For six weeks, from November 1 to December 13, 1993, I was 'writer in residence' at University College London. I quite liked the sound of it. It seemed as if I had managed to learn a trade after all.

I lived in an anonymous block of flats in the Barbican, and tried to achieve the status of real Londoner as soon as I could. It wasn't too hard. It took only a few days before people began to stop me on the street and ask me directions to destinations that were then still unknown to me.

The UCL Dutch Department is housed in one of the many large and small buildings that make up the College in Gower Street, a labyrinth in which you cannot find your way without help. My activities consisted of attending a weekly two-hour seminar on modern Dutch literature. The seminar focused for this occasion on my prose, in particular my novel *Out of Mind* (Hersenschimmen, 1984). The changing group of students, at most nine, at least five, had been assigned to study my work and to report on it. Some of them study Dutch as their major subject, others study it in conjunction with German or some other subject. Some of them were actually Dutch, but the great majority were native speakers of English. The seminars were therefore conducted mostly in English, even though most students were able to read and understand Dutch quite well. As a writer I felt a little out of my depth. You write a book and it goes its own way. The reader is allowed to do what he wants with it, and does. What could I add to the students' comments?

At a university people study the structure underlying a work of literature. You analyse, subdivide, seek and find themes that are supposed to be characteristic for a certain writer. But this analytical approach can easily foster the mistaken impression that works of art are composed in the same way. I therefore tried to tell the students something about the intuitive approach that is so central to writing, the trust a writer has to put in the 'unconscious knowledge' stored in his head.

A number of seminars dealt with the Dutch literary scene. How is an author's image constructed? What is the part played by critics and the media? I could not avoid some pessimism in my comments on the state of literature in the Netherlands. I see a situation gradually developing there in which more and more attention is focused on fewer and fewer writers. Both in the written press and in the visual media there is a tendency to repeat what others say. But things are not much better in England. In my opinion, the level of literary criticism is definitely lower there than in the Netherlands.

In addition to the seminars on modern Dutch literature I had convened a translation workshop, on my own initiative and with the support of Dr Theo Hermans, Reader in Dutch. More and more students participated in it as the six weeks went by. In five sessions of two hours each we translated three of my poems into English.

Compared to the other lectures and seminars, working on a text was a very concrete activity which confronted students with the 'hidden aspects' of the Dutch language, that whole spectrum of meanings and socio-cultural backgrounds that reverberates in a poem. Many of those hidden aspects were brought to light because we worked on the texts together. Together, because my position was equal to that of the students as far as translating into English was concerned. I would sometimes propose a specific translation that would be rejected by the students because 'you just don't say it like that here'. The difference between Dutch and English ears. I remember the translation workshop as a series of very animated meetings. The three poems we translated were read out in the course of a lecture on Poetry and Translation which I gave at the end of my stay, on an Open Day for which more than a hundred students of

Dutch from all over the United Kingdom had come to London. That translation workshop even gave me an idea that I elaborated on later, during a luncheon at the Dutch Embassy.

During my stay in London I had a long conversation with Faber & Faber, my English publisher. They would be quite happy to do more with Dutch literature but, they complained, competent translators were very rare. The initiative taken by the Foundation for the Production and Translation of Dutch Literature, sending writers for six weeks to various universities in Europe where Dutch is taught, is laudable indeed, but its effectiveness would be greatly increased if those writers could be actively integrated into the teaching of translation.

Several universities in the United Kingdom teach Dutch; during my stay I also visited the Universities of Hull, Sheffield and Liverpool. It would be of the utmost importance for Dutch literature if one of these universities were to be given the opportunity to start such a translation course. That course would obviously have to be concerned with more than purely literary translation.

If the Dutch authorities really want to stimulate the translation of Dutch literary work abroad, this would be the most effective method. One should not expect results after only a year or two, but in the long run the presence of a group of qualified translators would be certain to lead to the publication of more Dutch literature in (good) translations.

J. BERNLEF
Translated by André Lefevere.

J. Bernlef
A Dead Lizard

His death a fine pose
at the bottom of the well
magnified by the water:
lying on his back, legs
curled up, his graceful signature extends
through the swerve of his tail;
his hat, his umbrella discreetly
out of sight,
so a gentleman, a lizard, passes away.

The ticking of my watch almost
penetrates the calm surface of the water.

Translated by Jocelyne van Boetzelaer, Theo Hermans, Cate McPherson, Mandy Melse, Yasmin Penniall, Simon Ratcliffe and the author.

The Elephant Presently in My Keeping
Publishing Translated Literature in the UK

In 1962 and 1963 Cees Nooteboom, a young Dutch poet, was one star among the galaxy of writers, playwrights and poets, at those seminars at the Edinburgh

Festival which were the brainchild of the distinguished Scottish publisher John Calder. The world's press was enthralled by a naked woman (planted by Kenneth Tynan) cavorting in the gallery. The spotlight probably shifted away from Dutch verse, the city elders were wonderfully unamused, and funding for Jim Haynes' groundbreaking Traverse Theatre was suspended. Edinburgh, in those days, felt like Europe.

We made an assumption on *The Scotsman,* where I was Literary Editor in the middle of that decade, that if your city hosted the best international festival your readers would want to be kept abreast of what was published abroad. We reviewed French and American editions and theatre in Paris and (though I cannot recall why) in Buenos Aires. I commissioned a series of essays on the post-War novel. The editor, a cultivated and patient man, let it be known that if the study of the North Vietnamese novel ran to more than half a page I would be relieved of my post. We had dealt with the Japanese, the German, the Italian, the French and the American, and I suspect it was the detailed analysis of the post-War Dutch literary scene which brought the series to an honourable close.

Of all the writers cited in writer / translator James Brockway's admirable article I can only remember that we reviewed the books of Hella Haasse and Jan Wolkers in the paper. Wolkers, of course, was something of a cult hero in Britain at that time and his reputation made poignant Brockway's assertion that, 'Were Dutch a world language, Simon Vestdijk would long ago have become a world name in literature.' That was in 1966, and one sensed then – why else Brockway's piece? – that an exciting new literature was on the brink of escaping from the prison that was its language. The English-language part of that liberation is still far from complete, and the recent death of the very fine translator Adrienne Dixon is a cruel setback.

It is the German publishers above all who have rescued Dutch writers from the Netherlands. And one or two French publishers have played their part: notably the late Alain Oulman at Calmann-Lévy and the ubiquitous Actes Sud. What is wrong in England, and now also in America, is that there has ceased to exist, insofar as it ever did, an automatic curiosity about what is published in other languages. That the habit of publishing in translation has been kept alive since the last War in England is due in no small measure to a group of refugees from Middle Europe. That generation's retirement from active publishing coincides with the rise to the head of many houses of managers for whom the patient development of literary lists is by no means a priority.

I had the great good fortune to learn from Leopold Ullstein, in the view of many a nonpareil among European publishers, and when in due course I joined Harvill I took on the responsibility for rebuilding a list that had been founded by two ladies whose vibrant intellectual energies had been largely directed outside Britain. Indeed Manya Harari (the *Har* of Harvill: her partner was Marjorie *Vill*ier*s*) contrived to publish, sometimes in her own translations, the whole gamut of Russian dissident writing.

In one year Harvill published both *The Leopard* and *Dr Zhivago* but it was also the year that the firm sold itself to the substantial Scottish house Collins, now itself part of the multinational giant Harper-Collins. It is curious, with a list so strong as it was in Russian literature, and having published many French writers, chiefly theologians, that Harvill did not also establish bridgeheads into other languages. That it did not was attributable to the greater nimbleness in those days of their rivals of Secker & Warburg in particular, of André Deutsch, of Robert Knittell at Cape, later also of Faber & Faber, to some extent of Heinemann, and of course of John Calder.

When I arrived at Harvill nearly ten years ago the list was somewhat diminished with one of its founders dead and the other retired. There were, indeed, only two books on the stocks, one of them a new novel by the magnificent Yashar Kemal, from the only other language, so to speak, that Harvill had continuously embraced.

Now we publish in translation from twenty-two languages. Why?

Why? In the Netherlands the question would not arise; in every other part of the world it is taken for granted that a serious house will look in many languages for writers of quality. But: *Why?* when other English and American houses are cutting back their programmes of translation (while every now and again going berserk at book fairs and offering oil revenues to capture one elusive foreign essence rumoured to be, as they usually say, a cross between Marquez and Eco, and occasionally a cross between Eco and Jackie Collins); when the public library market has been savaged by one government after the other: when anyone who knows anything about the reality of modern publishing, which is to say the bottom line, will tell you not only that literature – unless it has a track record – is for the birds, but also that the extra time that has to be spent on translations, on dealing with authors and publishers in other languages is no longer cost-effective.

The answer perhaps lies in the list itself: in the last five years Harvill has published Claudio Magris, Jaan Kross, José Saramago, Torgny Lindgren, Javier Marías, Sebastiano Vassalli, Peter Høeg, Jean Rouaud, George Perec. We are reissuing the works of Marguerite Yourcenar, Leonardo Sciascia, Leo Perutz and Julien Gracq. We publish Raymond Carver, Richard Ford, Peter Matthiessen, Jonathan Raban, Martin Cruz Smith and Robert Hughes. And we are keeping up our Russian list with new poetry, with scholarly biographies and with the long-awaited translation of Lydia Chukovskaya's *Ahkmatova Journals.*

And then, out of the blue, over breakfast in St Malo two summers ago, Cees Nooteboom said that he would be willing to be published by Harvill and I rapidly and gratefully assented. He is not the only writer who has made his way through the outer perimeter and announced his intention to stay, but he is the only one who has come bearing the European Literature Prize in his knapsack. It is devoutly to be hoped that the Dutch Government will do what they can – not next year, *now*

– to ensure that the prize bears fruit, that the book and its author shall be celebrated throughout the world, or at least throughout Europe. It is deplorable, considering the energies and the money that have gone into the judging and the awarding of the prizes for authors and translators alike, that so negligible an effort is made to publicise the shortlists and the awards. And it is especially inept to be losing the opportunity to celebrate a prizewinner who can address almost every European in a language he can understand.

Nooteboom brings with him that rare accomplishment, which he nevertheless shares, among Harvill authors with Jaan Kaplinski, Peter Høeg and Jaan Kross, of being perfectly fluent in five languages at least. And he is willing to work very long hours indeed with his translators and he is willing to help the publisher sell his books by readings, by being in England, by *teaching* his work. This generosity is not always repaid in the short run, but in my experience it is always repaid in the end, even in Britain, but also all over the English-speaking world.

So here – a generation late, one cannot help thinking – the 'young Dutch poet' is reading from *The Following Story* in Heffers bookshop in Cambridge, is reading to a packed hall at the Dutch Embassy in London, is on the radio, is all over the newspapers (even in the gossip columns) where his English is more than once referred to as exasperatingly perfect, and in the course of his time here many regretful references are made to the late Adrienne Dixon, and many laurels are laid at the door of Ina Rilke who has made the beautiful translation of the new novel.

Harvill owes more than any other British house to its translators. Harry Willets, Solzhenitsyn's principal translator, has advised Harvill since before Cees Nooteboom was in Edinburgh in the sixties. He has read for Harvill in fourteen languages. He it was who read Harry Mulisch in Dutch for us, and who of all the Russian advisers we have had since Manya Harari died has done most to shape our list. Since our horizons have widened, other translators have assumed the role of counsellors to the house.

These gifted friends, Tom Geddes, Barbara Brav, David Bellos, Barbara Wright, Patrick Creagh, Margaret Jull Costa, seem to the publisher as much a part of what is Harvill as do our authors and our editors. Precisely what that is changes, grows, from year to year, and is most legible in the pages of the catalogue.

Matt Busby, the legendary football manager, once told a journalist who wanted to know how he made the *shape* of his teams that it was a friend of his, a sculptor, who had put it best: you begin with a huge block of marble and knock off it everything that doesn't look like an elephant.

As to the elephant presently in my keeping, I want it to be coherent only to the point that all the authors and translators should be content to share their English house with each other. It is *their* house. They must be at home in it.

CHRISTOPHER MACLEHOSE

For 32 million Americans, English is not their first but their second language. According to the 1990 census, the some 143,000 of them who speak Dutch are 24th on the list; of these, the highest percentage live in Pennsylvania. Of course this is not a large number, compared to the 17 million people who have Spanish as their first language. This handful of Dutch-speaking people, scattered across so many states, is too small a group to constitute a protected minority. In this respect, their position is quite different from that of the Spanish-speaking population, who are warned in their own language on the New York subway against the danger of AIDS and run their own radio and TV networks in California and Florida. The social relevance of Dutch consists, on the one hand, in maintaining a more modest but no less exciting social and cultural communications network in areas which have a high concentration of Dutch-speaking people, in some cases (e.g. Detroit) going back to the nineteenth century. On the other hand, there is a numerically small but highly motivated group of American academics for whom, for professional reasons, Dutch (or at least Dutch culture) has become a valuable instrument. Both communities have developed their own specific structures.

The first group (the immigrants) own clubs and media outlets, including their own newspaper, in regions with long established 'Flemish' or 'Dutch' traditions, such as Michigan, Wisconsin and Pennsylvania. This group is socially varied and includes workers and farmers, white-collar workers, business people and members of the professions. A new generation of Flemish and Dutch clubs has grown, in a sort of 'intellectual' way, out of Dutch Studies programmes at the universities, as for example Ms Reichenbach's at the University of Pennsylvania, and Johan Snapper's in Berkeley. In the case of the latter, and due largely to the efforts of Leni de Kesel-Lams, the wife of a Flemish businessman, greater social diversity among the members has led to the opening up of areas of activity that go well beyond academia. All these organisations, both the traditional and the more recent, receive support from associations such as the Flemish throughout the World and the Netherlands-America League, as well as from the Flemish and Dutch governments. Support from the governments is limited to the sending of publications and the establishment of academic chairs. In this case, Flanders is responsible only for two visiting Professorships: the Rubens Chair in Berkeley and the Brueghel Chair in Pennsylvania. With a little bit of creativity and a modest budget, logistic and moral support for those many spontaneous and unpaid cultural ambassadors for Flanders would allow them to further expand their activities.

The second group is made up of dozens of American academics, often with an excellent command of Dutch, who have chosen the history, culture and language of the Low Countries as their field of research. The main factor motivating their studies is the fact that the Low

Countries are extremely interesting from an international viewpoint. Their culture has reached great heights, both in the past and in more recent times, and socio-economic changes have often taken place there earlier, and gone further there than elsewhere. Van Eyck, Flemish Polyphony, Holland's Golden Age, the beguines, urban economics and the workers' movement in the Low Countries are the subjects of courses and doctorates in the universities mentioned above as well as in many others such as Duke, Columbia, Rutgers, Madison, Dartmouth and Minneapolis. Here too, an infrastructure has developed. American and Flemish medievalists have formed the highly regarded Society for Low Countries Studies, which, among other things, sees to it that one or more of the sessions at the yearly Medievalist Congress in Kalamazoo, at the meetings of the American Historical Association or at the Medieval Academy of America centre around the Low Countries. An Interdisciplinary Conference on Netherlandic Studies is also held, at regular intervals, at one of the twenty-seven American universities where the Dutch language can be studied. American academics are extremely interested in and fascinated by the culture and society of the Low Countries, and they are really getting down to it!

WALTER PREVENIER
Translated by Peter Flynn.

Dutch Cultural Policy A European Appraisal

For a number of years now the Council of Europe in Strasbourg has conducted a programme for the evaluation of the national cultural policies of its twenty-seven member states. In 1993 it was the Netherlands' turn to be assessed and as a first step a 220-page National Report was prepared by the Ministry of Welfare, Health and Cultural Affairs (WHC), entitled *Cultural Policy in the Netherlands.*

Traditionally, Dutch cultural policy has been one of benevolent neutrality: while funding was provided, the official doctrine was that 'the government is no judge of science and art', a creed first formulated in 1862 by the then prime minister Thorbecke.

In the past ten years, there have been a number of significant changes in this respect. Where formerly culture was seen as a national good, to be supported and promoted by the government, we now find a special law for culture, which defines quality and diversity as the two key principles of Dutch cultural policy. Where formerly there were open-ended funding arrangements and provision of social security for poor artists, we now find a new management structure, a professional planning and advisory process, modern financial arrangements and a government exerting control at arm's length through a number of executive funding agencies. Where formerly the administration would supply the funds and the artists would get on with producing art, they now have to persuade the advisory and funding bodies of the artistic quality and

the social relevance of the works they are producing. The most tangible outcome of this management revolution is the recent ministerial *Cultural Planning Document 1993-1996: Investing in Culture,* which presents the guidelines for cultural policy over the next planning period.

Having set out this central framework, the main body of the report is devoted to a detailed analytical description of what is going on in the various sectors for which WHC is responsible: museums, monuments, archives, archaeology, broadcasting and media, libraries, literature, visual arts, architecture, design, film, music, dance, theatre, amateur art, art education and international cultural relations. In 1993, the total WHC-budget for these cultural sectors was almost 2.2 billion guilders, which amounts to one percent of the national budget. Ninety percent of this goes to the five big sectors of Broadcasting, Libraries, Performing Arts, Museums and Art Education. Per sector the report contains information about historical developments, the aims of government policy, the statutory arrangements, the advisory and funding bodies involved, the financial situation, and data about supply and demand. For example, in the sector of Performing Arts in 1991 there were 21 orchestras with 1,688 performances, 4 ballet companies with 396 performances and 29 theatre companies with 3,800 performances. Together, they attracted an audience of 2.3 million, on a total of 238 million guilders in government subsidies. Over the past decade, the budget for culture has remained more or less the same in real terms, but while the amount of policy produced has increased, per capita spending for culture has actually decreased from 153 guilders in 1981 to 137 guilders in 1991.

The wealth of information in the report, much of which has been supplied by the Social and Cultural Planning Office (see *The Low Countries* 1993-94: 268), is put into perspective in a number of more thematic chapters, outlining the social and political background to Dutch cultural policy and its development over the course of Dutch history.

The closing chapters discuss the key challenges faced by Dutch society in the near future: the general decline in traditional religious and political loyalties, the rise of an underclass dependent on welfare, the accelerating information revolution, the internationalisation of culture, the growing number of immigrants (now 5.8 percent of the population), the changing economic and political climate. The strategies envisaged for meeting these challenges are a characteristic example of the dual approach of the Dutch to cultural policy making. On the one hand, steps are taken to preserve the national heritage with a new Delta Plan, to protect Dutch literature with a fixed book price agreement, and to encourage participation in Dutch cultural life by groups which are now clearly underrepresented: women, young people, immigrants, the less well educated. On the other hand, the challenge of free trade is welcomed too, and the Dutch government has not entered a cultural exception to the recent GATT agreement, which it sees as beneficial not just to Dutch multinational publishing and media companies, but for Dutch culture as a whole. It is, I believe, this dual approach which makes a useful contribution to the cultural debate in the Netherlands and in post-Maastricht Europe.

The second part of the evaluation programme involved an examination of Dutch cultural policy by a panel of European experts reporting to the Culture Committee of the Council of Europe. After a critical analysis and discussions with a wide range of people – the appendix to their report reads like a *Who's Who* of Dutch culture – the panel makes a number of sensible and constructive recommendations. In particular, they advocate a National Participation Plan in order to ensure a really multicultural artistic life: a closer integration of cultural, educational and other policies; a more targeted approach, both at the national and the regional level; and a strategy for developing the economic aspect of cultural enterprises, through a partnership between business and public funding. This latter point is raised because of the panel's concern at the diminishing public funding and their expressed opinion that further budgetary cuts are not acceptable.

All in all, this appraisal exercise has generated a lot of information and ideas, it has put the how and why of Dutch cultural policy more sharply in focus in two exemplary reports, it gives a boost to cultural-political debate, and above all, it should strengthen the resolve of the government to invest in Dutch culture.

REINIER SALVERDA

Cultural Policy in the Netherlands. National Report. European Programme for the Evaluation of National Cultural Policies of the Council of Europe. Zoetermeer: Ministry of Welfare, Health and Cultural Affairs, 1994; 223 pp.

J. Myerscough, *Cultural Policy in the Netherlands*. Report by the Panel of European experts. Strasbourg: Culture Committee, Council of Europe, 1994; 144 pp.

Film and Theatre

Kaaitheater A House of Many Rooms

HUMUS. Vijftien jaar Kaaitheater (1993) is a substantial art book, which provides an overall picture of the work of a unique artistic centre in Brussels. The Kaaitheater came into being in 1977 as a Festival to celebrate the hundredth anniversary of the Royal Flemish Theatre (KVS). The Festival was held five times between 1977 and 1985 – once every two years. This was not simply because its organisers felt that 'we've done it once so we can do it again' – it was a vision beginning to bear fruit. Artistic director Hugo de

Greef wanted to introduce Brussels and Flemish audiences to the avant-garde from abroad. Great names like La Cuadra de Sevilla, the Wooster Group from New York, the Bremer Tanztheater and others all visited Belgium for the first time. Performances by Teatr Stu (Poland), The Artaud Company (UK), Ro-Theater (The Netherlands), Unga Klara (Sweden), Jacques Lecoq (France), Jango Edwards (USA), Stuart Sherman (USA), Akademia Ruchu (Poland), Lindsay Kemp Company (UK), Bob Wilson (USA), National Theatre of the Deaf (USA), Carlos Traffic (Argentina), Falso Movimento (Italy) and others, were a revelation for many people.

De Greef understood perfectly well that bringing prominent foreign theatre to Brussels only made sense if its presence there could bring about a process of cross-fertilisation within the city's own theatrical culture. From the very beginning his aim was to give the sleepy Flemish theatre a 'vitamin shot' to increase its vitality. He succeeded.

Since this kind of work requires a certain continuity, he abandoned the festival arrangement after ten years. From September 1987 the Kaaitheater became a theatre production company operating on an annual basis. The organisation was supported by a merger with a non-profit association called 'v.z.w. Schaamte' (Shame), an important platform for production and distribution, which had also been principally inspired and guided by De Greef for ten years.

Everything depends on the choices one makes. The young Flemish artists brought in by the Kaaitheater not only acted as fertile soil (hence *HUMUS*) to enrich the field of Belgian theatre, in time they also began to shape the face of theatre and dance internationally. I am thinking here of the Radeis group, Anne Teresa de Keersmaeker (Rosas), Jan Lauwers (Epigonentheater, later Needcompany), Josse de Pauw, and Jan Fabre.

However, the Kaaitheater is not an institute, concerned with guarding its own fixed values. Artists working there operate under their own steam, but they are given financial, technical, dramaturgical and promotional support. There are regular coproductions, and these have involved (among others) Felix Meritis (Amsterdam), Theater am Turm (Frankfurt), Hebbeltheater (Berlin), Théâtre de la Ville (Paris), and Wiener Festwochen (Vienna). Once artists find their feet, both artistically and organisationally, they come out from under the wing of the Kaaitheater. However it is still a place of constant dialogue, where Belgian and foreign groups and artists all feel at home as they find an affinity for each other in the comments they make on society. Usually the relationship goes beyond just a single presentation of their work: De Greef follows their development and shows it to his own audiences. It was not until 1993-1994 that the Kaaitheater was finally able to use its own theatre in Brussels: the Lunatheater.

Dramaturgist Luk van den Dries points out in the book that De Greef, with his long-term objectives, has always aimed for 'a careful embedding in the structure of the Flemish theatre landscape'. In the 1970s, when Flemish theatre was openly seeking more social invol-

The Lunatheater building, home to the Kaaitheater (Photo by Ivo Lemaire).

A scene from *Maria Magdalena* (directed by Jan Decorte, 1981) (Photo Kaaitheater).

choreographers such as Anne Teresa de Keersmaeker, Michèle Anne de Mey and Marc Vanrunxt have quickly turned the Flemish handicap into a head start.

According to Luk van den Dries, the present consciousness of the physical body in the theatre is being translated in yet another way. Where modern theatre explores the self-contemplating and self-exposing body, it is engaged, in his words, in 'the digging out of the autobiographical and its use as a stepping stone to another, more authentic and transparent style of acting'. Relevant examples from the book reviewed here are the personal theatrical experiences of Spalding Gray, Rachel Rosenthal, Bob Wilson, Tim Miller, Steve Paxton, Tom Jansen, and in particular the Fleming Josse de Pauw, who has also emerged as a scriptwriter and film maker, together with Peter van Kraaij.

HUMUS. *Vijftien jaar Kaaitheater* has been written in Dutch, French and English. This book of text and photographs provides an exciting glimpse of a theatre which is making history, and which through its own range of theatrical publications is also contributing towards more scientific theatrical criticism.

FRED SIX
Translated by Steve Judd.

HUMUS. *Vijftien jaar Kaaitheater*. Bruges: Stichting Kunstboek / Brussels: Kaaitheater, 1993; 312 pp.

ADDRESS
Kaaitheater (administration)
Akenkaai 2 / 1210 Brussels / Belgium
tel. +32 (0)2 218 58 58 / fax +32 (0)2 218 49 65

vement, he confronted the Flemish group Internationale Nieuwe Scène with groups like the Kollektiv Rote Rübe and La Cuadra, which had a much more daring approach. By inviting great directors like Franz Marijnen, Gerardjan Rijnders, Jürgen Gosch, Peter Sellars, Anatolij Vassiliev, Jan Joris Lamers and Jan Ritsema, he entered into a dialogue with the repertory tradition, lending new meaning to concepts like ensemble, text and space.

In 1981 the Flemish production of *Maria Magdalena* (Hebbel) by Jan Decorte at the Kaai caused quite a stir and gave rise to a new and individualistic practice in the theatre, encouraging a generation of young dramatists working outside the framework of the large city theatres to carry out some innovative production work and a radical dramaturgical analysis. Repeated visits from companies like The Wooster Group (USA) or Discordia (The Netherlands) have in turn created an inspiring dramatic climate for new Flemish formations.

The Kaaitheater has always promoted increasing integration of artistic disciplines. Apart from music, mime, video, film, performing and plastic arts, dance also plays an important part in this. Among the most important foreign guests to make numerous visits are Jean-Claude Gallotta and Steve Paxton. Belgian

Dogtroep Nomads of the Wild Theatre.

Dutch fringe theatre flourished in the mid-seventies as never before. Young and inspired directors heeded the call for the democratisation of the institutionalised theatres and the criticism of conventional ways of directing, and tried to bring the theatre closer to the people once again, sometimes even literally so: by going out into the streets, singing and making music. Companies from abroad, mostly from the United Kingdom and the United States, also came to the Netherlands and left their mark on the new theatre culture that was developing there.

The strongly visual theatre of companies such as People Show from London, Welfare State from Yorkshire, and Bread and Puppet Theater from New York was a powerful source of inspiration for the founders of Dogtroep, an Amsterdam theatre company that staged its first show, *Hey That's Great Mister Silver,* in the streets in 1975. In its 'puppyhood' Dogtroep developed a brand of theatre all its own, not just in the streets, but also in the circuit of neighbourhood and youth centres; a brand which combined elements taken from the Anglo-American fringe theatre with European artistic currents from the beginning of the century, such as dadaism, surrealism, and futurism.

Young people in the centres mentioned above who were not really keen on seeing drama, and passers-by who found the way to their local blocked by theatre in the street, forced the members of Dogtroep to look for ways to survive in a noisy atmosphere and before an audience that was not always very cooperative. They therefore modified the company's style, so that the acts were more firmly based and the props and costumes became larger and more visible. Looking back, these early years proved a hard but fruitful apprenticeship for Dogtroep, after which it soon earned recognition from the organisers of theatre festivals at home and abroad.

In 1985 the company reached a turning point. Extreme pressure of work made many members decide to turn their backs on the company, after which the pioneers from the early period recruited new theatre people with a mixed artistic, technical, and organisational background. The company itself grew more professional, a non-committal attitude gave way to artistic daredevilry, and a greater variety of types of performance was created: spectacular plays in locations like empty factories, ad-hoc productions for all kinds of events and occasions, 'infiltrations' in the form of small, unexpected performances during, for instance, fairs or receptions.

During the years that followed Dogtroep grew into a company of experienced professionals. The company knows exactly what it is doing and can be very demanding, not just for itself, but also for the many producers at home and abroad who are interested in having it perform. In the meantime, Dogtroep has built up such an international reputation that many Dutch fans complain that the company is hardly ever to be seen in its own country. The touring list of the past few years bears this out. In 1992 the company performed in Albertville during the Olympic Winter Games and in Seville at the World Expo.

In the summers of 1992 and 1993 Dogtroep toured the Netherlands again with *L'Ascension du Mandarin,* an open-air performance first produced in France in

1991. This last production provides a good example of Dogtroep's unique total theatre which transcends ordinary theatrical limitations. The production is a wild explosion of multifaceted professionalism that simply bowls over the audience. With ironic reference to Beijing Opera and Japanese Kabuki, Dogtroep created a three-dimensional comic strip in which the elements, earth, water, air and fire constitute the background. The props are petrol, scaffolding and weird machines, and the actors are archetypal beings that cannot be seduced into text. The music is magically woven into the play and as such is also responsible for bombarding the spectator's senses. Rivalry and reconciliation are the basis of the dramatic action, but these themes are constantly made subservient to a form of humour that leaves nobody untouched.

In 1993 Dogtroep performed a new production for the Festival Kontakt in Torún (Poland), the first instalment of a triptych that was to be completed in Frankfurt as a special production for the Book Fair, the *Liebeslied eines Gehenkten.* Pictures of both the Frankfurt and the Poland performances were broadcast on television in various countries. In 1994 the company started *Laboratorium,* a project that gave young artists in the fields of theatre, music, sculpture and dance the opportunity to familiarise themselves with its *modus operandi,* while allowing them to develop their own ideas. The wild, visual and musical theatre of the Dogtroep nomads has already developed into an important Dutch export item; now the company is once again proving itself to be a launchpad for young artistic talent in the broadest sense of the word.

JOS NIJHOF
Translated by André Lefevere.

ADDRESS
Dogtroep
P.O. Box 15098 / 1001 MB / Amsterdam / The Netherlands
tel. +31 (0)20 632 11 39 / fax +31 (0)20 632 22 53

L'Ascension du Mandarin
(Photo by Kors van Bennekom).

Josse de Pauw Actor and Author

The Flemish actor Josse de Pauw (1952-) has played in ten or so films, among them *Crazy Love* (1987) inspired by the stories of Charles Bukowski, *Wait until Spring, Bandini* (1989) a screen version by Dominique Deruddere of John Fante's novel, *Sailors Don't Cry* (1988) by Mark Didden, *Toto le Héros* (1991) by Jaco Van Dormael, and the best known, *Just Friends* (1992) by Marc-Henri Wajnberg. All these films are the work of Belgian directors.

In his latest film, De Pauw has his most important role to date. He plays the part of a saxophonist, Jack, a character based on but not an exact portrait of the Antwerp jazz musician Jack Sels (1922-1970). De Pauw mimes blowing the saxophone so perfectly that the cinema goer is totally unaware that the music is, in fact, played by someone else: the American tenor-saxophonist Archie Shepp. For his part in this film, De

Josse de Pauw (1952-),
playing the saxophone in
Just Friends (1992).

Pauw received the award for Best Male Actor at the 1993 European Film Festival in La Baule.

Josse de Pauw also plays the main role in *Vinaya,* a film he made in 1991 with the director Peter van Kraaij. The footage was shot in the seemingly timeless landscapes of Mexico. De Pauw plays an unruly tramp with whom the youngster Vinaya wants to go 'to the other side of the mountain'. The two of them become friends. What follows is a sort of initiation story, in the course of which the youngster reaches maturity. The scenario is based on the script for a short film, written by De Pauw in the eighties.

De Pauw began his career as an actor with the company Radeis (a play on words: both radish and a swearword used by Brussels card players), of which he was a founder member. Between 1977 and 1984, this group of four, based at the Kaaitheater in Brussels, gave hundreds of performances in Belgium and the surrounding countries, as well as overseas in Venezuela, Hong Kong, Canada and the United States.

Following their parody of the circus, *Radeis due to Illness. Drama without Too Much Histrionics* (Radeis wegens ziekte. Theater zonder veel cinema), the collage of sketches, *I Didn't Know England Was So Beautiful* (Ik wist niet dat Engeland zo mooi was) marked the beginning of their breakthrough in 1979. In 1980, after being invited to the Festival of Fools in Amsterdam, Radeis took off internationally. There was more of a story-line in the productions that followed. *Birds* (Vogels, 1981) was about people 'who had forgotten that they were made to fly', and *Scaffoldings* (Echafaudages, the first version in 1981 and the second in 1983) was about the world of workers and tools. Radeis also made the series of sketches *United We Stand* (L'union fait la force) for the Dutch-language section of Belgian Radio and Television.

Their last performance (with *Scaffoldings*) was during the Olympic Arts festival in Los Angeles in 1984. They had already decided some time earlier to disband Radeis in order to prevent themselves from basking in their success while becoming stuck in a rut. Attractive offers from America did not make them change their minds.

After that Josse de Pauw went his own way. In his first solo piece, *Usurpation,* in 1985, the public were shown something other than the funny performances by Radeis. On stage a man and a woman confronted each other in a struggle for love. De Pauw has since performed with the Dutch company Hauser Orkater in Dylan Thomas' *Under Milkwood* and in the Flemish director Jan Decorte's works *Play Play* (Stuk Stuk) and *In the Meanwhile in the Meantime* (Inondertussendoor).

De Pauw's base is, as has already been mentioned, the Kaaitheater. There he has performed in various productions, such as *The Trio in E Diminished* (Het trio in mi bémol, 1991) by the French film-director Eric Rohmer, *Spanking the Maid* (De Meid slaan), a dialogue developed together with the Dutch actor Tom Jansen and staged in 1993, and James Joyce's *Exiles,* directed by Peter van Kraaij (1993). In other texts, also created for performances at the Kaaitheater, Josse de Pauw has proved himself to be a writer and story-teller. In 1991, he received the triennial State Prize for Playwrights for his two works *Ward Comblez. He Do the Life in Different Voices* (1989) and *The Blacksmith's Child* (Het Kind van de Smid, 1990). He was awarded the Dr Oskar de Gruyter Prize for the best actor of 1990, for his performances in those plays.

When writing the monologue *Ward Comblez,* De Pauw was assisted by Peter van Kraaij. Comblez, 'someone in trouble with himself who went travelling in his mind', tells a story which takes place successively in Algeria, Curaçao, Crete and again Crete. In the meantime, he quotes *in different voices* from conversations he had with a former lover who has left him. He also quotes from T.S. Eliot's *The Waste Land,* once much appreciated by his girlfriend.

The Blacksmith's Child was written and directed in collaboration with Peter van Kraaij. There are three narrators: the Blacksmith, Pomp and the Child. The latter are two children of the same Native American mother but of different fathers. Pomp, the son of a French-Canadian, witnesses the eradication of his (Indian) tribe while the Child, the son of an Irish blacksmith who emigrated to America, travels to Europe only to end up in penal servitude in Australia from where he escapes, finally meeting up with his half-brother again on a reservation. This fictitious story is placed in a historical context drawn from documents of the Lewis and Clark Expedition (1804-1806), commissioned by President Jefferson to explore the area around the Missouri, and from Robert Hughes' book *The Fatal shore, The Epic of Australia's Founding* (1986). There is no dialogue in the text, only stories placed beside and running into each other.

The beginning of 1994 saw the staging of *Momentum,* created by the Blindman Kwartet, at the Lunatheater where texts by De Pauw and others are combined with music by the Flemish composer Eric Schleichim (produced by the Kaaitheater). De Pauw also wrote the libretto for *The Soluble Fish* (De oplosbare vis), an opera by Peter Vermeersch, where a man is confronted by two fish, Coelacanth and Spek (produced in February 1994 by Walpurgis at Desingel in Antwerp). De Pauw is also preparing a project for mainly feminine roles based on *The Blind* (Les aveugles) by Maurice Maeterlinck and *The Women at the Tomb* (Les femmes au tombeau) by Michel de Ghelderode (production by the Kaaitheater). Both as actor and as author, his highly original talent has come of age.

JEF DE ROECK
Translated by Peter Flynn.

Oeroeg and the Dutch-East Indian Trauma

The Dutch writer Hella S. Haasse was born on 2 February 1918 in Batavia, then the capital of the Dutch East Indies. She has a sound reputation in the field of historical, often biographical novels.

Her recent *The Tea Lords* (Heren van de thee, 1992) was shortlisted for the AKO Literature Prize in 1993. This is one of her many novels set in the landscape of her youth – the former Dutch Indies – the Paradise Lost recalled with such melancholy by the old Indies hands of whom there are so many in the Netherlands. Unlike most of these, Haasse never indulges in nostalgia for *tempo dulu* (the good old days), but tries to describe not only the magic of the country and its people but also the inability of the Dutch to grasp its true essence.

The Tea Lords is set around the turn of the century in a world of colonial Dutch planters who, according to Haasse, should be judged not only on their greed and exploitation but also on their achievements. This even-handed approach is characteristic of her, and even at the beginning of her career as a writer – coinciding as it did with the birth of the independent Republic of Indonesia – it attracted quite some criticism. This was when Hella Haasse had her first breakthrough as a new young writer with the novella *Oeroeg* (pronounced 'Urugh'), the story of the impossible friendship between the planter's son Johan and the native boy Oeroeg. The novella appeared in 1948, three years after the Indonesian nationalist Sukarno had proclaimed the Republic of Indonesia, and a year before

The soldier Johan (Rik Launspach) in a tragic episode from *Oeroeg* (1992).

the actual transfer of sovereignty by the Netherlands. In the intervening period two Dutch so-called 'police actions' had created a great deal of bad feeling. Emotions ran high on both sides, and not everyone was grateful for Haasse's attempt to show both sides of the coin.

That 'the Indonesian question' can still cause a great deal of excitement over forty years after the event is clear from the suspicious response to plans to make a film of *Oeroeg*. Revelations about war crimes committed by the Dutch army during the police actions had already led to great consternation. When actor Peter Faber, Sergeant Van Bergen Henegouwen in the film, remarked during an interview that even Dutch soldiers had sometimes behaved like animals, the more conservative element in the population protested loudly against the film. They could have saved their breath. Director Hans Hylkema has outdone Hella Haasse in carefully balancing the points for and against both parties. The film *Oeroeg* begins where the book ends. Haasse's novel describes the friendship between Johan and Oeroeg, the son of the supervisor on Johan's father's plantation. They grow up together, they are close friends and, swept along by history, they see their friendship become impossible. Hans Hylkema presents this story in the form of flashbacks in the story of the soldier Johan (Rik Launspach) who returns from the Netherlands to the land of his birth to take part in the police actions. His old friend Oeroeg (Martin Schwab) has turned into a fanatical nationalist and freedom fighter. Throughout the film Johan is searching for this friend, aided by nurse Lydia (Josée Ruiter), his former childhood nanny, who plays an ambiguous (and not very clearly developed) part.

The main problem with the film *Oeroeg* is the rather simplistic approach to the Dutch-East Indian trauma, summed up by Johan in the comment: 'I have a right to a place in this country too'. The flashbacks show an environment of oppressors and oppressed, with native children being taught at school where the Rhine flows into the Netherlands and learning the Dutch national anthem off by heart. When Oeroeg comes home with an excellent school report, it is commented that he will make an excellent accountant on Johan's plantation; Johan's marks were much lower. And on top of that, Johan's father (Jeroen Krabbé) treats his native staff with marked disrespect and indifference. His attitude is not even spiteful, it is completely uninterested. The mysterious relationship between the colonial and the colonised embraced so much more than this, full as it was of fascination, hate, love, fear and prejudice. Here it is developed in a way that is much too facile.

In the parts which are set in the present day, everyone gets the benefit of the doubt. The Indonesian rebels certainly do carry on rather, but their rebellious attitude is understandable. The Dutch behave like bulls in a china shop, but they are also genuinely hurt. Nobody is right or wrong.

The way all this is worked into a film shows that Hans Hylkema has outgrown the world of television drama. *Oeroeg* has the feel of a fully-fledged feature film, with satisfactory acting performances, professional costumes, good camera work and rather unambitious but adequate editing. The scenario (by Jean van de Velde) is effective but not particularly refined, and the narrative structure using flashbacks is rather conventional. The film succeeds mainly in traditional terms, and for those with no prior knowledge it might lead to a better understanding of the history of the time. However those in search of detailed knowledge about the psychological mechanisms of colonialism may well be irritated by the film's superficial and over-explicit portrayal of externals. *Oeroeg* lacks repressed tension, mystery, ambiguity and absurdity, although these were the most obvious ingredients in the relationship between colonials and the colonised. It describes colonial history in the same rather schematic and straightforward way as, years earlier, Paul Verhoeven's *Soldier of Orange* (Soldaat van Oranje, 1977) had described the German Occupation of 1940-1945.

GERDIN LINTHORST
Translated by Steve Judd.

'The armies who endured that sullen swamp'
(Siegfried Sassoon).

History

Flanders Fields, Somewhere in France

The First World War was an event that did, quite literally, involve the whole world. There was fighting in Mesopotamia and Egypt, in the Italian Tirol and Bulgaria, in the Dardanelles, Eastern Poland and Jutland, in Africa and on the seven seas. But the most important theatre of war, the one which has provided the image of that war ever since, was and is the Western Front: seven hundred and sixty kilometres of continuous trenches and fortifications extending from the Swiss border right across Northern France to the North Sea at Nieuwpoort.

'We're off for France', the British soldiers said as they left for the Front, although a small part at the end of the line was not in France but in Belgium. Little did they care. The first bloody confrontation between the British Expeditionary Force and the Germans near Mons in late August 1914, and, almost simultaneously, the reports of atrocities perpetrated by the invading German armies in Aarschot and Leuven suddenly placed Belgium – 'Gallant little Belgium' – firmly on the map. 'We'll be back by Christmas', they had said; but it was to be Christmas 1918, four terrible years later, years during which that little bit of Belgian front would play such a major role that the names of obscure little Belgian villages like Sint-Jelijns *(Saint-Julien),* Zillebeke *(Hill 60, The Bluff)* or Passendale *(Passchendaele)* are still engraved on the collective memory of the British Empire and its descendants.

'We're off for France', they still said, and their letters (partly because of the censors) said 'Somewhere in France'. The language they used with those living along the Western Front was *franglais partoo: parleyvoo madmaselle, no bong, c'est un cheminglong to Teperaree* … but the Belgian front quickly became all too well known as a bitter reality.

The front line in West Flanders ran from the mouth of the IJzer near Nieuwpoort, upstream along that coastal river past Diksmuide as far as the old French barrier fort *Fort Knokke* (people had fought over *Flanders Fields* before*),* where the canal from Ypres entered the IJzer river. It followed that canal to Steenstrate and then went around Ypres in a broad curve like a backwards S, turned back through Wijtschate *(White Sheet)* and Mesen *(Messines)* and past Ploegsteert *(Plug Street)* where it plunged into France. Between Steenstrate and the sea the line was held by the Belgian army, which had been much weakened after the retreat from Antwerp in October 1914 and only survived because the German attack had foundered in the flooded IJzer plain. There the Belgian army defended itself honourably throughout the rest of the war, lent a hand where possible, as it did during the first gas attack near Steenstrate in April 1915, and three years later at Merkem during the German offensive of April 1918, but it was not to play a significant military role until the Final Offensive.

The French army supported the Belgian flanks in Nieuwpoort and near Steenstrate with a few divisions, and also plugged gaps for the British (Kemmelberg, April 1918).

However, the crucial area of the Belgian front was the Salient, the curve around Ypres. This was a British sector throughout the war, and it was only in the winter of 1914-1915 that the French replaced the decimated British Expeditionary Force in its northern part, between *Hill 60* and Steenstrate. The last divisions of these French troops had just been relieved on 22 April 1915 by newly constituted British and Canadian units when gas was used as a weapon for the first time in history. This time it was chlorine gas, but over two years later it was (and also for the first time) mustard gas. This gas was called Yperite; it was odourless, colourless, in mortar shells – and many times more effective. Flamethrowers were used here as early as the spring of 1915. Two years later the Battle of Messines Ridge (7 June 1917) would show that a massive attack with deep mines could be successful in breaking through positions which had been entrenched for years.

For the British Empire, it was above all the small Belgian front that came to symbolise the ugliness of the First World War. Ypres was to the British what Verdun was to the French. Nowhere else was so much sacrificed for so little, battles fought more brutally, lost positions held more obstinately. Nowhere else were conditions so inhuman and (therefore) orders so cynical or victories so futile. Of the almost one million British soldiers who died during the Great War, a quarter of a million fell in the Ypres Salient; the bodies of 45,000 of them were never even found. In October 1914 Ypres was chosen fairly arbitrarily as a last position to stop the German advance, and this position was maintained throughout the war, against all military logic, simply on the basis that it was not possible to give up something for which so many had already fallen. The best part of the British volunteer army was sacrificed on the Somme in the summer of 1916, but there was at least something to show for it: the German withdrawal to the Hindenburg Line in Spring 1917. There was nothing to show for the hundred days' blood- and mud-bath called *Third Ypres,* which consumed the rest of that army: a feverish swamp of madness, and on the far side an ugly hump of mud hardly eight kilometres from Ypres, with a sign on top saying 'Passchendaele'. At the first German attack the following spring all that had been gained – and more – was given up without a struggle.

Eighty years later all of this is well known, but it has also been forgotten. War tourism and misguided patriotism obscure the lessons which we might learn from this piece of Belgium *somewhere in France.* When the weekly *Punch* published the poem 'In Flanders Fields' in December 1915, the Ypres Salient instantly became world famous. The opening lines made it clear that this was the largest graveyard in the world: 'In Flanders fields the poppies blow / Between the crosses, row on row / That mark our place …' A Canadian army doctor, John McCrae, had written the poem in his field hospital during Second Ypres, as an immediate reaction to so much war misery. However, the last verse turned it into a pamphlet to crank up the war effort: 'To you from failing hands we throw / The torch (…) / If ye break faith with us who die / We shall not sleep …' Two years and a few hundred thousand poppies later the Salient had broken that faith forever, and with it the hope of a generation. There could be no more misunderstanding. Those war poets who survived (i.e. not Wilfred Owen, Edward Thomas, Isaac Rosenberg etc.) could only scream: 'in this sweet countryside amuck with murder', as Edmund Blunden wrote, and 'I died in hell (They called it Passchendaele)' (Siegfried Sassoon).

Eighty years later, the survivors have been reduced to a mere handful and all that can still be seen in this landscape is the cemeteries and the monuments. They are the best guides to understanding this 'corner of a foreign field / that is forever England': not as the witness to a glorious victory, but as 'the world's worst wound', a memorial to the ' unheroic Dead who fed the guns, / those doomed, conscripted, unvictorious ones…,' to use Sassoon's words once again.

PIET CHIELENS
Translated by Steve Judd.

John McCrae
In Flanders Fields

In Flanders fields the poppies blow
Between the crosses, row on row,
   That mark our place; and in the sky
   The larks, still bravely singing, fly
Scarce heard amid the guns below.

We are the Dead. Short days ago
We lived, felt dawn, saw sunset glow,
   Loved and were loved, and now we lie
      In Flanders fields.

Take up our quarrel with the foe:
To you from failing hands we throw
   The torch; be yours to hold it high.
   If ye break faith with us who die
We shall not sleep, though poppies grow
      In Flanders fields.

2 May 1915

A Pictorial History of the Grand' Place in Brussels

The Grand' Place in Brussels (1993) is, as its subtitle indicates, the story of 'a centre of five hundred years of history'. This story is an iconography: a number of episodes from the history of the Grand' Place are chronicled by means of illustrations which the author provides with a commentary.

After a short introduction on the origin of Brussels and the Grand' Place, the actual iconography begins with a miniature depicting the Entry of Joanna of Castile in 1496. The pictorial survey ends with photographs of the Japanese imperial couple being received at Brussels Town Hall in September 1993.

Between 1496 and 1993 many other princely visitors were welcomed in the Grand' Place – where the Town Hall is located – visitors such as William of Orange (1577) and the Spanish archducal couple Albert and Isabella (1615). In 1815 William I became King of the United Netherlands (the present-day Netherlands and Belgium) by virtue of the Treaty of London of 1814. The Hague and Brussels took it in turns to serve as the capital city. In his address, delivered in the Gothic Room in Brussels Town Hall in 1815, William I made a plea for harmony and cooperation. But to no avail: in 1830 the Belgian Revolution broke out. After several skirmishes in the Grand' Place, the Belgian tricolour (red, yellow and black) was raised over the Town Hall. A year later, on 21 July 1831, Leopold of Saxe-Coburg took the oath and became Leopold I, the first king of independent Belgium. Only in 1884 were relations between Belgium and the Netherlands completely normalised; William III, who was the Dutch king at the time, and his wife Emma were fêted in the Grand' Place. Dutch and Belgian flags flew together on the Town Hall and on the grand houses around the marketplace. So as not to offend the royal guests, it was decided that the Belgian national anthem, the *Brabançonne,* should not be played.

It is not only kings and members of the aristocracy who appear in the book. For example, there is a photograph of the visit of Thomas Woodrow Wilson to Brussels in 1919. Wilson, who was responsible for America's intervention in the First World War, was the first President of the USA to honour Europe with an official visit. During the reception at Brussels Town Hall, Burgomaster Adolphe Max referred to him as 'the champion of Right and Justice, the incarnation of our universal conscience'. In 1945 it was the turn of the 'liberators' Montgomery, Eisenhower, De Gaulle and Churchill, to be cheered by an enthusiastic crowd on the Grand' Place.

Unlike many other historical sites in the 'Old World', the Grand' Place came through both twentieth-century cataclysms unscathed. However, a couple of centuries earlier – on 13 August 1695, to be precise – it had known true devastation. On the orders of the French King Louis XIV, Brussels had been shelled by cannons and mortars in retaliation for the Dutch-British blockade of a number of French seaports. The Sun King's artillery reduced the historic city centre to ashes. Rebuilding work began barely two years later and before long the Grand' Place looked as it does today.

Approximately 130 years before this bombardment, another tragedy had taken place on the Grand' Place when the Counts Egmont and Hoorne were beheaded there on 5 June 1568 in one of the most dramatic episodes in the history of the Low Countries. In 1566, Egmont, Governor of Flanders under the Spanish King Philip II, had declared religious freedom, in an attempt to restore peace to the Low Countries, which had been torn apart by both the Spanish Inquisition and the Protestant Iconoclasm. Though Egmont himself remained a Catholic, Philip II considered him to be too lenient with the Protestants. He was arrested together with Hoorne, accused of high treason and put to death. In the centuries that followed Egmont was immortalised as a paragon of toleration by writers such as Voltaire, Schiller and Goethe. In 1864 a statue of Egmont and Hoorne was erected in the Grand' Place (the Belgian nation was still young and in need of national heroes). For aesthetic reasons, the city gov-

Gustave Simonau's lithograph of the Brussels Town Hall, c. 1835 (Town Museum, Brussels).

Sir Winston Churchill in the Grand' Place, 17 November 1945.

ernment decided in 1879 to move the monument to the Petit Sablon. However, two bronze plaques can still be seen on the facade of the King's House on the Grand' Place bearing the following inscription: 'In front of this building, Counts Egmont and Hoorne, victims of the oppression and intolerance of Philip II, were beheaded on 5 June 1568.'

Though one might not think so to judge by the above examples, the iconography is not restricted to 'great moments' in history. There is, for example, an engraving which illustrates the story of a sixfold murder. In 1694 a sergeant of Scottish origin butchered his landlord and the landlord's family. The engraving shows not only the bloody murders, but also the certainly no less bloody death by torture which the murderer met with on the Grand' Place. But there are also illustrations of a more lighthearted nature, like the lithographs of the charity ball held in the Town Hall in 1846 and the photographs of the triumphal reception of the Belgian national football team after their much-appreciated performance at the World Cup Finals in Mexico in 1986.

One might say that this book offers only a succession of anecdotes, but that is precisely its strength. Random pictures are used to provide an undoubtedly incomplete but always fascinating account of the historical significance of the Grand' Place. Unhindered by footnotes or detailed acknowledgments of sources, its readers can quietly dip into the beautifully illustrated chapters without feeling they have to read everything. *The Grand' Place in Brussels* is one of those marvellous books which invites you to browse unconstrainedly.

FILIP MATTHIJS
Translated by Alison Mouthaan-Gwillim.

Edgar Goedleven, *The Grand' Place in Brussels. Centre of Five Hundred Years of History.* Tielt: Lannoo, 1993; 286 pp.

Gerard Mercator and Cartography in Flanders

The Low Countries have played a leading role in the development of cartography. The area was the centre of European trade in the sixteenth century, and good mapmakers like Ortelius, Frisius, Mercator, Plancius, Hondius and others were all working there in that period. Of course it was not only trade which stimulated the demand for maps; there were also intellectual centres like Leuven and Mechlin where cartographical studies were carried out and the technique refined.

There is no doubt that Gerard Mercator, the four-hundredth anniversary of whose death was commemorated in 1994, was one of the most important of this generation of cartographers. Mercator was born Gerard de Cremer in Rupelmonde on 5 March 1512, to a family that originated from the Rhineland (the name

denotes a stallholder or merchant). When Gerard enrolled at the University of Leuven in 1530, he translated his name – as was the fashion in intellectual circles – and became Gerardus Mercator. In 1532 he completed his studies in the Faculty of Arts and obtained a degree in philosophy. After that he spent about two years in Antwerp, which was then the economic and cultural centre of the Low Countries. The reason why Mercator left Leuven is not clear, but it probably had to do with his dissatisfaction at the university's rigid adherence to the age-old teaching of Aristotle. The prevailing view of the world was partly determined by this teaching, which had been added to by, among others, the Greek astronomer Ptolemy in the second century. New discoveries, scientific research, recent publications, the search for new trade routes, and so forth, were changing this traditional view. Mercator eventually went back to Leuven to study mathematics, but he did not return to the University. He wanted to acquire a practical knowledge, rather than a theoretical one.

Under the direction of Gemma Frisius from Friesland, Leuven had become an important centre for scientific cartography. Frisius also brought Mercator into contact with the Leuven goldsmith Gaspard van der Heyden, who had already constructed and engraved a globe for Frisius. Van der Heyden imparted the necessary craftsman's and artistic skills to Mercator, who produced various globes together with Frisius and Van der Heyden.

The first map Mercator made in his own right was one of Palestine. This map was particularly useful for Bible study, but it was to put Mercator in prison for

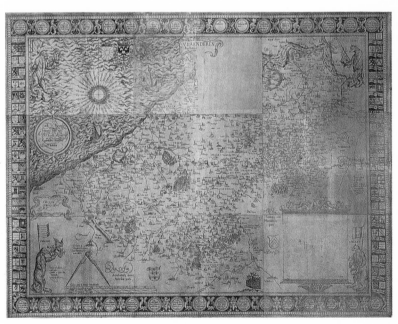

Portrait of Mercator by Frans Hogenberg (1574) (Museum Plantin-Moretus, Antwerp).

Vlaenderen Exactissima (Flandriae descriptio), a map of the County of Flanders, drawn by Mercator (1540) (Museum Plantin-Moretus, Antwerp).

several months in 1544 on suspicion of heresy. After all, in these unsettled times one could be accused of heresy merely for possessing a Bible. Probably this period of imprisonment was one of the reasons Mercator left Flanders in 1552 to settle in Duisburg where there was far greater religious freedom.

So while Mercator received his scientific education in Flanders, he accomplished the major part of his work in Duisburg. His most important map, which signified a revolutionary change in the prevailing picture of the world, was his 1569 world map; this was very reliable because of the projection he had developed. It is largely because of this 'Mercator projection' that he is rated as one of the fathers of modern cartography.

Mercator died in Duisburg on 2 December 1594. The following year his son published some of the maps under the name *Atlas sive cosmographicae meditationes de Fabrica Mundi et fabricati figura* – the first time the word 'atlas' was used to refer to a collection of maps. Mercator himself had, in fact, already published some of the maps under the title *Galliae tabulae geographicae* in 1585. In 1604 the Flemish publisher and cartographer Jodocus Hondius bought the engraved copperplates of the Mercator maps and reprinted them repeatedly. Hondius' successor, J. Janssonius, then took up the task and went on reprinting Mercator's work until 1673.

In addition to maps, Mercator also made various scientific instruments, wrote a little book about italic script, prepared a critical reissue of Ptolemy's maps and made a comparative study of the four gospels.

The image of the world that Mercator created with his cartography was not improved upon until the eighteenth century. Through his correspondence with the Englishmen John Dee and Richard Hakluyt, Mercator also had considerable influence in England. In the nineteenth century his memory was honoured with statues both in Rupelmonde and in Duisburg. He can be regarded as one of the most important scholars of his time.

DIRK VAN ASSCHE
Translated by Alison Mouthaan-Gwillim.

The Story of a Metropolis

Antwerp: Story of a Metropolis, 16th-17th century is the catalogue of an exhibition held from 25 June to 19 October 1993 as part of 'Antwerp 1993, Cultural Capital of Europe'. The catalogue itself is well-documented, luxuriously illustrated and offers interesting background information to the exhibition in the historic Hessenhuis. Moreover, the objects chosen tie in well with the earlier part of the book, which offers a series of articles on various aspects of Antwerp in the sixteenth and seventeenth centuries.

This relatively short period saw the meteoric rise of the city to a commercial and cultural metropolis, followed by its decline to a mere regional centre in the early eighteenth century. In an introductory historical article, Leon Voet places this well-known story within 'the context of the continual changes that shaped and reshaped the economic, social, and political structures of Europe and of the Netherlands'. When the annual fairs of Antwerp were opened up to the English Merchant Adventurers (whose products were boycotted elsewhere in Flanders and Brabant) Antwerp became the principal centre for English cloth on the continent and a meeting point for English, Hanseatic, Spanish and Italian traders. The town 'moved into the fast lane' with the discovery of the sea route to India, which made Antwerp a distribution centre for Oriental products brought to Europe by the Portuguese. By the 1560s, the city had become the linchpin of trade between Southern and Northern Europe, and, with over 100,000 inhabitants, the largest urban agglomeration in Europe after Paris and a few Italian cities. During the political and religious struggles of the second half of the sixteenth century, the city was a centre of Luthe-

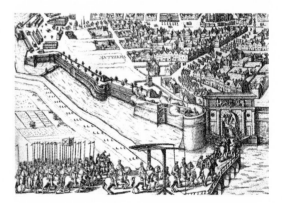

Entry of Alexander Farnese, Duke of Parma, at the head of Spanish troops in Antwerp on 27 August 1585 (Koninklijke Bibliotheek, Brussels).

Blazon of the Antwerp chamber of rhetoric *De Violieren,* on the occasion of the 1621 Landjuweel competition (Koninklijk Museum voor Schone Kunsten, Antwerp).

ranism, Anabaptism, and the more militant Calvinism, and chose to join the rebellion against the Spanish. In 1585, when the city fell to the Spanish, it was swiftly transformed into the bulwark of an equally militant Counter-Reformation. However, the strong commercial base of its export trade had disappeared. Voet mentions three main factors in this: the departure of many local Protestant merchants and skilled artisans to the religious tolerance of the Northern Netherlands, the closing of the Scheldt, in fact the imposition of heavy levies by the Zeeland and Holland authorities, and, most important of all, the disappearance of foreign merchants, except those from the Catholic, Southern European countries. The economic decline was temporarily halted by a boom in art and luxury goods as a result of the Counter-Reformation, but after 1650 Antwerp's international status deteriorated fast.

The article by Herman van der Wee and Jan Materné, 'Antwerp as a World Market in the Sixteenth and Seventeenth Centuries', uses statistical data to show that Antwerp's 'demographic miracle' – between 1496 and 1565 the population rose from 30,000 to 100,000 – in fact derived largely from a continuous immigration. The population then shrank drastically to 42,000 by 1589 (five years after the fall of Antwerp), before recovering to 68,000 by 1645. Antwerp's spectacular development as a North-South distribution centre had resulted in an improved infrastructure (a financial exchange, commodity markets, port installations), and the development of innovative financial techniques and a new banking system. After 1585, the integration of Antwerp into the Spanish Empire actually improved its position, while a new specialisation in luxury goods allowed the city to remain reasonably prosperous. However, the centre of the spice trade moved to the North, while the trade with the Spanish and Portuguese colonies in America inevitably moved southward again.

The other articles in the collection discuss this basic picture of 1585 as a watershed in Antwerp's history from a number of perspectives. Thus, Hugo Soly focuses on corporate organisations such as the craft guilds, and the behaviour of merchants as a social group, to sketch an outline of social relations in Antwerp. The sixteenth century had seen a sharpening of the contrast between wealth and poverty, with the 'proletarisation of many master craftsmen' going hand in hand with aggressive economic growth. After 1585, however, the cultural abyss between the rich and the poor widened even further as the wealthy merchants, who now chose to live off their landed estates rather than by trade, came more and more to play the part of aristocrats. The ideology of the common good which the city's government had subscribed to during the earlier period had all but disappeared. Anne-Marie van Passen discusses the representation of this metropolis in contemporary accounts, such as travel guides and diaries by English, Venetian, Florentine and Spanish visitors. 'Antwerp Portrayed', by Jan Grieten and Paul Huvenne, analyses the development of the new pictorial genres of maps and city portraits, in which Antwerp played a leading role in the mid-sixteenth century. Developed in analogy with human portraits, the cityscape became a stock item in an emerging art market. Similarly, Herman Pleij's article highlights the ideological function of the earliest printed almanacs and annual predictions, which were used by the city authorities to underpin the urban status quo. In the same way, the annual Landjuweel competitions (organised by the chambers of rhetoric) proffered idealised images of peaceful, hierarchical social relations in a sharply divided city. Francine de Nave draws the picture of a printing capital which initially disseminated both international humanism and the new religions, and later maintained a dominant role as the centre of Counter-Reformation literature. The inward-looking seventeenth century strenghtened Antwerp's luxury industries, discussed by Alfons K. L. Thijs. The European reputation of the studies of Rubens, Van Dyck and many immigrant painters, in combination with a vibrant art market and Italian inspiration, meant that Antwerp, in Arnout Balis' words, could be called the 'fostermother of the arts'. Lut Pil's article discusses the afterlife of this artistic fame, the myth of Antwerp's Golden Age that was developed with renewed self-confidence in nineteenth-century painting and civic celebrations.

Finally, Steven Jacobs' 'Epilogue: Story of an Exhibition' investigates the ideological place of this exhibition in the context of the 1993 cultural celebrations. With the 'cultural historical tale' as its starting point, the exhibition's aim was to combine objects of high art with commercial, proto-industrial items. The article warns the viewer not to regard these objects from a pre-museological past with the modern eyes of museum visitors accustomed to the isolation of 'Art' in exhibitions and museums. As an exhibition, then, *Antwerp: Story of a Metropolis* was to evoke the 'Kunst-und-Wunderkammers' of the period and be a 'self-conscious pendant' to those earlier art collections of the Golden Age. At the same time, it aimed at a critical questioning of the twentieth-century view of Antwerp's brief Golden Age.

This collection is an elegant, well-crafted and thoughtful contribution to our knowledge of the fortunes of the Southern Netherlands during the sixteenth and seventeenth centuries. *Antwerp: Story of a Metropolis* is to be appreciated even more for its attempt to take on board the ideological basis to the evaluation of an era and the creation of an exhibition.

SABINE VANACKER

Antwerp: Story of a Metropolis, 16th-17th century. (Includes Exhibition Catalogue Antwerp, Hessenhuis, 25 June-19 October 1993) (Gen. ed.: Jan van der Stock). Antwerp: Martial & Snoeck, 1993; 383 pp.

The Dutch Church in London Past and Present

'Only few church communities possess such a wealth of written documents bearing on their past history, or

have been the centre to the same extent of so many varied activities.' With these words, the Dutch church historian Lindeboom summed up the long, rich and continuing history of the Dutch Reformed Church at Austin Friars in the City of London.

The history of this Church goes back to 24 July 1550, when King Edward VI granted to the Dutch community in London the church which had been taken from the Augustinian Friars by his father Henry VIII. In King Edward's Charter, the Mayor, Sheriffs, Aldermen and Bishop of London are commanded to permit the Dutch *'freely and quietly to practice, enjoy, use and exercise their own rites and ceremonies, and their own ecclesiastical discipline, notwithstanding that they do not conform with the rites and ceremonies used in our Kingdom, without impeachment, disturbance or vexation'.*

The Dutch community at that time was the largest foreign community in London. By 1570 it numbered 5,000 people, out of a total population of 100,000. About half of these had come to London as religious refugees, fleeing the persecutions in the Low Countries. Others had come for economic reasons, bringing valuable skills to the expanding City. There were brewers, glassblowers, potters and tile makers; master weavers who produced luxury goods such as woven silk and tapestries; craftsmen who made fine leatherwork, jewelry, stained glass, paintings and sculpture; drainage experts and instrument makers; and mapmakers, printers and engravers, who all made prominent contributions. If Shakespeare was no Fleming, it is at least a Flemish engraver, Martin Droeshout, to whom we owe his most authentic and best-known portrait.

A second Dutch wave came to London towards the end of the seventeenth century, when William and Mary brought with them Dutch noblemen and courtiers, bankers and merchants, artists, architects and garden designers from the Dutch Republic. In later centuries, London again and again offered a safe haven to refugees from the continent: at the time of the Batavian Revolution towards the end of the eighteenth century, and in the present century, after Hitler's invasion of the Low Countries.

In October 1940 the Church was destroyed during the London Blitz. But the Dutch services continued almost without interruption in the Church of St Mary near Berkeley Square in the West End, which functioned as a focus for the Dutch refugee community throughout the war. The present Dutch Church was built between 1950 and 1954, and contains paintings, memorial plaques, stained-glass windows and tapestries symbolising the key elements of its history: the Christian religion and the Reformation, the history of the Dutch nation, and the relationship with the House of Orange.

The Church also has a small but fine collection of old books which miraculously escaped destruction in October 1940: early Dutch Bibles, works by the Fathers of the Reformation, books by Dutch historians from the Golden Age, atlases and encyclopedic descriptions of newly discovered continents. Among the highlights

Stained-glass windows with the pictures of William and Mary (Dutch Church, London).

of the collection are a beautiful Polyglot Bible published by Plantin of Antwerp in 1569-1571, and a magnificent Atlas of all the cities in the Low Countries, both in the North and in the South, published by Blaeu in 1649.

In the Library there is a case full of books on the history of this, the Mother of all Reformed Dutch Churches: volumes of Church correspondence, minutes of Church meetings, and monographs on the Church's role in the early Reformation both in the Low Countries and in London. The Church archives form a rich source of information, and there is a longstanding and ongoing tradition of scholarly publications, the latest example of which is the publication, in December 1993, of the *Acta* of the Church Council of the Dutch community in London from 1569 to 1585.

Today, the Dutch Church offers a place of worship to all who want to celebrate the Christian faith in the Dutch language. Every Sunday there is a Dutch service. And there is a wide range of other activities: discussion groups on Biblical themes, classes preparing for confirmation and confession, visits to the old, the poor, the sick, and the approximately 100 Dutch prisoners in British jails. There is a choir, a women's group, a discussion group on modern Dutch literature, and a weekly Open House for young people in the Church's Social Hall. Various associations in the Dutch community hold regular meetings there, and funds are now being raised to pay for the restoration of the Church organ.

True to its origins as a Refugee Church, members of the Church are active in writing to human rights prisoners and prisoners of conscience abroad, and in collecting money to support refugees and refugee organizations in present-day London. Characteristically, when the *Acta* just mentioned were presented, it was at a symposium in The Hague about refugees and refugee policies in modern Europe.

Another new initiative, now in its fourth year, is the

monthly Dutch City Lunch in the Social Hall, where speakers from the Netherlands – opinion leaders, business men and women, politicians, writers and church ministers – come and talk to an audience consisting of Dutch people who live or work in and around London. These City Lunches are quite successful in attracting a new audience to the Church. At the same time, they are an interesting continuation of the old Dutch tradition of the Minister and the Merchant, archetypes of the Dutch national character.

After 444 years in Austin Friars, the Dutch Church is alive and well – a corner of a foreign field that is forever Holland.

REINIER SALVERDA

ADDRESS
Dutch Church
7 Austin Friars / London EC2N 2EJ/ United Kingdom
tel. +44 (0) 71 588 1684

A Useful Synthesis on Medieval Flanders

The Flanders of the Middle Ages has been a source of fascination to international scholars for many decades. The reasons for this are legion: a strong tradition of urbanisation as early as the eleventh century, comparable only with northern Italy, which reflects an economic success story achieved through a technological edge (luxury textiles) and creative exploitation of the available transport opportunities; the permanent coupling of economic power and artistic creativity, culminating in the Maasland art and Van Eyck's *ars nova* in the fifteenth century; the early experiments, following those in England, with modern political institutions and parliamentary representation. This urban dynamic led, very early on, to polarisation, spilling over into thirteenth-century popular revolts and strikes against the feudal aristocracy.

The recent book by David Nicholas (Clemson University, South Carolina) entitled *Medieval Flanders,* is a product of the current high level of interest in this historical topic in the United States. Until the Second World War, Flanders was the subject of intensive study by German and French scholars, though in truth this had less to do with erudition than with politics. The two groups competed with each other to present the Flanders of the Middle Ages as a part of their own past – despite the fact that the feudal dependence of Flanders on the two superpowers was more a theoretical exercise than a social reality. Researchers in England and America have stayed largely aloof from these oldfashioned and somewhat unrealistic ideas; they have remained neutral, simply fascinated by an interesting and early economic and political model. I find it significant that, in the preface of his book, Nicholas distances himself from every ideological perspective. I also note that of Nicholas' excellent bibliography, which gives the essence of what is still important today, 95% consists of studies from the Ghent school and from English-language publications. Since the 1920s, when the eminent historian Pirenne 'tempted' large numbers of American and English scholars to Ghent, this flow of researchers has never let up.

Nicholas' book is a useful work in many respects. In anticipation of the soon to be published *New Cambridge Medieval History,* this is the only recent synthesis in English, written by a single author, and covering the whole of Medieval Flanders in all its facets. An English or American perspective on the Flemish past, as we can see in the unique publications of Patricia Carson, offers the advantage of intellectual detachment, unhindered by professional traditions and prejudices. In Nicholas' case, this originality is reinforced by the fact that, over the last twenty-five years, this author has published no less than five books on Flanders in the Middle Ages – all based on primary sources.

And yet this book offers less of a new vision of Medieval Flanders than one might expect; it is a well-worked, excellently documented synthesis of what has been achieved in recent times by dozens of researchers, including the author himself. Where he does venture to say something new or different (for example, about the earliest urban development) I fear that, as a result of understandable handicaps in his otherwise first-class information and technique, he has to bow to the superiority of a historian such as Adriaan Verhulst.

Nicholas' work lays clear emphasis on certain aspects: on landscape and agriculture during the earliest centuries. Socio-economic aspects receive wide attention in comparison to politics; culture and religion, with a meagre 42 out of the 460 pages, are very much the neglected children. This undoubtedly has to do with personal interest and experience.

Jan van Eyck, *The Virgin and Child with Chancellor Rolin.* c. 1435. Panel,

66 x 62 cm. Musée National du Louvre, Paris.

These comments, however, take nothing away from the great admiration which this excellent achievement deserves. Nicholas' obvious affection for and scientific interest in Medieval Flanders are symptomatic of a much broader swell in the United States.

WALTER PREVENIER
Translated by Julian Ross.

David Nicholas, *Medieval Flanders.* London / New York: Longman, 1992; 460 pp.

The Battle of Arnhem 17-26 September 1944

Arnhem: a medium-sized city in the heart of the Netherlands. The capital of Gelderland, the largest province, Arnhem is famous for its many parks and places of interest, some of which, such as the Burgers' Zoo, the Dutch Open-Air Museum and the Hoge Veluwe National Park with its Kröller-Müller Museum, are of international renown. But what made this provincial capital on the Rhine into an international household name was, above all, the dramatic conflict that took place there in September 1944: the Battle of Arnhem.

With the German troops in France retreating in disarray before his divisions and no longer offering any significant resistance, Field Marshal Montgomery thought there might be a chance of forcing Nazi Germany to surrender before the onset of winter. Working under extreme pressure, his staff produced a number of plans for a final offensive. Plans which were rapidly overtaken by the stormy developments of the following days, before there could be any thought of carrying them out.

The Allies' advance ground to a halt in the north of Belgium on about 4 September 1944 because of difficulties with the supply of fuel. Precious time was lost. On 8 September, the Germans launched their first V2 rocket on London from the west of the Netherlands.

Under these circumstances, Monty's plans for a bold attack took shape more and more clearly. The 30th Army Corps was to advance north from its bridgehead near Neerpelt in Belgium into the Netherlands along a line stretching from Eindhoven through Nijmegen and on to Arnhem. The main army would then turn eastwards and invade Germany. In this way, it would avoid the Siegfried Line, a strong line of defence along part of the Reich's western frontier. A smaller army would advance as far as the Zuiderzee, thereby cutting off the west of the Netherlands with the V2 launch sites.

However, there was the danger that the Germans would destroy the various bridges in the path of Montgomery's troops before the rapidly advancing infantry could reach them.

In order to prevent the Germans from carrying out such plans, airborne forces were to take and secure the bridges in a surprise attack. This combined attack by ground and airborne forces was codenamed Operation Market Garden.

As part of this offensive, on Sunday afternoon of 17 September, part of the 1st British Airborne Division was flown in to landing areas west of Arnhem. Thousands of parachutists were dropped and hundreds of gliders carrying vehicles and artillery landed in fields near Wolfheze, ten kilometres from their main objective, the bridge over the Lower Rhine at Arnhem.

In the days that followed, the rest of the division was flown in and part of the 1st Polish Independent Parachute Brigade was dropped south of the Rhine near Driel. But the Polish troops under Major General Sosabowski could only watch helplessly from their positions as their British comrades across the river were forced into an increasingly dangerous position.

Though the landings themselves had been a great success, the subsequent march on Arnhem did not go according to plan. The Germans reacted with unexpected speed and force. Only one battalion reached its objective that evening. This was the 2nd Battalion under Lieutenant Colonel Frost, which, in fact, only succeeded in taking the northern approach to the bridge. The southern approach remained firmly in German hands.

In the following days the Germans succeeded in preventing the rest of the allied forces from joining Frost's troops, who were still managing to hold their positions. Only a few small groups were able to reach Frost.

In this perilous situation, he and his men held out much longer than had been planned. They waited in vain, however, for the arrival of the 30th Army Corps, whose advance was much slower than expected.

During the night of 20 September, Frost was obliged to retreat in the face of the Germans' crushing superiority. The bridge was, once again, entirely in German hands.

The rest of the division was pushed back, during heavy fighting, into an ever decreasing area around Oosterbeek, a village a few kilometres west of Arnhem. Major General Urquhart, in command of the 1st British Airborne Division, managed for a few days to keep a bridgehead on the Lower Rhine. But when it became clear that the main body of the Army Corps would never reach it, he was ordered to pull back across the river, with the remnants of what, only a few days before, had been a proud division. This retreat, codenamed Operation Berlin, took place on the night of

The road bridge over the Lower Rhine: for Operation Market Garden, it proved to be 'a bridge too far'. Since 17 december 1977, it is officially known as the John Frost Bridge (Photo by W.H. Tiemens).

26 September 1944. Of the more than 10,000 troops of the 1st Airborne Division which had been deployed, only about 2,500 came back. The others were either killed in action or were rounded up, many of them wounded, and became prisoners of war. The Arnhem part of Operation Market Garden was a total failure, and went into the history books as the Battle of Arnhem.

The 30th Army Corps' push forward finally ground to a halt at Elst, a small village seven kilometres south of Arnhem. And the liberation which the Corps brought in its wake also stopped there. The area between Nijmegen and Arnhem became a no man's land; the Germans flooded it by breaking a dike on the Lower Rhine.

Arnhem became a front-line city. The population of this badly battered city and that of equally afflicted Oosterbeek was forced to evacuate. The long cold winter which followed brought much suffering to this occupied part of the Netherlands. Fuel became almost completely unavailable and the resulting lack of transport contributed to the total breakdown of food distribution. This winter of starvation claimed many victims, especially in the densely populated west of the Netherlands.

It goes without saying that the brave but hopeless fight put up by the British and Polish soldiers left an ineradicable impression on the locals, who watched these bringers of hope being defeated in the space of a few days.

Immediately after the liberation, the building of a military cemetery was begun in Oosterbeek. The Renkum council provided the land. The first service of Commemoration for those who fell was held there as early as September 1945. It was to be the beginning of an unique tradition: a commemoration stretching over several days, where the population of Arnhem and the surrounding areas, veterans and relatives of those who died, come together each year to honour the Allied soldiers who fell at the Battle of Arnhem.

It also goes without saying, that the many veterans present are welcomed and hospitably entertained during their stay by just as many families in the region. Strong ties of friendship have grown between them over the years.

Here, as in all the other areas involved in Operation Market Garden, the Battle of Arnhem was commemorated on a large scale in September 1994. But the Arnhem commemoration was different from, say, that of Eindhoven or Nijmegen, cities which, at the time, were able to welcome their liberators. There the emphasis was upon celebration, while in Arnhem it remained upon commemoration. And not only during those days in September, but all year round, as is apparent from the steady flow of visitors to the Airborne Cemetery and Airborne Museum in Oosterbeek and a number of other places where memories of the Battle of Arnhem are still strong.

W.H. TIEMENS
Translated by Peter Flynn.

'Safe, for the time being' The Dutch Language and the Language Policy of the European Union

The policy regarding the use of languages within the institutions of the European Union (the European Parliament, the Council of Ministers and the European Commission) was set out in 1958 in Regulation No. 1 of the Council of Ministers. The Regulation is legally binding and is directly applicable in all the member states. In the first of seven articles, the official languages and working languages of the twelve member states are set out. Here, the point of departure is that the official language of each member state is recognised as an official and working language of the European Union. This therefore includes the 'minor languages' such as Greek, Portuguese, Danish and Dutch. The Dutch language, with twenty million speakers in the Netherlands and Flanders, is the largest of the 'minor' languages in Europe.

However, the articles of Regulation No. 1 do not contain detailed and watertight directives for the use of languages within the European Union's institutions. The regulation should be seen as a framework within which a number of principles have been formulated. However, this framework does have a number of weaknesses. The first article contains no clear definition of the term 'working language'. In the following articles, only 'official languages' are discussed. Some claim that no explicit statement can be found to the effect that all the working languages must be used equally. Neither is there any mention of interpreting (which each institution deals with individually), and it is not clear whether all official documents must be translated into all languages at each stage in decision-making. These weaknesses in Regulation No. 1 render the position of Dutch within the European Union decidedly vulnerable. This, of course, is equally true of the other minor languages.

The European Parliament adheres fairly closely to the principles of Regulation No. 1, although a certain 'magnanimity' does prompt some MEPs to opt for the use of one of the main languages (English, French, German). This does not happen during plenary meetings, but during smaller meetings and trips by delegations. Dutch-speaking MEPs in particular change over more quickly to English on such occasions. Often, however, the use of faulty English considerably undermines the speaker's cogency and powers of persuasion. In addition, this well-meaning flexibility undermines the status of the speaker's native language. Despite these occasional compromises, the position of the Dutch language – and all other minor languages – within the European Parliament seems to be reasonably safe. Moreover, the Nyborg Report (1982) contained resolutions which confirmed the equality of the languages.

The situation regarding the Council of Ministers is

somewhat different. Here, at the intermediate level of the Committee of Permanent Representatives, only three working languages (French, English and German) are used on a regular basis, although at council and working-group level the situation is less precarious.

In the European Commission too, the minor languages are harshly treated: all final documents are drawn up in all languages, but the number of working languages is reduced to three. In addition, a better interpreting service is provided for the major languages.

The arguments for restricting still further the number of working languages are based on financial and organisational considerations. Some believe that the use of nine working languages hinders the development of the European Union. The creation of a new Tower of Babel will obstruct efficient, prompt decision-making, and in the long term may even make it impossible. Those arguing from a financial perspective point to the continuing growth of the European Union: the admission of new member states could increase the number of languages. The number of meetings will increase, and more documents will be produced. Inevitably, therefore, translation costs will also rise steeply.

The supporters of multilingualism dismiss these budgetary objections. The Nyborg Report had already established that although translation costs are high, they account for only 2% of the European Union's budget. Furthermore, no one has been able to calculate precisely how much money would be saved by restricting the number of working languages.

If the number of working languages were reduced, for example, to three, this would indeed be advantageous from a budgetary point of view. However, it would in no way lead to greater efficiency, which would require a resolute change to a single working language.

Multilingualism is also defensible from a legal point of view. Decisions made within the European Union do, after all, directly affect every citizen in every member state. They must therefore be able to understand them. There are also cultural and political objections to a restriction in the number of working languages. Multilingualism is both the expression and the guarantee of the rich cultural pluralism espoused in Europe's cultural policy, and within the political forum of the Union it ensures that all policy-makers have an equal negotiating position.

The Dutch and Belgian governments formally endorse Regulation No. 1, which legally accords Dutch the same status as the other official languages. They also maintain that this decision cannot be altered in any way. Yet in practice there appears to be a process of erosion: Dutch, together with all the other minor languages, is indeed under threat. The subordination of Dutch, a result of the preferential treatment given to the major languages, is not only damaging to the use of the language in European political discussions, but is also damaging to the international status of and self-confi-

dence in the Dutch language. One could even argue that an enforced restriction of multilingualism within the European Union's institutions could lead to an anti-European reaction among Europe's citizens.

In the Netherlands and Flanders, voices from many sides are calling for an increased awareness among the parties involved in order to prevent an erosion of the use of Dutch. Those involved must act according to principle and ensure that Regulation No. 1 is strictly adhered to. For example, in November 1993, the Belgian Minister of Defence, Leo Delcroix, threatened not to provide Belgian troops for the new Euro-army. He demanded the recognition of Dutch as an official language within the army, alongside French and English. Eventually, his demand was met.

The governments of the Netherlands and Flanders also have a 'policy for the nineties' which has been drawn up by the Dutch Language Union, a Dutch-Flemish intergovernmental organisation for the promotion of language and literature. One of the aims of this policy is to expand the number of traditional and electronic language aids (lexicographical works, a General Data Bank of the Dutch Language ...) which should help to strengthen the position of Dutch among international languages.

In December 1993, it once more became apparent that the language issue is still a controversial matter within the European Union. The discussion was prompted by the establishment of the Trade Mark Office in Alicante, Spain, for which five official languages (English, French, German, Spanish and Italian) were chosen. The Dutch protested strongly and eventually the Foreign Ministers reached a compromise on the Trade Mark Office's language policy: Dutch or Flemish companies may submit their applications to the Office in Dutch, but they must be accompanied by a translation into one of the five official languages. Furthermore, at the European Summit in December 1993, government leaders reaffirmed that all languages within the Union have equal official status. In the words of a headline in the Dutch newspaper *De Volkskrant,* the status of Dutch within the European Union was 'safe, for the time being'.

FILIP MATTHIJS
Translated by Yvette Mead.

REFERENCE

DUTHOY, WERNER, *Het Nederlands in de instellingen van de Europese Gemeenschap.* The Hague, 1993, 2nd ed.

The *Dictionary of the Dutch Language*
A Monument to the Culture of the Netherlands and Flanders

The *Dictionary of the Dutch Language* (Woordenboek der Nederlandsche Taal), known affectionately as the WNT, is likely to be finally completed in 1998, after almost 150 years of diligent labour. It will be the largest dictionary in the world.

Matthias de Vries (1820-1892) (Photo Sdu).

was founded in 1991. The society publishes its own journal under the characteristic title *Trefwoord* (Headword).

The lexicographical work of De Vries is highly comparable with that of his nineteenth-century contemporaries Sir James A.H. Murray and the brothers Jakob and Wilhelm Grimm. Murray was the first editor of the *New English Dictionary on Historical Principles,* the first volume of which (A-Ant) appeared in 1884. Since 1933 this standard work has been known as the *Oxford English Dictionary* (OED). A second edition in twenty volumes of this immense work appeared in 1989.

De Vries felt himself to be a kindred spirit of Jakob Grimm, in particular. The Grimm brothers, world-famous for their collection of fairy-tales, *Kinder- und Hausmärchen* (1812-1822), were the founders of Germanic philology. In 1852 they published the first part of the *Deutches Wörterbuch,* a thorough, historically based inventory of the vocabulary of the German language. This huge work, consisting of thirty-three volumes, was not completed until 1963.

The WNT and its English and German counterparts are all large, scholarly works based on historical-philological principles; all three were created in the nineteenth century, the Romantic period. It was a cultural period in which scholars developed a great interest in the vocabulary of their national languages, and in which new linguistic disciplines emerged: etymology, dialectology, comparative linguistics and phonetics. It was the perfect climate for lexicography to develop into a full-blooded science.

In the middle of the century, in 1849, the first Language and Literary Conference attended by Flemish and Dutch scholars took place in the Flemish town of Ghent. It was almost twenty years since the 1830 revolution which had led to the formation of Belgium as an independent state, separate from the Netherlands. However, many intellectuals from Flanders, the Dutch-speaking area of Belgium, had been

The WNT, in its forty weighty volumes, with 44,000 pages each divided into two columns, will then contain a complete record of the Dutch language from 1500 to 1921. It will give detailed definitions of almost one million words. For specialists, and especially for those interpreting and annotating literary texts, this gigantic dictionary is an indispensable aid. It is also the 'mother dictionary' of all contemporary explanatory lexicons in the Dutch language-area.

This dictionary is a mammoth work, a work which appeals to the imagination, and a work which is associated particularly with the name Matthias de Vries (1820-1892), professor in Groningen and later in Leiden. It was he who laid the foundations for the scientific study of Dutch language and literature using the stringent methods of classical philology. The most recent salute to this linguist is the Matthias de Vries Society, an association of dictionary collectors which

The WNT team at work in 1948 (Photo WNT).

campaigning since this split for 'unity of language in North and South'. It was at the Ghent conference that the Dutchmen Alberdingk Thijm and Gerth van Wijk, both friends of Flanders, advanced the idea of compiling a large, authoritative dictionary which would promote linguistic unity between the two parts of the Dutch language-area.

At the third conference, held in 1851, Matthias de Vries presented his *Design for a Dutch dictionary* (Ontwerp van een Nederlandsch woordenboek). De Vries was the real creator of the WNT. He set about this task with energy and vigour in 1852, together with the Dutch language specialist L.A. te Winkel. The Leuven professor J.B. David also helped with the preparatory work. The team's first activity for the WNT was to design the strongly historicising 'De Vries and Te Winkel' spelling system for the Dutch language, a system which, for reasons of uniformity and ease of cross-referencing within the dictionary, was maintained in all the volumes.

De Vries had to overcome a great many difficulties and a good deal of opposition. The first instalment did not appear until 1864, while the first thick volume (A-Ajuin) of his 'language museum' appeared in 1882, with a lengthy *Introduction* (Inleiding) which was largely identical to the earlier *Design*. The register of subscribers which precedes the actual text in Vol. I is very interesting, containing as it does a striking number of head teachers, teachers (some of whom refer to themselves as *instituteur)* and auxiliary teachers. And of course, the literary celebrities of the time in North and South are present, names such as Potgieter, Fruin, De Geyter and Conscience. One name which is missing is that of the great Flemish poet and lover of language Guido Gezelle, who is known to have sent memos on a good hundred thousand words typical of the Southern Netherlands to the editors of the WNT.

De Vries' famous *Introduction* influenced the work of all the later editors of the WNT. According to De Vries, the dictionary must contain no improper words or expressions and no overly obscure dialect words; French, German and English loan words were treated only cursorily, and only quotations from the best writers could be included. The dictionary was after all intended to play a role in shaping style, particularly among the young. The second generation of editors, however, distanced themselves from De Vries' overly normative and nationalistic attitude. From this generation on the WNT became a historical dictionary in which the development of the Dutch vocabulary since the sixteenth century was described in an objective, scientific way.

The structure of the lemmas has in principle remained unchanged, however: the grammatical details of each headword are first given, followed by its etymology; then comes a highly detailed definition of the meaning and the various distinctions of meaning, supported by large numbers of quotations; finally, the entry lists compounds and derivations. The quotations, taken from more than ten thousand sources, are arranged in chronological order; they often make for fascinating reading.

Compared with the *Oxford English Dictionary* and the *Deutches Wörterbuch,* the WNT gives the most extensive and thoroughly structured description of the headwords it contains. Nevertheless, it by no means offers a complete inventory of the vocabulary of the Dutch language since the Middle Ages; obvious words are sometimes missing – including, oddly enough, the Dutch words for 'Belgian'!

In 1969, the Belgo-Dutch Institute of Dutch Lexicology (INL) was founded in Leiden, with among its tasks the completion of the *Dictionary of the Dutch Language.* Apart from the WNT project, however, the INL is also working on a colossal computerised word archive, the Language Data Bank (Taaldatabank), which will ultimately contain the complete Dutch-language vocabulary from the earliest times to today. For the time being, however, we will look forward to 1998, the completion date for the WNT.

In 1992 the Hague publishing house Sdu brought out an affordable photographic reprint of the WNT, though obviously without the as yet untreated letters x, y and z. An unexpectedly large number of people – more than twelve thousand lovers of language (germanic scholars, Dutch-language scholars, historians, lecturers, etc.) – subscribed to this work. At the launch of this special facsimile edition, the Dutch linguist and columnist Hugo Brandt Corstius made this telling comment: 'The purchaser of this dictionary must not be someone in search of usefulness; it must be someone in search of beauty. Because the WNT is a monument.'

And indeed, the *Dictionary of the Dutch Language* is an impressive cultural monument, the fruit of 150 years of cooperation between Flanders and the Netherlands.

ANTON CLAESSENS
Translated by Julian Ross.

Pleasant Summer Days in Breukelen, Diepenbeek and Ghent

Each year thousands of young people from the Netherlands and Flanders leave for a British or American university or college and spend several weeks there improving their knowledge of the English language. But there are also a number of possibilities in the Netherlands and Flanders for non-Dutch speakers to study Dutch during the summer months. A large number of institutes run their own highly varied programmes. Three summer courses are of special interest, partly because they are subsidised either directly or indirectly by the Dutch or Flemish governments: the courses held in Breukelen (near Utrecht), Diepenbeek (near Hasselt) and Ghent.

Up until 1993, the course in Breukelen was organised by the Dutch Ministry for Education and Science. In 1994 it was run for the first time by the International Association for Dutch Studies (IVN), set up in 1970 to provide a focus and a platform for the rapidly growing community of 'international' university teachers of Dutch.

Responsibility for the content of the course lies with the Dutch Language Union, an inter-governmental organisation which coordinates the efforts of the Dutch and Flemish Authorities with regard to language and literature. Each summer some 150 students are welcomed from all over the world. They are lodged on a beautifully situated rural campus at the centre of which is the Nijenrode castle.

There are two courses run in Flanders. Each year Diepenbeek welcomes about a hundred students to the course there, most of them from Scandinavia, the German-speaking parts of the world and Eastern Europe. The Limburg University Centre looks after the organisation. At the other course, in Ghent, the number of participants in the course is limited; only fifty to sixty students are allowed to take part. They mainly come from the Latin countries such as France, Spain, Portugal and Italy. Here, the Ghent University Language Centre is responsible for the organisation. Both courses are subsidised by the Flemish Community's Department of Education.

The three courses target different groups. Those participating in the course in Breukelen are 'non-Dutch speakers who for study, career or other reasons wish to improve their knowledge of the Dutch language and culture'. In Diepenbeek the participants 'already speak Dutch, which allows them to really benefit from their stay in Flanders'. In Ghent, an essential condition for enrolment is that you should be 'studying Dutch as a main or subsidiary subject at a college for higher education'. Both of these Flemish iniatives can count on grants from the Flemish Community to cover the course and lodging costs. In Breukelen, too, a limited number of grants are available.

Those taking part in the Breukelen, Diepenbeek and Ghent courses are treated to impressive and diversified programmes. The Dutch language lessons are always held in the morning. The participants are divided into groups according to their level of proficiency in Dutch. A large number of educational tours to the main cultural cities, museums, artists' workshops and factories are also organised. From Breukelen, there are visits to Amsterdam, Utrecht etc. Cities such as Ghent, Bruges and Antwerp offer those attending courses in Flanders various opportunities for getting in touch with the wealth of local history. Another important feature of the programme is an introduction to contemporary society. To this end, there are debates and lectures by eminent people from the realms of politics, economics and culture. And there is even some time left for recreation. Diepenbeek students can go for walks in a nearby nature reserve and those from Ghent usually take much-appreciated bicycle trips along the banks of the River Leie.

Breukelen, Diepenbeek and Ghent see to it that, each year, about 300 students not only gain a better knowledge of Dutch, but also learn to appreciate the culture of the Low Countries. These summer courses are, from the point of view of Dutch cultural policy, an important investment for the future.

HANS VANACKER
Translated by Peter Flynn.

ADDRESSES
The International Association for Dutch Studies (IVN)
Raadhuisstraat 1 / 2481 BE Woubrugge / The Netherlands
tel. +31 (0) 1729 8243 / fax +31 (0) 1729 9925

Limburg University Centre
University Campus / 3590 Diepenbeek / Belgium
tel. +32 (0) 11 26 87 64 / fax +32 (0) 11 24 23 87

Ghent University Language Centre
Sint-Pietersnieuwstraat 136 / 9000 Ghent / Belgium
tel. +32 (0) 9 264 36 78 / +32 (0) 9 264 41 92

The Dutch Tradition in English Language Studies

English is undoubtedly the dominant international language in the world today. It is the language of power and diplomacy, of information and the media, of science and technology, of liberal democracy, trade and entertainment. And to an extent not seen before in history, English is now the global *lingua franca.*

In this English-dominated world, the Dutch are active in countless international organisations and networks. They are the second biggest foreign investors in the United States. They run some of the largest multinational companies, and Rotterdam is the biggest port in the world. As a corollary, the English language can be found almost anywhere in the Netherlands today. Cable TV provides direct access to CNN and the BBC. In education, English is the first foreign language for Dutch children from the age of ten, while in the universities an increasing number of courses, text books and theses are in English. In 1988, at least 24% of all new books published in the Netherlands were in English, and 70% of all films shown in Dutch cinemas were made in America.

It would be a mistake, however, to think that the Dutch are all speaking English now, or that they are shortly going to abandon their native tongue. The Dutch language is alive and well, as the natural medium of communication in politics and society, in the economy and in education, in literature, the theatre and the media, at work, at home and in public life.

There is of course also the European context, where multilingualism is a historical and contemporary reality. The same cable that brings CNN and the BBC to Dutch homes, also brings them programmes in German, French, Italian, Spanish, Portuguese and the Scandinavian languages. Some of these are taking on the role of regional *lingua francas,* the most important for the Dutch being German and French. But English occupies a special position: its rise, especially since the sixties, has been spectacular, and it is now the most widely used and needed foreign language in the Netherlands.

In this context, language skills are obviously of vital importance to the Dutch, and they will therefore have to continue to invest more time and money in the teaching of Dutch and of the three major modern languages, English, French and German (cf. also Uhlenbeck, in *The Low Countries* 1993-94: 31).

In the case of English in particular, the Dutch come well prepared to this task. The Netherlands has a long and distinguished tradition of scholarship in the field of English language studies. Dutch anglicists have made many important contributions to the study of English grammar, lexicography and linguistic analysis, and these have recently been highlighted in an interesting collection of biographical texts covering the period 1885-1990, entitled *Dutch Masters and their Era* (1993).

The volume opens with an *In Memoriam* of the first Professor of English Language and Literature in the Netherlands, Jan Beckering Vinckers (1821-1891), who was appointed at the University of Groningen in 1885. At that time, English studies were strongly influenced by the strictly historical-comparative approach of nineteenth-century German philology; indeed, until well into the present century Dutch anglicists often went to German universities in order to obtain their doctorates, since in the Netherlands they could not do so until after 1921.

Stuurman presents a chronological series of well-annotated articles on fifteen Dutch anglicists, the most important of whom are the grammarians H. Poutsma (1856-1937), E. Kruisinga (1875-1944), F. Th. Visser (1886-1976) and R.W. Zandvoort (1894-1990). It is their work which forms the core of the Dutch tradition.

Before the Second World War the most important contributions were Poutsma's *Grammar of Late Modern English* (1904-1926), Kruisinga's *Handbook of Present Day English* (1911-1932), and Zandvoort's journal *English Studies,* which was founded in 1919. Such was the reputation of these Dutch anglicists that in 1936 it was said that, while the English should certainly continue to speak and use their own language, they could safely leave the study and description of its grammar to the Dutch.

After the Second World War Zandvoort continued to play a leading role. His *Handbook of English Grammar* first appeared in 1946 and ran into many editions. It was phenomenally successful and became the most influential grammar of English by a Dutch anglicist. For many years, Zandvoort also took an active part in the international associations of Professors in English, American Studies and Modern Languages. And he expanded his *English Studies* into an international journal edited by a committee of anglicists from six European countries.

The last great representative of the Dutch tradition is F. Th. Visser, whose magnum opus, *An Historical Syntax of the English Language,* was published in three large volumes between 1963 (when Visser was already 77!) and 1973. This work is the last major product of the philological tradition in continental English language studies, and as Zandvoort put it in 1974, it marks the end of Dutch supremacy in this field.

Regarding this Dutch tradition, Sir Randolph Quirk notes, in his *Preface* to Stuurman's collection: *'Through the labours of a great generation in the Netherlands, English Studies (as witness English Studies) flourished both within and far beyond the Dutch frontiers, providing models of rich and immaculately accurate data-based research that transformed grammar-writing.'*

The pioneering efforts of these Dutch scholars have greatly contributed to the subsequent rapid and successful development of English language teaching in the Netherlands, for which they provided the handbooks, the grammars, the dictionaries, the phonetic manuals, the text editions, and above all the teachers. They also laid the scholarly foundations upon which the present generation of Dutch anglicists continue to build, not just in teaching but also in research, where they are in the vanguard of the electronic revolution and continue to pursue the study of English grammar through their active involvement in new projects and networks for international cooperation.

REINIER SALVERDA

Dutch Masters and Their Era. English Language studies by the Dutch, from the last century into the present (ed. F. Stuurman). Amsterdam: Amsterdam University Press, 1993; 200 pp.

Literature

The Netherlands Literature Museum and Documentation Centre Where Readers Become Spectators

Encouraged by the success of the 'Literary Exhibition' held in the Town Hall of The Hague in 1923 to mark Queen Wilhelmina's Silver Jubilee, the city's municipal archivist, Dr W. Moll, took a few tentative steps towards establishing a literary collection. Thirty years later he had an assortment of over 1,500 literary documents in his charge – a veritable cuckoo's chick. In 1953 this collection formed the healthy basis of the Netherlands Literature Museum and Documentation Centre founded in that year, which some forty years on has grown into a national literary archive-cum-museum containing some 20,000 manuscripts, over 1,000,000 letters and more than 60,000 photographs and 2,000 painted and drawn portraits relating to Dutch literature after 1750. Since 1982 the museum has been housed in the Royal Library complex, directly adjacent to the Central Railway Station. It confines its activities to more recent Dutch literature from the Netherlands. Flanders has its own Archive and Museum for Flemish Culture in Antwerp, founded in 1933, and in Leeuwarden, the capital of Friesland, the Frisian Literature Museum and Documentation Centre occupies the childhood home of the famous spy Mata Hari.

What does the Literature Museum do? It has more than 10,000 items in its care: gifts, permanent loans and – to a lesser extent – purchases, ranging from the literary estates of prominent Dutch writers (including Louis Couperus, Herman Gorter, Willem Kloos, Edgar du Perron and Simon Vestdijk), to not particularly important letters from not particularly important writers to ditto colleagues. Foreign writers are of course also represented in the collection, by virtue of their correspondence with Dutch writers: these include André Gide (corresponding with Jef Last), D.H. Lawrence (letters to and from Augusta de Wit), Jean Rhys (who was married to the Dutchman Eduard de Nève from 1919 to 1926), Rainer Maria Rilke, Jules Verne and Emile Zola. The main emphasis in the collection is on the period 1880-1950; besides letters and manuscripts, other items relating to writers are collected. Notes, reviews, proofs, publishers' contracts, portraits, book illustrations, busts, posters, videotapes, books containing dedications which because of those dedications have become literary documents, curiosities – in short, everything connected with the writers which is not a book. For books the Literature Museum relies on its neighbour, the Royal Library. All these items are not catalogued in strict order of acquisition; newly-acquired letters of, say, P.N. van Eyck, who in the 1930s was London correspondent of one of the principal Dutch dailies, are added to the existing P.N. van Eyck collection. The obvious advantage of this system is that the researcher can find all the documents relating to one writer in the same place, and does not have to consult what may be dozens of collections. Nevertheless, for fifty years after the writer's death, in order to study those documents not already published, he / she requires the permission of the copyright-holder(s): of the author himself / herself during his lifetime, thereafter of the heirs. It is true that the collections of the Literature Museum afford researchers the opportunity of studying writers in great depth and hence possibly – which is the object of the exercise – of gaining a greater insight into their work, but only with the permission of the copyright-holder(s). This of course also applies to the publication of letters, variants and other matter not primarily intended for the press. This brings us to the publications of the Literature Museum.

In the first place there are the *Writers' Picture Books* (Schrijversprentenboeken), usually literary exhibitions in book form devoted to one author or literary movement, of which thirty-five have appeared to date. As a rule they accompany an exhibition mounted by the Museum. Recent volumes were concerned with the grand old lady of Dutch letters, Hella Haasse, the celebrated children's author Annie M. G. Schmidt, so popular that she is sometimes called the real queen of the Netherlands, and Harry Mulisch, who with the publication of his magnum opus *The Discovery of Heaven* (De ontdekking van de hemel, 1992) was recognised as an author of European stature. The series *Behind the Book* (Achter het boek), aimed at a less general readership, contains mainly correspondence between important writers, provided with an extensive commentary. Up to now twenty-six annual issues of this periodical in book form have appeared. In addition the Museum issues postcards with portraits and manuscripts of writers and publishes a Yearbook.

Finally there are the exhibitions. There is a permanent exhibition illustrating Dutch literature since 1750, and temporary displays are organised to commemorate centenaries or writers' anniversaries. Children's literature, too, will shortly be given its rightful place within the Museum.

Though memorial houses of writers may be thin on the ground in the Netherlands compared with the United Kingdom – we can point to little apart from the Multatuli Museum in Amsterdam – there is nevertheless a Literature Museum which does its best to fill that gap. A place where readers can come and look. Before returning to their reading.

ANTON KORTEWEG
Translated by Paul Vincent.

ADDRESS
Netherlands Literature Museum and Documentation Centre
Prinses Irenepad 10 / 2595 BG / The Hague / The Netherlands
tel. +31 (0) 70 347 11 14 / fax +31 (0) 70 347 79 41
Correspondence:
P.O. Box 90515 / 2509 LM / The Hague / The Netherlands
Opening hours: 10 a.m. – 5 p.m. (Tuesday – Saturday)
1 p.m. – 5 p.m. (Sunday)

A Literary Peep Show

The Dedalus Book of Dutch Fantasy (1993) is not a sampler of a single, specific genre within Dutch literature. Its editor and translator, Richard Huijing, says in his introduction that he has put together an anthology which presents 'the Dutch literary imagination in as many guises as could be found'. The result is a hetero-

Looking at literature
(Photo Letterkundig
Museum, The Hague).

geneous collection of stories and novellas, 'from the weirdly improbable to the macabre, from fairy tales to pipe dreams, from darkest perversion to religious ecstacy'.

The concept of 'fantasy literature' is usually associated with supernatural themes such as witchcraft, vampirism and metamorphosis; and a number of the stories in this collection do indeed include such elements. The very title of Arthur van Schendel's 'The White Woman' (1938) indicates a typical Gothic tale. The two stories by Louis Couperus are entertaining sequels to the well-known tales of Bluebeard and Don Juan. In 'The Son of Don Juan' (1915) the ghost of the notorious lady-killer reminds Don Juanito, his pious and far from carnally inclined son, of his marital duties.

The humour in Jan Arends' 'Breakfast' (1969) is of an entirely different order. Old Mr Koopman turns into a monkey on his birthday, to the great displeasure of the nursing staff at an old people's home. The narrator laces his tale with such laconic observations as: 'It's surprising to see the way old gentlemen are able to climb trees when they change into monkeys.'

Fritzi Harmsen van Beek's 'The Taxi Pig' (1968) strikes the same note of absurdity from the very first sentence. The narrator remarks drily: 'As we were getting in, we hadn't noticed that there was a taxi pig in the car, along for the ride as well.' The casual tone of this statement is reminiscent of Kafka's *Metamorphosis* (Die Verwandlung): 'When Gregor Samsa awoke one morning from unquiet dreams, he found himself transformed in his sleep into a giant bug.' In her book *Fantasy: The Literature of Subversion* (1981) Rosemary Jackson wrote that in the story of the unfortunate Samsa 'strangeness is taken as a given, before the narrative begins'. The reader is caught up in a disorienting story which forms a 'closed mental space'. The same thing happens in the above-mentioned stories by Harmsen van Beek and Arends; here too the reader is transported to a closed mental space, an isolated world with new and strange laws.

However, in this anthology fantasy is not restricted to the supernatural or uncanny. In his foreword Huijing speaks of 'fancy' as the determining factor in his final selection for the anthology. In his view, 'fancy' includes 'the entire range of products of the imagination in fiction'; every author who does not adhere strictly to dogmatic realism writes, to a greater or lesser extent, 'fantastic' literature. This explains the inclusion of, for example, Frans Kellendonk's 'The Death and Life of Thomas Chatterton' (1983). Kellendonk looks at the biography of a historical figure – the poet Thomas Chatterton (1752-1770), famous for his forgeries of medieval verse – from a new angle. The story is in the form of a monologue, in which the critic who unmasked Chatterton as a literary charlatan debunks the heroic myth of the brilliant young poet driven to suicide by lack of recognition. Kellendonk held the view that literature was 'a form of research, research by means of the imagination'. The literary text is therefore a game of and with the imagination that also leaves room for creative input by the reader.

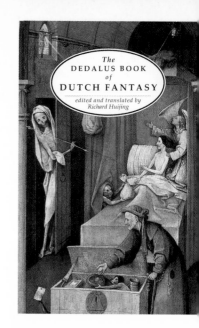

The best example of 'non-fantastic' fantasy is Gerard Reve's 'Werther Nieland' (1949). Huijing describes this novella as a 'tale in which all is hidden, suggested'. It is the psychological portrait of the adolescent boy Elmer, who realises 'that it must be impossible to understand all that happened and that there were things that remained mysterious, causing a fog of fear to arise'. Nothing really happens in the story. More important than the rather thin plot is the atmosphere of brooding threat, melancholy and aggression. Elmer's homo-erotic and sadistic daydreams and his preoccupation with physical decay are the typical romantic-decadent motifs which recur throughout Reve's oeuvre. The 'decadent', by the way, is one of Dedalus Publishers' specialities. An example of Dutch *fin de siècle* 'depravity' is provided by the highly blasphemous 'Concerning the Experiences of Hélénus Marie Golesco', published in 1907 by Jacob Israel de Haan. Despite his naturalistic debut this author, with some reservations, can be described as the Dutch Oscar Wilde. The metaphysical theme (the repudiation of God) is expressed in this tale in supernatural terms: Helenus is the devil's lover, both spiritually and physically. A lachrymose Christ tries in vain to win him over to God's Realm. Helenus relates how 'I mated him with the rage of my lithe body that jerked over his …'.

The wide range of stories in *The Dedalus Book of Dutch Fantasy* is not solely due to Huijing's broad definition of fantastic literature. His choice of authors is, to put it mildly, highly idiosyncratic. He has included a number of authors from the turn of the century who are virtually unknown in the Netherlands (Jan Hofker, Willem Schürmann), while there is no trace in his anthology of F. Bordewijk, whose *Fantastic Tales* (Fantastische vertellingen, 1919-1924, 3 vols.) may be regarded as the flagship of Dutch fantasy writing.

Alongside the stars of the past (Simon Vestdijk) and today (Harry Mulisch), Huijing has included such newcomers as P.F. Thomése and Maarten Asscher. The latter's 'The Secret of Dr Raoul Sarrazin' (1992) is reminiscent of Borges' intriguing stories.

Since Huijing makes no claim of objectivity or comprehensiveness – he even admits to having included a few of his 'personal highlights' – he can hardly be reproached for having produced a non-representative selection. First and foremost he has compiled a highly idiosyncratic anthology for a highly idiosyncratic publisher whose list includes such titles as *Tales of the Wandering Jew* and *The Dedalus Book of Femmes Fatales*. One might conclude from the foreword that the most important quality of Dutch fantasy is a kind of 'un-Dutchness': in other words, the fantastic stories resulted from a conscious or unconscious resistance to or preoccupation with the 'typically Dutch' phenomena of Calvinism and 'burgherdom' – to use the book's word for it. But this theory is too general and too vague to be the crux of the anthology.

The power of the individual stories in *The Dedalus Book of Dutch Fantasy* is more important than the book's overall cohesiveness. The collection could be considered a peep show of the Dutch literary imagination. The scenes presented to our gaze are sometimes exciting, often intriguing, more often than not pretty boring, but certainly worth seeing. And here, unlike in Real Life, one does not have to satisfy one's curiosity furtively. It goes without saying that fantasy beats life …

FILIP MATTHIJS
Translated by Scott Rollins.

The Dedalus Book of Dutch Fantasy (ed. and tr. Richard Huijing). Sawtry: Dedalus, 1993; 384 pp.

Back to the Netherlands

It's not that I haven't been back to the Netherlands, and it's not even that I haven't been back for a longer period of time; but my stay at the Translators' House, in January and February of 1993, was somehow so concentrated a time, so much an opportunity to be Dutch, so much an occasion to merge into a neighborhood and become part of a setting, a setting which ever since my childhood I wanted to be mine.

I was seven in 1942 when my family fled from the Netherlands and sixteen when I left Curaçao to go to the US. Somehow the Netherlands – and the Dutch language – were never truly forgotten, never really left behind, but inevitably they faded.

Take the matter of language. I continued to read Dutch without the slightest difficulty, spoke Dutch fluently, and as an American academic – teaching English literature at San Francisco State University – translated five books of Dutch poetry. But something happens when you don't use a language daily. You can find the words, yes, but you can't find the perfect words, the ones you need now, immediately. You want to say that

you can be *flexible* about your arrival time in Maastricht but the only word that comes to mind is *buigzaam* (bendable), and that's clearly not the word you want.

What happened at the Translators' House to bring about some of that linguistic and other acculturation? It's that I had to say something in Dutch about the way the in-house computer differed from mine at home. It's that I was invited to the weekly Thursday-evening drinks at a tavern in Amsterdam with other translators brought together by the literary magazine, *De Tweede Ronde*. It's that I went to the Nijhoff Translation Prize Awards in The Hague and afterwards lost my kindly host Rudi Wester, the deputy director of the Foundation for the Production and Translation of Dutch Literature, and suddenly there was a terrifyingly large reception where all my American-made cocktail party small talk was useless. And much more: I started to hear again the Dutch sounds that go with the language, the 'Cough, Hm, Ja, Nou, Dat valt nog mee' sounds, sounds that were familiar and reassuring. No amount of reading Dutch in a faraway place like San Francisco could accomplish that. And still more: what pleasure to read *De Volkskrant* in the morning and recognise the principals on TV at night!

As a small child in the Netherlands I was aware of being different, Jewish, a refugee already then, and wanting above all to be Dutch, to be indistinguishable from the other Dutch kids around me. Curaçao, the United States – it was not exactly exile, but the dream of the Netherlands was deferred, maybe displaced. I became an American. It's so much easier to become a real American than a real Dutchman, maybe because nobody is finally, fully, a 'real' American: we are all a bit estranged. Anyway, the longing for the Netherlands persisted on some level – and here, now, though with an identity clearly established in another part of the world, here I was free to become Dutch again, and somehow it worked.

Whether I walked through Amsterdam, visited my aunt in The Hague, took the train to see friends in Amersfoort, travelled to Limburg to give a lecture at an American institution, I felt what the Dutch poet Remco Campert called 'The spacious feeling of Holland / when evening falls …'. I could understand those lines: only someone Dutch could, I think.

For two months I translated Campert, completing fifty poems. Occasionally he and I would meet, either in his flat near the Concertgebouw or in my apartment within the Translators' House. We talked about words and phrases, he in his quiet, intense way, I somewhat more ponderous and academic. But the real gain was that the conversation took place at all; the gain was in all the conversations I had in those months in which I was working hard as a translator by slowly acculturating myself to Dutch turns of phrase, to Dutch tones, to Dutch ways of thought.

Funny little codes take longest to master. I remember, one late February evening, being told that a fragment from a show I watched on TV where a languid young man says, 'Het basismateriaal is kurk' ('Cork is the basic material') was not pure affectation, as I thought, but pure satire. Frank Ligtvoet, the Foundation's Director, and Pleuke Boyce, the charming Dutch-Canadian translator who lived in the other apartment in the Translators' House, burst out laughing. Well, it takes more than two months. No wonder I'm coming back.

MANFRED WOLF

Remco Campert

Praise for the Painters

With my friends the painters
I feel the greatest affinity,

for they see in a face,
a body, a landscape,

colour playing poker with a shape:
that raw stain of red ochre

turns out to be a languid thigh
in the light of the accomplished painting.

Translated by Manfred Wolf.

The Self and the Other The Novels of Marcel Möring

Mendel Adenauer is the only remaining member of his family. His father's identity is unknown and his mother and grandparents all died within a short space of time. 'My family? (…) that's a grave in the shape of a family': this painful fact is stated in Marcel Möring's first novel, *Mendel's Legacy* (Mendels erfenis, 1990). In this book Möring (1957-) describes the steadily increasing isolation of a Jewish adolescent who grew up in the rural eastern Netherlands of the post-World War Two period. Möring himself describes *Mendel's Legacy* as an *'Entbildungsroman'*: 'Mendel Adenauer has decided to follow his own path in life – but it is a dead end'. Usually a *Bildungsroman* relates, through psychological analysis, how a character is shaped by his environment and as a result gradually comes to terms with life. Mendel, by contrast, has chosen to work things out completely alone, without the help of others. He becomes messianic in his attempts to improve the world, increasingly isolating himself from his surroundings. His reactions to everyone and everything become stranger and stranger, and he eventually ends up in an institution. Here Möring is asking to what extent Mendel – as a survivor with this specific Jewish background and history – had been free to choose this path. In the book he tries to combine two opposing philosophical theories. The first theory, that of the French philosopher Emmanuel Levinas, is that a per-

son only exists in relation to others: it is the Other that gives content to our lives. The second, that of Jean Paul Sartre, is that man is always ultimately alone. Mendel is completely alone, but his conviction that his personal experience ought to have a universal validity leads him to adopt a messianic attitude: he is looking for what Levinas describes. Levinas' 'philosophy of the Other' is also known as the philosophy of the human face: we only acquire our identity through the perceptions of others. Mendel's tragedy is that he must get to know others, yet at the same time is also forced to withdraw because he cannot reach them. The lonelier he becomes, the more he comes to see his isolation as a reflection of the isolation of the Jews.

Möring's books deal with a surprising number of topics. In *Mendel's Legacy* these are Mendel's personal tragedy, the history of the eastern Netherlands since the industrial revolution, and the wider history of the Jews in Western Europe. His second novel, *The Great Longing* (Het grote verlangen, 1992), is also about the past, although not specifically about the Jewish past. This novel depicts both the presence of the past and its inaccessibility. 'Only the memory remains', we read, 'and the memory is not enough, memory is a great longing'.

The main character in *The Great Longing* is Sam van Dijk. Sam, his twin sister Lisa and older brother Raph are orphaned at an early age when their parents are killed in a car accident. Immediately afterwards they are separated; they grow up in different foster families. The three do not see each other again until their foster parents' guardianship comes to an end and they become independent. For Sam, Lisa comes to represent the wonder of memory: she tells him about the past they had shared until their parents died. It is Lisa who makes Sam aware that his emotional disabilities are due to his inability to remember anything from the past. He is particularly affected by her parable about someone whose memories returned when he realised that happiness can be attained through intense longing, for this is how it is for Sam. Just as Mendel searches for the truth in Jewish history, so Sam tries to discover the reality of his own past. At the end of the book, the cause of Sam's memory loss is revealed: Lisa tells him that he had been in the car with his parents when the accident happened. *The Great Longing* is also a *Bildungsroman* in other respects. During the course of the novel, Sam discovers both the Other and his own self in various ways. He comes to appreciate the value of his affection for his brother and sister, of friendship, compassion, of love and the erotic. And this illustrates Levinas' theory that longing is the force which impels the Self towards another.

The Great Longing is more deeply rooted in philosophy than Möring's first novel. The numerous quotations from thinkers such as Pico della Mirandola, Wittgenstein and Levinas reinforce the novel's existentialist theme. What drives us on? What does the Other mean to us? Sam is tormented by such tantalising questions. However, Möring's preoccupation is ethical rather than philosophical. Not only is Levinas'

Marcel Möring (1957-)
(Photo by Harry Cock).

concept of the Self and the Other primarily one of an ethical relationship, but in addition Möring's works are notable for their social commitment; he links the psychological alienation of his main characters with the political and social alienation of our society. Whereas the doom in *Mendel's Legacy* concerned the war-time past of the previous generation, in *The Great Longing* we have a degenerate, apocalyptic urban setting dominated by materialism and apathy – and all too recognisable.

With his first novel, Möring was already acclaimed as *the* rising young talent. For *Mendel's Legacy* he received the Geert Jan Lubberhuizen Prize for the best prose debut; his second novel *The Great Longing* received the AKO Literature Prize. Also, *The Great Longing* will shortly be published in an English translation by Flamingo. This seems to me a more valuable recognition of Möring's work than all the prizes in the world: the work of an original, passionate writer such as Möring should not remain unread because of language barriers.

JEROEN VULLINGS
Translated by Yvette Mead.

Music

The Alamire Foundation International Centre for the Study of Music in the Low Countries

From the mid-nineteenth century on, Renaissance music has interested musicians and musicologists. Since Gustave Reese's monumental synoptic work, *Music in the Renaissance,* appeared in 1954 (second ed. 1958), numerous specialised studies have been published about music in the fifteenth and sixteenth centuries.

Reese's book and similar studies give pride of place to vocal polyphony by composers from the Low Countries, who were renowned throughout Europe in their time, and whose imitative counterpoint set a standard for polyphonic music. Their contribution to genres which include the Latin mass and motet, Magnificat and hymn, the Italian madrigal and villanella, the

French *chanson* and the German *lied* are difficult to overestimate.

They learned to compose in any genre and language, hence their international appeal. Emperors, kings, nobles, princes and dukes, popes, cardinals and bishops all competed for the honour of acquiring the best polyphonists from the Low Countries as composers, choirmasters, singers and teachers at their prestigious Renaissance courts. From 1501, when the Venetian Ottaviano dei Petrucci brought out the first published collection of polyphonic music (devoted exclusively to composers from the Low Countries!), busy music presses encouraged the international distribution of their work. The prints replaced the luxurious manuscripts, beautifully illustrated with dazzling miniatures, which had circulated in the past. One of the most famous illustrators was Petrus van de Hove, better known as Petrus Alamire, who worked at the court of Margaret of Austria, Regent of the Netherlands, and was also a copyist, composer and diplomat. More than fifty beautiful choirbooks containing sacred polyphony have survived from between 1507 and 1530, either in his hand or from his workshop; most of them are kept in various libraries throughout the world as unique treasures, securely locked away in safes. This 'Renaissance man' gave his name to the 'Alamire Foundation', established at the Catholic University of Leuven in 1991 as the 'International Centre for the Study of Music in the Low Countries'. The University's musicology department is involved in the Alamire Foundation in collaboration with Musica (Peer, Limburg), a non-profit association led by Herman Baeten. An internationally known division of Musica is the Alamire Publishing Company, noted for publishing facsimiles of rare prints and manuscripts (including many with Renaissance polyphony). There are currently three researchers associated with the Foundation (Dr Eugeen Schreurs, Catholic University of Leuven, Professor Barbara Haggh, University of Maryland, USA, and Bruno Bouckaert, Catholic University of Leuven). The Foundation offers a limited number of fellowships to foreign and Belgian musicologists.

The Foundation's aim is to encourage scholarly research into music in the Low Countries from the Middle Ages until the end of the Ancien Régime, with the main emphasis on the Golden Age of polyphony in the fifteenth and sixteenth centuries.

Researchers in Flanders will be working with colleagues from the Netherlands, Great Britain, other European countries and America. The first stage of the project is now under way. The researchers are searching the archives of collegiate churches in the Southern Netherlands and what is now Northern France (as far as Arras) for information about music and musical activity. This information will be analysed and made available to researchers at home and abroad in database form. The collegiate churches were centres of excellence for the practice of both plainchant and polyphony. Each had its own choir of professional singers and often a choir school where boys were trained in singing and composition. The archives, many of which

A fragment of an 'Alamire' choirbook (MS 228 fol. IV) (Koninklijke Bibliotheek, Brussels).

With the Alamire Foundation, musicologists in Flanders are establishing a project which reaches across frontiers, in the same way as the Flemish composers of polyphony made their music known throughout Europe in the fifteenth and sixteenth centuries.

IGNACE BOSSUYT
Translated by Steve Judd.

ADDRESS
Alamire Foundation
Centrale bibliotheek / Mgr. Ladeuzeplein 21 / 3000 Leuven /
Belgium
tel. +32 (0)16 28 46 61 / fax +32 (0)16 28 46 91

Otto Ketting 'The good notes in our age'

The Dutch composer Otto Ketting (1935-) searches for 'the good notes in our age'. He believes that it is now almost impossible to shock people with music, as was done in the fifties and sixties. Everything has been done and everything is allowed. Why should a composer now experiment with the audience's listening habits, as Ketting did in *Collage no. 9* (and in his other collages) in 1963, on the occasion of the Concertgebouw Orchestra's 75th anniversary? Why not write music which begins before the conductor reaches the podium, an anti-anniversary piece in which the wind and string sections are supposed to organise a whist drive on stage?

Ketting wrote *Collage no. 9* when he was twenty-eight and provocation was part of his basic attitude and that of his contemporaries. Ketting was in fact an outsider in the world of young Dutch composers. He went his own way and did not study under Kees van Baaren, as Peter Schat, Louis Andriessen and Jan van Vlijmen did. He learned a great deal from his father, the composer Piet Ketting, but was otherwise largely self-taught. He studied trumpet at the conservatory and later played the instrument with the Residentie Orchestra in The Hague.

The idea behind *Collage no. 9* worked. Bernard Haitink, principal conductor of the Concertgebouw Orchestra at the time, refused to perform the piece. For three years it lay on the shelf, until the French conductor Ernest Bour dared to perform it – but without the notorious card-playing scene.

These days Ketting experiments with tradition rather than listening habits. A key work of recent years is *Symphony no.3,* whose premiere in 1990 was conducted by the composer himself. It is a large orchestral work with a traditional three-part structure, but it avoids easy resort to old forms and techniques. Ketting did not want to copy tradition shamelessly or plunder it for a fashionable, collage-like style. In his view that would be as disastrous as searching for a modern sound idiom by using vague hissing noises, clusters, tone clouds or unplayable rhythms, as many contemporary composers do.

In *Symphony no. 3* what seems at first sight to be an

had never before been studied, and which include *acta capitularia,* provide a rich picture of the triumphs and sorrows of the college of canons, in whose lives music played a vital part. The collection of thousands of names and of data about the choirboys, singers and composers will make it possible to place musical life in the Low Countries in a broader socio-cultural and religious context. At a later stage, research will be extended to cover the secular courts as well.

A second area of research concentrates on the music itself. Stylistic studies, publications in facsimile or in modern transcription, preferably of recently discovered, little-known or unknown compositions, are being prepared and proposed. Lectures, exhibitions, colloquia and conferences bring the results of this research to the public. One such conference was the international Orlandus Lassus Conference held in Antwerp 24-26 August 1994. By means of concerts and annual festivals concentrated on particular themes, scraps of old paper and parchment stored deep in the archives and libraries come ringing back to life.

To establish the Foundation as a truly international centre, where music and musical life are seen as part of society in general, interdisciplinary research is encouraged: musicologists work together with philologists, historians, art historians, classicists, liturgists and other specialists. The documentation centre with publications and a database is growing.

easy flirtation with the past is in fact a difficult struggle with traditional tonality. This is evident from the 'title'. Anyone calling a work a symphony these days is asking for a confrontation or at least a dialogue with the past. It is dialogue, rather than confrontation, that Ketting has deliberately sought in his work. His dialogue is a reflection on musical history, a grappling with the problem that composers themselves created when about the turn of the century they crossed over the borders of tonality and when not long ago they abandoned serialism, the structural anchor in which pitch, rhythm and timbre were arranged according to mathematical principles.

In *Symphony no. 3* Ketting uses not only a traditional form but also a true symphonic orchestra. Ketting says: 'The sound of the symphonic orchestra dates from the nineteenth century. You have to be quite honest about that. Of course I could have decided to leave out various instruments. That's the solution I would have chosen fifteen years ago. Through the word 'symphony' I want to emphasise reflection on tradition.'

As a result there is at first sight a sharp contrast with Ketting's earlier 'symphonies'. In 1959 he wrote his *First Symphony*. He says: 'With this piece I felt as if I was turning the world upside down, which in a sense I was. At that time no one in the Netherlands was influenced by the sound world of Alban Berg, almost everyone was still under the spell of Willem Pijper.' The *Symphony for Saxophones and Orchestra* (1978), which Ketting himself calls 'a rowdy piece that roars on and on', is also an untraditional work. In *Seventy Years of Dutch Music* (Zeventig jaar Nederlandse muziek) Leo Samama describes it as 'one of the high points in Dutch music: insistent, uncompromising, acidly witty, but also lilting and even dreamy'.

Yet Ketting's symphonies do show similarities, and these can also be found in his other works. Whether he is writing film music to escape from the solitary existence of the composer, opera (e.g. *Ithaka* written for the opening of the Amsterdam Muziektheater in 1986), orchestral works or compositions for smaller groups, his work is consistent and clear in structure, well thought out and colourful in sound. Ketting sometimes compares composing with the work of a director recording instructions so that the notes find their place. But as a true composer he works in the first place from a broad feeling for music.

PAUL LUTTIKHUIS
Translated by John Rudge.

BIMhuis A Concert Venue for Improvised Music

During the 1960s new forms of improvised music emerged in Europe for which, according to some observers, the term 'jazz' was no longer entirely appropriate. This new music was no longer based exclusively on American material, but took its inspiration equally from the achievements of European musical history.

The Dutch branch of this music developed successfully; over time it acquired an impressive reputation, both in the Netherlands and internationally, with names such as Misha Mengelberg, Han Bennink and Willem Breuker, Maarten Altena, Guus Janssen, Theo Loevendie and Ernst Reijseger. A large number of younger musicians followed in the footsteps of these trendsetters.

The increasing international appreciation of the quality of Dutch improvised music is inseparably bound up with the continuing system of subsidies operated by the Foundation for Jazz and Improvised Music in the Netherlands (SJIN – Stichting Jazz en Geïmproviseerde Muziek in Nederland), and the concert venue owned by this Foundation in Amsterdam, the BIMhuis.

These organisational structures came into being mainly on the initiative of the musicians themselves. Around 1970, musicians claimed key positions in SJIN and in the early years of the decade they founded the Professional Association of Improvising Musicians (BIM – Beroepsvereniging van Improviserende Musici), which attracted a membership of more than 250 musicians. BIM and SJIN then worked together to draw the attention of the Dutch government to the deprived position of jazz and improvised music and the poor social status of their practitioners compared with other, more accepted forms of music, which were at that time able to rely on large government subsidies and an extensive concert circuit.

The government accepted the proposals of SJIN and BIM; within a few years this led to the structured subsidising of jazz in the Netherlands via SJIN, and in 1974 the Foundation opened its own concert venue in Amsterdam, the BIMhuis. Today, SJIN subsidises more than a thousand concerts annually throughout the Netherlands.

The BIMhuis occupies a central position in the production activities of SJIN. In spite of its originally rather spartan facilities, from the moment of its opening, the BIMhuis functioned as the 'nerve centre' of the Dutch jazz world, and within a few years its name was also firmly established on the international scene. Following rebuilding work in 1984 the BIMhuis now has an attractive, well-equipped concert hall in the style of an amphitheatre, with an adjoining modern café which, depending on the type of concert, can be separated from the auditorium or incorporated in it. There are also intensively-used rehearsal rooms and recording facilities. In addition, as well as the offices of SJIN and BIM, the BIMhuis also houses the National Jazz Archive, which was set up in 1980 on the initiative of SJIN with the aim of acquiring as much material as possible relating to jazz and improvised music in the Netherlands, including sound and picture material, magazines and sheet music. In addition to collecting historical material, which it makes available for information or study purposes, the Archive also encourages the production of educational programmes, films and sound carriers, whose small circulations and sales make them less than attractive to commercial publishers.

The concert programme organised by the BIMhuis, with more than 150 events annually, offers an overview of developments and high points in the world of jazz and improvised music.These music categories are defined very broadly, and music by contemporary composers, 'impro-rock', blues, latin and other 'world music' can also be heard in the BIMhuis, especially when a substantial proportion of the music in question is based on improvisation. Apart from concerts, the BIMhuis also organises regular workshops and informal musical sessions.

Although in general the emphasis in the BIMhuis programme is on topical developments – it could even be described as having a laboratory function – it is also frequently possible to hear important representatives of the older schools there. Not only has virtually every European jazz musician of renown appeared there, but legendary American performers such as Charles Mingus, Max Roach, Dexter Gordon, Sun Ra and Art Blakey have also come to entertain the BIMhuis audiences. Many now famous musicians also performed at the BIMhuis early on in their careers, sometimes to only a small audience, and musicians such as David Murray and Arthur Blythe made their European debut there. Looking back, the BIMhuis programme over the past twenty years can be said to provide a historical overview of developments in jazz during this period.

Alongside the regular concert programme, special BIMhuis projects encourage artistic development in the sector; the unique cooperation and exchanges of musical information which these events generate in the diverse international participating groups regularly lead to new initiatives on the international circuit. In the *Carte Blanche* programmes, for example, musicians are given an opportunity to arrange a concert evening according to their own ideas and to invite guest musicians from home and abroad.

The most noteworthy events were undoubtedly the October Meetings of 1987 and 1991, to which more than fifty musicians were individually invited and which involved many other venues in and outside Amsterdam. Among those who took part were some of the most influential musicians from Europe and the United States, names such as Cecil Taylor, Misha Mengelberg, John Zorn, Louis Sclavis, Derek Bailey, Paul Bley, Anthony Braxton, Evan Parker, Richard Teitelbaum and Steve Lacy. For nine days these musicians worked together with colleagues from a younger generation on dozens of original works, some of which had been commissioned and some of which grew out of ideas born during the October Meeting. Here the organisers acted as intermediaries and allowed sufficient space in the programme for new initiatives to be added. This led on both occasions to more than a hundred performances, varying from duo to full orchestra, and resulted in fascinating confrontations between musicians with differing backgrounds and from different generations. The contacts established during the October Meetings resulted in many new plans and alliances on the international circuit. The exchange of information and artistic stimulus generated by projects

of this kind is therefore regarded by the BIMhuis as being just as important as the immediate musical result.

The efforts of SJIN and the BIMhuis are not directed simply towards organising as many concerts as possible for as many musicians as possible, nor to following blindly every new trend which appears – trends which, in jazz as in other spheres, are often the result of market mechanisms. Quality and possibilities for further development are paramount in all the activities undertaken. The greatest possible exchange of information and cooperation with other organisations within and beyond the Netherlands is a precondition for achieving this objective.

An important means of reaching this goal which has existed since 1987 is the Europe Jazz Network, a joint venture which has now taken on global proportions and which, by using an electronic communication system, effectively cuts to a minimum the distances between concert organisers, musicians and other relevant bodies and organisations. Common goals shared by the participants in this network include the upholding of high artistic standards, the promotion of professional codes of behaviour, improvement of organisation efficiency, maintaining a common databank and electronic mail service and using this to facilitate the exchange of ideas and the organisation of joint projects. By working together in Europe Jazz Network, the participants are able to exert a more direct influence on what is offered, and have become less dependent on the large commercial impresarios. This not only brings cost savings, but above all offers many advantages on the artistic front, such as the increase in the international concert opportunities for musicians who do not have 'star status' and who are therefore of little or no interest to commercial concert hall managements.

In the autumn of 1994 the BIMhuis marked its twentieth anniversary with a series of special events. From 29 September to 1 October, the one-off marathon programme *Greatest Hits* featured twenty-five leading Dutch ensembles with highlights from their current

The BIMhuis concert hall.

repertoire. In the second half of October the BIMhuis and Europe Jazz Network joined forces to present a third – now international – version of October Meeting involving performances not only in the BIMhuis but also in the other major European venues such as Cologne, Ghent, Parma and Ravenna. The organisers of these events decided against a retrospective of twenty years of the BIMhuis, but opted instead for a presentation of the artistic quality and diversity to be found in contemporary improvised music and a demonstration of the opportunities offered by international cooperation.

HUUB VAN RIEL
Translated by Julian Ross.

ADDRESS
BIMhuis
Oude Schans 73-77 / 1011 KW Amsterdam / The Netherlands
tel. +31 (0)20 623 33 73 / fax +31 (0)20 620 77 59

Science

An Institute for the Promotion of the Humanities and Social Sciences

Research flourishes when it stems from a combination of single-minded concentration and wide-ranging inspiration. It is a formula which provides the basis for outstanding results.

Each year, the Netherlands Institute for Advanced Study in the Humanities and Social Sciences (NIAS) invites forty carefully selected research fellows, both from within and outside the Netherlands, to its centre in the Dutch village of Wassenaar, where they are given an opportunity to work on their research projects undisturbed for one academic year. Each fellow is allocated a well-appointed study room in the Institute and has access to the various NIAS facilities, such as library services, secretarial assistance and data processing. During the research year there is ample opportunity for mutual contacts between the various research fellows. It is a way of working which NIAS has employed successfully for more than twenty years. But now there is more.

1 November 1993 saw the ceremonial opening by the Dutch Secretary of State for Education and Science, Dr Job Cohen, of a new conference building on the NIAS site. The building, completed earlier in the year, contains a large conference hall surrounded by twenty-three guest rooms (suitable for use as double rooms). The Institute's catering facilities were also extended at the same time. As a result of these additions, NIAS is now not only able to house the broad-based, annually changing research groups, but can also offer facilities for shorter and more specific scientific activities (workshops, conferences, summer schools, study centres, etc.).

NIAS's task is the promotion of the humanities and social sciences in the broadest sense. It is a task which NIAS fulfils in a variety of ways: by creating a working environment which facilitates advanced research by eminent scholars in a range of fields; by reacting at an early stage to new scientific developments, and by giving young researchers early in their careers an opportunity to participate in discussions on these developments at an international level.

NIAS was set up in November 1970 on the initiative of the Dutch universities. The driving force behind this move was Professor E.M. Uhlenbeck of Leiden University, in whose name a public lecture is now given every year at NIAS. The Institute began its activities in the spring of 1971, and the first NIAS research group was launched in October of the same year. On its foundation, the Institute was accorded interuniversity status; in times of economic austerity, however, when each university has to look very carefully at its own financial position, this is not a particularly advantageous situation. Consequently, in January 1988 NIAS underwent a change of status and became an institute attached to the Royal Netherlands Academy of Arts and Sciences.

NIAS is situated in the Rijksdorp residential area of Wassenaar, and consists of a cluster of buildings set on a well wooded site covering more than 1,5 hectares. The main building houses the fellows' study rooms and the staff offices together with all the support services. In addition, there is now the new conference building referred to above, with its meeting rooms and accommodation facilities. Also part of the complex is the Ooievaarsnest villa, containing a kitchen, restaurant, bar, fitness room and a number of guest rooms. Finally, there is the charming Uilenest cottage, which offers a further four guest rooms. The jewel in the NIAS crown is the Persian rose garden, which was completed in 1993. This paradise of quiet beauty was donated to NIAS by a former fellow, the Swiss psychiatrist Professor Kenower Bash.

During the course of a NIAS research year, fellows have an opportunity both to work on their own individual projects and to join forces around a joint research theme. In a normal academic year about three such theme groups are active, comprising a total of some twenty-five fellows. Recent themes which have formed the subject of study at NIAS have included 'Orality versus Literacy', 'The Reception of American Mass Cultural Forms in Europe' and 'Urban Change and Urban Policy'. Topics on the agenda for the coming years include 'Magic and Religion in the Ancient Near East', 'Dutch Conceptual History', 'Understanding Social Dilemmas' and 'The Pacific Rim'. It will come as no surprise that the research carried out at NIAS produces a veritable flood of books, articles, papers and lectures.

In addition to the research years, NIAS has also made a start on a range of programmatic activities, such as the advanced study programme 'Trends in Scholarship', which will be launched in 1994. This programme will offer an annual total of twenty researchers from

The NIAS premises in Wassenaar (Photo by Wim de Jonge).

Central and Eastern Europe an opportunity to spend two months at NIAS. During this time they can pursue their own study, and will be expected to take part in a series of lectures in which both major social issues and important developments within the various disciplines will be addressed. In addition, within the framework of a bilateral scientific collaboration arrangement with Hungary, a series of study centres will be set up based around research topics of common interest.

With effect from 1994-1995, two NIAS grants will also be available for Flemish and Dutch scholars who are conducting research into the language and culture of the Dutch-speaking countries in the context of the GENT accord.

NIAS is a unique institution in the Netherlands, but not in the world; there are several other countries which have institutes with similar aims. Six of these institutes for advanced study – three in the USA (Princeton, Stanford and North Carolina) and three in Europe (Berlin, Uppsala and Wassenaar) – have recently set up a system of annual consultation meetings. These are highly informal gatherings, at which topical scientific and social issues are discussed, along with all manner of collaboration options.

One of the results of this international academic collaboration has been the establishment of the *New Europe Prize for Education and Science,* which is awarded annually to one or more researchers from Central and Eastern Europe. The aim of this award is to contribute towards the institutional support of scholars in these regions, who have become entrapped by financial constraints. The prize of DM 75,000 therefore does not go to the winner, but to his – or her – institute or research group. The prizes were awarded for the first time in November 1993, to Professor Alexander Gravilov from St Petersburg and Professor Andrei Pleşu from Bucharest.

WOUTER HUGENHOLTZ
Translated by Julian Ross.

ADDRESS
NIAS
Meijboomlaan 1 / 2242 PR Wassenaar / The Netherlands
tel. +31 (0)1751 227 00 / fax +31 (0)1751 171 62

FURTHER INFORMATION
W.R. Hugenholtz (ed.), *22 1/2 Years of* NIAS. Wassenaar, 1994.

Tropical Medicine in Antwerp

The Institute of Tropical Medicine in Antwerp was founded in 1931 as a private institution. However, it took over the function of a School of Tropical Medicine which had been operating in Brussels since 1906. The initiative for the transformation of this school into an institute came from Crown Prince Leopold (who was to become King Leopold III) who undertook a study tour to the then Belgian Congo in 1926 and was appalled by the health risks and the medical facilities in Central Africa at that time. On his return, he asked Emile Francqui to take the necessary steps to establish an institute which would provide medical care for persons arriving from the tropics, as well as research laboratories and teaching. A Princess Astrid Institute of Tropical Medicine was founded in Leopoldville, now Kinshasa. Since the hospital was intended to accomodate persons arriving from Africa, it was decided to transfer this institute from Brussels to Antwerp, where it was located in the Art Déco buildings in which it still operates today, very close to where the 'Congo Boats' docked.

In recent years, it became obvious that the relatively small size of this hospital did not permit the investment necessary in order to keep medical standards at an adequate level. An agreement was reached with the University Hospital of Antwerp by which the hospital beds were transferred to that major hospital, while other medical services stayed within the Institute. This even allowed a considerable expansion of the outpatient department, which operates specialised medical consultations for patients with infectious and tropical diseases, a travel clinic and specialised consultations in such fields as tropical dermatology, tropical pediatrics and sexually transmitted diseases. The link with the University Hospital of Antwerp means that the most elaborate technical facilities can be offered to patients, while the Tropical Medicine component for hospitalised patients is provided by doctors of the Institute.

Postgraduate teaching takes place in Dutch, but also in French. Courses for medical doctors, veterinarians and graduate nurses are intended to prepare Europeans for work overseas. In recent years, it was realised that the Institute's work should increasingly be concentrated on the training of high level personnel from developing countries. This is done in a course in public health ('International Course for Health Development') which is held alternately in French and in English. There is a close collaboration with a similar course which is held every other year at the Royal

Tropical Institute in Amsterdam. Another course leads to a Master's degree in 'Tropical Biomedical Sciences'. This course is aimed at training persons such as epidemiologists, hospital administrators, research workers or medical school teaching staff. Practical training in research work, mainly concerning animal health, can lead to a Master's degree or even a Ph. D.

Research at the Institute has been concentrated on a number of priorities for the tropics. With its 240 staff – some thirty-five of whom are university-trained – the Institute is in no position to support the expensive fundamental research which is carried out at universities. However, it plays a vital role as a link between the populations in developing countries on one hand and the major research centres on the other. Its own research work is mainly aimed at solving the health problems of these populations, making use of the results of fundamental research.

A considerable effort has been made in recent years to concentrate research around a limited number of topics, in which different laboratories can collaborate. This has led to the formation of separate research departments: *Parasitology, Veterinary Medicine, Community Health, Clinical Research* and *Infection and Immunity*. The latter department, which concentrates on sexually transmitted diseases in the tropics, is also involved in AIDS research.

In fact, one of the very first cases of this disease to be observed outside the United States was seen by the Institute's medical doctors. Since the patient was an African, this led to an international enquiry, which led to the conclusion that the newly described disease was probably primarily of African origin. Research workers at this Institute, mostly affiliated with the Research Department for Infection and Immunity have since concentrated their attention on the means of transmission of the infection in the tropics, and on the particular aspects of the disease in Africa.

The Antwerp Institute, together with over thirty European institutes of tropical medicine, is a member of the TROPMEDEUROP association. This is an organisation in which Directors of Institutes meet on regular intervals. It is recognised as a non-governmental organisation with official links with the World Health Organisation, which enable it to advise the WHO on matters of health in the tropics.

LUC EYCKMANS

ADDRESS
Prince Leopold Institute of Tropical Medicine
Nationalestraat 155 / 2000 Antwerp / Belgium
tel. +32 (0)3 247 66 66 / fax +32 (0)3 216 14 31

Society

Open-Mindedness in Flanders

International and multicultural arts events and festivals have been mushrooming in Flanders in recent years. This is partly a reaction to the growth of neo-fascism throughout Europe, but it is also the continuation of a long standing tradition and a reflection of the open-mindedness of the Flemish arts world. Considering the way that Flanders has had to fight for its cultural identity and for Dutch language rights, this strikes me as being remarkable. Flemish nationalism is often seen abroad only as an extreme right wing movement, with all that that implies. It is often forgotten that it developed as a result of the suppression of the majority Dutch-speaking population by a French-speaking elite, and that the Flemish across the political spectrum are justifiably protective of their language and culture.

However, this has not led to either a closed or a parochial arts policy. Flanders has welcomed foreign artists from all disciplines, and this in turn has strengthened and enriched its own arts scene. When I first came to live in Flanders in the early sixties, Flanders was seen as an artistic backwater, particularly by its northern neighbours the Dutch. In fact it would be fair to say that as far as anyone else went Flanders, then just emerging from its language battles, hardly existed in the international arts world. But it was then, at the Wide White Space Gallery in Antwerp, that I was introduced to the work of such artists as Beuys and Fontana long before they became international names, and long before London or New York were aware of them. It was in Antwerp that Panamarenko and Vic Gentils were working, and according to Antwerp's contemporary art museum (MUHKA), it was then that Antwerp really was the cultural capital of Europe. They made this point by putting sixties art shown or created in the city alongside art from the nineties in the 1993 Antwerp Cultural Capital of Europe exhibition which had the somewhat indigestible title *On taking a normal situation and retranslating it into overlapping and multiple readings of conditions past and present* – a quotation from the American artist Gordon Matta-Clark.

It must however be said that in the sixties the level of the performing arts in Flanders was appalling, and it was not until the eighties that this changed. Obviously,

The Institute of Tropical Medicine in Antwerp.

various factors contributed to the theatre and dance revival. One of these was certainly the influence of organisations such as the Kaai Festival, a Flemish initiative which introduced Brussels to the best and most revolutionary international work in both theatre and dance. This helped to inspire Flemish artists: Jan Fabre and Jan Decorte started to create theatrical waves, groups such as De Tijd and Blauwe Maandag emerged, and the Dutch sat up and took notice. Flemish theatre was a force to be reckoned with. Flemish theatre companies began to receive invitations to the most influential international theatre festivals. Unfortunately language remains a barrier for them as it does for many Flemish writers. Dutch is a relatively unknown and not very fashionable language abroad. Moreover, while in Flanders audiences do turn up to see plays in English, French or German, languages understood by a large proportion of the population in this linguistically adroit country, and are prepared to accept translations of plays in other languages, the same cannot be said of the Anglo-Saxon or French speaking world. It seems to be a fact of life that the more dominant a language group, the less open people are to other languages. It is virtually unimaginable that an international literary event like *Het Andere Boek* (The Different Book) in Antwerp would generate the same amount of interest in much larger neighbouring countries. Here an enthusiastic public of several thousand come from all over Flanders to listen to and discuss the work of authors from around the world, and again in several languages. Equally, I have never been into a local public library in England which offers the extensive sections of foreign language literature available in the Central Library in Antwerp.

Dance of course has no such language limitations, and this made it easier for Flemish choreographers and dancers to achieve international acclaim. Anne Teresa de Keersmaeker is recognised as one of the most important figures in international dance. Wim Vandekeybus has received major awards in the United States. Jan Fabre has created works with the Frankfurt ballet. Here again the dance scene has been enriched by the number of international groups appearing in Belgium. The Kaaitheater, the Singel in Antwerp and the Klapstuk Festival in Leuven are just some of the organisations which have enabled the Flemish dance public to become one of the most discerning and well informed in the world, while Flanders' home grown dance talents have been able to develop in a really international climate with an individuality untrammeled by a stifling tradition. Of course there have been less glorious moments, and Belgium only gets wide publicity when things go wrong. The Mark Morris affair is one case which could refute my claim of open-mindedness. Gerard Mortier, then director of the national Munt Opera in Brussels, invited the American Mark Morris to become the house choreographer to replace the by then rather tired looking Maurice Béjart. Morris' somewhat irreverent sense of humour offended the Brussels bourgeoisie, which was still devoted to the decorative Béjart, and resulted in the Brussels French-

Sanfte Strukturen, a nomadic village of non-European architecture built for Antwerp 93 by the German artist M. Kalberer (Photo by Paul Verstreken).

language daily *Le Soir* coming up with front page headlines 'Mark Morris Go Home'. Of course the vast majority of the international press who reported this scandal did not, and do not, speak Dutch. Belgium was branded as 'intolerant' in spite of a more reasoned reaction from the more open-minded Flemish critics.

Not that this open policy has gone unremarked. Jan Hoet, director of Ghent's contemporary art museum and curator of the 1992 Documenta in Kassel, the most important contemporary art event in Europe, has often been criticised for ignoring Flemish artists in order to promote international figures. Hoet himself has always denied this, claiming he only looks for quality. Like anyone else he is governed by his own preferences, something not appreciated by those he dislikes. But Jan Hoet has done more than any other single figure in Flanders to stimulate discussion around and interest in the contemporary plastic arts, and those Flemish artists he does promote can be sure of an international showing. Perhaps the problem is that we only have one charismatic curator who has become a powerful public figure; but then of course most countries don't even have that.

Antwerp 93 came in for the same flak. It was said that its director Eric Antonis had rejected local Antwerp talent. He was determined to give Antwerp 93 a multi-cultural element and a European allure. In spite of glorious and inglorious failures the result was one of the most exciting cultural capital programmes ever. The relatively meagre budget forced his team to look for new and exciting projects since they could not depend on mega-stars or super-shows; and like other organisations in Flanders he managed to get some international co-productions off the ground, again making possible close contacts between local and international artists.

Flanders then is no longer seen as a artistic backwater by those in the know. It hosts events ranging from the biggest rock festival in Europe at Torhout and

Werchter to Ghent's much smaller but highly adventurous multi-disciplinary Time arts festival. Flanders has retained and strengthened its identity through successive invasions and occupations, its history has resulted in a stubborn individuality. The Flemish refer to themselves as *plantrekkers,* people who make their own way. It makes Flanders a difficult place to govern, but has given it a climate which creates independently thinking artists, prepared to be exposed to international influences without slavishly following trends. It is a climate in which creativity can flourish even when funds are in lamentably short supply. If the authorities ever do get round to realising that culture can be an investment and look at the increased tourist figures for Antwerp in 1993, it could get even better.

LIZ SANDERSON

Friesland Too Level-headed for Absolute Individuality

The people of Friesland are none too happy about the fact that the Dutch adjective 'Fries' applies both to themselves and the pride of Friesland: The Friesian cow (English, however, does discriminate by spelling the word two ways: 'Frisian' for the people and their language, 'Friesian' for their cattle.) When Friesian cattle were first exported to America (around 1850), breeders set up the Friesian herdbook, which would guarantee that a cow sold as 'Friesian' on the world market really did come from Friesland. True Friesians have a high milk-yield and are sturdy, which means that they can settle almost anywhere in the world. In Leeuwarden, the capital of Friesland, there is even a statue of a Friesian cow: *Ûs Mem* (Our Mother), by analogy with *Ûs Heit* (Our Father), the stadholder from Friesland's own branch of the House of Orange-Nassau from whom Queen Beatrix is directly descended. The Frisians are very proud of the fact that they saved the monarchy after the Dutch Stadholder King William III died childless in 1702.

It will by now be clear that Friesland has a special place among the twelve provinces of the Netherlands. It has been officially recognised as a bilingual province since 1954; in addition to *Hollands* (actually the Dutch spoken in the economically dominant province of Holland), Frisian is spoken there. Frisian is a form of West Germanic and is related to the Scandinavian languages. Dutch and German belong to the inland Germanic group, while Frisian and English belong to the coastal Germanic group. Until the early Middle Ages, the Anglo-Saxons and the Frisians could understand each other very well. This is probably part of the reason why there was contact between the two peoples from very early on, as we know because Anglo-Saxon jewellery has been found in Frisian graves. Neither was it coincidence that an Anglo-Saxon monk, Werenfried, brought Christianity to Friesland. He met a violent death in Dokkum in A.D. 754, and is now remembered as St Boniface.

Friesland has long enjoyed a special place within the Netherlands itself. The province was a democracy, jointly governed until 1498 by a body representing 11 towns and 30 *grietenijen*. Later Friesland was incorporated into the Republic of the Seven Provinces (1581-1795), but retained its sovereignty; for instance, Friesland did not participate in the Anglo-Dutch naval wars of the seventeenth century. A a result, the English fleet plundered Holland's Wadden island, Terschelling, but left Friesland's nearby Ameland untouched. The degree of Friesland's independence was such that, on 26 February 1782, the states of Friesland recognised the independence of the United States – the first European 'power' to do so.

Friesland's position was weakened somewhat when it became part of the (present) Kingdom of the Netherlands, established in 1814. The Dutch of Holland then became the new kingdom's official language. The Frisian Movement began to take shape at the end of the nineteenth century, strongly influenced by the German *Heimat* Movement, but also partly by analogy with the Flemish Movement. The Movement was not striving for political independence, but for cultural autonomy, particularly with regard to the Frisian language. Frisian was not recognised as an official language until after the Second World War, in 1954, and only then after conflict led to rioting because 'Holland' judges refused to accept statements in court in Frisian. Friesland's unique bilingual status also brings tensions, but comparison with movements such as those in Catalonia and the Basque region is unfair.

The population of Friesland is 600,000 – 4% of the Dutch population. 95% of Frisians understand the Frisian language, 80% can speak it (70% actually do so), 65% can read it, while only 10% can write and spell Frisian. In primary schools, one hour per week in Frisian language and culture is compulsory. In secondary schools the subject is optional from the third year, and there is very little interest. Professors of Frisian are to be found at the Universities of Groningen, Amsterdam and Leiden. Since 1938 the Frisian Academy (Fryske Akademy) has been setting down and documenting the Frisian language and has been working, among other things, on a Frisian historical dictionary. Nevertheless, attempts are being made

LEEUWARDEN
US MEM

to give substance to the province's bilingualism, for example by indicating the names of towns, villages and streets in both Dutch an Frisian: Sneek / Snits; Leeuwarden / Ljouwert; Kortezwaag / Koartsweagen, etc. The majority of the population is opposed to using only Frisian names, since this would cause confusion outside the province.

The Frisian language is influenced and undermined by, in particular, national radio and television. There is a regional radio station, but this is allowed to transmit for only a few hours every day. A Frisian television channel began broadcasting in 1994, but even this receives almost 50% of its funding from the European Community. Many Frisians take an active part in the European movement because they believe that Europe's regions will become more important in the near future; there are contacts with Wales in this context. 'Classic' Frisian is spoken mainly in the United States, where many Frisians have settled since the mid-nineteenth century. There the language has not been influenced by Standard Dutch. The astronaut Lousma was the grandson of a Frisian emigrant.

The rest of the Netherlands takes an endearing interest in Friesland. It is the only province with its own 'state' yacht. It has its own stirring 'national' anthem. The *Nasionale slokje* (national tipple), Beerenburger, is an excellent gin. The *Elfstedentocht* (Eleven Towns long-distance skating race) around Friesland is very popular and *skûtsjesielen* (sailing with Frisian 'tjalk' boats) attracts many spectators, as does the game of *kaatsbal* (fives). There is also *fierljeppen* – pole-vaulting over wide ditches – which non-Frisians cannot seem to master, to name but a few.

Individuality, then, yet the Frisian National Party has only 3 out of 55 seats on the Provincial Council. Only a few Frisians visit the national monument on 26 September to commemorate the Battle of Warns against the Hollanders (1345). The Frisian is too level-headed to make his individuality absolute.

KEES MIDDELHOFF
Translated by Yvette Mead.

The Story of *De Nederlandse Courant* in Canada

1954 was the year in which *De Nederlandse Courant* – Canada's oldest Dutch-language newspaper – was first published in Toronto. Dutch postwar immigration to Canada was at its height; the total number of newcomers reached 100,000 in May of that year and many more were to come. Most of them settled in Ontario. Often they received no news from their country of origin except for letters from family and friends, though many felt a need for continuing contact with the Netherlands and with other Canadians of Dutch origin. A Dutch journalist, Laura Schippers, became aware of this need, and set out to establish a newspaper, which was to be non-denominational, that could serve as a link between the newcomers and the old country. Thus

De Nederlandse Courant was launched from a small office in Scarborough. It started with 4 pages, with articles supplied by Laura, her husband and others, and focussed on community news and news from the Netherlands. It became an almost full-time occupation for Laura and her husband to publish the paper once a month, and later bi-weekly, for approximately 2,500 subscribers. These were not only from Ontario, but from other parts of Canada as well; at that time *De Nederlandse Courant* was the only Dutch newspaper.

Between 1959 and 1962 the paper led a precarious existence. Laura Schippers died in 1959, and it was continued first by her husband, then by another journalist, Ton Diening. In 1962 the paper was taken over by three businessmen, Nick Meulmeester, Henry McHill and Frans Schryer. Thea Schryer, Frans' wife, helped with redaction and typesetting. After some difficult years, Thea became sole owner and director, and under her direction the newspaper began to grow and expand. In the beginning the publication was a family business with Thea responsible for redaction, her sons helping with the lay-out, paste-up and typesetting, her daughter Frieda helping with administration, and others with mailing. The children were paid for their help. A room for an office was rented from Schryers Graphics. This combined effort proved successful and within a year the paper was financially sound.

The Dutch community continued to change and become more prosperous. A number of Dutch clubs had been established, there were more Dutch stores and businesses which advertised in the paper. Also, several other Dutch newspapers were being published. In Vancouver *The Windmill Herald* (which bought out *Hollandia News)* as well as *De Krant* (published once a month) had a wider western readership, while *Calvinist Contact* provided news for the Dutch Christian Reformed community. Federal multicultural policies were helpful. A survey made by Thea Schryer (questions were printed on the back of the invoices) indicated reader preferences for *De Nederlandse Courant.* There were now twenty pages, with sections for news from the Netherlands, sports, community news, interviews, travel. A number of paid contributors provided articles, while news from the Netherlands was selected from Dutch newspapers. One of the most popular columns was 'Nieuws van Thuis', with news about the homeland written first by Hans Kievid, and later by Mels van de Meeberg. Photographs of events in Toronto were usually supplied by Wim van Duyn. News from western Canada came from Mieke Hollenbach-Melcher. Editorials were written by Thea Schryer, who also reported interviews with well-known personalities. The paper was growing considerably, with close to 4,000 subscribers in 1979, including some from the U.S.; the number of readers was of course much higher.

In the meantime, mailing became more complicated because of changed postal regulations. For each postal code a separate mailbag had to be used, which meant fifty-two different postal bags; the sorting was now a full day's work for the three people. In 1987 *De*

DCA TRAVEL SERVICE INC.

wereld contact travel
with many free extras
Toronto 416-224-5211
Toll-Free 1-800-667-2525
Fax 416-224-0842
Bradford 416-775-6763
Grimsby 416-945-3301
Emergency Services Available
Business & Vacation Travel

De Nederlandse COURANT
DUTCH CANADIAN BI-WEEKLY

Martinair Holland
The other Dutch airline.

Postage Paid in
Burlington, Ontario
Canada

Publisher: Theo Luykenaar

Canada's Oldest Dutch Language Newspaper

Single copies $1.25 (GST incl.)

Second Class Mail
Registration No. 1807

November 27, 1993
Volume 38, Issue 24

Nederlandse Courant received the Lily Munroe Media Award for Excellence in Journalism. This award expressed appreciation for its content and lay-out, and its contribution to multiculturalism. In the same year the paper also received the Canadian Ethnic Journalist Award, in recognition of its professional standards of content and lay-out.

In 1991 Thea felt it was time to sell, and buyers were found in two businessmen from Burlington, Bas Opdenkelder and Theo Luykenaar. There have been some changes in format: the paper is now of twenty-four pages or more, and appears twenty-six times per year in tabloid form with short articles in English and Dutch; travel news is an important feature. The paper is aimed primarily at the Ontario market. Definite strategies are in place: conservative policy, positive reporting about the Netherlands, increasing the advertising base, and sponsoring cultural events such as choirs, a visiting Dutch soccer team and a touring family theatre from the Netherlands. With effective marketing, *De Nederlandse Courant* continues to grow; it now has more than 4,000 subscribers, and is also widely distributed through Dutch stores. The present editor, Theo Luykenaar, sees the paper as a business, 'not a passion'. It is a newspaper that also meets the interests of the younger generation. This means that there is a somewhat larger percentage of articles written in English than before, while at the same time support is given for Dutch language classes and Dutch cultural events. With this strategy, the future of the paper remains promising.

WILLEMINA SEYWERD

ADDRESS
De Nederlandse Courant
3019 Harvester Road / Burlington, ON L7N 3G4 / Canada

Feminists in a Church

Since 11 December 1993, the International Information Centre and Archive for the Women's Movement (IIAV – Internationaal Informatiecentrum en Archief voor de Vrouwenbeweging) has been housed in Gerardus Majella Church in Amsterdam East. This massive church, which is no longer used for religious purposes, has been completely rebuilt and restored under the aegis of the Amsterdam Heritage Trust, and space in the building is rented out. the IIAV has leased not only office space but the entire dome of the church, and is thus the principal tenant.

The IIAV's history goes back to 1935, when a number of Dutch feminists decided to assemble an international women's archive. By doing so they sought – successfully – to breathe new life into the women's movement. Under the motto 'No documents, no history' they established the International Archive for the Women's Movement (IAV – Internationaal Archief voor de Vrouwenbeweging).

The IAV's independent nature caused it some difficulties during the Second World War. The occupying Germans, who regarded the IAV as a threat, confiscated most of the collection. Some of their archive material has recently surfaced in Moscow; the books have not as yet reappeared.

Despite this serious reverse the IAV continued to collect, preserve and document the cultural heritage of women. On 8 March (International Women's Day) 1988 it agreed a merger with the Information and Documentation Centre of the women's movement (IDC – Informatie en Documentatie Centrum), founded in 1969, and the feminist journal *Lover* (Foliage) estab-

The new home of the IIAV
(Photo by Jan Carel
Warffemius).

lished in 1973. Thus the International Information Centre and Archive for the Women's Movement (IIAV) was born, and soon found itself in urgent need of more spacious accommodation.

Five years later, in December 1993, the IIAV moved into its new quarters. The spacious Majella Church provides a splendid home for its extensive collection. the new location offers space for – among other things – 61,000 books, the 625 periodicals from the Netherlands and abroad to which the IIAV subscribes, 15,000 photographs, other pictorial material, numerous posters and 430 metres of archive material on the position of women today and in the past. The spaciousness of the church also lends itself extremely well to the activities which the IIAV organises. Exhibitions are held in the dome, and the various reading rooms can also be used for lectures.

Among the IIAV's treasures are a splendid book on the pleasures and problems of women which dates from 1578 and a picture book of the female body by Aletta Jacobs (1854-1929), arch-feminist and the Netherlands' first woman graduate. The many old posters with feminist slogans and the vast quantity of documentation on current issues also catch the eye.

The IIAV's international orientation makes it of considerable value not only to the Dutch but also to interested individuals from outside the Netherlands; a sizeable part of the collection is in English. Anyone who wants to know about, for instance, the history of the Australian women's movement can find illumination at the IIAV.

The IIAV can look back on more than half a century of efficient documentation and archiving on both a national and an international level. Because of its international outlook, the organisation can justifiably be called unique.

SANNE CLAESSENS
Translated by Tanis Guest.

ADDRESS
IIAV
Obiplein 4 / 1094 RB Amsterdam / The Netherlands
tel. +31 (0)20 665 08 20 / fax +31 (0)20 665 58 12

Visual Arts

Dawn of the Golden Age

During the past year the city of Amsterdam has been drawing particular attention to its 'Golden Age' by means of exhibitions and musical and other events. The highpoint of this tourist programme was the exhibition *Dawn of the Golden Age* held at the Rijksmuseum in Amsterdam. It was an ambitious exhibition of nearly 350 works of art giving an overview of Dutch art between 1580 and 1620, the period which led up to the Golden Age itself. Visitors could admire not only

paintings but prints, drawings, silver, tapestries, glass and furniture.

It was, therefore, an exhibition which provided a general overview in the broadest sense of the word. This has become something of a tradition at the Rijksmuseum – in 1958 there was an exhibition entitled *Medieval Art of the Northern Netherlands,* with some 400 works of art. This was followed in 1986 by *Art before the Iconoclasm,* dealing with Northern Netherlandish art between 1525 and 1580. The title *Dawn of the Golden Age* differed from its two predecessors in that it seemed to indicate that the works on display were only harbingers of the art of the Golden Age. Or did this title perhaps contain some unspoken promise of a future exhibition dealing with the Golden Age itself?

The large number of impressive works of art in Wim Crouwel's elegant setting would, however, have quickly driven any such consideration from the mind

Hendrick Goltzius, *Venus and Cupid with Two Satyrs.* 1599-1602. Canvas, 105 x 80 cm. Philadelphia Museum of Art.

Abraham Bloemaert, *The Death of Niobe's Children.* 1591. Canvas, 203 x 249.5 cm. Statens Museum for Kunst, Copenhagen.

of the visitor to the exhibition. On entering the exhibition the visitor immediately came face to face with the overwhelming *Death of Niobe's Children* (1591) by the Utrecht artist Abraham Bloemaert. It measures over 6 feet by 8 and is an outstanding example of the so-called Dutch Mannerism, which developed from 1585 on in the young Protestant Republic of the Netherlands during the turbulent years of the Eighty Years War. The Mannerists frequently chose dramatic subjects, depicting nude figures in mannered postures; Joachim Wtewael's *The Deluge* (c.1590-1592) demonstrates this very clearly. The Mannerists' main source of inspiration was the work of the Flemish artist Bartholomeus Spranger, who worked at the court of the German Emperor Rudolph II in Prague. Rudolph II was a great lover of the arts who not only employed many Dutch artists but also bought a great many works of art. The exhibition contained a number of showpieces by his court artists including gold and silver work by the goldsmith Paulus van Vianen and sculptures by Adriaen de Vries.

Mannerism was, however, only a shortlived movement in the history of painting; around 1600 interest shifted to the portrayal of reality. This change brought with it the development of new genres, such as the portrait, landscape, the town view and still life. These new genres were introduced by immigrants from the Southern Netherlands, who for religious and economic reasons moved to the North in large numbers. They were important not just for painting, but for other forms of art as well, such as the weaving of tapestries and damask.

The word 'dawn' seems particularly appropriate for the process of development which these different genres went through. The traditional sober portrait changed into the more dashing compositions of Frans Hals; imaginary mountain views gave way to the prototypical Dutch scene. These and others were the genres which were to reach their zenith in the golden years of the seventeenth century with such masters as Rembrandt, Van Ruisdael and Vermeer.

Alongside the development of specialisations in painting there was also a great interest in new techniques. This was the period in which the technique of etching was first widely used and when Hendrick Goltzius produced his famous pen-drawings. These were pen and ink drawings on linen, which have the appearance of engravings. We know that Rudolph II bought one such drawing and marvelled at its consummate technique. That same picture, now owned by the Philadelphia Museum of Art, could be admired at the exhibition. That says something about the generous attitude of those museums which loaned their works for the exhibition; for as well as the Goltzius other works of the highest quality from foreign museums were on display. Clearly, the organisors of this exhibition were able to assemble a splendid and unique selection of works of art; and the massive catalogue in English is a lasting reminder of it.

YVETTE BRUIJNEN
Translated by Michael Shaw.

Dawn of the Golden Age. Northern Netherlandish Art 1580-1620 (ed. Ger Luijten et al.) Zwolle: Waanders, 1993; 718 pp.

Art in the Brussels Metro

In 1969 the Belgian Minister of Transport decided to set up a committee to advise him in selecting and commissioning graphic artists to beautify Brussels' metro stations. The so-called 'Metro Committee' was and is composed of people who are considered to be familiar with the Belgian artistic landscape, and thus qualified to choose between the best artists in the country. They also have to be able to link architecture and graphic art with the concept of 'public art'.

The great challenge was to present underground graphic art not as in a museum of modern art but rather as a humanising element in cold, anonymous metro stations. An important limitation was that the committee had no influence on the architectural design of the stations. These were determined by the technical requirements of the engineers, and the architects' involvement was restricted to the internal appearance of the stations. The ideal solution – a proper integration of art and architecture – therefore remained a purely theoretical and frustrating concept. However, as the projects spread to more and more locations, attempts were made to arrange consultations between the various authorities concerned in order to move towards an integrated concept. However, due to the lack of a creative dialogue a completely satisfactory solution has never been found.

Nevertheless, by 1993 the Brussels metro could still boast fifty-five stations which had been 'humanised' by artists, some of whom can be counted among the foremost representatives of Belgian art, such as Vic Gentils, Paul Delvaux, Christian Dotremont, Pierre Alechinsky, Roel D'Haese, Octave Landuyt, Pol Bury, Jean-Michel Folon, and comic-strip artist Hergé, the spiritual father of Tintin and others. Although most of them had rarely or never had any opportunity to design monumental works on this scale, many still met the challenge splendidly and produced some of their very best works. The fact that others did not entirely succeed in their intentions was due more to the technical limitations inherent in the assignment than to lack of talent.

In broad terms we can say that the assignments have been a success overall. They certainly improve the atmosphere of stations which are otherwise neutral, so that travellers are less likely to get the impression that they are waiting for a train in a purely functional tube. They are given an opportunity to become acquainted with an artistic project which they did not know existed.

Let us say it straight out: these works of art cost less than 0.2% of the total investment, and they do contribute to the positive image of underground transport in the Belgian capital, both in Belgium and abroad. Many foreign specialist journals have devoted articles

Octave Landuyt, *The Final Traffic – Because You Are Going to Die Anyway* (Naamsepoort Station, Brussels).

Vic Gentils, *Aequus Nox* (Thieffry Station, Brussels).

to this phenomenon, and it has been discussed at numerous conferences on transport problems. To put it rather simply, we might say that the function of wall paintings in caves and later in catacombs has now been taken over by art in the metro.

LUDO BEKKERS
Translated by Steve Judd.

Painting on the Couch

Is there such a thing as typical Dutch art? This is a question which is posed with some regularity in catalogues and books about Dutch art, and it comes up again in *Dutch Art and Character* (1993). According to the introduction, the various essays in this volume will not provide the answer because their subject matter differs too much and the approaches are too varied to enable conclusions to be drawn about the character of Dutch art. *Dutch Art and Character* comprises articles on Brueghel, Bosch and Rembrandt and about the modern artists Van Gogh, Mondrian and Willink. The collection also includes an essay on assemblages, while a contribution on Queen Wilhelmina of the Netherlands, who reigned from 1898 to 1948, falls rather outside the theme.

The essays themselves hardly touch on the question of 'the Dutch character'. So it is not clear why the subject is ever raised, or why Dutch history is outlined in the introduction. What the essays do have in common is a psychoanalytical approach to art. Consequently, it would have been more useful if the foreword had included a short introduction to the history of psychoanalysis and its significance for art history, particularly since the collection is not intended specifically for psychoanalysts.

Psychoanalytical approaches to art have been subject to some criticism. One of the most frequent objections cited is that the artist himself is not lying on the couch and that there can therefore be no real analysis. Further objections are that the artist is regarded as a patient and his or her psyche as a clinical picture, and also that psychoanalytical approaches to art produce a one-sided picture.

Arseen de Rijck examines this criticism in his article on Hieronymus Bosch (1450-1516). In his view, psychoanalytical studies about art are often criticised because of their tendency towards reductionism. The wealth and originality of art are at issue; as, for example, in studies by the early psychoanalysts, who tried to derive universal truths about human nature from art.

In his article De Rijck examines how inner conflicts are visualised in the work of Hieronymus Bosch. Here the artist and his work are being closely linked. Based on an analysis of the work, the conclusion is drawn that the central theme of Bosch's work is human nature exposed to demonic temptations. It is above all the black side of human nature that is portrayed. According to De Rijck, there are indications of a paranoid personality structure. He goes on to describe the technique, style and symbolism of the work, seen as an expression of the artist's inner world. On the subject of form, for example, he says that in his work Bosch created a certain distance between himself and his subject. The space is not illusionist, as it was for example in the baroque. This line of reasoning finally confirms the one-sidedness of the psychoanalytical approach. No consideration is given to the historical development of art itself. In the time of Bosch the way of portraying space and human figures was totally different from the baroque period and so has little to do with Bosch's choice, conscious or otherwise.

In the article on Hieronymus Bosch, the key issue is the artist's work. The article on Pieter Brueghel the Elder (1528-1569) elaborates on the question whether the contemporary psychoanalyst is a preacher in disguise. Phenomena such as gluttony, lust and aggres-

Hieronymus Bosch, *The Cure for Folly.* Fifteenth century. Panel, 48 x 35 cm. Museo del Prado, Madrid.

Carel Willink, *The Yellow House.* 1934. Canvas, 100 x 75 cm. Gemeentemuseum, Arnhem.

and menace has hitherto been explained by the social and economic situation of the time. But the author prefers to look for the explanation in the personality of the painter. Feelings of aggression are suppressed, and at the same time expressed, in his paintings. According to the writer, creativity played an important role in Willink's life. One of her conclusions is that this creativity allowed Willink to introduce order and equilibrium into his life and provided a solution to his inner conflicts.

Freud, the father of psychoanalysis, explained cultural phenomena as a form of sublimation. Passions and emotions are raised to a higher level and in this way made manageable and acceptable to the outside world. As in the article on Willink, the idea of sublimation also plays its part in the articles on Van Gogh (1853-1890) and Mondrian (1872-1944). According to Pieter van den Berg, sublimation did not cause Mondrian to lose all contact with reality. The central question in this article is whether Mondrian's ideas about horizontal and vertical lines have their origin in problems of identity. The author refers to a duality in Mondrian's personality which stems from his relationship with his father. Mondrian reacted against his father and his father's world by leaving the Netherlands and turning his back on Calvinism and figurative painting. At the same time he identified with his father in his straightforwardness and in his sober, committed and isolated way of life.

It is quite possible that Mondrian had a dual personality, but this observation does not explain the use of horizontal and vertical lines. Mondrian's art is much more complicated than that, and a whole range of factors are involved, such as the development of his work, the work of contemporaries, modern life, the metropolis, theosophy, his own carefully formulated ideas about art, and so forth.

Whilst I have some reservations about the application of psychoanalysis in art history, I can imagine that as an auxiliary, provided that it is used with care, psychoanalysis can sometimes be of some significance. However, after having read this collection of essays, that significance has not become clear to me. Psychoanalytical explanations have not clarified art – let alone Dutch art – but rather art has been used to illustrate psychoanalysis. It is the artists, rather than the works of art, that are central to *Dutch Art and Character*. It is they who are on the couch.

SASKIA BAK
Translated by Alison Mouthaan-Gwillim.

Dutch Art and Character. Psychoanalytical Perspectives on Bosch, Brueghel, Rembrandt, Van Gogh, Mondrian, Willink and Queen Wilhelmina (ed. Joost Banneke et al.). Amsterdam / Lisse: Swets & Zeitlinger B.B., 1993; 220 pp.

sion are the realm of psychoanalysts. But they also play a role in Christian ethics, as engravings of the seven cardinal sins by Brueghel illustrate.

Very little is known about the lives of Bosch and Brueghel. In the articles on modern artists, on the other hand, the facts of the artists' lives play an important role. Information taken from the lives of the artists forms the basis for an analysis which is subsequently used to explain their work.

Yvonne van de Graaf-Slijper, author of the article on Carel Willink (1900-1983), is very explicit. Willink produced very smoothly and accurately painted canvasses with elements depicted very realistically in a sharp, cool light, suggesting threat and alienation, as in *The Yellow House* (1934). Many of the paintings were produced in the thirties, in a time of crisis and threat. Although his work does not refer directly to the crisis and anxiety of the thirties, the feeling of oppression

Bart van der Leck Architectural Painter and Fine Artist

It must have been particularly difficult for Bart van der Leck to make it clear that he saw his painting not as a separate discipline, but rather as an element alongside architecture. For him the painter and the architect complemented each other. The architect provided the space and the painter provided colour to define that space. Van der Leck did not succeed in winning much support for this point of view, to which he held uncompromisingly throughout his life. The public knows him as the artist who painted a few well-known works such as *The Cat* (1914) and *Horseman* (1918) in which abstraction was made to seem natural. The architects with whom he worked often gave him only a subordinate role.

In 1919, after a period of working with De Stijl which was cut short because of his uncompromising attitude, Bart van der Leck withdrew to a house which he built himself and where he could follow his own principles as a painter. His subjects, which until then had been mainly aimed at society, now took on a more homely character, with still lifes, portraits and even nature motifs. He went more in search of reality, while remaining true to his principle of monumentalism. He was never exclusively a painter of pictures. He created murals and also gave colour and shape to space with floor coverings and ceramics, as a glass painter and interior decorator.

This was in fact the way Bart van der Leck had begun his career. After attending junior school he became an apprentice at a glass workshop in Utrecht, where he had been born, the fourth of a family of eight children, in 1876. He worked for eight years in various studios, using bright colours in precise shapes, isolated within the black contours of the lead against the background. Afterwards he attended an industrial art school and the Amsterdam National Academy of Fine Art.

As an artist, Van der Leck restricted himself after 1904 to flat surfaces and almost entirely to primary colours. Like several of his contemporaries, he was excited about Egyptian art and also about the poor social conditions of workers in his own society.

He translated this interest into figure studies, in which the individual increasingly gave way to common features in groups of people, such as workers leaving the factory or four soldiers in a row. He placed these against a realistic background, which after 1912 was replaced by a monochrome surface. In this way Van der Leck took the first steps towards a new style of painting which could be used in architecture. His experiments with casein paint on asbestos cement were also part of this process. The paintings increasingly developed into murals. Form and colour were gradually reduced to pure elementary proportions and primary colours: red, yellow and blue as well as black.

During the course of this development, Van der Leck was given his first monumental commissions for posters, mosaics, typographical designs and particularly colour construction designs, for the company Müller and Co and Mrs Kröller-Müller. While living at his new home he also met Piet Mondrian, who had a different background as a landscape painter but was also moving along the same path towards abstraction. From this time on, Van der Leck called his work 'composition' and began to break open the shapes into fragments of geometric elements. Through the 'destruction of the plastic natural', as he himself called it, reality was transformed into separate areas of primary colour against a white background. Van der Leck did not follow Mondrian in limiting himself to a horizontal and vertical division of the surface; diagonal and sloping lines continued to suggest some movement. Mondrian took over the white background from Van der Leck, but did not completely abandon spatial suggestion. Mondrian remained too much a painter to do this, and mixed the background in various shades. Van der Leck preferred to use the surface and positive colour as he strove to compensate for architecture and its definiteness with open, spatial areas of colour. The two articles which Van der Leck published in *De Stijl* were entirely devoted to a plea for fine art and architecture to come together. However for Bart van der Leck this did not mean that he wanted completely to abandon reality as a starting point.

Van der Leck's eccentric attitude quickly distanced him from De Stijl again. In his own home in Blaricum

Bart van der Leck, *Horseman*. 1918. Canvas, 94 x 40 cm. Rijksmuseum Kröller-Müller, Otterlo.

he remained an obstinate supporter of the integration of fine art within architecture, continuing to translate visual reality into geometric shapes, without sacrificing recognisability. On the contrary: in Van der Leck's work after his short period with De Stijl he again turned away from the far-reaching abstraction which he had used in 1916-1917. As a result his designs were better suited to the taste of his main customer: Mrs Kröller-Müller. In 1928 she placed her collection in the care of a foundation, which ten years later opened the Rijksmuseum Kröller-Müller in the Hoge Veluwe region of the Netherlands. The museum has a large Van der Leck collection, with over four hundred paintings, drawings, designs and objects.

Van der Leck did not receive much recognition for his artistic efforts during his lifetime. His ideas were too idiosyncratic, and he was also too firmly bound to a single patron, the Müller company. For this reason his later works especially are virtually unknown. Van der Leck remained active until his death in 1958, working towards increased refinement, with white increasingly coming to denote silence.

He achieved a great monumentalism with minimal means. In this way his art fits in with minimal art from America after the Second World War.

For various reasons, Bart van der Leck has remained largely unknown. In an attempt to change this situation the Rijksmuseum Kröller-Müller has organised an exhibition of one hundred and fifty works of both 'free' and applied art, which is being held from 10 September until 27 November 1994 at the museum in Otterlo.

ERIK SLAGTER
Translated by Steve Judd.

ADDRESS
Rijksmuseum Kröller-Müller
Houtkampweg 9 / 6731 AV Otterlo / The Netherlands
tel. +31 (0) 8382 1241

The Tulip 400 Years in the Netherlands

A few special tulips here and there, set some distance apart in a border, or displayed indoors in a special tulip vase. It is difficult to imagine now, when every year in the Dutch bulb growing area colourful bulbfields stretch as far as the eye can see. Nevertheless, that was how it was done in the seventeenth century. In those days the tulip was a rare and highly desirable product, and worth its weight in gold to many a Dutchman.

The Frans Hals Museum in Haarlem commemorated the 400th anniversary of the tulip in the Netherlands with an indoor and outdoor exhibition held from 26 March to 29 May 1994. In the courtyard garden of the former Old Men's Home the Parrot tulip, the Blue Ballad and many other choice varieties of tulip could be admired in a historically authentic setting, while inside the museum an alternative bulb route led the visitor past all sorts of prints, paintings and objects connected with the tulip mania.

The history of the tulip in the Netherlands begins in the spring of 1594. That was the year in which the tulips of the renowned botanist Carolus Clusius first flowered in the botanical garden of the University of Leiden. Within forty years the exotic bloom imported from the Turkish Empire was to conquer the Netherlands. Tulip growing led to a frenzied trade in the bulbs which reached its height around 1635. At first the bulbs were beyond the means of all but scientists and well-to-do tulip fanciers; later they also came within the reach of ordinary tradesmen and craftsmen. A lively trade grew up, most of it on paper. Options to buy were traded with up to 100% premium long before any actual tulip bulb could be seen. In 1636 a single specimen of the popular pink Semper Augustus could fetch a sum equal to the price of an average canal property in the centre of Amsterdam. In February 1637 this speculative market suddenly collapsed. Many speculators lost their entire fortunes and were reduced to beggars from one day to the next.

Poets and painters were also affected by the tulip mania, as the exhibition in Haarlem made clear. In a painting by Jan Brueghel the Younger of 1640 the speculators are depicted as foolish monkeys. The tulips are listed, weighed and traded by striking hands. The dealers are so prosperous that they ride horses, carry swords and can afford expensive dinners. We are also shown what happened after the crash. One monkey is portrayed urinating on a now worthless contract. Another is haled before the Bench on account of his debts. Several brawls are in progress, and one speculator is even being borne to his grave.

In a very different category are the seventeenth-century Tulip-books. Artists and botanists cooperated to depict the different species of tulip in watercolour. Magnificent illustrated catalogues thus came into being, which were a godsend to the traders, since it always took great expertise to predict which variety lay concealed in which tulip bulb. One of the famous Tulip-books is that illustrated by the Haarlem artist Judith Leyster, which has been preserved in the Frans Hals Museum. Craftsmen as well as dealers made use of these 'floral anthologies'. In the applied arts, tulips were a favourite decorative motif for all kinds of products. Tiles in particular were often decorated with tulips, but we also find the flower on stained-glass windows and furniture.

Not surprisingly, the brilliant colour combinations of the different species of tulips also inspired painters to produce colourful still lifes in oils. The flower still life as a separate genre came into being during this period. The tulips are frequently combined with all kinds of other flowers from different seasons, showing that the painters often did not work directly 'from life', but on the basis of previously made studies. On occasion they may also have used specimen books for the time-consuming painting of fine detail. It is striking how meticulously, almost scientifically, the flowers are usually reproduced.

In fact, to have a bouquet of flowers in the living room was extremely unusual. They rarely appear in

Jan Brueghel the Younger, An Allegory of the Tulip Trade. c.1640. Panel, 31 x 49 cm. Frans Halsmuseum, Haarlem.

Eduard Hermans, Vase (untitled). 1994. Stoneware, 58 x 49 x 58 cm. Frans Halsmuseum, Haarlem.

paintings of interiors from that time. Flower vases as we know them did not yet exist either. There were, however, special tulip vases with a number of openings or spouts, in which the flowers were displayed individually. These vases were designed in Delft and came in a variety of shapes. Sometimes a tulip vase would consist of sections stacked one on another; the lid of a bonbonnière, for instance, might do service as a vase. The tall obelisk form, which was copied from the Chinese, was also popular.

It was a pleasant thought of the Frans Hals Museum to invite thirteen Turkish and thirteen Dutch artists to provide a contemporary comment on the theme of the tulip vase for this occasion. Some of these works were elaborations on the traditional forms, with spouts, openings, stacking and pyramid forms unmistakeably inspired by the past. Other artists took the shape of the tulip itself as the basis for their work. All the vases were on display, complete with fresh tulips, during the period of the exhibition.

JULEKE VAN LINDERT
Translated by Rachel van der Wilden.

Bibliography

of Dutch-Language Publications translated into English (traced in 1993)

Berge, H.C. ten
The white shaman: selected poems / by H.C. ten Berge; ed. by Theo Hermans; transl. [from the Dutch] by Theo Hermans … et al.. London: Forest Books, 1991. X, 85 p.

Berger, Thomas
Stan Bolivan and the dragon / Thomas Berger. [Edinburgh]: Floris, 1992. [32] p.
Translation of: Stan Bolivan en de draak. 1992.

Bernlef, J.
Driftwood house: poems / by J. Bernlef; transl. by Scott Rollins. Francestown N.H.: Typographeum, 1992.

Bos, Burny
Ollie, the elephant / Burny Bos. New York: North-South Books, 1991. [32] p.
Originally published in Dutch as: Tetkees zoekt een baby. 1989.

Bruijne, Peter de
Siberian miracle / Peter O. de Bruijne / transl. by Adrian Peetoom. London: Marshall Pickering, 1991. 237 p.
Translation of: Loutervuur. 1990.

Bruna, Dick
Miffy / Dick Bruna. London: Little Mammoth, 1991. [32] p.
Drawings originally published in: Nijntje. 1955.

Bruna, Dick
Miffy at the zoo / Dick Bruna. London: Little Mammoth, 1991. [32] p.
Drawings originally published in: Nijntje in de dierentuin. 1955.

Bruna, Dick
Miffy goes flying / Dick Bruna. London: Little Mammoth, 1991. [24] p.
Drawings originally published in: Nijntje vliegt. 1970.

Claus, Hugo
The sorrow of Belgium / Hugo Claus; transl. from the Dutch by Arnold J. Pomerans.
London: Penguin, 1991. 608 p.
Translation of: Het verdriet van België. 1983.

De Ke, Andre
A safe place / Andre De Ke; transl.: Leon Meersseman, Arnold Strobbe. Roseville-Detroit: Belgian, [1993]. 49 p.
Contains five short stories.

Dros, Imme
The journeys of the clever man / Imme Dros; transl. from the Dutch by Lance Salway. Woodchester [etc.]: Turton & Chambers, 1992. 135 p.
Translation of: De reizen van de slimme man. 1988.

Durlacher, G.L.
Stripes in the sky / Gerhard Durlacher / transl. by Susan Massotty. London: Serpent's Tail, 1991. 108 p.
Translation of: Streifen am Himmel: Geschichten aus Krieg und Verfolgung. 1988.
Translation of: Strepen aan de hemel: oorlogsherinneringen. 1985.
Originally published in: De Gids.

Durlacher, Gerhard L.
Drowning / Gerhard L. Durlacher; [transl. from the Dutch: Susan Massotty]. London: Serpent's Tail, 1993.
Translation of: Drenkeling: kinderjaren in het Derde Rijk. 1987.

Elders, Leo J.
The philosophical theology of St. Thomas Aquinas / by Leo J. Elders S.V.D.; [transl. from the Dutch]. Leiden [etc.]: Brill, 1990. IX, 332 p. (Studien und Texte zur Geistesgeschichte des Mittelalters; Bd. 26). Includes index.
Based on: Filosofische godsleer. 1987.

Emmelkamp, Paul M.G.
Anxiety disorders: a practitioner's guide / Paul M.G. Emmelkamp, Theo K. Bouman, Agnes Scholing. Chichester [etc.]: Wiley, cop. 1992. VI, 202 p.
Includes bibliographical references and index.
Translation of: Angst, fobieën en dwang. 1989.

Faverey, Hans
Against the forgetting / Hans Faverey; [transl. from the Dutch: Francis R. Jones]. [S.l.]: Anvil Press Poetry, 1993. [96] p.
Translation of: Tegen het vergeten. 1988.

Frank, Anne
The diary of Anne Frank / Anne Frank. Oxford: Heinemann, 1990. 221 p. (New windmills).
Originally published as: The diary of a young girl. London: Constellation Books. (Vallentine Mitchell & Co.), 1952.
Translation of: Het Achterhuis: dagboekbrieven 14 juni 1942 – 1 augustus 1944. 1947.

Gogh, Vincent van
Letters from Provence / Vincent van Gogh; sel. and introd. by Martin Baily. London: Collins & Brown, 1990. 160 p.
Originally written in Dutch.

Halkes, Catharina J.M.
New creation: Christian feminism and the renewal of the earth / Catharina J.M. Halkes London: SPCK, 1991. 177 p.
Includes bibliographical references: p. [163]-174 and index.
Translation of: … En alles zal worden herschapen: gedachten over de heel-wording van de schepping in het spanningsveld tussen natuur en cultuur. 1989.

Halkes, Catharina J.M.
New creation: Christian feminism and the renewal of the earth / Catharina J.M. Halkes. 1st American ed. Louisville, Ky: Westminster/John Knox Press, 1992. 177 p.
Includes bibliographical references: p. [163]-174 and index.
Translation of: … En alles zal worden herschapen: gedachten over de heel-wording van de schepping in het spanningsveld tussen natuur en cultuur. 1989.

Hamaker-Zondag, Karen
Handbook of horary astrology / Karen Hamaker-Zondag. York Beach, Me.: Weiser, cop. 1992.
Includes bibliographical references and index.
Translation of: Handboek voor uurhoekastrologie. 1983.

Hermans, Toon
Prayer bundle / Toon Hermans; transl.: John F. Jansen. Kansas City: Sheed & Ward, 1992.
Translation of: Gebedenboekje. 1986.

Herzberg, Judith
But what: selected poems / Judith Herzberg; transl. by Shirley Kaufman with Judith Herzberg; introd. by Henk Romijn Meijer. [Oberlin Oh.]: Oberlin College Press, cop. 1988. 116 p.; 19 cm. (FIELD translation series; 13).
Translation of selected poems from: Zeepost. 1963, Beemdgras. 1968, Strijklicht. 1971, Botshol. 1981 and Dagrest. 1984.

Heymans, Annemie
The princess in the kitchen garden / Annemie and Margriet Heymans. New York: Farrar, Straus & Giroux, 1992.
Translation of: De prinses van de moestuin. 1991.

Hin, Floris
The colour book of knots /
Floris Hin. 2nd ed. [S.l.]:
Adlard Coles Nautical,
1991. 157 p. (This is …).
Originally published:
London: Macmillan, 1982.
(This is series). (Nautical
books).
Translation of: Dit is
knopen en splitsen. 1982

Hol, Coby
Henrietta saves the show /
written and ill. by Coby
Hol. New York: North-
South Books, 1991. [32] p.
Simultaneously published
in Dutch as: Het avontuur
van de kleine witte pony.
1991.

Hol, Coby
Tippy bear goes to a party /
written and ill. by Coby
Hol. New York: North-
South Books, 1991. [32] p.
Simultaneously published
in Dutch as: Tippie viert
carnaval: een verhaal van
Coby Hol. 1991.

Hol, Coby
Tippy bear hunts for honey /
written and ill. by Coby
Hol. New York: North-
South Books, 1991. [32] p.
Simultaneously published
in Dutch as: Tippie zoekt
honing: een verhaal van
Coby Hol. 1991.

Kempers, Bram
Painting, power and patron-
age: the rise of the professional artist in the Italian
Renaissance / Bram Kem-
pers; transl. from the Dutch
by Beverley Jackson.
London [etc.]: Allen Lane
The Penguin Press, 1992.
XIV, 401 p.
Includes bibliographical
references: p. [373]-389 and
index.
Translation of: Kunst,
macht en mecenaat: het be-
roep van schilder in sociale
verhoudingen, 1250-1600.
1987.

Kopland, Rutger
A world beyond myself:
selected poems / Rutger
Kopland; transl. from the
Dutch by James Brockway;
with a forew. by Jeremy
Hooker; and an introd. by

the translator. 1st ed.
London: Enitharmon Press,
1991. 80 p.

Krabbé, Tim
The vanishing / by Tim
Krabbé; transl. from the
Dutch by Claire Nicolas
White. New York: Random
House, cop. 1992.
Translation of: Het gouden
ei. 1984.

Krabbé, Tim
The vanishing / by Tim
Krabbé; transl. from the
Dutch by Claire Nicolas
White. London: Signet,
1993.
Translation of: Het gouden
ei. 1984.

Kuitert, H.M.
I have my doubts: how to
become a Christian without
being a fundamentalist /
H.M. Kuitert; [transl. John
Bowden]. London: SCM;
Valley Forge, Pa.: Trinity
Press International, 1993.
288 p.
Translation of: Het alge-
meen betwijfeld christelijk
geloof: een herziening. 1992.

Lammen, Hanny
Haiti: island in the waves /
Hanny Lammen; [transl.
from the Dutch by Karen
Bakker]. London: Excali-
bur, cop. 1991. 202 p.
Translation of: Haïti, eiland
in de branding.

Limburg, Astrid
Women giving birth / pho-
togr. by Saskia van Rees;
text by Astrid Limburg and
Beatrijs Smulders. Berke-
ley, Calif: Celestial Arts,
1992. 122 p.
Includes bibliograhical
references.
Translation of: Baren: verti-
cale baring, eerste contact,
invloed van water, compli-
caties. 1984.

Lindwer, Willy
The last seven months of
Anne Frank / Willy Lind-
wer; transl. from Dutch by
Alison Meersschaert. New
York: Pantheon, 1992. XIII,
204 p.
1st English edition: New
York: Pantheon Books,
1991.

Translation of: De laatste
zeven maanden: vrouwen in
het spoor van Anne Frank.
1988.

Louf, André
Tuning in to Grace: the
quest for God / Andre Louf.
[S.l.]: Darton, Longman and
Todd, 1992.
Translation of: Inspelen op
genade: over God-zoeken.
1983.

Louf, André
Tuning in to Grace: the
quest for God / Andre Louf;
transl. by John Vriend.
Kalamazoo, MI: Cister-
cian Publications, 1992. (Cister-
cian studies serie; 129).
Translation of: Inspelen op
genade: over God-zoeken.
1983.

M.
M. C. Escher, his life and
complete graphic work / ed.
by J.L. Locher. New York:
Abradale Press/Harry N.
Abrams, 1992.
Includes bibliographical
references and index.
Originally published: 1982.
Translation of: De werelden
van M. C. Escher: het werk
van M. C. Escher. 1971.

Maertens, Freddy
Fall from Grace / Freddy
Maertens and Manu
Adriaens; [transl. from the
Dutch: S. Hawkins]. [S.l.]:
Ronde Publ., 1993.
[x, 214] p.
Translation of: Niet van
horen zeggen. 1988.

Matthysen, Donald
December 1944: roman /
Donald Matthysen. London:
Excalibur, 1993. 93 p.
Translation of: December
1944: roman. 1987.

Minnen, Cornelis A. van
American diplomats in the
Netherlands, 1815-50 /
Cornelis A. van Minnen.
New York: St. Martin's
Press, 1993. 204 p.
(Franklin and Eleanor
Roosevelt Institute series on
diplomatic and economic
history; 5).
Includes bibliographical
references and index.

Translation of: Yankees
onder de zeespiegel: de
Amerikaanse diplomaten in
de Lage Landen en hun
berichtgeving, 1815-1850.
1991. Dissertation Leiden.

Nederlander, Munin
Kitezh: the Russian grail
legends / by Munin Neder-
lander; transl. from the
Dutch by Tony Langham;
forew. by John Matthews.
London: Aquarian, 1991.
[304] p.
Translation of: Kitesj: de
legende van haar hemel-
vaart, of nederdaling in het
Swetli Jarr, in samenhang
met de bylígni over o.a. de
tafelronde van Wladimir
van Kiev als voorspelling
van een christelijk kommu-
nisme in Rusland. 1988.

Nierop, H.F.K. van
The nobility of Holland:
from knights to regents,
1500-1650 / H.F.K. van
Nierop; transl. by Maarten
Ultee. Cambridge; New
York: Cambridge Univer-
sity Press, 1992. (Cambridge
studies in early modern
history).
Includes bibliographical
references and index.
Translation of: Van ridders
tot regenten: de Hollandse
adel in de zestiende en de
eerste helft van de zeven-
tiende eeuw. 1984. Dissertation Leiden.

Nooteboom, Cees
Following story / Cees
Nooteboom; [transl. from
the Dutch Ina Rilke]. [S.l.]:
Harvill, 1993. [150] p.;
22 cm.
Translation of: Het vol-
gende verhaal. 1991.

Nooteboom, Cees
Rituals: a novel / by Cees
Nooteboom; transl. [from
the Dutch] by Adrienne
Dixon. London: Penguin,
1992. 145 p. (Penguin inter-
national writers).
Originally published: Baton
Rouge: Louisiana State
University Press, 1983.
Translation of: Rituelen.
1980.

Over
Over the hills and far away /
ed. by Els Boekelaar and
Ineke Verschuren. [Edin-
burgh]: Floris, 1991. 236 p.
Translation of: Kabouter-
sprookjes. 1985.

Palmen, Connie
The laws / Connie Palmen;
transl. from the Dutch by
Richard Huijng [S.l.]:
Secker & Warburg, 1992.
240 p.
Translation of: De wetten:
roman. 1991.

Poortenaar, Jan
An artist in Java and other
islands of Indonesia / by
Jan Poortenaar; transl. from
the Dutch by Horace Shipp;
in collab. with the author;
with a forew. by Frank
Brangwyn. Singapore [etc.]:
Oxford University Press,
1989. XIV, 178 p. [55] bl.
Previously published as:
An artist in the tropics.
London: Sampson Low,
1928.
Includes index.
Translation of: Een kunst-
reis in de tropen, 1925.

Poortvliet, Rien
The ark / Rien Poortvliet;
[transl. from the Dutch].
New ed.. Lion: Oxford,
1992. [242] p.
Previous edition: 1986.
Translation of: De ark van
Noach, of Ere wie ere toe-
komt. 1985.

Rol, Ruud van der
Anne Frank, beyond the
diary: a photographic
remembrance / Ruud van
der Rol and Rian Verhoeven;
with introd. Anna Quindlen.
New York: Penguin, 1993.
113 p.
Translation of: Anne Frank.
1992.

Schierbeek, Bert
Keeping it up: the countryside / Bert Schierbeek;
transl. [from the Dutch] by
Charles McGeehan; introd.
by William Jay Smith. 1st
American ed. Rochester,
MI: Katydid Books, Oak-
land University, 1990.
191 p. (European writing in
translation. The Nether-
lands; 2).

Schillebeeckx, Edward
Mary: yesterday, today,
tomorrow / Edward Schille-
beeckx and Catharina J.M.
Halkes; [transl. from the
Dutch J. Bowden]. London:
SCMP, 1993. [96] p.
Translation of: Maria:
gisteren, vandaag, morgen.
1992.

Schubert, Ingrid
The monster problem /
Ingrid and Dieter Schubert.
London: Red Fox, 1991.
[32] p.
1st English edition: London:
Hutchinson, 1989.
Translation of: Wie niet
sterk is … 1989.

Schulte Nordholt, Jan Willem
Woodrow Wilson: a life for
world peace / Jan Willem
Schulte Nordholt; transl. by
Herbert H. Rowen. Berke-
ley [etc.]: University of
California Press, cop. 1991.
VII, 495 p., [16] p. of plates.
Includes bibliographical
references and index.
Translation of: Woodrow
Wilson: een leven voor de
wereldvrede. 1990.

Smit, Daan
Plants of the Bible: a gardener's guide / Daan Smit.
Batavia, Ill.: Lion Publ,
1992.
Includes bibliographical
references and index.
Translation of: Planten uit
de Bijbel: hun herkomst en
hun gebruik door de eeuwen
heen: gids voor het kweken.
1990.

Spierenburg, Pieter
The broken spell: a cultural
and anthropological history
of preindustrial Europe /
Pieter Spierenburg. New
Brunswick, N.J.: Rutgers
University Press, cop. 1991.
X, 313 p.
Includes bibliographical
references and index.
Translation of: De verbroken
betovering: mentaliteits-
geschiedenis van preïndu-
strieel Europa. 1988.

Spierenburg, Pieter
The broken spell: a cultural
and anthropological history
of preindustrial Europe /
Pieter Spierenburg. Basing-
stoke: Macmillan Educa-
tion, 1991. X, 313 p.
Includes bibliographical
references and index.
Translation of: De verbroken
betovering: mentaliteits-
geschiedenis van preïndu-
strieel Europa. 1988.

Sprong, Edo
Hand analysis: the diagnos-
tic method / Edo Sprong.
New York: Sterling;
London: Cassell [distribu-
tor], cop. 1991. 176 p.
Includes index.
Translation of: Handanalyse
en zelfherkenning: alles in
de hand. 1988.

Straaten, Peter van
How was it for you? / Peter
van Straaten. London:
Fourth Estate, 1991. [47] bl.
Originally published in
Dutch.

Vels Heijn, Annemarie
Rembrandt / Annemarie
Vels Heijn. London: Scala
in association with the
Rijksmuseum Foundation,
1989. 128 p.
Includes index.
Translation of: Rembrandt:
met 60 afbeeldingen in
kleur naar werken van de
meester, zijn leermeesters,
leerlingen, vrienden en
tijdgenoten. 1973.

Velthuijs, Max
Crocodile's masterpiece /
Max Velthuijs. London:
Andersen Press, 1991.
[26] p.
Translation of: Krokodil en
het meesterwerk.
Amsterdam: Leopold. 1988.
Uitg. van de Stichting van
de Collectieve Propaganda
van het Nederlandse Boek
t.g.v. de Kinderboekenweek
1988.

Velthuijs, Max
Frog and the stranger /
Max Velthuijs. London:
Andersen Press, 1993.
[26] p.
Simultaneously published
in Dutch as: Kikker en de
vreemdeling. 1993.

Velthuijs, Max
Frog in winter / Max Velthuijs. London: Andersen,
1992. [26] p.
Simultaneously published
in Dutch as: Kikker in de
kou. 1992.

Editor:
Dutch Books in Translation
Koninklijke Bibliotheek,
The Hague
The Netherlands

Contributors

Dirk van Assche (1955-)
Editorial secretary
Ons Erfdeel
Murissonstraat 260,
8931 Rekkem, Belgium

Saskia Bak (1964-)
Staff member of the Fries
Museum, Leeuwarden
Radesingel 14 b,
9711 EJ Groningen,
The Netherlands

Ludo Bekkers (1924-)
Art critic
Tentoonstellingslaan 6,
2020 Antwerp, Belgium

Els de Bens (1940-)
Professor of Journalism and
Communication Studies
(University of Ghent)
Vogelheide 6,
9052 Ghent, Belgium

J. Bernlef (1937-)
Writer
Valeriusstraat 104",
1075 GC Amsterdam,
The Netherlands

Ignace Bossuyt (1947-)
Professor of Musicology
(Catholic University of
Leuven)
Lostraat 40,
3212 Pellenberg, Belgium

José Boyens
Art critic
Hogewaldseweg 33,
6562 KR Groesbeek,
The Netherlands

Ton J. Broos (1947-)
Lecturer in Dutch
(University of Michigan,
Ann Arbor)
1405 Harbrooke Avenue,
Ann Arbor, MI 48103, USA

Yvette Bruijnen (1967-)
Art critic
Joost Banckertsplaats 8B,
3012 HA Rotterdam,
The Netherlands

Wiep van Bunge (1960-)
Lecturer in the History of
Philosophy (Erasmus
University Rotterdam) /
Research worker for the
Dutch Organisation for

Scientific Research
Prins Bernhardkade 22/a,
3051 AJ Rotterdam,
The Netherlands

Piet Chielens (1956-)
Bank employee / Chief
editor *Gandalf*
Zevekotestraat 32,
8970 Reningelst, Belgium

Anton Claessens (1936-)
Teacher / Member of the
editorial board *Ons Erfdeel*
Honkersven, 29,
2440 Geel, Belgium

Sanne Claessens (1971-)
Law student
Oudezijds Voorburgwal 239,
1012 EZ Amsterdam,
The Netherlands

Pierre Delsaerdt (1963-)
Head of Archives and
Historical Collections
(UFSIA Library, Antwerp)
Prinsstraat 9,
2000 Antwerp, Belgium

Paul Depondt (1953-)
Journalist *(de Volkskrant)*
Korenmarkt 25,
9000 Ghent, Belgium

Marc Dubois (1950-)
Lecturer (St Lucas
Architecture Institute,
Ghent) / President of
Stichting Architektuur-
museum
Holstraat 89,
9000 Ghent, Belgium

Pierre H. Dubois (1917-)
Writer
Thorbeckelaan 551,
2564 CD The Hague,
The Netherlands

H.M. Dupuis (1945-)
Professor of Medical Ethics
(University of Leiden)
P.O. Box 2087, 2301 CB
Leiden, The Netherlands

Luc Eyckmans (1930-)
Director Prince Leopold
Institute of Tropical
Medicine
Nationalestraat 155,
2000 Antwerp,
Belgium

Dirk de Geest (1957-)
Research worker for the
Belgian National Fund for

Scientific Research
(Catholic University of
Leuven)
Poortveldenplein 17/4,
3200 Aarschot, Belgium

Henk van Gelder (1946-)
Journalist
Leidsegracht 93,
1017 NC Amsterdam,
The Netherlands

Sarah Hart (1950-)
Gardening columnist
(NRC Handelsblad)
Lange Mare 64, 2312 GS
Leiden, The Netherlands

Jan van Hove (1953-)
Journalist *(De Standaard)*
Dambruggestraat 6,
2060 Antwerp, Belgium

Wouter Hugenholtz (1952-)
Executive Director NIAS
Meijboomlaan 1,
2242 PR Wassenaar,
The Netherlands

Hans Ibelings (1963-)
Staff member of the
Netherlands Architecture
Institute (Rotterdam)
Curierekade 50,
1013 CH Amsterdam,
The Netherlands

Geert van Istendael (1947-)
Writer
Kruisdagenlaan 58,
1040 Brussels, Belgium

Steven Jacobs (1967-)
Art critic
Burgstraat 118,
9000 Ghent, Belgium

Deborah Jowitt
Dance critic *(The Village
Voice)* / Professor of Dance
History (Tisch School of
the Arts, NYU)
78 Christopher Street,
New York, NY 10014, USA

Anton Korteweg (1944-)
Director Netherlands
Literature Museum and
Documentation Centre
(The Hague) / Writer
Wasstraat 23, 2313 JG
Leiden, The Netherlands

Connie Kristel (1955-)
Historian
Sarphatistraat 201,

1018 GJ Amsterdam,
The Netherlands

Ilse Kuijken (1966-)
Art critic
K. van Hulthemstraat 92,
9000 Ghent, Belgium

Pieter Leroy (1954-)
Professor at the Faculty of
Political Science, section
'Environment, Nature and
Landscape' (University of
Nijmegen)
Grameystraat 4, 6525 DP
Nijmegen, The Netherlands

Juleke van Lindert (1956-)
Art critic
Roosje Vosstraat 5,
1069 RA Amsterdam,
The Netherlands

Gerdin Linthorst (1946-)
Film critic / Chief editor
De Filmkrant
Admiraal de Ruyterweg
274, 1055 MR Amsterdam,
The Netherlands

Paul Luttikhuis (1959-)
Musicologist / Journalist
(NRC Handelsblad)
Vossegatselaan 39 bis a,
3583 RP Utrecht,
The Netherlands

*Christopher MacLehose
(1940-)*
Publisher (Harvill
Publishers, London)
77-85 Fulham Palace Road,
London W6 8JB,
United Kingdom

Filip Matthijs (1966-)
Editorial secretary
The Low Countries
Murissonstraat 260,
8931 Rekkem, Belgium

Kees Middelhoff (1917-)
Radio commentator /
Journalist
Sterrelaan 13, 1217 PP
Hilversum, The Netherlands

*Anne Marie Musschoot
(1944-)*
Professor of Dutch
Literature (University of
Ghent)
Nieuwkolegemlaan 44,
9030 Ghent, Belgium

Jos Nijhof (1952-)
Teacher / Theatre critic

318

Berkenkade 14,
2351 NB Leiderdorp,
The Netherlands

Max Nord (1916-)
Literary critic / Writer
Banstraat 26hs,
1071 KA Amsterdam,
The Netherlands

Cyrille Offermans (1945-)
Literary critic / Writer
Doonweg 15, 6097 CX
Heel, The Netherlands

Frits van Oostrom (1953-)
Professor of Dutch
Literature before the
Romantic Period
(University of Leiden)
P.O. Box 9515, 2300 RA
Leiden, The Netherlands

Rudi van der Paardt (1943-)
Lecturer in Latin
(University of Leiden)
Jacob van Ruysdaellaan 3,
2343 EN Oegstgeest,
The Netherlands

Marc Peire (1953-)
Musicologist / Collaborator
BRTN-Radio
Polderhoeklaan 31,
8310 Bruges, Belgium

David A. Pinder (1944-)
Professor of Economic
Geography (University of
Plymouth)
Dept. of Geographical
Sciences, Drake Circus,
Plymouth, Devon PL4 8AA,
United Kingdom

Walter Prevenier (1934-)
Professor of History
(University of Ghent)
Vlieguit 14, 9830 Sint-
Martens-Latem, Belgium

Huub van Riel (1951-)
Artistic co-ordinator
BIMhuis (Amsterdam)
Derdeloversdwarsstraat 10',
1016 VE Amsterdam,
The Netherlands

*Pieter C. Ritsema van Eck
(1938-)*
Curator of the Glass
Collection (Rijksmuseum,
Amsterdam)
Carel Reinierszkade 3,
2593 HK The Hague,
The Netherlands

Jef de Roeck (1930-)
Theatre critic
Tervuursevest 123/20,
3001 Heverlee, Belgium

Reinier Salverda (1948-)
Professor of Dutch
Language and Literature
(University College
London)
69 St James's Lane,
Muswell Hill, London N10
3QY, United Kingdom

Liz Sanderson (1944-)
Journalist BRTN (Radio
Vlaanderen Internationaal)
Hoogstraat 36,
2000 Antwerp, Belgium

*Lydia M.A. Schoonbaert
(1930-)*
Chief curator Royal
Museum of Fine Arts
(Antwerp)
Leopold de Waelplaats 1-9,
2000 Antwerp, Belgium

D.H. Schram (1952-)
Lecturer in Literary Theory
(Free University of
Amsterdam)
Leerdamhof 252,
1108 BX Amsterdam,
The Netherlands

Willemina Seywerd (1928-)
Lecturer in Dutch
(University of Toronto)
265 Scarboro Crescent,
Scarborough, ON M1M 2J7,
Canada

Fred Six (1943-)
Teacher / Theatre critic
Roggelaan 68,
8500 Kortrijk, Belgium

Erik Slagter (1939-)
Art critic
Eemwijkstraat 1, RC 2271
Voorburg, The Netherlands

W.H. Tiemens (1944-)
Insurance company staff
member / Writer
Barendrechtstraat 26,
6843 NC Arnhem,
The Netherlands

Lauran Toorians (1958-)
Historian
Mozartlaan 623, 5011 SP
Tilburg, The Netherlands

Hans Vanacker (1960-)
Editorial secretary
Septentrion
Murissonstraat 260,
8931 Rekkem, Belgium

Sabine Vanacker (1962-)
Lecturer in Dutch
(University of Hull)
Dept. of Dutch Studies,
Cottingham Road, Hull
HU6 7RX, United Kingdom

Paul Vermeulen (1962-)
Architect
Kwaadham 18, 9000 Ghent,
Belgium

Jeroen Vullings (1962-)
Teacher / Literary critic
Madelievenstraat 25,
1015 NV Amsterdam,
The Netherlands

*Arthur K. Wheelock, Jr.
(1943-)*
Curator of Northern
Baroque Painting (National
Gallery of Art, Washington
D.C.) / Professor of Art
History (University of
Maryland)
National Gallery of Art,
Washington D.C. 20565,
USA

August Willemsen (1936-)
Writer / Translator
Gouden Leeuw 249,
1103 KE Amsterdam,
The Netherlands

Paul de Wispelaere (1928-)
Literary critic/Writer
Moerhuizestraat 64,
9990 Maldegem, Belgium

Manfred Wolf (1935-)
Professor of English
(San Francisco State
University)
2531 – 21st Avenue,
San Francisco,
CA 94116, USA

Aart van Zoest (1930-)
Writer
Broekerwaard 154,
1824 EW Alkmaar,
The Netherlands

Translators

Geoffrey Ball,
Ghent, Belgium

Jocelyne van Boetzelaer,
London, United Kingdom

James Brockway,
The Hague, The Netherlands

Inge van Eijk,
Nijmegen, The Netherlands

Jane Fenoulhet,
London, United Kingdom

Peter Flynn,
Ghent, Belgium

Lesley Gilbert,
London, United Kingdom

Tanis Guest,
London, United Kingdom

Theo Hermans,
London, United Kingdom

Francis R. Jones,
London, United Kingdom

Steve Judd,
Haacht, Belgium

Peter King,
Cottingham, United Kingdom

André Lefevere,
Austin, TX, USA

Ria Leigh-Loohuizen,
Dordrecht, The Netherlands

Cate McPherson,
London, United Kingdom

Yvette Mead,
Canterbury, United Kingdom

Mandy Melse,
London, United Kingdom

Frank van Meurs,
Nijmegen, The Netherlands

Elizabeth Mollison,
Amsterdam, The Netherlands

Alison Mouthaan-Gwillim,
Antwerp, Belgium

Yasmin Penniall, London,
United Kingdom

Simon Ratcliffe,
London, United Kingdom

Scott Rollins,
Amsterdam, The Netherlands

Julian Ross,
Wassenaar, The Netherlands

John Rudge,
Amsterdam, The Netherlands

Michael Shaw,
Haslemere, United Kingdom

Paul Vincent,
London, United Kingdom

Theodoor Weevers (+)

Claire Nicolas White,
St James, NY, USA

Rachel van der Wilden,
Rijswijk, The Netherlands

Manfred Wolf,
San Francisco, CA, USA

ADVISOR ON ENGLISH USAGE

Tanis Guest, London, United
Kingdom

As well as the yearbook *The Low Countries*, the Flemish-Netherlands foundation 'Stichting Ons Erfdeel' publishes the following booklets covering various aspects of the culture of the Netherlands and Flanders:

O. Vandeputte / P. Vincent / T. Hermans
Dutch. The Language of Twenty Million Dutch and Flemish People.
Illustrated; 64 pp.

J.A. Kossmann-Putto & E.H. Kossmann
The Low Countries. History of the Northern and Southern Netherlands.
Illustrated; 64 pp.

Jaap Goedegebuure & Anne Marie Musschoot
Contemporary Fiction of the Low Countries.
Illustrated and with translated extracts from 15 novels; 128 pp.

Hugo Brems & Ad Zuiderent
Contemporary Poetry of the Low Countries.
With 52 translated poems; 112 pp.